The Comprador in Nineteenth Century China:

Bridge between East and West

Harvard East Asian Series   45

The East Asian Research Center at Harvard University
administers research projects designed
to further scholarly understanding
of China, Japan, Korea, Vietnam, and adjacent areas.

YEN-P'ING HAO

The Comprador in

Nineteenth Century China:

Bridge between East and West

Harvard University Press   Cambridge, Massachusetts   1970

Distributed in Great Britain by Oxford University Press, London

Preparation of this volume has been aided by a grant from the Ford Foundation.

Library of Congress Catalog Card Number 70-105372

SBN 674-15525-4

Printed in the United States of America

For My Parents

Preface

For better or for worse, Sino-Western contact during the past century significantly reoriented China, and one instrument of that contact was the comprador. He served as a bridge between China and the West. Although this figure has now vanished from the scene, he remains a controversial subject. Usually he was condemned by his fellow-countrymen as a traitor, first for serving persons who were not Confucian, and later for assisting those who were not Chinese. Yet in many ways his versatile and important role in modern China has too often been slighted.

In dealing with the social and economic institutions surrounding the comprador, this book enters the comparatively neglected field of modern Chinese socioeconomic history. It inquires into the comprador's role in effecting social change, economic development (especially early industrialization), and intellectual transformation in China. Finally, it touches on the broader theme of acculturation. Based primarily on documentary sources, the work is intended to put the intricate issue of the comprador in clearer perspective and to throw light on the relationship between East and West at large.

Prepared originally as a dissertation at Harvard, this study owes a great debt to John K. Fairbank, without whose guidance and encouragement it could not have been accomplished. For his bibliographical knowledge as well as his ideas, I am especially grateful to Liu Kwang-Ching, who pioneered in the study of China's treaty ports through an examination of their business firms. His influence on this study has been far greater than he may realize.

Preface

Ramon H. Myers made substantive economic and historical contributions, and Dwight H. Perkins offered valuable suggestions on major points relating to the problems of economic history. My wife, Pin-han, has been of inestimable help throughout the preparation of the manuscript.

Many others have helped in diverse ways. Robert N. Bellah, Waldo H. Heinrichs, Ezra F. Vogel, and Yang Lien-sheng read part of the manuscript and made useful suggestions. I benefited from fruitful discussions with Thomas A. Metzger in connection with the general problems of Chinese socioeconomic history, and with Don C. Price in regard to improving the style. I am obliged to the following scholars for their help and encouragement during various stages of research: Ronald Yen-ling Cheng, LeRoy P. Graf, Ichiko Chūzō, Kuo Ting-yee, Lawrence F. Silverman, Eugene Wu, and Wu Hsiang-hsiang. In making the final revision, I benefited from the editorial acumen of Mrs. Virginia LaPlante and Mrs. Olive Holmes. For expert aid in the preparation of the manuscript, I am indebted to Mrs. Eileen Cave and Mrs. Margaret Forestell. Cheng Yen-fen, Li Hsiao-t'ing, Liang Chia-pin, and Liang Tzu-heng were helpful in arranging interviews with several former compradors and their family members, to all of whom I am grateful.

Stephen C. Lockwood kindly permitted me to read his paper on Augustine Heard & Co., and Robert W. Lovett of the Baker Library, Harvard University, assisted me in the use of the library's archives of various American firms. The gracious permission of Matheson & Co., Ltd., London, enabled me to work among the Jardine, Matheson & Co. Archives at the University Library, Cambridge, England. For other assistance, I am grateful to the staffs of the Harvard-Yenching Library, the Houghton Library, and the Baker Library of Harvard University; the East Asiatic Library of Columbia University; the Library of Congress; the Essex Institute; the Hoover Library; the Library of the Institute of Modern History and the Fu Ssu-nien Library, Academia Sinica, Taipei; the Tōyō Bunko, Tokyo; the Feng P'ing-shan Library of the University of Hong Kong; the Hong Kong Supreme Court Library; and the University Library of the University of Cambridge.

For financial support, I am grateful to the East Asian Research Center of Harvard University, the American Council of Learned

Preface

Societies, the Social Science Research Council, the American Philosophical Society (the Penrose Fund), and the University of Tennessee (the Faculty Research Fund). I am indebted as well to the Harvard-Yenching Institute for a traveling fellowship, arranged by Glen W. Baxter, which I held as a graduate student at Harvard in 1962–1963.

Y.P.H.

Knoxville, Tennessee
September 1969

Contents

I   Introduction: The Comprador in Chinese Society   1

II The Western Merchant and His Chinese
    Comprador   15

The Western Mercantile House   15
Reliance on the Chinese Comprador   24
Further Benefits of the Comprador   36

III The Rise and Fall of the Comprador   44

Origins of the Comprador   45
Rise of the Modern Comprador, 1842–1900   48
Spread of the Comprador Outside China   54
Decline and Fall, 1900–1943   59

IV Functions of the Comprador in the Foreign Firm   64

House Steward   65
Business Assistant   68
Upcountry Purchaser   75
The Chief Comprador Tong King-sing   83

V   The Comprador as a Nouveau Riche   89

Accumulating Wealth as a Comprador   89
Accumulating Wealth as an Independent Merchant   94
Total Income of the Comprador   99

VI   The Comprador and Modern China's Economic
     Development   106

     Foreign Economic Intrusion   106
     Modern China's Commercial Development   112
     The Comprador as Industrial Investor   120
     The Comprador as Industrial Manager   136
     The Comprador as Entrepreneur   146

VII The Comprador System as a Socioeconomic
     Institution   154

     The Process of Becoming a Comprador   154
     Mechanism of the Institution   161
     Characteristics of the Institution   171

VIII Beyond a Purchaser: Noneconomic Activities of
     the Comprador   180

     Style of Life   180
     Sociopolitical Activities   184
     Intellectual Response to the West   195

IX   Conclusion: Significance of the Comprador as a
     Middleman between East and West   207

     Appendices
     A. Augustine Heard & Co.'s Compradors, 1850's–1860's   227
     B. Russell & Co.'s Compradors, 1830's–1870's   229
     C. Jardine, Matheson & Co.'s Compradors, 1850's–1900's   231
     D. Dent & Co.'s Compradors, 1830's–1860's   233

     Bibliography   235

     Notes   246

     Glossary   295

     Index   301

Illustrations

Ex-comprador's market report from Hankow: Augustine Heard & Co.,
    Shanghai, 1863   38
Plan for house at Yokohama, Japan: Augustine Heard & Co., 1866   60
Shanghai property: Russell & Co., probably early 1860's   67
Receipts kept by comprador for money paid: Augustine Heard & Co.,
    Hong Kong, 1853   70
Comprador's order: Augustine Heard & Co., Hong Kong, 1866   72
Comprador's security chop: Augustine Heard & Co., Hong Kong, 1859   156
Comprador's security chop with free English translation: Augustine
    Heard & Co., Hong Kong, 1860   158
Comprador's agreement: Augustine Heard & Co., Hong Kong, 1860   162
Plan for house at Shanghai: Augustine Heard & Co., 1846   163
Comprador portrayed as a mandarin: Hsü Yü-t'ing (1793–1859),
    comprador to Dent & Co., Shanghai, 1840's   185
The honorific arch with which the Ch'ing government honored Hsü
    Jun (1838–1911), comprador to Dent & Co. (1861–1868), for his
    efforts in famine relief in the 1860's   187

Tables

1.	Diverse activities of Jardine, Matheson & Co.	23
2.	Cash account with the comprador, Augustine Heard & Co., Hong Kong, 1871	41
3.	The decline of Canton in foreign trade, 1860–1865	50
4.	Duties collected at the treaty ports, 1865–1867	50
5.	Cash account with the comprador, Augustine Heard & Co., Hong Kong, 1870	71
6.	Monthly salary of the comprador and his staff, Augustine Heard & Co., Hankow, 1866	91
7.	Total income of the compradors, 1842–1894	105
8.	Noted compradors as native bankers, Shanghai, 1840's–1880's	115
9.	Major commodities shipped between Shanghai and Kiukiang on foreign vessels, 1866, with division between Chinese and foreign ownership	118
10.	Chinese produce shipped on foreign vessels between Shanghai and Chinkiang, 1866, showing division between foreign and Chinese ownership	119
11.	Steamship investments of Choping (comprador to Russell & Co. at Shanghai), 1862–1863	121
12.	Compradors' investments in the China Coast Steam Navigation Co., Shanghai, 1873	122
13.	Compradors' investments in steamship companies in China, Shanghai, 1862–1875	124
14.	Compradors' investments in Chinese-owned steamship companies, 1872–1893	125
15.	Yü Hsia-ch'ing's investments in steamship enterprises, 1909–1918	126
16.	Compradors' investments in China's modern coal mines, 1863–1886	127
17.	Compradors' investments in China's modern mines, 1863–1898	128
18.	Compradors' investments in China's cotton textile enterprises, 1890–1910	129
19.	Compradors' investments in China's machine-manufacturing industries, 1883–1913	131

20. Investments of the comprador Chu Ta-ch'un, 1870's–1913   134
21. Investments of the comprador Chu Chih-yao, 1897–1910's   135
22. China's first large-scale modern enterprises promoted and invested in by the compradors   137
23. Social background of the merchant directors of the China Merchants' Steam Navigation Co., 1873   142
24. Comprador's deposits required by foreign banks, Shanghai, 1907   160
25. The number of comprador's clerks in foreign banks, Shanghai, ca. 1900   165
26. Noted bank compradors from Soochow, Kiangsu, in Shanghai, 1870's–1920's   176

The Comprador in Nineteenth Century China:
Bridge between East and West

I Introduction: The Comprador in Chinese Society

It has been maintained that "East is East and West is West, and never the twain shall meet."[1] Yet in a sense they did meet at the treaty ports in late Ch'ing China, with the Chinese compradors as middlemen. Their middleman role was both symptomatic and strategically important in the process of Sino-Western economic intercourse and cultural diffusion, although the result of such contacts was not always happy. The compradors, by virtue of their wealth and expertise, constituted a new type of merchant, who played a significant role in modern China.

The history of modern China has been in many ways a process of responding to the Western impact. This impact originated and manifested itself most clearly in the treaty ports. Diplomatic negotiations and military encounters were usually prompted by conflicts arising out of trade relations, and behind the trade, which was the main reason for the foreign presence in China, stood Western merchants. Their contacts with a society drastically different in nature from their own required the aid of natives. After the abolition of the monopolistic Cohong system in 1842, the compradors supplanted the hong merchants and became the commercial intermediaries between China and the West. The comprador (*mai-pan*) was the Chinese manager of a foreign firm in China, serving as middleman in the company's dealings with the Chinese.

As the intermediary between foreign and Chinese merchants, the comprador had first and foremost an economic function, which was

1

the springboard for his social, political, and cultural activities. With the increase of China's foreign trade after 1842, the need for a commercial middleman became urgent. Yet the difficulty of the language and the complexity of the currency, coupled with China's great variety of commercial practices and social customs, proved major impediments to free and direct Sino-foreign transactions. The comprador provided the necessary link between the foreign firms and Chinese commerce. Within the foreign firm, he recruited and supervised the Chinese staff, served as treasurer, supplied market intelligence, assumed responsibility for native bank orders, and generally assisted the foreign manager in transactions with the Chinese.

This type of commercial middleman was by no means a unique and foreign institution, but developed within the context of traditional Chinese economic institutions. In fact, a purely native institution of licensed brokers known as *ya-hang* had long been performing such functions. Thus, even if the foreigners had been as knowledgeable as, say, a Hopei merchant in Canton, they would still have used an institution like the ya-hang. Indeed, it was not uncommon for a foreign merchant to have his business conducted through the official Chinese ya-hang before 1842. The comprador differed from the broker in the sense that while a ya-hang was an independent commission agent, a comprador was in the main contractually employed by the foreign merchant. Yet the newly emerged comprador owed his experience to the Cohong system, and thus the institution did not grow in a vacuum, but either shoved other institutions aside or absorbed them to make way for itself.

In the Ch'ing period (1644–1912) there existed a vast complex of Chinese mercantile activities, and the more powerful merchants were those who handled the tea, salt, silk, cotton, and opium transactions. Among these, the monopolistic salt merchants seem to have been the most notable.[2] Next came the hong merchants. In the early Sino-foreign trade the Chinese merchants who handled trade with Europeans gradually became organized into the merchant guild of Cohong (*kung-hang* or officially authorized merchants). The guild was licensed by and responsible to the officials, and had a monopoly over all trade with Western merchants. Members of the Cohong were known as the hong merchants, who formed one of the

Introduction

largest commercial elements until 1842. After China was defeated by Britain in the Opium War, the Treaty of Nanking brought the foreign trade oligopoly of the hong merchants to an end.[3]

The arrival of foreign merchants in relatively large numbers at the treaty ports created a new professional area for individual pursuit. Against this setting the new comprador class took shape. Before long, the Taiping uprising (1851–1864) accelerated the decline of the salt merchants. Thus, both foreign and internal factors combined to create a situation more conducive to independent enterprise. The rise of the comprador, although not of so powerful an influence as to shift the commercial center entirely from inland to the treaty ports, epitomized this tendency. The rise of the treaty ports themselves added a major new dimension to a largely unanalyzed complex of mercantile activity.

A proper business climate is of vital importance to economic development. Western history since the Middle Ages shows that security under a stable government or the lack of it has been the most important single influence on entrepreneurship.[4] For its part, however, the Ch'ing government failed to perform several functions important to the context of economic activity, such as the maintenance of peace, of a commercial law, of a regulated money supply, and of a system of weights and measures. The lack of peace and order seems to have been the most crucial hindrance to economic development. Although the Sino-Western treaty system of the nineteenth century opened China to various forms of imperialistic encroachment, including extraterritoriality, treaty tariff, and foreign settlements and concessions, the system also provided a milieu favorable to business expectations in certain respects. It furnished stable conditions for business pursuit, because, owing to foreign protection, funds in the treaty ports were secured against the depredations of Chinese officials, and the merchants thus became personally safe from China's social and political disturbances. While some facets of Chinese economic history remain unknown to us, it seems probable that the compradors were the first group of merchants in Chinese history to accumulate great wealth through a commercial career free in theory and practice from official "squeeze" or exaction.

Handling most of China's foreign trade in the nineteenth century, the compradors accumulated by various means, both legal and illegal, a considerable sum of funds. Individually, they could hardly compare with the former hong merchants in wealth, but they certainly outnumbered them. At the same time, they learned from Westerners the methods of managing modern businesses and had an opportunity to apply this knowledge. Consequently, the comprador was able to combine the roles of passive owner and active manager of capital, which distinguished him from the traditional rich man, who lived a gentry life and entrusted the operation of his investments to the socially inferior managers. Although there had been exceptions to the traditional pattern, the comprador clearly constituted a new type who combined wealth with entrepreneurial expertise.

One characteristic of China's traditional merchants was their marked reluctance to enter a new field. This tendency may have reflected the traditional attitude toward competence, expressed in the distinction between those who are *nei-hang* (within the trade, in the know) and those who are *wai-hang* (outsiders, laymen). Thus, when one had become established in a particular line, he dared not jeopardize his career by shifting into new and unfamiliar undertakings.

This reluctance is indicated by the fact that the former hong merchants seem to have disappeared quickly from the scene once the trade pattern had changed. Later, the Shansi bankers also refused to make the necessary change and consequently had passed into total eclipse by the end of the Ch'ing period. Even Hu Kuang-yung, the noted banker who negotiated foreign loans for Tso Tsung-t'ang, failed to respond to the challenge of the new when he turned down an invitation from Li Hung-chang to participate in the management of the China Merchants' Steam Navigation Co.[5] The company was finally put under the charge of two ex-compradors, Tong King-sing (1832–1892) and Hsü Jun (1838–1911).[6] This aversion to change suggests why the salt merchants seldom participated in the financing and operation of new-style enterprises, and why the traditional Shansi bankers could not meet an altered economic situation, as could the Japanese Zaibatzu. Against this background, can the compradors be considered a new type? Were they entrepreneurs? On the same line, the generally accepted assertion that the entrepreneurial spirit was singularly absent in late Ch'ing China will also be examined.[7]

Introduction

The significance of the comprador in the crucial period of China's early industrialization lay not only in his being rich but also in his ability to combine ownership of capital with entrepreneurial skill. Still more important was the fact that, as one of the first Chinese to experience direct and extensive contact with Westerners, he first saw the profits and promises of modern industry. Such knowledge was invaluable at the time, since it could hardly have been acquired otherwise. It was not that he had become disillusioned with traditional businesses, but that he had become familiar with the superior advantages of modern enterprises. He accordingly was the first to enter the modern fields of steamship navigation, mining, milling, and finally manufacturing, and thus became a pioneer in China's industrialization effort.

As an economic institution, the comprador system contributed in another way to China's early industrialization. Some businesses, capitalized and owned purely by Chinese and organized on modern Western lines, also employed compradors. The two most notable examples were the China Merchants' Steam Navigation Co. and the Imperial Bank of China. In contrast to their fellow-compradors in foreign business houses, compradors in Chinese firms dealt with most matters relating to foreigners. Thus, an institution, at first created mainly to meet the needs of foreign merchants, finally wound up in the service of China's modern business.

The complex and important position of the comprador in late Ch'ing history prompts a number of questions about the implications of his purely economic role for China's economic development. How rich were the compradors? What was their total income? How did they achieve and spend it? Rendering services to the foreign merchants, were they the spearheads of foreign colonialism and economic imperialism? Or, by virtue of their experience, were they able to compete with the foreigners in the management of modern enterprises, and thus in a way to prevent unchecked foreign incursion? Did they help foreigners by selling imported goods, or did they benefit the Chinese by selling native produce to the foreigners? In short, were they essentially responsible for the stimulus that foreign economic intrusion gave to China's economic development as a whole? The comprador was more than just an individual; indeed, a socioeconomic institution was gradually formed that centered around him. How did the comprador system embody and modify Chinese and Western institutions? As for his economic pursuits, to what extent were they connected with his social activities? In order to deal with these questions in proper historical perspective, it is necessary to consider the position of the comprador against a broader social and political background.

Although the main concern of this study is the economic activity of the comprador, his role cannot be separated from that of the merchant in general, just as the merchant cannot be isolated from the society within which he found himself. Moreover, the comprador's economic pursuits were closely related to his other varied activities within society. Since the economic aspect of life is intertwined with practically all other aspects, the social, political, and ideological factors also have to be taken into account.

The rise of the comprador class must be viewed from the perspective of the rise of the merchant class as a whole. In the hierarchy of Chinese social values, merchants were at the bottom, artisans were a step higher but still below the farmers, and scholars were at the apex. This does not mean, however, that the government was indifferent to merchants, nor that their activities did not affect government policy. But in a Confucian society based mainly on agrarian economy, merchants were by and large regarded as parasitic and without moral worth. The rise of the merchant class in the late Ch'ing was therefore remarkable. Fiscal difficulties forced the Ch'ing government to seek revenue through the sale of rank or degree status. About a third of the lower degrees (below the *chü-jen* or "provincial graduate") were purchased, that is, they were granted in reward for "contributions" that had been solicited for famine relief, public works, or military needs. In time of emergency, the actual sale of offices was resorted to. Although purchased ranks or titles seldom, if ever, involved real authority or responsibility, they nevertheless made it possible for the rich merchants, including the compradors, to raise their social status, at least nominally, to that of the gentry class. The theoretically low status of the merchant was thus somewhat misleading. Indeed, the discrepancy between the social ideals, embodied in the legal texts, and the social realities was very great, even in traditional China.[8] Actually, the wealthy merchant had been influential in society in the sense that he could, by his wealth, manipulate to some extent the persons of higher social prestige; he bought his power.

At the same time, the comprador's pivotal economic role also led to the rise of the merchant class. The term *shang*, translated "merchant," usually referred to traders in traditional China before the rise of the comprador. They were generally divided into *hsing-shang*, the "traveling traders," and *tso-ku*, the "stationary traders." But by the late Ch'ing the term *shang* carried a broader meaning. Within its scope were included persons who engaged in various forms of commercial, financial, or industrial pursuits. Since the comprador was typically the one who engaged in broader economic activities than a trader and yet was called a shang, such a shift of meaning was largely owing to the rise of the comprador in the treaty ports.

The rising social status of the comprador was by no means solely a result of his economic activities. Unlike his predecessors, who had usually not been allowed to participate in the governing process, he gradually took part in local government affairs, together with other merchants. He performed many gentry functions, such as the maintenance of social order, and assumed responsibility for many traditional gentry-led activities, such as famine relief.[9] Thus, although gentry functions continued, the gentry now came partly from the merchant class. The rise of the comprador was illustrated by the fact that Tong King-sing, comprador to Jardine, Matheson & Co. at Shanghai (1863–1873), was later officially appointed a bureau commissioner (*tsung-pan*), to take charge of China's first steamship company in 1873.[10] Now that merchants, through purchase, had joined the gentry in the ranks of the social elite, the two were frequently mentioned together as "gentry-merchant" (*shen-shang* and *shen-tung*).[11]

The arena of the comprador's activity was by no means limited to economic pursuits and local politics. With his expertise, his economic power, and the rising influence of the merchant class as a whole, the comprador became involved in China's politics on the national level. His help, based on his knowledge of pidgin English and of "barbarian affairs" (*i-wu*), was enlisted both by the Chinese government and by foreign diplomats. He is also known to have participated in modern China's reform (1898) and revolutionary

(1911) movements. Thus, the rise of the comprador was owing less to the rise of the merchant class as a whole than to his own special qualities. Indeed, the comprador's competence in the field of foreign affairs actually accelerated the social rise of the merchant class.

Even more noteworthy was the comprador's new social attitude. Because of his unique knowledge and experience, he had a different outlook from his contemporaries. Unlike the orthodox scholar-officials, he was among the first to emphasize the importance of commercial and industrial development rather than of military equipment and the Confucian social order. Less indoctrinated in the Confucian classics, he turned out to be a vigorous challenger of some of China's traditional values. To some extent he departed from, and even turned against, traditional society.

For example, aside from the fact that he combined the roles of both passive owner and active manager of capital and that he showed a readiness to take risks in a new field, he tended to view his economic undertakings as a family business. The traditional Chinese merchant tried to raise his family out of the merchant class by educating his sons to pass the civil service examinations. The comprador, however, differed from this tradition in several respects. On the one hand, it was he, not his sons, who would probably be appointed a high official, and such an appointment was based precisely on his competence as a merchant. On the other hand, unlike other merchants, he was quite content to remain a merchant, and in some cases even refused invitations to become an official.

The comprador's departure from tradition can also be seen in the way in which he educated his children, especially during the nineteenth century. He either made them private students of Westerners, or sent them to Western-style schools, without paying much attention to the Confucian classics and civil examinations. With such an education, they were better suited to continue the career of a comprador. Indeed, he expected his profession to continue in the family for generations. However, unlike the hong merchants' descendants, who were often required by the officials to continue the profession, the comprador's "family business" was a matter of choice.

All in all, since the comprador's activities involved an interaction between two cultures at a variety of levels, he can be said to represent the "marginal man," who assumes the role of both a cosmopolitan and a stranger.[12] Of course, the comprador was by no means the only kind of marginal man living in the treaty ports. Side by side with him arose another new type, the "treaty port mandarin."[13] With the opening of the ports, there emerged a group of "barbarian experts" to handle the new foreign relations—men like P'an Shih-ch'eng, Hsüeh Huan, and Ting Jih-ch'ang. Before the 1880's these experts were still separated from the bulk of the scholar-gentry class. They specialized in foreign affairs and had no intimate ties to the main strata of society. Like the compradors, they were "cosmopolitans" in the sense that they were less ethnocentric, and "strangers" in the sense that, identifying less intimately with their own world, they were able to look at it with a certain critical detachment. Both the comprador and the treaty port mandarin might lack a thorough mastery of the Confucian classics, but they were quick to respond to the new situation and grasp opportunities when they presented themselves. In the hybrid treaty port society, both types gained advancement through contact with the foreigners and thus made their careers outside the traditional channels.

The compradors occupied a lower position in society than the treaty port mandarins and generally mediated between the two cultures at a lower level. But precisely for this reason, they were better examples of the marginal man. Indeed, their importance should by no means be underestimated on the grounds of their relatively lower social status and more prosaic role. On the contrary, acculturation is composed of a variety of "situational circumstances" rather than of fundamental interchanges between "systems" (including value systems). Cultural interaction is usually effected piecemeal in the workaday world of human affairs, rather than by wholesale abandonment or adoption of fundamental social structures. But fragments merge into larger themes, and, in the last analysis, a process of great cultural change is seen to arise from the everyday activities of very ordinary men.

The comprador's noneconomic activities raise a number of issues. The rise of the comprador was a product of the treaty system, which provided places and opportunities for Chinese and foreign merchants to pursue their calling. The treaty ports remade Chinese life. It was in them that China met the West, and through them flowed Western goods, people, and ideas. While foreigners dominated the scene, the day-to-day texture of Sino-Western contact was an interweaving of Chinese and Western ways and values. To what extent did the comprador exemplify this mix? How did he affect cultural interaction in general and the hybrid "treaty port culture" in particular? He has been criticized for being unorthodox, but did his significance not lie in the very fact that he deviated from the tradition as a middleman? What role did he play in China's modernization, apart from its industrialization? To what extent did he, compared with the early Jesuits, affect the Western image of China and the Chinese image of the West? What were his own views and attitudes as a middleman between cultures?

The answer to these questions may be that after all he worked at the ragged edges of two cultures and was thus not in position to mediate in a full and adequate way. The foreign merchant was not always the best spokesman of his civilization, just as the comprador did not always represent the Chinese orthodoxy. In the process of cultural diffusion, people who serve the intermediary functions are often "inadequate" groups—the "adequate" people being either unwilling to act or lacking the opportunity to do so.[14] Just as foreign traders and missionaries could transmit no more of their culture than they themselves knew, so the compradors were unable to introduce any more of the West to China than what they had learned. Moreover, like their Western counterparts, the compradors were not the best qualified representatives of their own culture. Unfortunately, their limited contribution was further hindered by the fact that their social position, while improving, was still in most cases relatively low. For instance, the Yale-educated Yung Wing (1828–1912), although sometimes hard put to make a living, nevertheless maintained his honor by declining an invitation in 1859 to become a lucrative comprador to the prominent British firm of Dent & Co. And every comprador used his *hao* (the style of a man or the name by which he is generally known) instead of his *ming* (a man's official name) in his business dealings.[15] Therefore, the new cultural elements introduced or represented by the compradors could immediately acquire undesirable associations from their low social status, which might outweigh any intrinsic advantages.[16]

Indeed, one should not overemphasize the rise of the comprador.

Like any marginal man, he had his limitations. He was shrewd and talented but not always honest. Not an independent merchant per se from the beginning, he hung his hopes for success too closely on his connections with foreigners and thus on China's unstable foreign relations. He was still generally associated with the "parasitic" merchant and was criticized for deviating from social norms. Limited by his background, he was perhaps culturally and intellectually more imitative than creative. Although alive to new ideas and capable of criticizing his cultural heritage, and thus to some extent liberated from tradition, he was still moved by many traditional values, such as familism and regionalism.

The comprador was often condemned as a traitor, first for serving persons who were not Confucian, and later for assisting people who were not Chinese. After the rise of modern nationalism, he was particularly held in contempt by Chinese patriots, being regarded as the running dog of foreign economic imperialism and hence identified with foreign incursion. But a closer look shows that the anticomprador movement was an anachronism, since the slogan "Down with the comprador class" was in vogue during the nationalistic movement in the 1920's—a time when the comprador had already declined and was soon to disappear completely. Today, when the profession has been defunct for more than a generation, the meaning of the word "comprador" has moved one step further from its original commercial sense. It now means any Chinese who betrays China and "sells out" his country's interests to foreigners. Thus, there have arisen such terms as "compradorial tendency" and "compradorial character," with highly scornful connotations.[17] Like so many people in history whose fame, or notoriety, begins only after death, the comprador's presence in China's national consciousness is vividly felt now that his importance has passed. This after-image will remain for years to come.

Created by necessity, the compradors were at first indispensable as commercial middlemen. But gradually they became an obstruction to a freer, more direct and thorough Sino-foreign economic contact. In fact, at the turn of the century when Chinese and foreign merchants tried to carry on direct trade, both parties suffered reprisals from the compradors. During the initial period of acculturation, when intermediaries between the two cultures were most needed, the compradors were also of benefit to Chinese society. However, with time their historical significance as cultural mediums greatly decreased. On balance, taking into account all the activities of the comprador, he appears to have been an essential economic middleman and a valuable cultural go-between in the nineteenth century, while gradually becoming more of a hindrance in the twentieth.

In entering the comparatively neglected field of modern Chinese socioeconomic history, this study is not intended to provide corroborative evidence for a genetic theory, though it may well throw light on the subject.[18] Designed as a study of the relation between foreign and Chinese merchants in general, and of the activities and influences of the compradors in particular, this book is also not intended as a treatment of the ramified problems of China's foreign trade, although any study of Sino-foreign commercial relations cannot be entirely separated from the trade that formed its basis.

While some compradors remained in the profession all their lives, others in the course of time turned their wealth into business and industry and thus became independent businessmen. Their later careers were nevertheless intimately connected with their comprador years, both the accumulated capital and the special experience having resulted from contact with foreigners. Moreover, most compradors maintained their own separate businesses while they served in the foreign houses. Thus, since the comprador was not only a commercial middleman but also usually an independent merchant in one way or another, the term "comprador-merchant" is also used. No uniformity appears in the spelling of the word "comprador." In the records of the American and British firms, both "comprador" and "compradore" were used. I have chosen the simpler form.

The meaning of the word "comprador" has also kept changing. Today it has been drastically altered to depart even further from its original sense. It is used to refer to all persons who associated with foreigners in one way or another, acting as traitors. Not only are merchants who tried to operate mining enterprises and silk factories with the foreigners labeled as compradors, but also high officials (like Li Hung-chang), bankers (like Hu Kuang-yung), and warlords (like Ch'en Chiung-ming) are regarded as "compradors of high class.''[19] Such figurative usage is avoided in this study, and every effort is made to adhere to the term's original commercial sense.

Although this study covers the history of the comprador—the man and the institution—in nineteenth century China, most emphasis is put on the period 1860–1890, owing to the nature of the primary sources used. Also, it is confined mainly to the compradors of Western establishments, since the role of the Japanese business firms in China was insignificant until the twentieth century. Although Hong Kong was a British colony from 1842, it is here included in China geographically, for most of the foreign firms situated in Hong Kong actually conducted business in China. A great majority of China's compradors, especially before the 1880's, came from Canton. By this is meant the Canton prefecture (Kuang-chou fu), which administratively included fourteen hsien. Half of these districts were not close to the sea, while the other half were, among which Hsiang-shan (Heung-shan), Nan-hai, and P'an-yü were the homeland of most of the Cantonese compradors.

The information in this study of merchants' activities is drawn by necessity from scattered sources, including archives, journals, and biographies. An American commercial attaché in China once aptly remarked, "It seems strange that in the various books written on China, more especially those of a commercial character, so little should have been said by way of description of one of the most important institutions of the country in its relations to foreign trade—that of the comprador."[20] A number of explanations may be given for this silence. In spite of the important role played by the comprador, he was relatively unknown in China beyond his own circle, for the commercial world was generally outside the pale of official history, which centered its interest on the throne and the top levels of society.[21] What is more, few compradors were men of letters, and their own accounts are particularly scarce. Finally, the Westerners showed their great interest in China's commerce by keeping voluminous and vivid records of the hong merchants and the Hoppo (the superintendent of customs for Kwangtung province), but they seldom wrote about the compradors' activities. Even the correspondence between foreign partners in China seldom mentioned their compradors unless in connection with concrete problems. Perhaps the foreigners regarded the compradors' activities as unspectacular or took them for granted. More likely, they did not know exactly how the comprador system worked, or they would have abolished the costly operation at an earlier date. Thanks to the records of some Western mercantile houses in China, however, it is possible to obtain a fairly satisfactory picture. These original sources include the archives of Russell & Co., Augustine Heard & Co., and Jardine, Matheson & Co., supplemented by contemporary Chinese and English newspapers and the writer's interviews with former compradors.[22]

II The Western Merchant and His Chinese Comprador

The Treaty of Nanking in 1842 marked the beginning of the Western invasion of China, and the opening of the treaty ports provided more places and opportunities for foreign merchants to pursue their calling. At the China end of the trade, they now faced the problem of establishing, conducting, and promoting a business. When free trade replaced the monopolistic Cohong system after 1842, however, they found that it was by no means easy to initiate direct contact with their Chinese counterparts. A variety of reasons made it necessary to employ a Chinese to work for them as a comprador.

A successful foreign mercantile house in China required the presence of an energetic managing partner on the local scene, but even more essential was the employment of an able Chinese comprador. For the comprador not only rendered diverse and extensive services, but he also was an independent merchant in his own right. For these reasons, he was particularly cultivated by the foreign partners. An exploration of the development of foreign business in China will show how much it owed its success to the Chinese comprador.

The Western Mercantile House

Vasco da Gama's voyage around Africa to India in 1498 ushered in the age of European expansion in the East, and the successful industrialization of Europe during the nineteenth century initiated the period of economic imperialism. After the opening of China in

1842, most foreign China-trade firms organized their business in China as an agency house—or a commission house, in American business terminology. The house made money chiefly from commissions, earned at rates varying from one-half to five percent on a wide diversity of operations.[1]

Organization and Business. Most of the big Western firms in China, such as Russell & Co., Augustine Heard & Co., and Jardine, Matheson & Co., were organized primarily on a family basis. Partners usually headed the main and branch offices, so that managers and investors were identical. Business was conducted largely through correspondence, which is especially important in understanding the history of the Western firms. Among the approximately 82,000 letters of the Jardine, Matheson & Co. archives, about 57,300 fall under the heading of "Local Correspondence" written from the China coast, the rest being mainly from India, Africa, America, Australia, and Europe.

The correspondence portion of the Augustine Heard & Co. archives was originally divided into two categories. The "European and American" letterbooks consisted of "House Letters" through which regular transactions were handled. These impersonal firm-to-firm business exchanges included advice, proposals, and semi-contractual agreements, besides fulfilling the responsibility of the house to keep its Western constituents and creditors supplied with market information, on the basis of which orders were placed with the house. The bulk of the letter writing, however, fell in the category of "Chinese and Eastern Ports," which dealt with local communications.

The Western partner in charge of business at the China end (called "Head in the East" in Jardine's case) usually resided at the main office in Hong Kong, while branch offices and agencies in different treaty ports kept in close contact with him through correspondence. In the case of Heard's, according to its partnership agreement, any matter that involved money had theoretically to be cleared with the head of the house.[2] However, in fact decentralization was common, and the branch managing partners had to rely heavily on their independent judgment. Both Albert F. Heard and Edward Cunningham in Shanghai could act independently of the main offices of Heard's and Russell's in Hong Kong in 1861.[3] Actually, with the opening of the Yangtze and the rise of Shanghai in the sixties, the foreign partner at Shanghai gradually took charge of the business of the treaty ports on the Yangtze (Chinkiang, Hankow, and Kiukiang) and in the north (Chefoo, Tientsin, and New-chwang).

Desirability of a partner was assessed not only on his ability or the amount of capital he could bring with him, but also on the number of constituents that would follow him to the house.[4] Another factor was his willingness to go to China, for the success of a foreign firm depended heavily on the entrepreneurship of its partner on the local scene. William Cole, an American merchant, described in 1860 how he changed his impression of Russell & Co.: "My intercourse with the partner of Russell & Co. has been uniformly agreeable. I have a higher impression of the house than before. It must vary with the characters of the individuals at the head of its management from time to time . . . I consider Mr. [Thomas] Walsh particularly a man of high tone as well as business capacity."[5] A partner in China not only had to keep close watch on the home market and observe business trends, but also to think fast, develop initiative, and have imagination. The mentality required in China was not a provincial one, since the most crucial task for a foreign merchant on the local scene was to achieve a better connection with Chinese commerce—through the comprador.

The heart of the business was the merchandise trade—the sale of Western manufactured goods, primarily wool and cotton, and the export of tea and silk from China. Acting chiefly as agents on orders from constituents and supplying services at the risk of capital located in London or New York, the agency houses handled considerable imports and exports. Whereas the larger houses maintained their own fleets, the smaller ones chartered vessels for single voyages. Being concerned mainly with the sale or purchase of goods in China on behalf of principals in Europe or the United States, the agency houses kept their business free from risk.

The main function of the agency house was the handling of manufactured goods, opium, and the specie paid to Chinese in exchange for tea and silk. Thus, the agency house required a modicum of capital with a maximum of enterprise. The fact that the house paid for regular and large purchases of native produce out of Chinese bank accounts, which were built up through the sale of its imports, increased house prestige and influenced both Chinese merchants and Western constituents. Indeed, an energetic foreign constituent was most desirable for an agency house. Witnessing the sizable tea purchases by his fellow American merchants of Olyphant & Co., Russell's Shanghai partner wrote with envy in 1860: "I only wish we had such enterprising constituents as that commission house, for I don't know any thing to prevent our being enterprising too, if we are at liberty to be so."[6]

Although the commission business involved minimum risk, it also enjoyed minimum control and profits and consequently restricted entrepreneurial activities. One alternative was marketeering, which, however, involved both risk and extra effort. Market estimation was a tenuous business at best. While the comprador provided market intelligence on the China end, a foreign merchant had to keep a close and constant watch on the market situtation at home. For instance, with the English tea market in mind, Thomas Larken, Jardine's Foochow partner, wrote to Joseph Jardine in 1856 comparing Foochow tea with that of Canton: "The scented Capers [of Foochow] are well made and clean but I am afraid the scent is not exactly what it should be . . . The scented Orange Pekoes made here I do not like. They draw a fair liquor and taste *strong scented* & *strong burnt* but the leaf is too *yellow* and *short* and wants the blackness of the Canton Teas, which although not the natural color of the Tea, it is what people have been accustomed to in England and I think it will be found difficult to persuade them of the fact, and of the actual superiority as far as *trueness* goes of the Foochow Teas."[7] And the English tea taste kept changing. These Canton Pekoes, which were favorites in England in the fifties and sixties, gradually went "out of favor," and in 1870 the tea memorandum of Jardine's London office stated, "we should not advise shipment to any extent."[8] Instead, it went on to make clear that the Kiukiang tea was preferred to that of Foochow: "The sorts which pleased best last year were the rich, flavoury Pekoe Souchong kinds, mostly shipped from Kiukiang . . . If the crop [at Foochow] is no better than that of last year, we could not recommend large purchase on any terms."[9]

In order to reduce the risk in large speculative investments but at the same time keep them under their own control, the foreign agency houses usually engaged in the system of "joint-account" shipping, with the firm and another party or parties investing jointly. Under this arrangement, capital was contributed by two or more parties and the profit or loss was divided by the ratio of investment. Heard's, as shown on its 1859 balance sheet, had sixty-seven running accounts with European, American, and Chinese constituents. It also proposed joint-account monopolies with a Taiwan mandarin for camphor export and with the Prince of Satsuma, Japan, for produce shipments.[10] This system was even more widespread among the British houses.[11] As early as 1849 Jardine's contracted for a joint-account shipment of tea with the Chinese tea merchant Manfoong Hong.[12] This kind of compromise arrangement was especially useful as a means of sharing risk and encouraging business.

The activities of an agency house were by no means limited to general transaction business, and it commonly managed a great diversity of operations. In order to carry on the normal commission business of buying and selling, the house was forced to provide all the necessary ancillary facilities, particularly shipping and insurance. The uncertainty of the political and economic scene in China in the fifties undoubtedly encouraged this tendency to diversity, since no one source of income in the trade was reliable enough to risk specialization.

Thus, by the 1850's most Western houses were not only concerned with the normal commission business of buying and selling, importing and exporting, but also acted as banks, serving both the depositors and the house; handled exchange operations, negotiating bills and converting dollars and pounds sterling into taels; served as agents, managing shipping, insurance, and freighting; acted in legal matters; and engaged in a number of investments. Jardine, Matheson & Co., for example, not only traded itself but also "acted as banker, billbroker, shipowner, freighter, insurance agent [and] purveyor" all at once.[13]

Among these activities, the exchange function provided the main purchasing power for the house's agents in the treaty ports. Some exchange business was conducted on a barter basis— with manufactured goods being consigned in exchange for native products—but the house also handled the exchange operations on a "higher" level. Opium sometimes served as a convenient medium of exchange, but the selling of bills was the most important means of gaining purchasing power, as for Heard's in the fifties. For a Western agency house, the exchange operations—such as negotiation of bills, conversion of one currency into another, remittance of returns in goods, bills, or treasure, guarantee of bills and bonds—were not only important means to get more orders from the constituents, but also were remunerative in themselves.

At the same time, it was advantageous for the house to make full use of all its resources, both monetary and managerial, and to expand its foreign trade functions to include local services. Augustine Heard & Co. in the late fifties acted for others in almost all capacities in which it acted for itself. Smaller firms, individual agents, house employees, and Chinese merchants were all customers for the services and facilities of the house. Indeed, the services designed for one purpose were easily employed in others.

Changes in Business Patterns. The ways of doing business kept changing. In the fifties and sixties, China trade was dominated by a small group of powerful foreign houses, as the Customs' Report described in retrospect: "In old times, business was done in Shanghai by men having command of large capital, who bought heavy consignments here and stored them till there was a chance for sale."[14] The larger houses also functioned as banks, issuing dollar notes and providing deposit and remittance facilities, as in the case of Jardine's. A well-known American merchant, Edward Cunningham, wrote in 1873: "Twenty to twenty-five years ago the prominent houses, including one American, did a flourishing exchange business . . . One English bank had less business than one of the mercantile houses."[15]

But the 1860's saw one of the greatest changes in China trade. The era of the clipper ship ended with the advancement of the more efficient steamship, and in 1869 the Suez Canal halved the distance to Europe. The gradual extension of telegraphic communication was to have an even more profound effect on the commission business. All in all, the rapid development of communication methods accelerated the change in old business patterns, as Jardine's London office observed in 1870: "In considering the prospects for the importation of Tea during the season 1870 and 1871, we would first remark that *the conditions of trade have materially altered of late years* . . . There has been a want of keeping quality in the teas, and a consequent unwillingness on the part of Importers to hold. There has been much less disposition to speculate in the article, even when figures have looked favourable, because of the rapid communication with China rendering any prolonged scarcity nearly impossible."[16]

Thus, the once gigantic houses, which were few in number and financially self-sufficient, gradually lost their monopolistic position in the China trade after the sixties. The newly established, smaller foreign firms, with loans from the steadily growing foreign banks in the treaty ports, now had the opportunity to compete with the older houses. The opening of the Yangtze and other new ports, with the new regulations, shifted the commercial center to Shanghai. The growth of business in a new direction in the sixties saw the concomitant decline of the traditional commission agency business, as Edward Cunningham of Russell & Co. observed in 1861: "I think we are sliding into a great change. The American business is following or had followed the English and like that can no longer be done on commission . . . I see all our business gone and I look around to find who has it. Not Heard's or any house on commission. It is being done by parties on their own account . . . The business has become too complicated to be done by agents."[17] Four months later, Albert F. Heard of Augustine Heard & Co. also acknowledged the new business trend toward specialization and house investment. He wrote, "I am becoming more and more convinced that we must change somewhat our style of business . . . Comm. [Commission] pur. [purchases] . . . are a myth. How have Olyphant & Co. and others wheedled away the floating constituency which we had?"[18]

In the course of time, Western firms gradually became more and more involved in operations at their own risk. Commenting on the recent depression in merchandise business, F. B. Forbes of Russell & Co. wrote in 1872: "The trade in tea and piece goods has also got worked down to the barest trifle of commission or expected profit. In all the old staple branches of China commerce, the broker is taking the place of the merchant . . . When the period of transition is over, no doubt most of the larger firms with capital and credit will have transferred themselves from produce to industrial and financial enterprises . . . Those of them, who, like ourselves have the management of steam lines and insurance offices are the luckiest, and it is significant that Jardines, Heards and others are all struggling to develop this branch of business."[19]

Indeed, local shipping was perhaps the most outstanding and successful branch of business to be fostered. The ascendancy of Western shipping in the coastal trade is well known, and the story of the rivalry has been vividly told.[20] The trend toward diversification was best illustrated by the establishment of ancillary commercial facilities on an independent basis; thus, both banks and steamship companies grew out of what had originally been merely a sideline or composite part of a complete agency business. Whereas banks developed so fully and rapidly as to be beyond the control of a single house, the steamship business retained a closer connection. The Shanghai Steam Navigation Co., a joint-stock company promoted and established by Russell's partners in 1862, declared that "the house of Russell & Co. will act as permanent agents and treasurers of the Company."[21] Russell's were also to furnish all the managerial personnel and the offices for the steamship company. For the purpose of competing with American merchants for the Yangtze steamship business, Butterfield & Swire founded the China Navigation Co. in 1872, and Jardine's reorganized the various steamers under its management into the China Coast Steam Navigation Co. the next year, both parent companies serving as "general agents."[22] The China Steam Navigation Co.'s business developed so successfully and on such a scale that it finally overtook the usual business of Butterfield & Swire as an agency house concerned chiefly with the merchandise trade.

Besides shipping, foreign firms invested in other activities, especially industrial undertakings after the 1880's. Heard's, for example, made investments in such enterprises as an ice company, a rice cleaning mill, barges, pile-drivers, and a floating dock.[23] Jardine's engaged in an even broader scope of activities, ranging from utilities and railroads to silk filature and sugar refining. In this way an agency house gradually developed as a nexus of trade, shipping, insurance, finance, and investment activities, which may be illustrated by the diverse operations of Jardine, Matheson & Co.[24] (See Table 1.)

Reliance on the Chinese Comprador

A variety of reasons prevented the Western merchant from trading directly with his Chinese counterpart, causing him to depend on the

The Western Merchant

Table 1. Diverse activities of Jardine, Matheson & Co. (est. 1832).[a]

---

1. Trade
    A. Export Department (Tea, Silk, China Produce, Export Credits Guarantee)
    B. Import Department (Timber, Fertilizers, Metals, Liquor, Food)
    C. Auxiliary Departments (Accounting, Correspondence, Delivery, Shipping)
2. Shipping
    A. Hongkong Whampoa Dock Co. (1863)
    B. China Coast Steam Navigation Co. (1873)
    C. Indochina Steam Navigation Co. (1882)
    D. Shanghai Dock and Engineering & Co. (1900)
3. Wharf and Godown
    A. Shanghai and Hongkong Wharf Co. (1875)
    B. Hongkong and Kowloon Wharf & Godown Co. (1886)
    C. Ewo Cold Storage Co.
    D. Ewo Press Packing Co.
4. Insurance
    A. Union Insurance Society of Canton (1838)
    B. Hongkong Fire Insurance Co. (1868)
5. Finance
    A. Matheson & Co., Ltd., London (1848)
    B. Hongkong and Shanghai Banking Corp. (1864)
    C. British and Chinese Corp. (1898)
    D. Central Chinese Railways, Ltd. (1904)
6. Industry
    A. Ewo Silk Filature (1881)
    B. Ewo Cotton Mills (1895)
    C. Ewo Brewery Co.
    D. Hongkong Dairy Farm Ice and Cold Storage Co. (1899)
    E. Hope Critall (China) Ltd.
    F. The China Sugar Refining Co.
7. Miscellaneous
    A. Shanghai Land Investment Co. (1888)
    B. Hongkong Electric Co. (1889)
    C. Hongkong Tramways, Ltd. (1902)

Source: Jardine, Matheson & Co., *An Outline of the History of a China House for a Hundred Years, 1832–1932;* Uchida Naosaku, "Yōkō seido no kenkyū;" Uchida Naosaku, "Zai-Shi Eikoku shōsha."

a. Date in parentheses indicates year of establishment. Unfortunately, further quantitative data about the degree of diversification of activities, such as sales data for each category, are not available.

help of his Chinese comprador. Employed on contract to handle the Chinese side of the firm's activities, the comprador headed and guaranteed the Chinese staff and served as the foreign merchant's middleman in his dealings with the Chinese. As such, he played a pivotal role in the mercantile world in the treaty ports. In the words of a Western newspaper editor in China, "the comprador may be regarded as not only the axle on which the whole wheel of the foreigner's business with the native turns, but in many cases also the hub, the spokes, the rim, and in fact, the whole wheel, save the paint, which may be taken to represent the firm which gives it the colour of its name."[25]

Although the importance of the comprador may here be somewhat exaggerated, the Western merchant's dependence on the comprador can certainly be seen from the relative number of his Western and Chinese employees. At Augustine Heard & Co. in 1860, for example, its Western employees numbered eight assistants at the head office in Hong Kong, which included a tea taster and a silk inspector. There were six clerks in Shanghai, and three or four at Ningpo and Foochow. Single agents or representatives were stationed at Canton, Amoy, and Macao. But each office was outnumbered by a comprador department, ranging from about thirty in Hong Kong, a score or so at Shanghai and Canton, to about six in other places. The comprador's indispensable position in the Western house was revealed in a letter from George F. Weller, Heard's Foochow manager in the fifties and sixties, to the head of the house in Hong Kong in 1862: "When the comprador [Akit] was ill, everything ground to a halt."[26]

Reasons for Employing a Comprador. The monopolistic nature of the Cohong system was one basic reason for the Sino-British Opium War of 1839–1842. The Canton system of trade was abolished after the Treaty of Nanking in 1842, whereupon the Western merchants hoped to initiate a free trade. But there were fundamental obstacles to free and direct transactions, which necessitated the employment of the comprador.

The Western merchant in China was confronted at the outset by the language problem, which he preferred not to tackle. Other factors that served as major impediments to economic activity included the complexity of the currency. In the silver sector, for instance, the major unit of account, the tael, was not uniform but varied from place to place and trade to trade.[27] Aside from the sycee (*wen-yin* or monetary silver), dollars gradually found a place in the system—first by the import of Spanish, Mexican, American, and other dollars, then by coinage in China.[28] Jardine's accounts sent from Hong Kong to Shanghai in 1861 did not make the necessary distinction between tael and dollar and consequently had to be returned, as James Whittall wrote from Shanghai: "I regret to have to return you the accounts sent up for Yakee & Eukee, as there is no difference made by you between Taels and dollars, the balances of all of them being therefore totally incorrect. You debit them with so many Taels advanced, as only so many dollars, then charge commission on drawing so many taels and carry it as dollars . . . This confusion unfortunately runs through the whole of these accounts."[29]

The complexity of the currency was coupled with the varying systems of weights and measures.[30] J. Henderson, the first foreign merchant to reside at Tientsin, recalled the difficulty when he first arrived there in 1860: "Being the first arrival, and the only [foreign merchant] at the time, I found on applying to H. E. Chun How [Ch'ung-hou] that there were neither standard weights nor a scale of relative weights with Shanghai and Canton, nor with the Haiquan [Haikwan] weights; all these, with the aid of my compradore, I had to settle for my self."[31]

Lacking the necessary information, the Western merchant could hardly understand the Chinese market, especially the unregulated issue and circulation of money certificates and credit bills by old-fashioned native banks. The financial status of the various native banks and of the leading Chinese merchants was unknown to him. It also seemed impossible for him to comprehend China's extraordinary variety of commercial practices and social customs.[32] China's strong mercantile and geographical guilds, reinforced by regionalism and familism, made it virtually impossible for him to trade directly with the Chinese. All in all, the existing indigenous economic and social conditions, coupled with cultural barriers, made it necessary for a Western merchant to employ a Chinese comprador for the purpose of doing business smoothly with the Chinese.

Efforts to Promote Chinese Connections and Secure Efficient Compradors.

The Comprador in China

In a time of keen competition at the treaty ports, an agency house in China had to demonstrate its entrepreneurial skill as well as its ability to obtain compradorial talent of a high quality. Its success or failure was determined to a great extent by its ability to maintain good relations with the Chinese—to cultivate the native merchants in general and the compradors in particular. The Chinese constituents were important to the house not only for doing business but also for subscribing to the shares of certain enterprises undertaken by the house. In view of the diverse and extensive services rendered by the comprador to the house, the house clearly owed its success in large part to him.

The American firm of Russell & Co. provided a good example of the Western merchants' efforts to promote Chinese connections. It enjoyed particularly cordial relations with the Chinese merchants in the sixties, and at the same time the firm employed valuable and efficient compradors. The insight and effort of the Shanghai managing partner, Edward Cunningham (1823–1889), was instrumental in establishing and maintaining the firm's successful Chinese connections.[33] After an absence for a long honeymoon in Europe and a visit with his relatives in Milton, Massachusetts, Cunningham was back in China in January 1861, to resume his former position. He now proposed to concentrate the firm's resources in steamship enterprise in Chinese waters for the carrying trade, but P. S. Forbes, the head of the house in America, showed little interest.[34] Cunningham then demonstrated his promotional abilities not only by raising the necessary capital in China but also by operating the business successfully—in both cases relying to a high degree on his ability and willingness to cultivate the Chinese merchants, including the compradors, in the treaty ports.

As American vice-consul in Shanghai in 1850-1854, Cunningham had been active in the treaty ports.[35] Having been with Russell & Co. in China for years, he was well versed in the China coast patois of pidgin English and could rely on his friendship with Chinese merchants and compradors. Around August 1861 he took a step designed to foster the interest of his Chinese friends in the steamship business. At a time when the freight rates on the Yangtze River were spectacularly high, he arranged to have his Chinese friends share the ownership of an immediately profitable steamer. In a letter to P. S. Forbes, he later explained: "Though I took the risk myself, I took none of the profits, dividing her up, as soon as she [the steamer *Willamette*] was safely running, among our Shanghai Chinese, in order to induce them to enter upon the grander scheme of the SSN [Shanghai Steam Navigation] Company."[36]

Cunningham's success lay in the fact that he could persuade his "Chinese friends and constituents" to make investments. In 1861–1862, he successfully raised the necessary funds for the Shanghai Steam Navigation Co., with the Chinese merchants subscribing more than one-third of the total capital of one million taels. This was of particular significance in view of the fact that in the same period three other houses were contemplating a similar project but could not find the necessary capital.[37]

For the purpose of maintaining a closer relation with the Chinese merchants, Cunningham decided to purchase properties for waterfront sites near the Chinese business sections at the various ports for the steamer business. The Kin-lee-yuen (Chin li yüan) wharfage site in the Shanghai French Concession, which turned out to be the main base of Russell & Co.'s steamer business, was chosen because of its convenience for the foreign merchants as well as for the Chinese. Situated next to the Chinese city, it proved to be one of the Shanghai Steam Navigation Co.'s strong attractions for the Chinese shippers.[38] In order to promote business one step further among the Chinese shippers, a "shipping office" was built in 1870 at Kin-lee-yuen—an arrangement intended to "please the Chinese."[39] Indeed, the firm's partners, such as Edward Cunningham, F. B. Forbes, and Frederic D. Hitch, devoted considerable attention to maintaining contact with the Chinese. In selecting the clerks in charge of the shipping business, they placed emphasis on ability "to talk to the Chinese."[40] Cunningham in 1871 even proposed that, in the future, those who recommended sons or relatives to be clerks should be told that the young men were required to learn Chinese at their own expense.[41]

The bulk of the firm's business, of course, was through the comprador. In the sixties, Russell's compradors were among the best of the time, and this favorable situation could be traced back to the firm's former close relations with the hong merchants at Canton.[42]

For example, soon after the firm's Shanghai branch office was established, Howqua (1810–1863) recommended in late 1858 a fellow-Cantonese, Ahyue, as the new Shanghai comprador.[43] Ahyue could speak English and was considered honest and faithful to the house.[44] He brought in another Cantonese named Sunchong as his partner, who in the words of a Heard's partner was a man of "big face" or wealth and social standing.[45]

In early 1865, Russell & Co.'s new Shanghai partners, George Tyson (1832–1881) and Frank B. Forbes (1839–1908), effected changes in the Chinese staff. They chose a Chekiang man named Choping as the firm's new chief comprador, replacing Ahyue, "the old compradore."[46] Tyson reported to P. S. Forbes on March 24, 1865: "We have also made a complete change of our steamer compradore office and none too soon—Frank [B. Forbes] will tell you all about this when he sees you. It is too long a story to write!"[47] As "one of the largest [richest] men" in Shanghai and an eminent silk merchant in his own right, Choping greatly promoted the firm's Chinese business, including that of the Shanghai Steam Navigation Co.[48] Koofunsing, one of the firm's compradors in the 1860's, was a noted tea and silk merchant of good reputation and standing.[49] In Tientsin, Russell's engaged Sunkee, whose ability as a comprador was unquestioned.[50] The compradors of Russell's on the Yangtze must have been generally efficient, for F. B. Johnson of Jardine's wrote to William Keswick in 1872 complaining of the ever-deteriorating situation at Hankow: "Russell & Co. are taking all the cargo from us."[51]

By the seventies, however, this favorable situation had gradually worsened. After Cunningham's departure, according to F. B. Forbes, the new Shanghai managing partner, H. H. Warden, "did not seem to care, or was not perhaps the man to extend our connections as Mr. Cunningham did."[52] Russell's loss of business was also ascribed partly to the inefficiency of the firm's chief comprador. Energetic in business and valuable to the house in the sixties, Choping was by 1872 aging and weak in health. As F. B. Forbes observed, "Choping himself is beginning to show signs of failing . . . I fancy he is asthmatic."[53] This unfavorable situation continued for some time, as F. B. Forbes wrote from Shanghai the next year: "I am sorry to say that our Chinese connections here are not very powerful. Choping is getting rather feeble in health and more timid, though his *loyalty* is unbounded. Koofunsing, the younger, is worthless except to screw and hoard away dollars. These are our only people."[54]

By late 1874 the unfavorable situation had still not improved. F. B. Forbes wrote to Cunningham, "We could hardly be worse off than we are with Choping's people."[55] In Tientsin, Sunkee was deeply immersed in his own speculative activities by the early seventies and thus proved an inefficient comprador. He was finally discharged in 1873, but his successors were far from satisfactory. The situation in the upper Yangtze ports was even worse. Apunn, the Hankow comprador, "went away, owing much money [to the House]."[56] Realizing that the firm's loss of business was partly owing to the ever-deteriorating relations with the Chinese merchants, F. B. Forbes tried in June 1873 to engage Hsü Jun, former comprador to Dent & Co. (1861–1868), as the firm's chief comprador in Shanghai: "I am working hard to get Ayun [Hsü Jun], and hope to succeed, though his connection with the Chinese company [China Merchants' Steam Navigation Co.] is a serious difficulty."[57] Forbes' efforts were unavailing.

Heard's connections with the Chinese were never as successful as Russell's, and its partners felt the disadvantage constantly. This inadequacy did not mean, however, that the firm neglected to promote relations with the Chinese. In fact, business with native traders was much sought after, as A. F. Heard wrote on February 28, 1858: "I am anxious to get up a shipping business among the Chinese but never have been able to do it . . . The few who have ever tried never have repeated the attempt . . . Some houses have very large connections of this description and it is the best commission business we can have."[58]

The foreign merchants' idea of operating a steamship business in China in the early sixties was not new, but the lack of funds constituted a difficulty. During 1861–1862, when Cunningham was promoting the Shanghai Steam Navigation Co. and finally succeeded in raising the capital locally, Heard's was engaged in a similar project but failed for lack of money. After learning of Cunningham's success, John Heard wrote to a partner on February 20, 1862: "Our plan for a Company has always been to get Chinese interested, and this we tried to do, but could not to any considerable extent."[59] On March 3, he wrote to another partner: "We have often thought of the same scheme in connection with Chinese, but have never been able to obtain sufficient encouragement."[60]

During Heard's thirty-odd years of trading in China (1840–1875), it failed to employ a valuable comprador comparable in ability or wealth to Tong King-sing of Jardine's or Choping of Russell's. Tong Loong-maw, the most able of Heard's compradors because of his familiarity with the tea business, only took charge of the upcountry purchases in Foochow—in contrast to the dynamic role played by Tong King-sing and Choping as chief compradors at Shanghai. Unfortunately, Tong's service as a comprador did not last long. When his own business affairs became pressing, he resigned and went to Hankow in 1862.[61] In a letter to a partner dated April 18, 1862, A. F. Heard complained: "We are unfortunate in our Chinese connections . . . and we feel the effect of it constantly. Our men are good workers but they are small men and have not the 'face' of men like Luncheong, Suncheong [comprador to Russell & Co.], Ahone and others. The Foochow comprador [Tong Loong-maw] is an exception, and I wish we had a dozen like him."[62] Although Heard's did not have a valuable comprador in Shanghai, A. F. Heard tried to compensate by establishing connections directly with eminent Chinese merchants. In the same letter, A. F. Heard continued: "The sale of *Shangtung* was a great hit, as it has opened a connection with Chun Yue Chong (alias Choping) who is one of the largest [richest] men here."[63]

The fact that the Western merchant depended heavily on the Chinese comprador was demonstrated by a letter of Jardine's Shanghai manager. After the old comprador, Asam, had resigned in 1846 because of illness, A. G. Dallas wrote to the main office at Hong Kong, applying for a new comprador, who would be "absolutely necessary" in Shanghai: "I must again apply to you for a Comprador and also for a warehouseman . . . and a responsible Comprador would have saved all the trouble I had with the stolen silk. . . . From want of a head Comprador we have also a great deal of trouble with coolies and all our servants. If you can only get a steady respectable man who can shroff dollars and will promise to remain and look after the house and godown I do not care whether he is a business man or not, but someone is absolutely necessary."[64]

Jardine's business with the Chinese was ably promoted by its compradors. Since the firm was the largest foreign house in China, the position of comprador there was extremely attractive to Chinese merchants. Its compradors, like Takee (d. 1865), Acum, Tong King-sing (1832–1892), Tong Mow-chee (1827–1897), and Ho Tung (1862–1956), were among the ablest and richest in the treaty ports. Jardine's enjoyed particularly good relations with its former compradors. The bulk of its transactions in the sixties was carried on through direct and constant contact with them, including Acum, Aleet, Yakee, and Yowloong.[65]

The efforts made by partners of Heard's and Russell's to promote business with the Chinese were paralleled at Jardine's. In the sixties, Jardine's enjoyed close contact with other Chinese merchants, who together with their excompradors were frequently mentioned in the partners' correspondence as "our native friends."[66] The firm did business with Ahone, a noted silk merchant regarded by A. F. Heard as having "big face."[67] Ekee, who formerly served in Jardine's, purchased tea and silk for the firm from the interior.[68] Jardine's also did business in tea with Hsü Jun, Dent & Co.'s former comprador and now an independent merchant.[69] The most important purchaser of the firm's manufactured goods in the sixties seems to have been Tucksing, "the best informed Native," who in 1867 had been doing business with the firm for fifteen years.[70]

The effort made by the partners of Jardine's to cultivate the compradors could be seen from their relations with Tong King-sing. Although they did not completely trust him as a treasurer, they took various steps to encourage him as an assistant in business transactions. In 1867, four years after Tong became comprador, F. B. Johnson proposed to James Whittall to give him a share of the Canton Insurance office: "I hope to allot the 10 shares you place at our disposal for Shanghai in a way to increase business here. Overweg & Co. have applied for one and A. Wilkinson & Co. for another, and I propose to give one to Tongkingsing who is exerting himself to obtain China business."[71] One year later, Johnson appealed to William Keswick on the same ground: "Tongkingsing seems to be doing what he can to influence Chinese business and I shall be glad if you will take into consideration some plan for giving to him or any other influential Native a share in the profits on premia which he may collect for the office."[72] Tong was of particular importance to the firm's shipping business for soliciting both capital and freight. In order to encourage him, Johnson reported to Whittall on October 2, 1871: "I have arranged to allot 350–400 shares [of the China Coast Steam Navigation Co.] to Tongkingsing and his native friends."[73]

Tong King-sing not only functioned ably as a comprador in Shanghai but was also instrumental in improving the efficiency of the Tientsin comprador office. In 1871 he recommended his brother Tong Mow-chee as the firm's Tientsin comprador, in which capacity he was a great help to William Forbes, the firm's agent at that port. F. B. Johnson wrote to Willian Keswick on June 22, 1871: "With regard to the Agency at Tientsin, I imagine that the increased efficiency of Mr. Forbes's management is due in no small degree to Tong King-sing's staff."[74] Jardine's successful relations with the Chinese was owing mainly to Johnson's effort and insight. In view of the keen commercial competition in China, he realized the necessity for foreign merchants to learn Chinese. In a letter to Keswick dated September 27, 1871, he wrote: "Foreigners will probably be unable to cope with the difficulty until they learn the language and looking to the future of the firm, I believe that the success in China of those who are to follow us will in no slight degree depend on their acquirement of the Native tongue."[75]

Thus, it is clear that in many ways the foreign business firms greatly relied on, and benefited from, the compradors. Although it is quantitatively impossible to prove that those firms who employed compradors, or the most effective compradors, made more profits than did firms without compradors or with less effective compradors, the fact that they continually hired them substantiates this contention.

Rivalry in Obtaining Able Compradors. The Western merchants competed vigorously for able compradors and potential constituents. The fight between Heard's and Russell's to get Apunn as their Hankow comprador in 1865 gave eloquent testimony to this rivalry. H. G. Bridges, the Hankow agent of Heard's, reported to A. F. Heard on June 20, 1866: "Apunn was shipping quantities of stuff to Shanghai, and Atong [Heard's Kiukiang comprador] wanted to get him here [Hankow] as compradore or otherwise that we might have his freight, but in the meantime R. [Russell] & Co. nobbled him and made him compradore."[76] Meanwhile, Heard's had promptly employed Russell's former Hankow comprador, Coe Lun, as Bridges continued: "Coe Lun . . . was disgusted at being superseded by Apunn, and would be happy to be King Kee [Augustine Heard & Co.] Comprador . . . on a commission for what freight he could get. I wrote Mr. [R. I.] Fearon he would be a desirable compradore, and it would be well to get hold of him."[77]

The competition for hiring able compradors and potential constituents also existed between Russell's and Olyphant's. Through its comprador at Canton, Russell's so successfully competed with Olyphant & Co. that Chinese merchants lost their confidence in the latter's steamship line. In a letter dated May 27, 1868, John M. Forbes of Russell's wrote from Canton to Edward Cunningham with regard to their Canton comprador Ahyue: "He has been working the S. [Shanghai] S. N. Co. versus Olyphant's line lately and the result is he finds no one with confidence eno. [enough] in it [Olyphant's line] to pay for a share."[78] At the same time, however, Achea, one of the firm's able freight brokers at Canton, was tempted by Olyphant's promise to "give him a much better chance," as Forbes continued: "Olyphants have been trying to get hold of one of our freight brokers (Achea) and I sent him there to find out what they wanted. They told him, as a great secret!, that they had bought four steamers and had a large capital subscribed, that they would give him a much better chance than we could, etc., etc. I told Achea that he must decide which company should have his freight for himself, but that my advice to him was to wait a short time until the four steamers came, before deciding any thing."[79]

For the purpose of cultivating Chinese traders, Sunkee, Russell's Tientsin comprador, wanted to catch up with Jardine's in the practice of "entertaining the customers . . . every New Year at dinner." In a lawsuit that Sunkee brought against Russell's in 1875, he asked the firm to pay back his expenses for such entertainment: "Item No. 8 was a charge for entertaining the customers of the firm every New Year at dinner. It was a 'large dinner.' In 1869 it cost $63; 1870, $53; 1871, $49; 1872, $42. A second dinner was given in one year, 'because E-wo [Jardine, Matheson & Co.] wanted to be level with them.' "[80]

In the contest for better Chinese connections and higher compradorial efficiency, foreign partners closely watched the developments in other firms. In contrast to the special efforts made by his American counterparts to promote Chinese relations, James Whittall, Jardine's Head in the East stationed in Hong Kong, admitted his inability to do so. In February 1867 he told a partner of Heard's that he himself "can't cultivate the Chinese as R. & Co. & A. H. & Co. do!!!"[81] However, in the early 1870's when Choping, Russell's Shanghai comprador, was aging and sick, F. B. Forbes wrote: "In the matter of obtaining information, or in persevering drumming among Chinese, Jardines with Tongkingsing or Heards with their comprador could beat us hollow."[82]

Although occasionally foreign firms cooperated over mutual interests, suspicion persisted. An agreement concerning uniform freight rates was reached between Russell & Co. and Butterfield & Swire in August 1873, but when a number of old patrons of Russell's were enticed away, F. B. Forbes suspected that the latter had not abided by the agreement: "We cannot get *legal proof* of Butterfield's bad faith, but when cargo promised to us is taken away to their steamers . . . the evidence is complete enough for us. We have repeatedly brought the cases to [William] Lang's [Butterfield's Shanghai manager] notice. He himself denies everything and says that the same rumors are brought to him about us."[83] Forbes' suspicion was not without reason, for Butterfield & Swire did try hard to drum up Chinese freight. Forbes noticed in April 1873: "[The compradors to] Butterfields have given a big *chin-chin* [goodwill] dinner to all the freight brokers, at which the foreign clerks assisted."[84]

From the account of Cheng Kuan-ying (1842–1923), comprador to Butterfield & Swire in 1873–1881, it appears that the firm had other ways of developing Chinese business: "We either gave them [freight brokers] an extra commission of 5 per cent, or gave them allowance for expenses such as [office] rent, or permitted them to recommend men to serve as steamer compradors—the best posts going to men recommended by those who brought the largest amount of freight."[85] The good relations between the Chinese and Butterfield & Swire was mainly owing to William Lang's ability to find a competent foreign shipping clerk in charge of relations with the Chinese, namely, Henry B. Endicott, a Chinese-speaking American, who was employed in 1872 and then worked closely with the firm's comprador Cheng Kuan-ying.

Up to the middle sixties, Jardine, Matheson & Co. was singularly unsuccessful in its steamer operations on the Yangtze, chiefly because of the firm's inability to cultivate Chinese business. The situation changed after Tong King-sing became the comprador at Shanghai in 1863. Soon its partners were trying to catch up with Heard's in cultivating the Chinese, as William Keswick wrote to James Whittall in 1865: "Your purchases on a/c [account] of Ekee's friend are quite satisfactory. I may mention here that Heard & Co. are doing the utmost to encourage business of this nature on Native a/c . . . Their object is of course to secure freight for their steamer, and business for their receiving vessel."[86] Jardine's connections with the Chinese were threatened by the aggressive management of Heard's in this period. Tucksing, one of Jardine's old customers, was being lured away, as Keswick wrote on February 4, 1866: "Heard tried very hard to get Tucksing to promise to become connected with the Coast Steamer scheme."[87]

Jardine's gradually shifted to a more active role. In the late sixties, the firm had a close connection in the silk business with Choping of Russell's.[88] F. B. Johnson even arranged with him to purchase produce from the interior for the firm—"Choping will act for us in the country if necessary."[89] In 1870, Jardine's was friendly with Chongfat, Russell's former comprador, who "at Canton was the most influential shipper."[90] Jardine's thus showed that it could, with the aid of able compradors, successfully develop the steam freighting business among Chinese merchants. Indeed, by the early seventies, the inefficiency of Russell's Choping contrasted strikingly with the capability of Jardine's Tong King-sing or of Butterfield & Swire's Cheng Kuan-ying—two of the most able and influential compradors of the time.

In the shipping business on the Yangtze, Jardine's came from behind in the sixties and finally triumphed over the others. Their Hankow comprador, Sow Moey, was replaced in 1885 by Wun Hing, with a view to improving freight: "I think we are getting a much better proportion than formerly. Wun Hing has hardly been with me long enough yet to judge, and give an opinion on his capabilities as Compradore, but from what I have seen so far he appears to be taking a great interest in the Steamer & Insurance business, so I hope things will improve."[91] Things did improve, as Jardine's Hankow agent reported to Shanghai three weeks later: "Our new Chinese staff has proved a great improvement on the old regime; the Compradore Wun Hing seems to have a great deal of influence with the teamen, and has been very useful to us, in conjunction with his broker Acheong, in securing us any teas we fancied. . . . The godown staff seems also very efficient, and capable of putting through any amount of business, and everything has worked very satisfactorily."[92]

Jardine's Kiukiang comprador functioned efficiently as well. He not only looked after the freight interests of Jardine's but also procured much of the freight from Butterfield & Swire's comprador. Jardine's Kiukiang agent reported in 1886: "It is a matter of great satisfaction to me that you are pleased with our freight returns . . . and I have great pleasure in speaking to the efficiency of our compradore and the energy displayed by him. The accusation made by Messrs. B & S's compradore are unfounded, I assure you. He considers himself aggrieved because he cannot now secure for their steamer the large proportion of freight that he was last year in a position to influence."[93]

In view of the keen competition of the foreign firms on the Yangtze, B. A. Clarke, Jardine's Hankow manager, urged James J. Keswick at Shanghai to visit the Yangtze before it would "by and by be too late": "It is very necessary that you come here [Hankow] to see for yourself the why & the wherefore of certain changes which I would strongly recommend in the interests of the Indo-China S. N. Co. I feel confident that your visit will amply repay you in many ways, & it will enable you to see the necessity of certain changes which are requisite in your interests as Agents of the Company,—that is if you wish to keep your place on the River. Some of our friends are making a big bid for the Trade, and unless you make a stand now, it will by & by be too late."[94] It is thus clear that the Western merchants, realizing the importance of the Chinese connections to their success in business, competed sharply in obtaining able compradors and potential constituents.

Further Benefits of the Comprador

The Western merchants not only depended on the comprador for their usual business transactions with the Chinese, but also benefited from him in many other ways. For one thing, a Western firm usually maintained close commercial relations with its former compradors. After having become a fully independent merchant, the former comprador, being familiar with the firm he had once served, maintained close contact with it. In the late sixties, Chongfat, Russell & Co.'s former comprador, was "the most influential shipper at Canton," and his business was much sought after.[95] John M. Forbes, Jr., wrote to Edward Cuningham in 1868: "At present I am trying to get Chongfat to give the S. [Shanghai] S. N. Co. the support of his patronage."[96]

Heard's also endeavored to maintain relations with its former compradors. After Tong Loong-maw resigned his compradorship at Foochow in April 1862, he went to the upper Yangtze to trade on his own account. Heard's Shanghai office kept in close contact with him, and in this new capacity he actually helped the firm even more than before, as John Heard wrote on April 4, 1862: "The old Compradore will be worth twice as much to us on the Yangtze, I propose to establish him there as a Tea-hong, but to act through and for us, and be our factotum in every way, but not to act as Compradore."[97] From the upper Yangtze ports, he frequently supplied market information on such items as tea, sugar, pepper, and opium.[98] This information was provided to the firm in letters written in Chinese (see illustration), which were translated by G. B. Dixwell, the firm's clerk at Shanghai. Two days after Tong's arrival at Hankow, for instance, he wrote to Dixwell: "I arrived at Hankow on the 5th of 1st month [Feb. 22, 1863] and looked into all kinds of business but found the market not opened since the [Chinese] New Year. But . . . they began to deliver sugar—the article should give some profit if sent from Shanghai. I beg you to consider this and write to Mr. [John] Heard at Hongkong."[99]

Relations between Jardine's and its former compradors were even closer, and a considerable part of the firm's business was done through its ex-compradors. When Yakee was to resign Jardine's Shanghai compradorship in 1859, James Whittall reported from Shanghai to Joseph Jardine, head of the firm, at Hong Kong: "Yakee, I am sorry to say, has made up his mind to leave me after the end of the year. . . . He intends commencing again as a Merchant

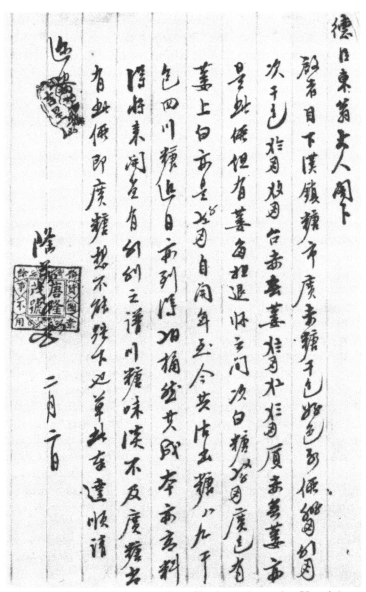

Ex-comprador's market report from Hankow: Augustine Heard &
Co., Shanghai, 1863. Letter of Tong Loong-maw to G. B. Dixwell.
Source: G. B. Dixwell (Shanghai) to Albert F. Heard (Hong Kong),
April 1, 1863, HM-60, HC.

and promises to take the same interest in the Hong [Jardine, Matheson & Co.] as heretofore, coming around every day."[100] The firm later frequently contracted for tea and silk with him, together with other former compradors, as William Keswick wrote in 1864: "Yakee will be my principal man this year, and with Ekee and Aleet I should have no difficulty in buying very largely in the country for sale in the market and for shipment to Hong Kong."[101] The comprador Acum was adept at upcountry purchase. After he had been succeeded by Tong King-sing in 1863, he still did business with Jardine's. The firm advanced to him and Yakee about $100,000 for the purchase of tea and silk in 1867 and the next year Acum alone was advanced $100,000 for a silk contract.[102]

Jardine's continued to do part of its business with its former compradors because in this way it could purchase native produce cheaper than could its neighbors. James Whittall reported from Shanghai in 1861: "I regret equally with yourselves that these teas do not hold out a more favorable result—but on comparing Yakee's & Aleet's accounts, both acting perfectly independent of each other, I find that they agree pretty well, and from what I hear of similar transactions on account of our neighbours, I am satisfied that ours are cheap in comparison."[103]

In the same way, Western merchants did business with their current compradors. Although a comprador's normal duties did not require his acting as a principal with his Western employers, this was often done, which resulted in many benefits to the employers. Since the comprador's activities as an independent merchant were on a complementary basis, Western merchants welcomed wider connections between their compradors and other Chinese merchants. As a broker, the comprador brought more business to the firm.[104] Or as a principal in a transaction, he bought produce and then "resold" it to his own Western employers.[105]

In the capacity of a merchant trading in his own right, the comprador was valuable to the Western firm in still another way. As marketeering and investment activities took the place of pure commission business for the agency house after the sixties, Western firms felt the need to reduce the risk of large investment and at the same time try to control it. For this purpose, they introduced a system of joint account. Both British and American agency houses carried out this type of operation with their Chinese and Western constituents, including the compradors. See Yong of Heard's and Tong King-sing of Jardine's are known to have been engaged in joint-account shipments with their firms when they were compradors.[106] The joint-account system was not limited to shipping. Jardine's had a "joint account contract" with Ekee for the upcountry purchase of tea in 1865.[107] Heard's also tried to operate jointly with Atai a copper mine in Hainan Island in 1873.[108]

The comprador sometimes helped the Western firm financially when it was short of money. Heard's frequently obtained loans from its comprador and paid him interest. At the time of the Taiping uprising, however, it was no longer easy for a firm to get money in this way. In a letter to C. A. Fearon, Heard's Shanghai partner, Augustine Heard, Jr., wrote from Canton on June 10, 1853: "Can't send you any money yet. The Comprador [Achen] says the bankers and rich men are carrying their money all away, and he can't get any yet. He will be able to tell in a day or two."[109] The quest turned out to be unsuccessful, as Heard wrote nine days later: "I suppose we must trust to Providence for money. I can't get any more from the comprador."[110] The significance of the correspondence lies in the fact that it was probably common practice for Heard's to get money through its Canton comprador. In fact, in 1855 after the Taipings left Canton, Heard's was able to receive at least $140,000 worth of deposits through the comprador.[111]

Other compradors of Heard's were valuable to the firm in this respect. When Augustine Heard, Jr., could not get money from the Canton comprador in 1853, he was finally able to "borrow through the [Hong Kong] comprador."[112] When the firm was desperately in need of money in 1863, A. F. Heard wrote: "I must say the [Hong Kong] comprador [See Yong] has come out like a brick. I can count upon . . . certain $23,000."[113] The firm's cash account with the Hong Kong comprador shows that for six out of twelve months in 1871 the balance was in the comprador's favor. (See Table 2.) This practice of borrowing money from the comprador also existed in Shanghai. In 1861, A. F. Heard and Edward Cunningham considered an abortive proposal to undertake jointly for Heard's and Russell's the lucrative transportation of the tribute rice to Peking.

Table 2. Cash account with the comprador, Augustine Heard & Co., Hong Kong, 1871 (Mexican dollars).

Month	Cr. by comprador[a]	Balance[b]
January	$222,328.18	$606.40
February	201,432.75	5,524.95
March	154,397.86	*267.45* [due comprador]
April	101,813.68	23,897.87
May	49,492.49	3,994.09
June	24,763.81	10,522.15
July	111,541.72	*14,486.98* [due comprador]
August	219,404.44	1,784.80
September	215,782.29	*13,147.14* [due comprador]
October	309,657.05	*3,806.57* [due comprador]
November	327,427.41	*32,625.92* [due comprador]
December	157,574.35	*15,251.37* [due comprador]

Source: Cash Account, vol. 56, HC II.

a. This column represents the total monthly disbursements—or payments—made by the comprador on the company's behalf.

b. The nonitalicized figures in this column represent the cash amount due the company still held by the comprador at the end of each month. The italicized figures refer to the amount that the comprador had spent for the company in excess of what he had received from the company.

Out of the $600,000 cash advance needed, A. F. Heard expected to get $100,000 from the comprador.[114] In 1870 when Heard's was "short," G. B. Dixwell borrowed 15,000 taels from the Shanghai comprador: "Before I went down to Hong Kong I borrowed 15,000 taels of the Comprador, as we were short. This sum he says he wants in a couple of months and I think as a matter of policy we had better pay it up as soon as we can conveniently."[115] The practice of getting a loan from the comprador was true not only for Heard's but for other firms as well. In 1862, E. M. Smith, an American merchant in Shanghai, borrowed through his comprador, Wang Yüeh-ting, 78,940 taels and $15,400, paying an interest of 12 percent per annum.[116]

The comprador's connection with other Chinese merchants was often encouraged by the agency house, for it might bring profits not only to him but to the house as well. His close association with the native banks was a typical example. From the fifties many compradors were partners of native banks, such as Takee, Hsü Jun, and Tong King-sing. This relationship was natural, since imported goods were often sold on credit against the native bank order, which matured in periods varying from three days to one month, usually with the comprador's guarantee. His connection with the native banks, however, had another advantage for the Western employers. For those firms with extra capital (like Jardine's), it was possible to make money through the comprador by lending the extra capital to native banks through him—in a system of "chop loan" that was institutionalized after the sixties. For those firms lacking capital (like Heard's), the comprador could borrow from the native banks. Thus, his running account with a native bank was valuable to the firm and was encouraged by the Western partners. John Heard wrote of his comprador in 1859: "He is ready to find for us a considerable sum at any moment and he can't do this unless he has his running account at the [native] Bank and [otherwise] he becomes a mere accountant of no use that any boy could be who knows how to figure."[117]

In like manner, the comprador in charge of a firm's shipping sometimes carried on a private business as a ship chandler to provide the necessaries for the firm's ship.[118] Or, more often, he would operate a freight-brokerage hong. Cheng Kuan-ying, chief comprador to Butterfield & Swire in 1873–1881, operated freight hongs in Szechwan, Hankow, and Shanghai after 1875.[119] During the 1880's the comprador's freight-brokerage hong also performed the function of a customs broker, helping native traders to declare at the customs and to transport goods down the Yangtze.[120] Thus, the comprador gained his commission and the Western firm profited from the transport and insurance income. By the eighties this kind of hong was called a *Yü-hang* (Szechwan hong), for its aim was mainly to befriend the Szechwanese traders.[121] Large Western firms like Butterfield & Swire frequently loaned from 10,000 to 60,000 taels to their compradors for the establishment of Yü-hang at Hankow, Chungking, Wan-hsien, and K'uei-chow.[122] The compradors to the China Merchants' Steam Navigation Co. and to Jardine, Matheson & Co. were similarly helped to establish their Yü-hang in the late eighties and nineties, respectively.[123] In such ways the Western merchant relied on his Chinese comprador not only as a comprador but as an independent merchant as well.

III   The Rise and Fall of the Comprador

Although the comprador's rise started in 1842, his role as a commercial middleman between China and the West did not become significant until after the treaties of Tientsin in 1860, when more treaty ports were opened on the Yangtze and the northern China coast. In the sense that his activity was not confined to China alone but extended to other parts of Asia, he was a true middleman between East and West. The comprador thus survived the conditions that had brought him into existence and remained indispensable to foreign merchants for years to come. By the turn of the century, however, when Chinese and foreign merchants had become more knowledgeable about one another, and when business patterns were changing, the position of the middleman-comprador began to decline. The First World War accelerated this decline, until in 1943, after a century's existence, he symbolically disappeared when the so-called "treaty system" formally came to an end.

A study of the comprador poses a number of problems. The word itself was used with much confusion throughout the comprador's hundred-year history. Being a borrowed term from the Portuguese, it had no traditional meaning. Thus, a "ship comprador" might refer to a man furnishing provisions for any ship, or to a man taking care of Chinese affairs on a particular steamship. It also meant a person in charge of the Chinese staff in a steamship navigation company, or, strangely enough, a shop providing ship necessities.[1] Besides foreign firms, other foreign organizations employed compradors. For example, the comprador to the Shanghai Municipal

44

Council acted mainly as a treasurer.[2] Nor were the Chinese equivalents for the term free from confusion. Besides being generally called *mai-pan* (purchaser), a comprador was also known as *k'ang-pai-tu* (from the sound of "comprador") in Shanghai, a *Hua chang-fang* (Chinese treasurer) or *pan-fang* (comprador office) in Hong Kong, and a *ling-shih ti* (he who takes charge of things) in Tientsin.[3] He was mentioned in official documents as *shang-huo* (merchant-partner), and he regarded himself as *tsung-li* (manager in general).[4]

To explore the conditions that gave rise to the comprador and the factors that brought about his decline also raises a methodological problem. What are the criteria to indicate the change? It would be desirable to compile quantitative data for presentation in a table, and one such measure would be the number of compradors. But the available historical sources do not provide this information. What is more, the quantitative approach has its limits. Since both the size of foreign firms and the functions of the compradors changed considerably with the passage of time, the number of compradors would be a misleading index of their rise and fall. The discussion must therefore be confined mainly to the compradors' functions and activities.

Origins of the Comprador

The Portuguese were among the first Europeans to trade in the East, and the term "comprador," meaning "purchaser," was Portuguese in origin.[5] *Mai-pan*, the general Chinese term for "comprador" which also means "purchaser," was not new in Chinese history. It originally referred to the official broker who purchased supplies for the government in the Ming dynasty (1368–1664). This practice derived from two former institutions of governmental procurement—the *ho-mai* (negotiatory purchase) in the Northern Sung dynasty (960–1126), which in turn originated in the *kung-shih* (palace purchase) of the T'ang dynasty (618–907).[6] At the time of the Cohong system the word *mai-pan* was generally used as a verb, meaning "to buy," and thus *mai-pan chih-jen* referred to a man who purchased provisions for foreign merchants, otherwise known to them as "comprador."[7]

Within the framework of the tribute system, old China's maritime trade had from the early eighteenth century been channeled through the hong merchants in Canton, who enjoyed a special position of monopoly in China's maritime trade.[8] It was from the Cohong system that many of the early compradors acquired their business experience. Under this system, the Chinese officials at Canton required the hong merchants to guarantee the linguists (*t'ung-shih* or "translators"), the linguists to guarantee the compradors, and the compradors to guarantee the servants and workmen—all in an interlocking hierarchy. There were two kinds of compradors, both of whom were licensed agents engaged in purchasing the foreigner's daily supplies. The first kind was the ship comprador (a ship chandler), who was selected from well-to-do native families by local officials, and who furnished provisions for foreign ships.[9] On the arrival of a ship at Macao, for example, the master or supercargo would engage a ship comprador licensed by Chinese local officials at Macao or the district of P'an-yü, who had the sole privilege of supplying the ship with provisions and all other necessities. He would accompany the ship to Canton, hire workmen there, make purchases, and in general act as clerk and local purveyor while the ship was anchored at Whampoa.[10] Compared with the second type of comprador, he was so important that from 1835 to 1843 the term "comprador" generally referred to the ship comprador.[11]

However, there was a sudden growth of foreign "free" merchants in China after the ending of the British East India Company's monopoly in 1834, as shown by the following figures for the number of foreign merchants at Canton during 1826–1837:[12]

Year	Total foreign merchants at Canton	British	American	Connected with BEI Co.	Number of houses
1826	76	25	19	20	4
1831	83	32	21	20	6
1837	213	158	44	0	18

The rapid growth of foreign merchants made possible the rise of the house comprador—the steward-treasurer in a foreign house. This comprador was a house steward, furnishing provisions and taking care of "the thousand small articles called 'chow chow.' "[13] He also served as a treasurer, assisted by a shroff (silver expert).[14] At first his activities were strictly confined by the Chinese officials, but eventually he was allowed to hire and guarantee a limited number of servants for the foreign merchants. For instance, in 1809 a house comprador secured one godown-keeper, two gate-keepers, and four coolies for a foreign factory.[15]

As one obligation of his license, the comprador was supposed to report to the local officials, through the linguist, on the foreign merchant's personal conduct, especially his misdoings, such as opium selling, tax evading, and silver purchasing.[16] The local officials were responsible for the faithfulness of these reports. However, the comprador's financial integrity was secured by the linguist, who in turn was guaranteed by the hong merchant. Thus, in 1823 Howqua, a hong merchant, was held responsible for the sum of $50,000 in a case of default by a comprador.[17]

Although the comprador worked under the supervision of the linguist, he himself was more likely to become rich. This was owing to the fact that a linguist, who was mainly an interpreter and an expert in customs affairs, had fewer opportunities to make extra money, while a comprador, being able either to handle some trade on his own account (as ship comprador) or to obtain access to the treasury (as house comprador), could easily acquire wealth. This was the main reason that the hong merchants often found it difficult to recruit a sufficient number of linguists and requested local officials to supply them instead.[18] For the same reason, local officials required the linguist to pay only 30–50 taels of the customary fees (*lou-kuei*) for each entering foreign ship, while a ship comprador had to pay 50–100 taels.[19] As with the Ch'ing officials, the main sources of income for both ship and house compradors were outside their regular salaries. Although a ship comprador's annual stipend was 50–100 taels, he is known to have been milked by officials for more than 3,000 taels a year for a single foreign ship anchored at Whampoa.[20] The house comprador's annual salary was only 250–300 taels, so that he clearly depended on his two percent shroffing commission for examining the purity of the silver.[21]

The comprador's position in foreign trade was thus well established. On the one hand, he was familiar with the transactions, and on the other, he steadily accumulated funds. Aming, a ship comprador and later a house comprador, "in process of time, by both fair and underhand trade . . . amassed a large sum of money. He was considered one of the wealthiest men in the province [of Kwang-tung]." Since only men of wealth were likely to be appointed compulsorily by the Chinese officials as hong merchants, Aming was later named one.[22] In 1862 he assumed Augustine Heard & Co.'s Kiukiang compradorship.[23] This switch was unusual, because former hong merchants seem mostly to have dropped out of foreign trade after the Cohong monopoly was replaced by the "treaty system" in 1842. Aming's case was one of the interesting exceptions, which might be attributable to his former experience as a comprador. Indeed, it was not the linguist but his subordinate, the comprador, who expanded his functions and took the place of the former hong merchants after 1842. Although at that time both the function and the status of the comprador changed, his rise was owed in part to the experience he had acquired under the Cohong system.

Rise of the Modern Comprador, 1842–1900

The comprador's new role between East and West originated in 1842 with the conclusion of the Treaty of Nanking. That treaty states in part: "The Emperor of China agrees to abolish that practice [Cohong system] in future at all Ports where British Merchants may reside and to permit them to carry on their mercantile transactions with whatever persons they please. . . . It shall be lawful [for them] to hire at pleasure servants, compradors, linguists and without interference on the part of the local officers of the Chinese government."[24]

After the abolition of the Cohong system, some of the former hong merchants engaged in private tea or silk business, while others disappeared entirely from the China trade scene.[25] The former linguists, after leaving the hong merchants, served mostly as clerks of the new maritime customs or as customs brokers.[26] The comprador, however, enlarged his function to supplant the hong merchant as the Chinese collaborator of the foreign trader. The role of the comprador gradually shifted from a house steward to a business assistant. Meanwhile, the status of the middleman in

China's foreign trade also changed. He was no longer licensed by Chinese officials and guaranteed by the hong merchants, but instead was employed by the foreign mercantile house.

However, the Treaty of Nanking had little immediate effect. The new trade of the treaty ports did not start overnight and the former Canton system seems to have shown great inertia.[27] John Heard, 3rd, complained in 1844: "Although a treaty had been signed for some months, trade continued to go on in the old manner, as there had been no time to organize a new system. We learned its (new system) working but never liked it as well as the old Hong system, and never had the same feeling of safety in our transactions."[28] But the Western merchant's worry about safety in business transactions subsided when his Chinese comprador began to guarantee them.

The Cantonese first showed themselves able to meet the need for compradors. Because of their earlier experience under the Cohong system, the Cantonese compradors assumed a particularly active and important role, in which they were to dominate China's foreign trade for about forty years. It was in the other treaty ports, however, rather than in Canton, that their main role was played, and their rise on the national scene was possible only after the decline of Canton as the center of China's foreign trade.

The history of Canton's prominent position in China's foreign trade goes back for centuries.[29] Its prominence was owing mainly to its advantageous geographical position. Besides being a relatively good port, it served, as an ideal first station for ships coming from Europe. In addition, being far from the capital, it was a suitable place for foreigners' activities that might otherwise pose a serious threat to the central government at Peking.

The abolition of the British East India Company in 1834 encouraged the movement of foreign "free traders" to Canton, and foreign firms suddenly increased.[30] But the Sino-British military encounter there in 1856 was a severe blow to Canton's prosperity, as Augustine Heard, Jr., recalled: "Up to 1856, Canton was the chief place of business in China, and all the mercantile firms had their headquarters [there], with the exception of the two leading English houses (Jardine, Matheson & Co. and Dent & Co.), whose heads were in H.K. But with the destruction of the [foreign] factories [in Canton], all were driven there [Hong Kong]."[31]

The war damage and destruction could be restored, but Canton's leading position in China's foreign trade was gone forever.[32] The rise of Shanghai was another early factor in its demise, as was the Taiping uprising in the 1850's. The opening of Foochow (1854) and Hankow (1861) as shipping ports for tea, and the proximity of Hong Kong and Macao to the delta of the Canton River, with its unrivaled facilities for smuggling, further robbed Canton of the preeminence it had so long enjoyed in commercial prosperity. Many factors thus combined to undermine the Canton position, and its decline in the foreign trade was clear and steady.[33] (See Table 3.) When Canton is compared with other newly opened ports in duties collected, it falls behind Shanghai, Foochow, and Hankow.[34] (See Table 4.)

Table 3. The decline of Canton in foreign trade, 1860–1865 (Mexican dollars).

Year	Imports	Exports	Total
1860	$18,400,000	$16,200,000	$34,600,000
1861	12,900,000	15,800,000	28,700,000
1862	10,500,000	17,700,000	28,200,000
1863	9,500,000	16,000,000	25,500,000
1864	8,100,000	13,600,000	21,700,000
1865	7,900,000	13,500,000	21,400,000

Source: IMC, *Returns of Trade at the Treaty Ports of China.*

Table 4. Duties collected at the treaty ports, 1865–1867 (Mexican dollars).

Port	1865	1866	1867
Shanghai	$2,166,841	$2,162,446	$2,310,889
Foochow	1,642,201	1,543,351	1,712,430
Hankow	943,437	1,010,175	1,033,549
Canton	843,893	889,479	934,775
Tientsin	358,023	541,336	411,298

Source: *North China Herald*, Oct. 13, 1868, p. 489.

Rise and Fall of the Comprador

The Cantonese merchants had been active in other large trade centers by the middle of the nineteenth century, but they did not dominate the scene until after 1860 when China's foreign trade became based on more stable relations with the Western powers. With the establishment of new branch offices of foreign firms in the new ports, the Cantonese compradors went to them as hangers-on with the foreign merchants. Partly because of their former connections, and partly because of their taste for Cantonese food, foreign merchants usually brought along their Cantonese compradors and other employees, including cooks, when they went to the other newly opened ports.

The Chinese system of financial guarantees also favored the continued employment of the Cantonese as compradors. After the fifties almost every comprador had to be "secured" or financially guaranteed. His surety was fully responsible for his honesty in business transactions and financial solvency. Because the Cantonese merchants were familiar with foreign trade, they naturally guaranteed their fellow-townsmen as compradors. That it was to the interest of the foreign employer to have such guarantees is illustrated in a letter from John Heard to Albert F. Heard in 1859: "The Shanghai Comprador is not secured at all. He was, by our old Comprador [in Canton, See Yong] when we first went to Shanghai."[35]

Augustine Heard & Co. provided a good example of the Cantonese spread to other treaty ports. When the firm established a branch office in Foochow in 1854, its old comprador at Hong Kong, See Yong, recommended and secured a fellow-Cantonese, Tong Loong-maw, to go with the company as a new comprador.[36] Tong Loong-maw's brother Akit succeeded him when Tong became too involved in his own business to fulfill his comprador duties.[37] Heard's main office was located in Canton from 1840 to 1857, when they moved it to Hong Kong on account of the Sino-British war, taking with them their comprador, a Cantonese named Atchu.[38] In Shanghai as well, Heard's new comprador, Chu-u-teng, was "a former Canton boy."[39] In the same manner, most of the firm's compradors in other treaty ports were Cantonese, such as See Kai (Shanghai, 1850's); Aming, Agunn, Ahee, Atong, and Achow (Kiukiang, 1860's); Coe Lun and Seating (Hankow, 1860's). (See Appendix A.)

51

Russell & Co.'s case is as clear as Heard's. Its Canton comprador, Ayow, began his service as early as 1831.[40] After the firm established a branch office in Shanghai in the 1840's, the old hong merchant Howqua in late 1858 recommended a Cantonese named Ahyue as the new Shanghai comprador.[41] Ahyue in turn asked a fellow-Cantonese, Sunchong, "to take half the responsibility and profits."[42] The Cantonese Koofunsing and Chongfat are also known to have been compradors of Russell's who followed the firm to Shanghai.[43] Russell's Cantonese compradors constituted the main body in other treaty ports as well. (See Appendix B.)

Jardine's Cantonese compradors, like their colleagues in the American houses, went northward with their companies. Soon after Shanghai was opened for foreign trade on November 11, 1843, Alexander Grant Dallas, Jardine's junior partner (1843–1854), established a branch there. He brought along Cantonese servants, but before long realized the necessity of having a comprador as well. He applied for one to the main office at Hong Kong in 1844, and in response to his request, a Cantonese named Asam was sent to him.[44] Asam left Jardine's in 1846 because of illness.[45] Atow, another Cantonese, was dispatched to Shanghai to take his place.[46] Most of Jardine's subsequent Shanghai compradors are known to have been Cantonese—men like Yakee (late 1850's), Acum (until September 1863), Tong King-sing (Sept. 1863–June 1873), Tong Mow-chee (June 1873–July 1897), and T'ang Chieh-ch'en (1897–1904). Many Cantonese served as the firm's compradors in other treaty ports, such as Foochow (Acum and Allum), Hankow (Yowloong), and Tientsin (Tong Mow-chee). (See Appendix C.)

The use of Cantonese compradors was also common at Dent & Co., another gigantic British firm. One of its partners, T. C. Beale, employed a Cantonese in Macao (in Hsiang-shan district) named Hsü Yü-t'ing as its new Shanghai comprador in the 1840's, when the branch office was first established there. He was succeeded by his brother Yungkee. Their nephew, the famous comprador Hsü Jun (1838–1911), continued to act as comprador at Shanghai. The firm's compradors in other ports were also mainly Cantonese, especially in the early sixties. (See Appendix D.)

The supremacy of the Cantonese compradors in the treaty ports was gradually challenged, first by the Chekiang men and then by the Kiangsu group. This change was partly due to the fact of regional commercial specialization. The Cantonese were particularly good at the tea business, and it was mainly for this reason that they were employed as compradors at Foochow, Shanghai, Kiukiang, Hankow, and Japan. The Cantonese comprador's expertise in the tea business was illustrated by the fact that, in order better to satisfy the Western customers' taste, M. A. Daly, Heard's representative at Foochow, asked his Cantonese comprador, Akit, to experiment in preparing a new "chop" or kind of tea, with the assistance of the firm's foreign tea-taster.[47] Daly wrote to A. F. Heard on April 7, 1863: "I am glad you are going to allow Akit to attempt the new style of Souchong, as I think the experiment an important one, and well worth trying. I have told him to spare no pains in making the chop."[48] However, China gradually lost much of her international market to India, and the tea trade assumed a downward course, especially after the 1860's. The decrease in tea export probably somewhat curbed the activities of the Cantonese compradors. At the same time, silk maintained its importance in China's exports (30–40 percent) until 1908, which accounts for the gradual but steady rise of the Chekiang compradors, who seem to have specialized in the silk trade. Jardine's Takee was a prominent silk merchant at Shanghai, and through him the firm developed the so-called "Soochow system" of silk purchase in the fifties. Russell's Choping, a native of Hu-chow, Chekiang, which achieved a reputation for silk production, was one of the most prominent silk merchants at Shanghai in the sixties. A. F. Heard wrote of him from Shanghai in 1862: "He has grown up in *Silk* and all the wealthy men here are *silk* men."[49]

Foreign banking, like shipping, grew out of what had once been a sideline activity of the old agency house and developed into a full-fledged institution on its own after the eighties. This new business increased the importance of the rising Chekiang compradors. Because the natives of Chekiang were noted for their banking talents and influence, some of the foreign banks employed them as compradors.[50] Wang Huai-shan was the first comprador to the Hongkong and Shanghai Banking Corporation in 1865, and in the twentieth century Yü Hsia-ch'ing served as comprador first to the Russo-Chinese Bank and then to the Netherlands Bank at Shanghai.[51] Indeed, the popularity of a comprador staff from Chekiang (especially Ningpo) was next only to that of one from Canton.[52] By the early twentieth century, although the Cantonese still constituted the main body of compradors at Hong Kong, the Chekiang compradors overshadowed the Cantonese compradors at Shanghai, as shown in the following breakdown of the place of origin of ninety noted compradors in the 1920's:[53]

Place of origin	No. of compradors
Chekiang	43
Kiangsu	31
Kwangtung	7
Anhui	5
Kiangsi	1
Unknown	3

The rise of the Kiangsu comprador, compared with his fellow-compradors from both Kwangtung and Chekiang, was less spectacular and of a later date. This is attibutable to the fact that he was prominent in neither the silk business nor the tea trade, and that his contact with the foreign merchant was delayed. Few compradors of the big foreign mercantile houses in the nineteenth century seem to have been natives of Kiangsu, though some of the minor firms occasionally employed them.[54] An exception was Chu Ta-ch'un, who became Jardine's comprador at Shanghai at the end of the nineteenth century.[55] The prominence of the Soochow compradors at the foreign banks started late, only after the Taiping uprising forced them to flee to Shanghai, where they eventually dominated in the foreign banks.[56]

Thus, the geographic location, the regional commercial specialization, the domestic political scene, and the international market all played a role in bringing about the rise or decline of different groups of compradors. China's social customs, familism, and regionalism also played a part.[57]

Spread of the Comprador Outside China

The Chinese comprador was not only an intermediary in Sino-Western trade but also a commercial middleman between East and West at large, since his activities extended far beyond China's treaty ports and reached other parts of Asia. In an article entitled "John Comprador" published in 1878, Thomas Knox, an American merchant engaged in the Far Eastern trade, stated that the Chinese comprador was active in Japan, Cochin China, Bangkok, Rangoon, Penang, Malacca, Singapore, Java, and Manila, and that his influence was even felt in India.[58]

The records of Heard's and Jardine's bear this out. As the China-based Western business firms expanded their activities to Japan, Korea, and Southeast Asia, they employed Chinese compradors to accompany them. On May 12, 1860, an agreement was made between Augustine Heard & Co. and two Cantonese, Leong A Tien and One A Cheong. They would act as compradors and "agree to go to Saigon . . . to be under the entire control of J. N. King, Esq., agent for Messrs. Augustine Heard & Co."[59] In like manner, Heard's engaged in December 1866 two other Chinese, Ho Ch'ien and Wang Ch'ang-chieh, who would follow Jonathan Russell to Manila.[60]

In order to expand their business to Korea, Jardine's sent B. A. Clarke to establish a branch office at Jenchuan in June 1883. The Chinese staff who went with him included a comprador, a shroff, and a godownman.[61] With a view to finding a larger place for all of them to live, Clarke changed the office in 1884, as he reported from Jenchuan: "Since the [steamship] 'Nanzing' left, I have had to take another office, as the place we were in leaked so badly that it was impossible to work in it when it was raining. The place I have taken is in the Japanese settlement and though not very good it is larger and there is room for the Shroff and Compradore to live in it."[62] One of the comprador's functions at Korea was to get hides, as Clarke reported on Sept. 16, 1884: "I have not yet got any Hides, but now that the weather is getting cooler, the Compradore hopes shortly to secure some."[63] The importance of the comprador to Jardine's representative was expressed by Clarke's letter of Sept. 20, 1884, regretting that the comprador could not be at Seoul and Jenchuan at the same time: "I would come up myself, but I have the Co. to attend to, & can't possibly get away, so it is as you may imagine very awkward for me not to have the Compradore here at this time, however I must do the best I can without him."[64] As the Korean business was not profitable, Jardine's wound up its office at Jenchuan in October 1884.

After establishing head offices in either Hong Kong or Shanghai, some of the Western houses developed their businesses one step further by setting up branch offices or agencies in Japan. Western merchants in Shanghai were deeply concerned about general conditions in Japan, and market intelligence about Yokohama and Nagasaki appeared frequently in the Shanghai English newspapers.[65] Nagasaki was the only port where Chinese merchants could do business during most of the Tokugawa period, and thus Chinese merchants had more influence there. Hsü Jun helped Dent & Co. in opening an agency at Nagasaki in the late fifties, and at the same time the Shanghai comprador of Sassoon & Co., a certain Loo, went to Japan and acted as their Nagasaki comprador.[66]

Yokohama was the other center for Chinese compradors. In the late fifties, Heard's founded branch offices at Nagasaki and Kanagawa, and in 1859 E. M. Dorr, their representative at Kanagawa, applied to A. F. Heard at Shanghai for a Chinese comprador.[67] The firm's most important agency at Japan, however, was the one at Yokohama. When it was established in 1861, John Heard, the Hong Kong partner, employed in Macao a Cantonese named Akow as the new comprador to go to Yokohama "to further and assist in their [Heard's] business in every way in his power."[68] When Akow became sick in 1865, he recommended a fellow-townsman, Sow-no, as his successor, "who was for something like three years a merchant at Nagasaki, and was employed here [Yokohama] by Walsh Hall & Co. for a time during the absence of their Comprador."[69]

Akow took four staff members—one shroff, one cook, and two coolies—who represented his functions as a treasurer and house steward as well as a business assistant.[70] He was required to be in constant attendance at the comprador office, for the purpose of redeeming the comprador's orders.[71] As a business assistant, his role in Japan was even more important than that of his fellow-compradors in China, since he seems to have been the only channel of business transaction, handling all the sales and purchases. In a letter dated May 27, 1866, A. O. Gay, Heard's Yokohama agent, reported of Akow's activities in the early 1860's: "He sold all the goods, and received payment himself, bought cotton, tea, etc., and settled with the silk men in his own room."[72] The comprador also provided market information, for Sow-no was regarded by Gay as "a very useful man in my intercourse with the native [Japanese] merchants, as he understands the Import Market very well."[73]

In the case of Jardine's, William Keswick went to Kanagawa in 1859 to establish a branch office. At the end of that year, a comprador was sent to him from China at 30 taels per month.[74] Two years later, the comprador added another three assistants to his staff, as Jardine's Shanghai office informed Keswick in 1861: "There are three Chinamen going, who have been engaged for servicing at Mexican $20 per month each; one half of their wages to be paid here, the other half to be received by themselves in Japan."[75]

Like Heard's, Jardine's most important branch office in Japan was at Yokohama, where Chinese compradors' services were enlisted by most of the firm's representatives—S. J. Gower, C. S. Hope, H. P. Austin, Edward Fisher, and Herbert Smith.[76] Edward Whittall went there from China as the new manager in 1871, bringing a comprador who later proved to be expendable, as Whittall reported to Hong Kong in 1871: "The Compradore I brought up with me is of no use and I find I can do better without him; and he will return to Hongkong by the mail steamer."[77] He had earlier asked whether Yowloong, Jardine's comprador at Hankow, could be sent to him: "I shall be very glad if you could send me Yowloong to be the Compradore here, for he would be very useful, and a much better class."[78] But this arrangement did not work out.

The spread of Chinese compradors outside China raises some perplexing questions. It was natural for the Western merchant to employ a Chinese comprador in China, but why did he use one outside China, especially in Japan? Why did Chinese, instead of Japanese, serve as compradors? One reason was that Chinese merchants and emigrants were already influential in East and Southeast Asia. With regard to Chinese merchants at Nagasaki, a British consul reported from Japan in 1869: "I am glad to be able to report that the Chinese . . . who have been formidable and successful competitors with the foreign merchants in their commercial transactions are now all placed under the strict jurisdiction of the local authorities. . . . The [Chinese merchants'] guild in Nagasaki, which had existed for ages . . . was burnt down during the past year."[79]

In addition, the Chinese comprador was familiar with China's market, which was the main basis for the Western merchant's operations in the Far East. Jardine's shipped Swatow sugar and New-chwang peas to Japan, and Japan's tea and silk were occasionally processed in China.[80] In Korea, it was because of the comprador's substantial information about China's market that B. A. Clarke shipped chestnuts and ginseng to Shanghai and Hong Kong in 1884: "By this trip I am sending across a small shipment of Chestnuts, which the Compradore says will sell well in Shanghai &/or Hong-kong. There are only 36 piculs, but if you can recommend a further shipment, I would try & get 100 piculs for next trip. The Compra-dore is very anxious that I should buy some ginseng if I can get permission to export it. It costs here $6.00 per catty, & he says it sells in Hongkong for *$9.00* per catty, so a shipment of 2 or 3 piculs might answer."[81]

Another reason for using Chinese compradors was that a Western merchant in Japan found it more difficult to employ a Japanese as comprador. When Akow, Jardine's comprador at Yokohama, re-turned to Canton for a home visit and became too sick to go back to Japan in 1866, A. F. Heard asked the firm's Yokohama agent about the possibility of employing a Japanese as comprador. In reply, A. O. Gay explained the difficulties: "With regard to the Compra-dore and his staff, my observation since I have been here and com-paring it with the experience of others long resident at the place, leads me to believe that to find Japanese to take their place will be [a] difficult matter. I do not find that there are any who employ Japanese as Compradores as we do the Chinese."[82] There were a number of specific drawbacks to employing a Japanese comprador, involving reliability, suitability, and cost, as Gay continued: "It is extremely difficult to find reliable Japanese to enter foreign service. . . . They would not take as much care to prevent the coolies from stealing as the Chinese do. . . . A gentleman who has been here almost since the opening of the port, told me the other day, that he thought, if such could be found they would cost more than Chi-nese."[83]

Finally, the Chinese, especially Cantonese, compradors were better qualified than the Japanese in the tea business, which in the sixties seems to have been the chief element of the Japanese trade for Western merchants (especially Heard's and Jardine's). In order to process tea at Japan, William Keswick at Yokohama ordered tea-firing and coloring equipment through Jardine's Shanghai office in 1862, and in response, a Chinese teaman was also sent over at $24 per month.[84] In 1859, two years before Heard's established its Yokohama agency, A. F. Heard sent his comprador to Japan to investigate the tea business. He was greatly encouraged by the comprador's report, and in a letter to F. A. Field, dated August 17, 1859, he instructed the Yokohama agent: "My Chinaman Chu-u-teng by name has been here and the result of my conversation with him is that nothing can be done in tea save by permission of the Japanese official. . . . Chu-u-teng says the [tea] leaf is excellent, can be picked four times [a year]. . . . If we can join partnership with the [Japanese] Emperor and monopolize for ten years the tea pickings of Japan, we shall make our fortunes and I pray you to take the matter seriously in hand."[85]

Heard's final arrangement with the Japanese authorities is not known, but the firm's tea business in Yokohama went well from that time forward. The branch maintained a tea-firing house, a tea go-down, and a packing house of its own (see illustration), and later a tea taster arrived from Hong Kong.[86] In 1862, A. F. Heard planned to spend "$5,000 a month to fire tea in Japan," and in 1872 the Yokohama office handled tea business worth about $614,000.[87] Although A. O. Gay of Heard's admitted that a Japanese comprador would have helped the sale of imports, the employment of Japanese "as 'runners' to find buyers for imports" served the same purpose. More important to the firm was the tea business, in which the Cantonese comprador was particularly good, as Gay observed at Yokohama in 1866: "The Japanese do not understand the manipulation of Tea, as those Canton people do, who have been brought up to it, and they do not seem to take interest enough in it to learn. . . . Smith, Ascher & Co., who have had such long experience here, tell me that they have a Tea Firing Staff of 14 or 15 people, and even employ Cantonese to the packings, because the work is done better by them than by the Japanese."[88]

Decline and Fall, 1900–1943

Although the archival materials of Heard's, Russell's, and Jardine's do not go beyond the 1890's, so that it is impossible to examine

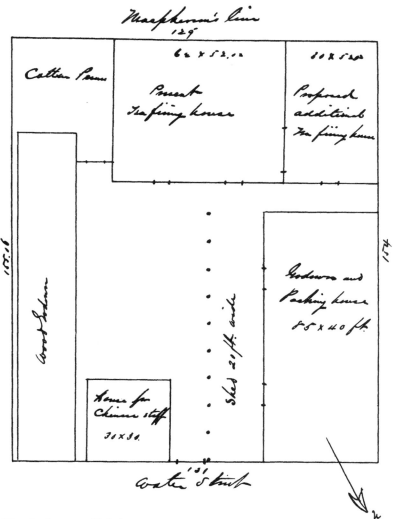

Plan for house at Yokohama, Japan: Augustine Heard & Co., 1866.
Note "House for Chinese staff" and "Tea firing house." *Source:* A. G.
Gay (Yokohama) to Albert F. Heard (Hong Kong), Feb. 25, 1866,
HM-55, HC.

their subsequent operations in detail, the decline of the comprador
was obvious by the turn of the twentieth century. For one thing,
few prominent compradors achieved their success in the twentieth

century. The decline of the comprador is also evidenced by the relative frequency with which he appeared in the Hong Kong and Shanghai newspapers. In contrast to earlier times, after the nineties little news or advertising concerning the comprador is found in the *Hongkong Daily Press,* the *Hongkong Telegraph* and the *North China Herald.*[89]

The decline of the comprador in China resulted from a number of factors both within and without the country. As time went on, the foreign merchants became more and more knowledgeable about China. Commenting on ways of coping with the comprador's "squeeze" or exaction, the British consular report of 1867 singled out the possibility of learning the Chinese language: "The most hopeful permanent remedy will be an increased knowledge of the [Chinese] language on the part of foreign mercantile employees, to which the necessities of the times and their future altered position are both pointing."[90] This proved to be a sound prediction. Both F. B. Johnson of Jardine's and Edward Cunningham of Russell's, as already shown, encouraged their foreign clerks to learn Chinese in the sixties. Continental Europeans, especially the Germans, also showed energy in the pursuit of linguistic competence. Chinese language schools were opened by the British Chamber of Commerce in Shanghai and Hong Kong in 1915 and 1916, respectively. During the period between the two world wars, some Western firms required their staffs to attend Chinese classes and paid bonuses to those who passed the examinations. They were then sent by the firm to deal directly with their Chinese agents in the interior.[91]

The decline of the comprador was accelerated by the First World War, which curtailed China's imports as well as foreign investment in China. Foreign merchants greatly reduced their China trade: Western powers were occupied with the war, and Japan was enjoying prosperity at home. The effect of the war could be clearly seen in the *Hua-tzu jih-pao,* the largest Chinese newspaper in Hong Kong. In the late nineteenth century a large volume of advertising appeared in this newspaper either by foreign merchants for employing compradors or by compradors for expanding their business. In contrast, only one such advertisement appeared in 1915.[92]

But the basic factor in the trend away from the comprador lay less in external changes than in China's new social and economic setting. For one thing, the Chinese merchant, like his Western counterpart, gradually became more experienced in foreign trade. A Chinese firm at Amoy, C. G. Lin & Co., traded directly with Jardine's Hong Kong office in 1890: "If you have some white shirtings according to the sample which we enclose herewith, please let us know at your convenience, how many bales you have got in stock, also give us your price. . . . If you can send us some samples of grey shirtings, T. Cloth and Camlet &c. with prices attached we will see whether we can buy and deal with you *directly*. . . . We herewith send you $1.70 to square up our account. You will be pleased to inform us the different prices of white shirting Nos. 600, 700, 800, as well as No. 900 and also a red mark *8* both printed in English and *Chinese*."[93]

The decline of the comprador must also be related to the contracting role of the middleman owing to changes in trade and the integration of markets. His position in China's foreign trade was further threatened with the development of modern Chinese banks which, increasing from 17 in 1914 to 102 in 1926, put the old-style Shansi banks out of business. One important function of the comprador was to guarantee credit, which became less necessary as the Chinese merchants began to utilize a modern banking system. This system enabled them to transform their personal credit into the credit of a bank that was known to the whole community as a sound and reputable institution. Side by side with a decline in imports which was further affected by the upward revisions of Chinese tariffs in 1918 and 1922, the economy of China boomed during and after the First World War, especially in the field of native industry. In addition, the monetary reform in 1933 abolished the tael, the multiform unit of account. The currency system was further simplified two years later when nationwide paper currency was introduced.

The Japanese were the first foreign merchants in China to dispense with their compradors. The abolition of the comprador by the Mitsui Company in 1899 was followed by the Yokohama Specie Bank in 1907.[94] The British-American Tobacco Company and the Standard Oil Company were among the first Western firms to discard their compradors.[95] The compradors further declined in the late 1930's after the nationwide war broke out with Japan. Finally, China's new equal treaties with the Western powers in 1943, which put an end to the old treaty system, symbolized the disappearance of the comprador from the China scene.

Although the comprador himself declined and finally disappeared, the commercial intermediaries between East and West continued. For one thing, the role of the independent Chinese brokers became more important. Foreign merchants continued to employ Chinese for help, but not with the functions of a comprador. Unlike the former comprador, the Chinese employees' functions and responsibilities were greatly reduced. They guaranteed neither the business transactions nor the personal integrity of other Chinese employees in the firm, and at the same time no longer handled the upcountry purchase which finally lost its importance.[96] Rather, they served as commission agents or commercial factors, and in most cases they were simply salesmen or commercial advisers. In the large foreign firms, the Chinese who supervised other Chinese staff members now changed his title from "comprador" to "Chinese manager" (*Hua ching-li*, still operating in Hong Kong today), so as to disassociate himself from the compradors, who were discredited and severely attacked during the nationalistic twentieth century.

IV   Functions of the Comprador in the Foreign Firm

Twenty years after his return from China, Augustine Heard, Jr., of Boston wrote about the comprador: "The comprador, to whom allusion has frequently been made, was a most important element in the large China house. In these there was a Chinese Firm, subordinate to the Foreign, of which the Comprador was the Head."[1] Why was a Chinese firm maintained within a foreign firm? What did the comprador do for the agency house? To what extent did he make China's foreign trade work?

Since the ever-changing business methods and patterns of the foreign firm generally determined its dealings with the Chinese, the functions of the comprador, which usually reflected those of his Western employer, also changed from time to time. Before the sixties, most Western firms in China organized their business in an agency house, and their compradors generally handled the import-export transactions of the firm. After the sixties, when foreign banks were developing rapidly into independent institutions, the bank comprador began to play an important role. During the period when the agency house was managing a variety of operations, its comprador's role was thus multi-functional; and when its investment activities overtook the commission business, his function became even more diverse. Thus, the comprador not only took care of the transaction business but also after the sixties handled matters concerning steamships, insurance, and factories. When some Western firms grew too gigantic and became considerably more complex, each of the firms' departments (such as import, export, and machinery) acquired a comprador of its own.

The comprador was the head of the foreign firm's Chinese staff, whom he recruited and guaranteed, as Augustine Heard, Jr., recalled: "He engaged all the native servants and employees, and was personally responsible for their honesty and general good conduct. The foreigner of course had no means of ascertaining the character of his Chinese servants, and relied implicitly on the selections of his Comprador, who as implicitly accepted the responsibility."[2] With this staff, the comprador performed extremely diverse functions. "It would be much shorter to tell what the comprador did *not* do than what he did."[3] However, his functions may be classified as those of housekeeping steward and business assistant.[4] While keeping the house clean and in good order, he also acted as treasurer, salesman, interpreter, freight broker, and intelligence provider. In addition, he handled the purchase of native produce from the interior—the so-called "upcountry purchase" system.

Special functions nevertheless differed among the individual compradors, depending on their special qualifications. Although the comprador had general functions, there was no particular rule limiting his specific activities. A contemporary newspaper observed, "there is no exact rule concerning transactions between Chinese producers and foreign firms through compradors," and "each foreign hong made its own agreement."[5] Such differences resulted not so much from the different foreign houses whom he served as from the different places in which he worked.

House Steward

After the abolition of the Cohong system in 1842, the new comprador assumed the responsibility of the former "house comprador" (as distinguished from the "ship comprador") and acted as a house steward, supervising other Chinese servants in the house. A Bostonian named Osmond Tiffany, Jr., who visited Canton in 1844, later recalled: "The housekeeping [of a foreign firm] is entirely under the charge of a comprador, and he is a very important functionary." As the steward of both the firm's offices and living quarters, the comprador "had under his thumb the cooks, the cooleys [coolies], the purveyors and the servant boys." All these servants were recruited and personally guaranteed by him, as the Bostonian continued: "The comprador must look out for honest men and rogues at the same time; he is responsible for all the moveables in the house, and is obliged to replace the plate of the establishment if lost. Once the table silver happened to be stolen from the sideboard after dinner was over, and new glittering substitutes were in use at tea time. The comprador has to bear the loss himself, and say nothing."[6] This practice of personal guarantee on the part of the comprador was also witnessed by Augustine Heard, Jr.: "If, for instance, a robbery were committed in the house—a watch or money was stolen—the foreigner simply notified the Comprador, who was expected to find the thief and the property, or to make good the loss out of his own pocket."[7]

Acting as a house steward, the comprador's duties ranged from house renting, repairing, and cleaning to the purchase of land.[8] He was also in charge of purchasing the miscellaneous ("chow-chow") things for which Seating, Heard's Hankow comprador, got 960 taels a year, as H. G. Bridges reported in 1866: "Seating informed me that he had spoken to you about the renewal of the allowance of Tls. 960 per annum to the comprador for [buying] 'chow-chow.' . . . Dent & Co. stopped their comprador's chow-chow allowance long ago and even make him pay his own market men. Our pay and allowances to Chinese [comprador] are very fair."[9] Besides, a comprador "in mercantile establishments . . . usually made arrangements for the supply of provisions, out of which he made his own profit."[10] In the Heard's archives, there are five volumes of "chow-chow" books recording the prices of such items as milk, fowl, eggs, grapes, and soupmeat during the 1861–1873 period.[11] The "Hongkong poisoning case" of 1856 also illustrates such responsibility.[12]

The comprador was held responsible for all the details in the house that were taken care of by the "boys," or household servants. Russell's Shanghai comprador office, in fact, was next to the servants' room. (See illustration.) "They [servants] have a horror of offending the comprador, who would cut them off with a wink of his eye, but they fear no one else."[13] Augustine Heard, Jr., had to send for the comprador in order to punish his careless servant "boy":

When we were living at Canton [before 1856] I had a "boy" who was very careless, and constantly annoyed me by neglecting to see that there

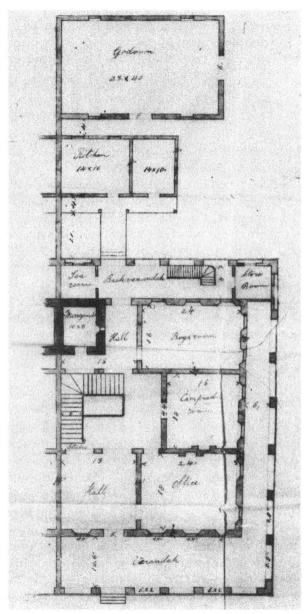

Shanghai property: Russell & Co., probably early 1860's.
Note comprador room and boys' room. *Source:* Case 26,
RA.

were no mosquitoes under my curtain. I spoke to him frequently about it, to no avail. . . . No punishment that I could inflict would be equal to having him well laughed at by his fellows. . . . One night I ordered all the servants of the house to come up to the verandah. . . . When they were all gathered I called for the comprador, who lived two miles away. . . . Finally, he rushed in, all agog to know what was wanted at two o'clock in the morning, I said, "Comprador, have got one piecy musket inside my bed."[14]

The comprador did not complain in this instance, since he regarded the matter as within his responsibility. However, he might refuse to obey an order if he considered it unreasonable. At the time when Heard's head office was at Canton, as Augustine Heard, Jr., later recalled, "the end of this house was on the 'Creek,' which ran up towards the city from the river, and every night it was crowded with sampans which came there for shelter." One night, he continued: "In one of these sampans was a child who cried all night in such a way as to render sleep impossible. I stood it until patience ceased to be a virtue, and then asked the compradore if he could not do something to have the child removed. The compradore said he did not think it could be done. 'No got reason,' he said. 'The child has as much right to cry as you have not to want him to cry.' I could not gainsay this."[15]

Business Assistant

With the expansion of the Western agency house after 1860, the comprador's main function shifted from that of a house steward to a business assistant. The shift was so great that he was sometimes referred to as a "Chinese manager" or "Chinese business-manager."[16] As such, his most important function was to guarantee the solvency of the native banks and Chinese businessmen. Because of the inconvenience of coin and bullion and the shortage of cash for the requirements of the trade, Chinese constituents paid Western firms for imported goods in the form of a native bank order, with which the Western merchants were not at all familiar.

That a comprador was held responsible for the native bank order was illustrated by Heard's Hankow office in 1866. Compared with the native bank at Shanghai, the one at Hankow was much more shaky and insecure. As H. G. Bridges explained in his report to

Functions of the Comprador

A. F. Heard on June 28, 1866, "An opium shop or any other buyer of goods establishes what he calls a bank, so he can give one of these orders in payment of purchases." As a result, several native banks went bankrupt. Realizing the seriousness of this financial crisis, Heard's Hankow comprador Seating "talked plainly" with the firm's Western reprsentative "and said he would not secure sales." Bridges quoted Seating as arguing: "If you remit money to a constituent in a Bank Bill you do not secure it; a foreign bank is made of iron, and how can I secure a Chinese bank that is made of paper? If I sell your goods to a man who takes them to his shop up the back street and they burn up, I cannot pay; I am not an insurance office."[17] However, Seating's request for not securing the native bank orders was not acceptable by Heard's, as Bridges continued: "My opinion is that 9/10 of Hankow would feel no doubt as to their compradors' liability to make good losses arising from his taking bad banker's orders or giving credit to a firm that could not pay. . . . When I first came to Hankow Soyseng, Seating's predecessor, acknowledged his liability for all sales made by him."[18]

This practice was by no means limited to Heard's, but was universally accepted in other foreign firms as well. Bridges wrote the next day: "I beg to say that I have made enquiries of other parties, and there is but one opinion, namely, that the compradore is entirely responsible, and Taytnabb & Co. and Sassoons say their compradores' security papers are worded to fully cover all such risks. In fact, there is no doubt as to what is the custom and universal usage, and I never supposed there was any doubt."[19] Indeed, this practice was the main reason for employing a comprador, for without such security the Western firm's business could not have operated smoothly, if at all. Bridges explained: "My own opinion is that if the money for or rather payment for goods sold is not secured, it would be better to do no business, as the losses some day will more than eat up the profits. The idea [of Seating] is absurd, for if the [native] Banks are so shaky that the compradore does not know who to trust, we can know nothing about it."[20]

The comprador also acted as a treasurer. The well-known comprador Hsü Jun was reminded of this duty on the first day that he became Dent's Shanghai comprador.[21] The comprador-treasurer was of particular importance before the fifties, as a Heard's partner

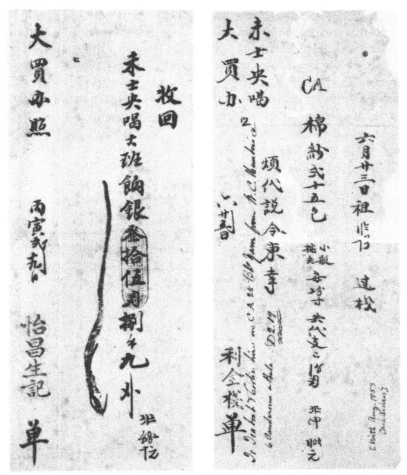

Receipts kept by comprador for money paid: Augustine Heard & Co., Hong Kong, 1853. *Source:* Case 30, HC II.

wrote: "In those days [1840–1846] there were almost no Banks. Each House was its own Bank, of which the Comprador was Cashier. All money was in his charge."[22] (See illustration above.) Heard's Hong Kong comprador, for instance, usually handled $100,000 or more per month in 1870–1871.[23] (See Tables 2 and 5.) Russell's Shanghai comprador similarly "had charge of their Treasury."[24]

Functions of the Comprador

Jardine's operated the same way, until they discovered the malpractices of Tong King-sing in 1871 and then deposited most of their money in the Hongkong and Shanghai Banking Corp.[25] While taking care of the treasury was the comprador's main duty, he also "acts as the banker of the establishment, strangers deposit with him their specie, and check on him when they want money."[26] Heard's Canton comprador received at least $140,000 in deposits in 1855.[27]

The fact that the comprador handled most of the firm's business money almost entirely eliminated the need for its hard currency transactions. The salary of foreign employees was paid by a check drawn on the comprador, who held the funds against which the employee wrote "chits," or memoranda acknowledging debts for retail transactions.[28] In this way both the firm and the foreign employees might owe money to the comprador, as frequently

Table 5. Cash account with the comprador, Augustine Heard & Co., Hong Kong, 1870 (Mexican dollars).

Month	Cr. by comprador[a]	Balance[b]
January	$293,350.47	$11,787.30
February	141,294.45	36,973.27
March	176,898.22	15,314.53
April	180,535.89	*8,377.28* [due comprador]
May	87,276.29	20,098.97
June	249,241.92	12,206.32
July	111,018.16	23,383.01
August	297,519.55	12,006.79
September	238,022.95	18,992.27
October	242,639.68	22,385.52
November	281,821.17	7,885.37
December	179,542.40	*1,440.03* [due comprador]

Source: Cash Account, vol. 55, HC II.

a. This column represents the total monthly payments made by the comprador on the company's behalf.

b. The nonitalicized figures in this column represent the cash amount due the company still held by the comprador at the end of each month. The italicized figures refer to the amount that the comprador had spent for the company in excess of what he had received from the company.

happened. (See Tables 2 and 5.) The comprador-treasurer's function was also to facilitate business transactions for which "orders, or cheques, were drawn on him, precisely as on a modern Bank."[29] This order or cheque was called a "comprador's order." The use of a comprador's order was universal, as evidenced by both Jardine's

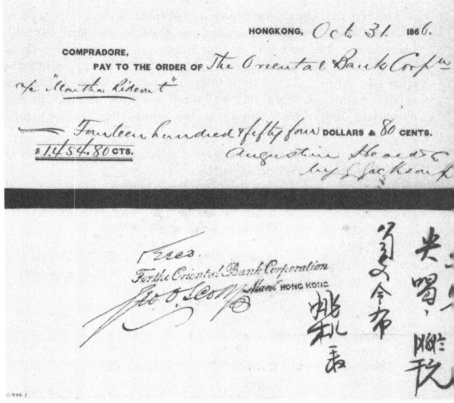

Comprador's order: Augustine Heard & Co., Hong Kong, 1866. *Source*: Case 1, HC II.

and Dent's.[30] In the Heard archives there are about 45,000 such comprador's orders (see illustration), in six boxes, covering the period from 1844 to the 1860's, all drawn by the firm's managers.[31] After it was duly signed, either in Chinese or English, the holder could get money from the comprador. The comprador's order was occasionally in the form of a promissory note at three days' sight, but was usually to be paid immediately by the comprador.[32] The earliest comprador's order available in the Heard archives was one concerning opium dealings at Canton in 1844:[33]

Comprador,

Pay for 3 chests of Patna	
at 630	1,890
7 chests do.	
at 635	4,445
	$6,335

April 1, 1844   [signed] AH & Co.

Since "all the money was in his charge" and since a variety of currency was handled in the treaty ports, another function of the comprador-treasurer, who was himself usually an expert on the intricacies of the money, was to examine bullion, coins, and other specie collected for the firm, with the assistance of a shroff.[34] He also handled the exchange business among gold, silver, and copper coins, as well as different treaty port silver dollars. T. S. Odelly, Jardine's Canton representative, "settled thro the Comprador 30,000 Foochow Dollars" in 1861.[35] Because of an advance in the gold quotation at Shanghai in 1863, Jardine's William Keswick instructed the Hankow representative to buy 5,000 taels worth of gold, with the help of the comprador: "Gold has advanced in this Market to Tls. 16.4 per Tael weight for Pekin Bar. I do not know what description of Gold is current at Hankow, or of what purity it is, but I think it probable that a fair remittance might be made on it, and I beg you will look into the matter with your Compradore, and if you find the metal of a high standard & you can buy it at a good margin on the above quotation, you will please interest us to the extent of about Tls. 5000. Your Compradore must observe great caution in buying."[36]

Before long, Keswick found that, owing to the local official policy, he had to secure more copper cash outside Shanghai. This task was to be undertaken by the comprador, as he reported two months later to Alexander Perceval: "We are now finding the want of Copper cash very much & the [Chinese] Authorities have refused to allow more to leave Shanghai for the Cotton districts. I have instructed Mr. [Edward] Whittall to purchase Tls. 50,000 worth at Ningpo [through his comprador], & I think I shall tomorrow request Messrs. C. Wilson & Co. of Chinkiang to purchase a similar amount or to contract for them. It is almost impossible to purchase Cotton without Cash, & I beg you will ascertain if it be possible to send them to this [port] from the south."[37]

The comprador-treasurer also handled different kinds of bills and drafts. James Keswick at Shanghai sent a telegram to Jardine's Hankow representative in 1885 which read: "Request Comprador secure more favorable exchange for Mercantile Bank Shanghai drafts."[38] The most important of these bills and drafts, as already shown, was the "native draft," or the native bank order. Since the comprador handled different kinds of bills, he was also known in Shanghai as a bill broker.[39]

In addition, the comprador provided market intelligence. Concerning the fluctuating price of peas, John Heard asked the advice of the Hong Kong comprador, as he wrote to A. F. Heard in 1860: "One can find out about as little of the future of peas as rice, both most uncertain articles. I asked the comprador [what] to say about it. He said, 'That price just now $2.30, suppose got 10,000 pls. [piculs], much come down little.' "[40] When Heard's was considering signing a contract with the Ch'ing government for transporting the tribute rice to Peking in 1861, its Hong Kong comprador wrote a note both in Chinese and English concerning different kinds of rice.[41] The comprador supplied exchange information as well, as Heard's Foochow representative wrote in 1865: "The Comprador [Akit] suggests to me that *sycee* is likely now to be very low."[42]

As the activities of the Western houses in China gradually diversified, so did the comprador's role. One of his newly developed functions was to take care of the shipping business for the firm. This was the main function of Sunkee, Russell's Tientsin comprador (1862–1873). Because Russell's served as the general agent for the Shanghai Steam Navigation Co. and had to furnish its managerial and office facilities, the firm's Tientsin comprador also worked for the steamship company. T. Moore, Russell's Tientsin agent, stated that

Functions of the Comprador

Sunkee's "special business at Tientsin was to procure freight and passengers for the S. [Shanghai] S. N. Co."[43] This was likewise the case for Heard's Yangtze compradors. H. B. Bridges, Heard's agent at the upper Yangtze ports, reported from Kiukiang in 1862: "One of the principal uses of a compradore here is to keep good terms with these northern fellows and get freight from them."[44] He must "always be on the sharp look out for cargo."[45]

Enlarging his functions so as to replace the Cohong linguists, the comprador now also acted as an interpreter.[46] In his correspondence to the head of the house at Hong Kong, Heard's Shanghai partner sometimes enclosed Chinese letters of business intelligence received from its Chinese representatives on the upper Yangtze, to be translated by the Hong Kong comprador.[47] The comprador performed further varied functions, ranging from customs reporting to entertaining constituents by providing dinners and women.[48] When the firm had business to conduct with the Chinese authorities (especially with regard to selling them military products, such as rifles, powder, and ammunition), one of the comprador's special duties was to deal with the Chinese officials.[49]

In addition, the comprador handled the actual business transactions. Besides acting purely as a commission agent, he occasionally became an independent broker, helping the foreign firm in buying and selling.[50] For instance, if a Chinese merchant intended to purchase certain imported goods, he would contact a comprador and inform him of the price that he was willing to pay in terms of Chinese currency. Then the comprador would check with the foreign merchant about the current price and the probable date of delivery. If, after converting the price into Chinese currency according to the rate of exchange, he calculated that the transaction would allow him a profit, he would accept the order of the Chinese merchant on the one hand and close the deal with the foreign merchant on the other.[51] However, his more important function, especially during the nineteenth century, was to buy Chinese produce from the interior.

Upcountry Purchaser

The activities of the compradors were not limited to the treaty ports. In the sixties, Heard's compradors occasionally went to

Yüeh-chou, Hunan, to investigate mining possibilities and to Wei-hsien, Shantung, to buy "straw braids" for them.[52] The firm's Foochow comprador, Tong Loong-maw, tried to get a monopoly license from Taiwan officials and rented land for the firm in Tamsui for producing petroleum.[53] In February 1873, the firm employed Atai, former comprador to Dent & Co. in Hong Kong, to go to Hainan Island to "obtain the consent of the authorities and the inhabitants near and in Cheong-fa-hien to his working sundry copper and other mines in that vicinity."[54]

The comprador's main duty in the interior, however, was to buy tea and silk, a system known as the upcountry purchase, which was extensively developed at Shanghai and Foochow in the sixties. Before the Treaty of Nanking, the Western merchants used to obtain the Chinese produce from the hong merchants at Canton. However, things changed after 1842. On February 24, 1850, Russell's Robert B. Forbes at Canton wrote to Joshua Bates, a London constituent: "We are also about raising commission on American business. . . . The fact is [that] . . . the labour is now much increased since the Hong monopoly failed."[55] One reason for the labor increase was the fact that the Western agency houses had to purchase the Chinese produce from the interior by themselves. An eye-witness report of the situation in the fifties read in part: "It has lately become a custom in Shanghai and Foochow, and to a small degree in Canton also, to intrust very large sums of money to Chinese [compradors] for the purchase of tea and silk in the interior. The money is lost sight of for months in a country where a foreigner could not follow; yet, such is the honesty of the Chinese, that the instances are rare in which the man intrusted with it has made off."[56]

Actually, as the British consular report of 1849 indicated, this system started at Shanghai in the late forties as "one of the surest means of securing a fair proportion of the best qualities [of tea] for the Shanghai market."[57] The system developed so rapidly that by the mid-sixties the compradors were "despatched into the country with sums of money large enough to buy up the produce of whole districts."[58] This was also true with silk, about which a foreign commissioner of the Chinese customs reported in 1867: "The system of contracting [silk] beforehand for delivery has prevailed to a large extent of late years, and now, instead of [foreign] merchants waiting the arrival of the produce on the market, they send large sums of money into the country by their Chinese servants [compradors], who make advances to and secure contracts with the [local silk] Hongs."[59]

It was at Foochow that the upcountry purchase of tea was conducted on the largest scale in a sophisticated way. Augustine Heard, Jr., wrote: "Years after the Hong system had ceased to exist, foreigners were in the habit of sending large sums, both in the shape of money and opium, into the country districts from Foochow for the purchase of teas."[60] Several large Western houses were engaged in such upcountry purchases, and Heard's case in the period from the 1840's to the 1860's clearly illustrates the role of the comprador.

Heard's established its Foochow office in 1854.[61] The old Canton comprador See Yong recommended Tong Loong-maw as the new Foochow comprador to accompany George F. Weller, the firm's Foochow agent. Tong, his brother Akit, and Weller were to handle the upcountry tea purchase for the house. Tong's upcountry activities were diverse and on a large scale, as indicated in the following comprador's upcountry purchase account of 1857, prepared by Heard's office at Foochow:[62]

Items from Compradors, particularizing this season's contract purchases in the Kiaso District.

[Comprador's] Expenses [in the Upcountry]	T. [Taels]
Rent of our six houses for one year at 250 taels each	1,500
Small houses and market places	150
Wages of head men and all parties hired to manipulate &c &c for 12 months each house 1500 taels	9,000
Boat hire, Coolie hire for transportation, charcoal, wood &c &c about 235 each chop (12 chops)	2,820
Expenses Canton coolies taking treasure to country and otherwise assisting, say T. 75 each chop	900
Inside country duty or better called squeeze T. 51 each chop	612
Powder, guns spears &c &c say	275
forward	15,257
Iron pans, fire places & other appurtenances, Tea paper and sundries about	1,200
	16,457

First cost of leaf

3654 piculs at 22.5 T	82,215 T.		
630 ″ at 19.5	12,285 T.		
(last) 536 ″ at 11.	5,896 T.	100,396	
Suey How duty & squeeze 7.5 m. per picul		3,615	
Boxes and Leads 8 m. per picul, avg. 25.8 T. per picul		3,856	

Tls. 124,324

[*Comprador Owed to the House*]	[*Taels*]
Amount credit compradors as reported short cost of all Teas produced from the above mentioned leaf	107,213
Amount gain upon treasure sent to [the District of] Kiaso, the difference in weights used there & Foochow being about 2% in favor of F. [Foochow]	2,500

forward 109,713

Amount allowance made to the compradors	3,000
Expenses firing and packing 200 piculs siftings not taken by us but *kept by compradors*	1,500
Cash received by compradors in Foochow for sale of siftings	3,000
Gain on Lead, house Tea and Sundries	1,000
Compradors asserts that he has lost 3,000 taels & so on	3,000
Amount which the compradors cannot account for and which may arise from the cost of the leaf being 3,111. A few mace less than the compradors makes it by his proportioning	3,111

Tls. 124,324

The upcountry operations were handled only by the large Western houses, as a Heard's partner explained: "In the early days every House was its own Bank, and it sought no facilities outside of its own resources. Consequently, the old House with large capital had a practical monopoly of the business. For instance, a few Houses could never have maintained so long their monopoly at Foochow if banks had been ready, as they were afterwards, to lend assistance to those less strong."[63]

Equipped with plentiful funds, Heard's, like other large houses such as Jardine's and Russell's, carried on upcountry tea purchasing on a grand scale at Foochow, only two hundred and fifty miles away from the Bohea (Wu-i) tea district. Augustine Heard, Jr., recalled: "Huge amounts of money went into the country [in the hands of the comprador] . . . in February and March, and did not come back in the shape of teas till May. It was a great risk to run. We had no right by Treaty to buy produce in the interior, and could make no redemption in case of loss."[64]

Heard's at Foochow seems to have had two kinds of arrangement with the comprador concerning the tea purchase. The first was to advance the funds to him, while the house took the risk of gain or loss. The comprador and his staff, with the advance money in hand, went to the tea-growing area in early spring. Purchases lasted from May to August, and the tea arrived in Foochow from June to September.[65] Around $70,000 out of the $200,000 annual upcountry purchase money was thus sent upcountry before any tea appeared in port.[66]

The second arrangement was to negotiate a contract with the comprador, and through him, with other teamen as well. M. A. Daly, Weller's assistant at Foochow, reported: "Pekoes—we have contracted for the quality refined . . . dividing our order equally between [comprador] Akit and [teaman] Siequa, and this arrangement I think offers our best chance of getting fine tea."[67] Both comprador and teaman might get financial help from the house and use its facilities; the house in turn would have the "right of first refusal" for purchasing the tea—"they will not sell them [teas] to any one until we have refused them."[68] In a letter dated June 18, 1859, Weller reported: "I have told the comprador [Tong Loong-maw] that if any Oolong men wish to put their teas in our godown under our advance, we will do so, provided we have the refusal of the same at market price."[69]

Once the tea houses were set up in the tea-growing area and the upcountry system was well established by the comprador, Heard's could easily draw up more tea contracts with him. John Heard wrote to A. F. Heard on April 4, 1862: "He [Tong Loong-maw] has established [tea] houses in the Tea Country. . . . Having finished the 6 chops [shipments], the [tea] houses are available all through the season for getting down Teas if they promise well. Contract pegion [business] is done up at Foochow."[70]

For Heard's, the upcountry business was profitable not only for the commission, as Heard continued: "He shall get down 7 chops of finest Congous which we shall probably resell on the market, and I think they will make a fair profit, besides our earning fat on them down in our steamers. If they promise better to England, we can ship them, but this we can see when the time comes."[71]

Tea market estimation was a difficult and important business for the agency houses. The time from order to shipment was usually six months, and under the contract system at least four months were necessary from the advance of money to the arrival of the tea. The comprador not only took care of purchasing but also provided market information for the house. George F. Weller reported from Foochow in 1859: "The Compradore [Tong Loong-maw] has returned [from upcountry] and will begin at once to make arrangements for the contract. . . . The Compradore says that if our order is likely to be increased, the sooner it is done the better, as at a later period of the season we shall not stand much for a chance."[72] In Foochow, the supply of market information by the comprador was indispensable to Heard's, especially as the upcountry purchase system gradually increased and became standardized. In 1860, Heard's spent almost a quarter of a million dollars for the upcountry purchase, handled by the Foochow comprador Tong Loong-maw. However, in 1862 the partners decided to discontinue the upcountry purchase for that year, mainly on the basis of Tong's market report: "The Foochow Comp. [comprador] says prices will be very high, and that there are as many houses in the country now being prepared as last year, and this prospect was in favor of active competition in the interior—so I think it safer to stand aloof."[73]

The upcountry purchase, though important, was only one part of Heard's tea business. Augustine Heard, Jr., recalled: "We performed all tea operations of the tea-merchant—buying the leaf, firing it, making the chests and packing them."[74] Some of the tea was fired upcountry on the spot of purchase, but usually firing and repacking were done in the firm's Foochow godowns, lasting from July to November, and entirely carried out by the comprador. Weller had a special regard for the Foochow comprador on account of his important role as a teaman. When Tong's own business affairs became too pressing for him to continue as a comprador,

Functions of the Comprador

Weller expressed concern about his successor: "I note that the Comprador [Tong Loong-maw, now in Hankow] will not return here. I have not much confidence in Akit. He is too fond of 'squeeze' and besides is unpopular with a great many tea men. However, we can try him and he may change his ideas and do very well."[75]

Yet Heard's was certainly not the biggest tea purchaser at Foochow. After 1854 and through the sixties, Jardine's secured a great amount of tea through its compradors Ahee and Acum and its teamen Taishing, Yunta, and Tonghing.[76] In 1855, "the amount of treasure that Ahee had with him in the country . . . including Drug [opium], was $440,065."[77] The Foochow upcountry system was also entered into by other large Western houses. In fact, it was the American firm of Russell & Co. that took the initiative in sending its comprador "into the interior with large sums of money" to make purchases directly from tea growers.[78] In 1855, the firm's upcountry purchase there was handled entirely by its comprador Ahone.[79] Meanwhile, the British firm of Dent & Co. in the same year spent about $400,000 for the upcountry purchase at Foochow.[80]

Before the upcountry purchase system became standard procedure in Foochow, it had apparently been in existence on a small scale in Shanghai. In some instances Heard's got tea by advancing money to the teamen and in return had the right of "first refusal"—a system similar to that of Foochow. One of the firm's agreements with teamen reads: "Augustine Heard & Co. agree to advance such teamen . . . to any amount under $1,000. . . . Such advance to be repaid when the chop is sold with the interest at the rate of 1 per cent per month. . . . The teamen are to have the liberty of selling their tea to any other foreigners, but in all case Augustine Heard & Co. are to have the preference, and where they became purchasers of tea advanced upon, the advance is considered as part payment for the chop and interest and all charges to cease from the day it is settled."[81]

Heard's also sent the Shanghai comprador into the interior. In the days of the Taiping uprising tea was occasionally transported under Western protection, but the comprador's staff usually handled such tasks.[82] The comprador, as a rule, gave a report to the manager from the interior, as in the following upcountry tea report by Heard's Shanghai comprador in 1859:[83]

Crop of Moyaw will be	80,000 h/c [half chest]
Crop of Eychow will be	120,000 h/c
Crop of Twankay, Setyune &c.	130,000 h/c
	330,000 h/c
If high prices sale in Shanghai, this amount may be increased 10 c 20,000 h/c, not more	20,000 h/c
	350,000 h/c
Crop of Taiping will be	90,000 h/c
	440,000 h/c
In addition we here estimate Pingtueg &c., say	60,000 h/c
Soochow pack	20,000 h/c
Gives a Total of	520,000 h/c

Takee, Jardine's noted comprador at Shanghai (1849–1851), partly handled the firm's upcountry tea purchase. As A. G. Dallas reported in 1851: "Takee has been assuring me that he will have a cargo of Tea down *very early* of the season, and he has more than once spontaneously urged upon me to have fast ship ready. He is now up the Country making his arrangements."[84] However, his more important duty seems to have been the handling of upcountry silk rather than tea purchases. During the late forties and early fifties, compradors to Dent's and Jardine's at Shanghai gradually worked out a method of silk purchase. Under the so-called "Soochow system," the compradors brought opium for sale from Shanghai to the silk-producing region of Soochow, where silk was purchased. A. G. Dallas wrote from Shanghai in 1851: "It is not usual to send more than five chests [of opium] in one boat, so the risk is divided. The arrangement will be to take delivery of the Opium at Woosung, settle weight and quality there, and [settle] the price at Soochow. The proceeds to be paid here cash in a fortnight, or transferred to accounts if produce is being purchased."[85] Through the initiative of Dallas, who tried to compete with the firm's British competitor Dent and Co., Takee consented to engage in this kind of business for the firm in 1851. Being anxious not to fall behind, Dallas continued:

"The Honan men and other large dealers resort to Soo-chow [Soochow] to make their purchases [of silk], and I see nothing for it but to adopt the system cautiously. . . . I intend in the meanwhile to make an early trial."[86]

By 1852 Dallas thought that Takee was no longer capable of "monopolizing" the silk market in Shanghai, although he still regarded Takee highly: "My confidence is a good deal shaken in his *ability*, or in that of any other Chinaman here, to conduct such a large operation as a monopoly of the Silk Market in the present day; but . . . I still think him one of the best of them."[87] Jardine's upcountry silk purchases through Takee in fact gradually decreased. Dallas reported the comprador's explanation: "He complains of want of capital—having so much of his means locked up in Teas . . . and he says that with larger advances from me he could secure the Silk; but these I am not inclined to grant for various reasons. A strong one is the very precarious state of his health from fever."[88]

Takee's successor, Yakee, handled the upcountry purchase of tea, silk, and cotton on a comparatively small scale in the late fifties.[89] Acum, the next comprador (1859–1863), engaged mainly in the upcountry purchase of tea. James Whittall reported to Alexander Perceval (Head in the East, 1860–1864) on November 24, 1863: "Acum (my Compradore) started again for the Country this afternoon, the steamer Pootung conveying him and about a lac [$100,000] of treasure. He has instructions to act promptly & boldly, and as he is neither wanting in sense or *enterprise,* I am very sanguine he will do well for us. I expect he will be back in 4 or 5 days, when I intend transmitting to the same district another lac or thereabouts."[90] However, most is known about Acum's successor, the renowned Cantonese comprador Tong King-sing (1863–1873).

The Chief Comprador Tong King-sing

The rise of Shanghai as an entrepôt increased the importance of the Western firm's Shanghai office, and consequently the Shanghai comprador came to hold a particularly important position. He was usually referred to as the chief or general comprador (*tsung mai-pan*).[91] As such, he loosely supervised the firm's northern compradors, took charge of interport matters, and performed other varied functions.

In the sixties, Jardine's Tong King-sing, Dent's Hsü Jun, and Russell's Choping all acted as the "heads," as it were, of the firms' northern compradors on the Yangtze and North China coast.[92]

Heard's Shanghai comprador was another such chief comprador. Performing the interport liaison function, he frequently not only visited other treaty ports personally but also maintained close contact, through correspondence, with the compradors there.[93] In a letter to John Heard dated February 26, 1858, A. F. Heard wrote from Shanghai on the tea contract with Kiukee: "Our compradore will write to yours about the matter with all the necessary particulars, names of Kiukee's men, &c."[94] The comprador also had to write to the firm's Chinese customers, as A. F. Heard wrote to the Captain of the *Fire Dart* in 1862: "The man in charge of them [junks at Chinkiang] is called Ip Chee Hing and we enclose a letter for him from our [Shanghai] Comprador, informing him that the *Fire Dart* will tow the Junks, &c."[95]

Tong King-sing's activities best illustrate the functions of a chief comprador. In September 1863, Tong succeeded Acum as Jardine's Shanghai comprador, but his area of activity was not confined to Shanghai.[96] He frequently visited other treaty ports, either to develop general business or on a special mission assigned by the foreign manager.[97] He helped the firm to settle disputes with Chinese merchants in other ports.[98] Sometimes he acted as an interpreter, for in the view of an American merchant, he spoke English "like a Briton."[99] When Hsü Jun recommended him in 1872 as treasurer of the Cantonese Guild in Shanghai (Kuang-Chao kung-so), Tong declined to accept on the ground that he was too often out of Shanghai.[100]

Unlike the Foochow comprador, whose business was mainly the upcountry purchase, the Shanghai comprador had to take charge of the firm's diverse operations. In 1870, Tong began to manage Jardine's newly established shipping agency. F. B. Johnson, Jardine's Shanghai manager, wrote to the Hong Kong partner, William Keswick, in 1870: "I have arranged with Tong King-sing to establish in connection with his office a shipping agency on the premises which involves no expense to us and I think will work well."[101] The next year, a Chinese-owned steamer was consigned to Jardine's through Tong's arrangement. F. B. Johnson wrote: "The consignment of the steamer *Norna* owned as you are aware by Chinese has been offered to us through Tong King-sing & I have accepted it subject to your arrival. The owners will probably call upon you with reference to details and as I understand that the vessel is not mortgaged any advances we may be called upon to make for ordinary disbursements would not be jeopardized."[102]

One year later, Tong went to Hankow and employed a freight broker "to assist in the management of cargo" for Jardine's.[103] Indeed, Tong's help in the shipping business was highly valued by the firm. His suggestion to operate the Shanghai-Foochow line was adopted by Johnson, and he even suggested international operations. Johnson wrote from Shanghai in 1871: "Tong King-sing tells me that we can engage through cargo to Manila for the *Peiho* via Amoy either by our direct boats from here or by the *Yuentsefei* & Lapraik [Douglas Lapraik & Co.] boats."[104]

Besides shipping, Tong also helped with the firm's insurance business. In a letter to James Whittall, Jardine's new Head in the East (1864–1874), Johnson proposed to give one share of the Canton Insurance Office "to Tong King-sing who is exerting himself to obtain China business."[105] As was usually the case, Tong also served as a treasurer. Each morning he prepared the cash book, which was then examined by the foreign manager. William Keswick reported to James Whittall on September 27, 1864: "The rough one [Cash Book] is written up to last night—by Tong King-sing, who writes English well. A Cash Book is kept which every morning is written up, and this book is frequently examined by me, though I must admit, hitherto not daily. A form such as the one enclosed is handed me every morning with the balance of Coin and Silver distinctly stated."[106]

According to the instructions of the Shanghai manager, Tong, as treasurer, secured copper cash from Chinkiang in 1863 for the upcountry purchase at Hankow.[107] He also handled the native bank order, as evidenced by F. B. Johnson's words in 1869: "Your remarks regarding Native Draft for Taels 14,800 have my attention and the matter has been referred to my Comprador."[108] By the late sixties, the comprador-treasurer Tong King-sing began to assume a further responsibility in helping Jardine's develop a "new business" —the "chop loan" (*ch'e-p'iao*) to native banks.[109] This system had been introduced by Wang Huai-shan, comprador to the Hong-kong and Shanghai Banking Corp. at Shanghai.[110] Jardine's immediately followed suit in 1868, as Johnson wrote: "I find that I can occasionally invest our Cash balances in Chinese Bankers' orders at short dates say 3 c [to] 7 days at rates of interest varying from 12% to 15% with, I think, perfect safety, as I should not discount the paper of any one Bank to a greater extent than Tls. 10,000 or 15,000. . . . I am aware that the success of such business will depend upon the acumen and trustworthiness of our Compradors."[111] It is not known to what extent Jardine's was engaged in the chop loan business, but Johnson clearly showed a great interest. He so strongly advocated the new system that he even suggested that it replace "the hard driven competition for the export of Tea and Silk."[112]

Like other compradors, Tong also guaranteed the solvency of the firm's Chinese constituents. For instance, he guaranteed Achew, comprador to Jerdein & Co., who was Jardine's agent at Hankow. In a letter to Jardine's Shanghai office on August 22, 1868, Tong wrote: "In consideration of your having released Achew, Compradore to Jerdein & Cy., Hankow, from the custody of the Mandarins, and since you have agreed to press your claim for the Tls. 4000, on the Shingyuetah Bank and Ahone the real debtors, I hereby bind myself, that should you not be able to recover through H. B. M.'s Consul the whole of your claim or any part thereof from the said Bank and Ahone, to pay you on behalf of Achew the whole or such portion of the claim that may be unsatisfied in installments of one thousand taels each in every six months commencing on the 31st December 1868."[113] Four years later Tong went to Hankow to recover the claim. F. B. Johnson wrote in 1872: "Our compradore Tong King-sing proceeds to Hankow today for the purpose of recovering if he can a claim which he guaranteed for us some years ago upon one of the Hankow banks which failed. We released Achew the compradore from liability because Tong King-sing paid us but he (TKS) now stands in our shoes & we have the right to claim payment of the order on his behalf."[114]

Compared with the other varied services he rendered to Jardine's, Tong's function as an assistant in business transactions was less important. He handled some purchases and sales, but it was probable that the bulk of Jardine's transactions did not go through him. The firm's main channel of buying and selling by the sixties was through direct and constant contact with a body of Chinese merchants, many of whom were the firm's former compradors—men like Yakee, Acum, and Yowloong.[115] Although Jardine's had been in close contact with native merchants and occasionally received market intelligence from them, the firm still relied greatly on Tong's information on many aspects of the Chinese market.[116] He provided market intelligence for sugar and wood oil, and frequently went to Chinkiang and Canton to handle the rice business.[117]

Although Tong himself did not handle Jardine's opium transactions, the firm's opium intelligence seems to have depended mainly on Tong's report. Johnson wrote to Keswick on September 11, 1868: "I enclose a memorandum drawn up by Tong King-sing regarding the production of Native Opium, which seems trustworthy in its information excepting only as regards the important point of quality. I have no doubt that it is very difficult if not quite impossible to collect true statistics as to the supply likely to compete with Indian drug this year or next."[118] Johnson had to maintain close contact with the main office in Hong Kong, because the supply of Indian opium in Shanghai was mainly transported by sea from Hong Kong. In 1869 when a ship was to depart for Hong Kong, he wrote to Keswick: "I have requested Tong King-sing to send you under this cover the latest quotations of the opium market at noon to-day when the bearer will leave."[119] Tong's quotations from Shanghai in 1869 were as follows:[120]

Sunday 14 March 1869
1/2 Past 11 A. M.

Opium market quiet.

On account of the larger portion of the drug being in 2d (Chinese) hands.

Malwa is quoted at Tls. 600.

Foreign holders are asking Tls. 610, but are willing to sell at Tls. 600 if they get a bone fide offer. Chinese holders are willing to part at Tls. 590.

Patna (old) is quoted at Tls. 530.

Sassoons people are asking Tls. 540—but Chinese holders are selling at Tls. 525 to 527.

New drug—nothing doing.

Tong King-sing

Tong was consulted on the financial condition of Chinese merchants as well. F. B. Johnson reported to James Whittall in 1867: "I have made all the enquiry I can through Tong King-sing as to the origin of Ekee's difficulties which he asserted in the first place to the fact that Ekee was involved when he first came into connection with the Hong, and in the second to reckless trading and speculation. I enclose a statement of his affairs as given me by Tong King-sing."[121]

Thus, although the comprador had general functions, the importance of each function differed from place to place. For instance, the compradors at Canton and Hong Kong acted mainly as house bankers, while the comprador at Foochow chiefly handled up-country purchases. The value of the Shanghai comprador lay in his ability to perform effectively the role of a chief comprador—supervising the compradors at the Yangtze and North China ports and contributing entrepreneurially to the firm's diverse operations. The comprador at Tientsin or on the Yangtze acted as a commission agent for the sale and purchase of goods as well as for the shipping business, whereas the comprador in Japan helped the foreign house with his special knowledge of the tea business.

V The Comprador as a Nouveau Riche

Taking advantage of the lush opportunities afforded in the treaty ports and fully utilizing his close relationship with the foreigners, the comprador was able to accumulate a great deal of wealth in a surprisingly short period of time. The newly-emerged comprador-merchant thus turned out to be a *nouveau riche* in modern China. It is important to understand how the compradors achieved their fortunes, as well as to estimate their total income and assess its significance.

One salient feature of the comprador was that, in his different capacities, he could accumulate wealth through various ways. First of all, he made money by acting as a comprador. While the success of the foreign merchants depended to a great extent on the comprador, he too profited substantially from them. Besides his salary, commission, and other legitimate income, he usually "squeezed" his employers. At the same time, the comprador accumulated wealth by operating as a merchant in his own right. Enjoying the unique privileges of a comprador, he was better able than most to develop his private business.

Accumulating Wealth as a Comprador

How did the comprador accumulate wealth in his primary capacity? First, a comprador was usually paid a fixed salary, covering his services and expenses in maintaining a staff. His annual salary, which usually ranged from 500 to 2,000 taels, averaged at 1,000 taels. An ordinary comprador received 40 taels per month in

1878, and a bank comprador's average annual salary was 1,200 taels at the end of the nineteenth century.[1] Great diversity existed in the payment arrangements. Tong Mow-chee, Jardine's Tientsin comprador, observed in 1875: "There was no rule as to payment of compradors. Each foreign hong made its own agreement."[2] Thus, the amount of a comprador's salary actually depended on other arrangements, such as whether he could get commission, or who paid the expenses of the comprador's office. Tong King-sing was allowed 5,744 taels per annum for expenses in 1865, including 1,500 taels for his own salary, and theoretically he had no right to exact commissions.[3] In Tientsin, his comprador brother Tong Mow-chee was allowed 1,800 taels per annum for himself and staff in 1871–1873, with an additional 300 taels for renting a hong.[4] The salary of Sunkee, comprador to Russell's at Tientsin in 1862–1873, was 1,200 taels a year from 1867, paid monthly or quarterly, but the house was to pay his other expenses, such as the rent for a hong and the wages of his staff.[5] During the early sixties, Akow, Heard's Yokohama comprador, was paid 170 Mexican dollars monthly, which covered the wages of his staff, consisting of a shroff, a cook, and two coolies.[6]

In contrast to the comprador's office expenses, his salary was small. Commenting on the allowance of 5,744 taels per annum for Tong King-sing's office, William Keswick explained to James Whittall in 1865: "The sum required by the Comprador, though in the aggregate it appears large, is not when taken item by item so much out of the way."[7] This was particularly true in the case of Seating, Heard's Hankow comprador from 1866, whose salary of 20 taels monthly constituted only about ten percent of the expenses of his office. (See Table 6.) In the early seventies at Tientsin, according to Tong Mow-chee, "it would be a very good salary for a comprador to clear Tls. 1,000 a year, having all his expenses paid."[8]

The salary constituted only a small part of the comprador's total income. He accumulated a substantial amount by receiving commissions from both Chinese and foreign merchants on each actual business deal. Although in some instances he was theoretically not allowed to exact commissions from his foreign employer, he generally received one to five percent commission, with an average of two to three percent.[9] One of the foreign commissioners of

Table 6. Monthly salary of the comprador and his staff, Augustine Heard & Co., Hankow, 1866 (taels).

Comprador [Seating]	20
Shroff	15
Godown man	10
Godown assistant	10
Godown assistant	10
Tea office boy	12
Market man	10
Market man	10
Market man	10
Writer	10
Canton watchman	8
Hankow watchman	3.90
Chair coolie	5
Chair coolie	5
Porter for front gate	5
Porter for street gate	5
Table boy	12
Table boy	5
Cook	15
House coolie	6
House coolie	6
Total	190.90

Source: H. G. Bridges (Hankow) to A. F. Heard (Shanghai), June 14, 1866, HC.

the customs reported in 1866: "The compradors not only survive but also charge 2 to 3 percent on trade for doing so."[10] This income was especially important in Canton in the forties just after the Cohong system had been abolished, as a Heard's partner recalled: "Nearly all the mercantile transactions with the natives, buying and selling, passed in some shape through his [comprador's] hand, or under his supervision, and on very many of them he received a commission."[11] In Foochow, Augustine Heard & Co.'s comprador charged the firm one percent commission on securing tea trade, and this was an established "custom" there in the sixties.[12]

In Shanghai, however, the comprador theoretically had no right to charge a commission from his employer in the mid-sixties. In 1864, fifty-two compradors wrote to the foreign merchants' Shanghai General Chamber of Commerce, proposing "to charge certain commissions," but their effort did not succeed.[13] William Keswick of Jardine's also found that "it would be better to allow . . . [a] fixed charge than to admit a right on the part of the Compradore to exact commissions from the Native trading with us."[14] The fact remained, however, that it was very common for the comprador at Shanghai to exact around two percent commission on each transaction.[15] After the "chop loan" system was introduced in the late sixties, he likewise received a commission from it.[16]

It was assumed by the foreign partners that commissions would encourage the comprador to bring more business to the house. Although Sunkee, Russell's Tientsin comprador (1861–1873), preferred to be paid exclusively by wages rather than by commission, Edward Cunningham offered him a low salary of 100 taels per month with the right to receive one percent commission from the firm on transactions.[17] This arrangement was similar to that made between Jardine's and its Tientsin comprador Tong Mow-chee.[18] Besides, a comprador at Tientsin in the sixties could get 5 taels from his employer for each chest of opium sold, and "two per cent also on passengers and Chinese freight."[19] In 1862 Sunkee received from Russell's 4,616.8 taels for his wages and commissions, as shown in the following tabulation:[20]

Wages—12 x Tls. 100		Tls. 1,200.0
Commissions		
Goods sold—1% x Tls. 247,933		2,479.3
Opium sold—55 x Tls. 2.5		137.5
Freight and passenger solicited	ca. Tls.	800.0
	Total	Tls. 4,616.8

Compradors on the Yangtze ports had a similar privilege. In addition to salary, Heard's comprador received a one percent commission from the firm on sales and purchases handled. But since the steamship rivalry was keen, he received two percent on both freight and passengers.[21] The agent of Heard's at Hankow reported to A. F. Heard in 1866: "In October of last year, I wrote to Shanghai that R. [Russell] & Co. paid their compradore 2% on all cargo obtained and . . . in further I should pay 2% on freight and passengers, unless it was objected to, in order to increase the Compradore's zeal."[22] Trying to compete with other firms, Jardine's J. J. Keswick instructed from Shanghai that the firm should pay its Hankow comprador a two percent commission. B. A. Clarke reported from Hankow in 1885: "Your instructions relative to the payment of 2% commission to the Compradore will be carried out, & I think with this he can smooth away difficulties which have hitherto worked against us, by paying a proportion of the extra expenses incurred through bringing Cargo to your Steamers."[23]

In order further to cultivate the comprador, foreign firms sometimes offered him an even higher commission. For example, to the Canton comprador Ahyue, Russell & Co. once offered a "5% commission on all the freight business he procured."[24] Thus, a commission from foreign merchants of one percent on transactions and two percent on freight and passengers was generally accepted, although not without exception. While receiving a commission from the foreign merchants, the comprador also "scraped his earnings from his own countrymen . . . and earned a fat commission for every transaction."[25] He therefore exacted an average commission of three percent on freight and other transactions. When his importance as a commercial middleman decreased at the beginning of the twentieth century, the commission on transactions was gradually reduced to from one-half to one percent.[26]

Yet the comprador's main source of income came from neither salary nor commission, but from "squeeze." It should be emphasized that as a middleman between Chinese and foreigners, a comprador's "opportunities for doing mischief were tenfold more numerous than those enjoyed by an ordinary Chinese or an ordinary European."[27] Consequently, he "milked" his foreign employers in many ways. One of the comprador's important functions was acting as treasurer, in which capacity he could make extra money for himself. Since he managed the cash and native bank orders for the agency house, he might put them into reliable native banks and collect the interest for himself. In this way, as John Heard estimated, the comprador could make an extra of $5,000 to $6,000 per year.[28] Another unique privilege enjoyed by a comprador was the private use of the firm's funds to finance his own business. Furthermore, because foreign merchants were only familiar with the main produce and imported goods of their business, the comprador, as a business assistant, could further "squeeze" his Western employer by, for instance, forging a higher price list of other native produce and pocketing the surplus money himself. The practice of "squeeze" was widespread, as Tong King-sing wrote to Jardine's William Keswick in 1868: "I never have robbed or squeezed you in the slightest degree as most of Chinese servants do."[29]

While the actual total income, both legal and illegal, of a comprador is unknown, it is certain that he earned money in many ways. One contemporary source estimated in the sixties that he profited more from a transaction than did the foreign house.[30] His income might in this case have been over-estimated, but he undoubtedly could gain by various means from a single transaction—through salary, commission, "squeeze," and the increased opportunities for his own business. In a way, the small salary actually forced him to abuse his position. He is thus reminiscent of the Ch'ing officials, whose salaries were small but all of whom were comparatively wealthy.

Accumulating Wealth as an Independent Merchant

Just as the comprador got a handsome income directly from the agency house, so he benefited indirectly from his position. On the one hand, the influence he exerted on Chinese constituents made him valuable to Western houses, and for this reason he got money as a go-between for Chinese and foreign merchants.[31] On the other hand, he was well paid for acting as a spokesman for Chinese merchant-investors who had business with a foreign house. For instance, Tong King-sing, who spoke perfect English, was requested by native merchant-investors to accept the directorship in several Chinese-owned steamship companies and thus received "an income of about Tls. 1,000 per annum."[32]

In addition, the comprador accumulated wealth as an independent merchant in his own right. He could develop his own business in many ways by utilizing his power as a comprador. Being the treasurer of an agency house, he could secretly use its funds to finance his own business, as in the case of Tong King-sing, who in 1871 improperly discounted about 80,000 taels of native bank orders not due, which Jardine's had entrusted to his care, in order to tide over a financial crisis in his own business.[33] Or a comprador might privately use the facilities of the foreign house for his own sake.[34] But his greatest asset was the reputation he enjoyed from his close connection with foreign firms.

Why was this foreign connection so important to the development of the comprador's own business? To answer this question, one must understand how inseparable his role as a comprador was from his role as an independent merchant. This confusion was pointed out in 1867 by both Rutherford Alcock, British minister at Peking, and Charles A. Winchester, British consul at Shanghai. Since "the same individuals . . . [were] constantly employed in different capacities as Comprador and broker, and allowed to conduct commercial operations on their own account," the Chinese merchant "might well be perplexed as to which of the three characters he was to ascribe to the middleman in each individual bargain."[35] For this reason, many disputes arose between Chinese merchants and foreign firms after a comprador had absconded. In 1860, Chinese tea merchants at Foochow brought suit against Jardine, Matheson & Co. after the defalcation of Acum, the firm's Foochow comprador, who owed 900,000 taels to the teamen. Jardine's claimed in court that Acum was not a comprador or an agent for the firm at the time, but rather a broker from whom the firm bought tea. The teamen, on the other hand, asserted that Acum was the firm's comprador, and thus Jardine's had bought tea *through* him, not *from* him. One of the teamen explained why, after hearing that Acum had run off, he did not take steps to find him: "Because E-ho hong [Jardine, Matheson & Co.] and Acum are considered identical . . . Had Acum died, we should have done the same . . . He is known all over the place as such [comprador to Jardine's], or he would not be trusted . . . Acum was the E-ho hong . . . E-ho and Acum are identical."[36]

This argument was not without reason, since a comprador at Tientsin in the seventies usually "used the seals of the foreign hongs for . . . [his own] private business chits."[37] This confusion lasted into the twentieth century.[38] Rutherford Alcock admitted in 1867 the difficulty of handling these cases: "No Court of Law can unravel the complication and confusion of interests necessarily resulting, nor can any judge, however able, determine the proportionate degrees of responsibility attaching to the various parties mixed up in the same transaction, through the middleman, or in several operations, in one of which the same individual appears as the salaried servant of a foreign firm, in another as broker, with doubtful powers, and in a third as principal."[39]

As was usually the case, Jardine's finally lost the suit. Disputes between Chinese and foreign merchants arising from the absconding of a comprador were not uncommon after the sixties, and in most cases it was the Chinese merchants who won the suit in court, although the assessors often favored the foreign firms.[40] As C. A. Winchester pointed out in a letter to the Shanghai taotai (intendant of circuit) in 1867: "A comprador who receives a monthly salary from the Foreign merchant, who resides in his house, and has openly in the face of the world the position of a servant of the firm, is a person whose acts in the ordinary course of such business as his master carries on, English law will hold to be the acts of the master."[41]

This being the case, one could hardly distinguish whether a comprador's efforts to cultivate constituents were for the house or for himself. In a letter dated June 4, 1868, Edward Cunningham of Russell's wrote to John M. Forbes, Jr., about comprador Ahyue: "He was already disposed to do anything he could for the house, but looks rather to advantage to himself from any fresh connection, than to us."[42]

Russell & Co.'s agent had the same feeling about the comprador. In the suit Sunkee brought against the firm in 1875, he argued that he should be repaid for expenses he had incurred for New Year's dinners given to Chinese customers. Refusing his claim, T. Moore, the firm's Tientsing agent at the time, argued that the dinners were given more in the interest of Sunkee's own business than in the firm's: "Sunkee never made any claim for payment for cost of New Year's dinners at the time. They were given in the interest of his own business more than in that of Russell & Co. He had a large constituency."[43] In fact, according to Moore, the business of the house was "very bad," whereas Sunkee's own business was "very good." Moore attributed Sunkee's success in his own business to his position as the firm's comprador. Actually, this was not far from the truth, since Sunkee's business suddenly "fell off" when other Chinese merchants learned that he would soon be discharged by Russell & Co. A Tientsin merchant testified in court in 1875: "Sunkee's business fell off [in 1873], because it was rumored that Russell & Co. were going to change their compradore; everybody thereupon came down upon him at once, some withdrawing their goods from his godowns, and others demanding payment of money due to them from him."[44]

Tong King-sing found himself in a similar situation in 1871. The three native banks of which Tong was a co-partner were "subjected to pressure from all who had claims upon them," because there was a rumor that Jardine's were to wind up their business soon and Tong consequently would lose his comprador position. F. B. Johnson reported to William Keswick on June 1, 1871: "I was informed that three Banks, 'Taiwo,' 'Taising' & 'Chingyih' . . . had been for a week past subjected to pressure from all who had claims upon them, & that this 'run' had in the first place arisen from an absurd rumour which has lately been extensively circulated among the Chinese to the effect that Mr. Jardine having lost some millions the House here is about to close."[45]

The comprador's accumulation of wealth as an independent merchant was greatly helped by the fact that he was by and large free from mandarin's control. It was generally true in nineteenth century China that one got one's wealth by cultivating official ties and acquiring the gentry's cooperation.[46] But such connections were a drain on one's financial resources. It was common practice for officials, when under pressure for funds, to collect contributions, or in other words, make levies on merchants known to have money. The Liang-Huai salt merchants, for example, contributed 36,370, 963 taels to the government between 1738 and 1804, not counting the 4,670,000 taels spent by them on the Ch'ien-lung emperor's southern tours. One salt merchant, Chiang Ch'un, raised several monetary contributions that helped to finance the military compaigns of the Ch'ien-lung era. For his efforts he was awarded the title of financial commissioner. Kingqua (Liang Lun-shu, 1790–1877), one of the hong merchants, contributed 95,000 taels to the government in 1828 and another 20,000 taels in 1832, and in consequence was awarded the title of salt comptroller.[47]

But the comprador differed from his predecessor merchant prince in this respect. Acting either as a comprador or as an independent merchant, he need not resort to official channels to accumulate wealth. In fact, he maintained his wealth by keeping away from them, because he enjoyed a privilege denied to ordinary Chinese merchants. Living in the foreign settlements and working for the foreign firms, he was in theory as well as practice free, to a great extent, from mandarin's control. Before he could be arrested, the Chinese officials had to consult his foreign employers, who enjoyed the right of extraterritoriality. After 1869, according to F. L. Hawks Pott, he could be summoned only with the consent of the foreign consul concerned.[48] Although foreign consuls were not always willing to take a firm stand to protect their Chinese employees, the comprador nevertheless benefited from this connection.[49] In 1854, for example, the British consul at Shanghai dispatched two armed boats in order to release a British Indian's comprador who had been arrested by the Shanghai taotai for selling gunpowder to the Taipings.[50] In 1882, Wang K'o-ming, comprador for W. S. Wetmore, an American merchant, was arrested by Tso Tsung-t'ang for his former connections with the Taipings, but was released as a result of the foreign consuls' joint protest engineered by the American consul J. R. Young.[51] Chang Chao, the Chekiang governor, tried in 1907 to arrest a Japanese firm's comprador at Shanghai named Kao Ch'ing-t'ang for smuggling rice, but did not achieve his aim until Kao had been lured out of the foreign settlement.[52]

Fully utilizing his close association with foreigners, the comprador had other ways to free himself from China's domestic politics and the officials' "squeeze." One way of achieving this end was to trade under foreign names. This practice, already quite common in the 1860's, was best illustrated at Chinkiang in the 1870's.[53] Nearly every foreign firm there had several different Chinese hong names under which the comprador could trade, the profits being shared by both. Li Chih-chee, comprador to W. F. Walker, for example, testified at court in 1879: "It was the general practice of foreign firms at Chinkiang to have three and four Chinese names to trade in. Mr. Walker himself had three. The capital and the business carried on in the three different hongs belonged to the compradores and not to Walker. Walker was recompensed by what he made out of commissions, applications for transit passes, etc. By using Walker's name the compradores saved certain taxes, and Walker received half of this amount for the use of his name. Nearly all the [foreign] firms carried on their business in that way."[54]

In the early sixties, when the main tea-producing areas were disturbed by the Taipings, the comprador often transported his own tea from upcountry to Shanghai under foreign protection.[55] Or he might ask foreigners to have his own enterprise registered as foreign property. For example, when the China Merchants' Steam Navigation Co. bought the entire fleet of the American firm of Russell & Co. in 1877, the Chinese share-holders of Russell's ships, most of whom were comprador-merchants, refused to go along and finally formed the Ningpo Steam Navigation Co., registered as an American firm. Jardine, Matheson & Co. made a similar kind of arrangement in 1870.[56] The foreign merchants under whose names the compradors were operating such businesses accepted the obligation to protect these properties, and occasionally backed them up by the military strength of their own countries. German troops landed at Swatow in 1883, in order to support a German firm's claim to a piece of disputed land that probably in fact belonged to the firm's comprador.[57] While it is thus clear that the presence of foreign merchants in China inhibited the normal growth of China's indigenous capitalism by diverting its capital, the point is that, being the first group of Chinese merchants who were generally free from close government control, the compradors were not liable to be mulcted of their gains, and this fact was conducive to their accumulation of wealth.

Total Income of the Comprador

The compradors were among the richest Chinese merchants not only in the treaty ports, but also in China as a whole. A number of indications bear this out. First is their total personal income. In about a decade during the 1850's, Jardine's Shanghai comprador Takee accumulated several million taels—a surprising amount for for the time.[58] Choping, Russell's Shanghai comprador in the sixties and seventies, was another example. In a letter regretting the fact that their compradors were "small men" and did not "have the

'face' of men like Luncheong, Suncheong, Ahone and others,"
A. F. Heard wrote from Shanghai on how rich Choping was in 1862:
"The sale of *Shantung* was a great hit, as it has opened a connection
with Chun Yue Chong (alias Choping) who is one of the largest
men here. He has 130,000 T. [taels] in R. [Russell] & Co.'s scheme,
owns the *Scolland*, the *Contest*, and *Shantung*, the *Sir Charles Forbes*,
and in house and lands, half of the foreign settlement.—He is now
very friendly with us, and from his control of money is a man to whom
we kowtow!"[59]

The wealth of Takee and Choping was soon to be challenged
by their fellow compradors. The "scholarly comprador" Cheng
Kuan-ying, comprador to Butterfield & Swire at Shanghai in
1873–1881, probably invested 400,000 taels in China's modern
enterprises in the late nineteenth century.[60] In 1877 Jardine's Tong
King-sing (1863–1873) invested some 300,000 taels in the Kaiping
coal mines, which proved to be a successful *kuan-tu shang-pan* (government supervision and merchant operation) enterprise.[61] According
to the autobiography of Hsü Jun, Dent's Shanghai comprador
(1861–1868), by 1883 he had a total investment of 1,275,000 taels
in the shares of various modern enterprises. He was also co-owner of
eight pawnshops in Shanghai, involving a total investment of
348,000 taels. In addition, he had an interest in real estate in the
foreign settlement in Shanghai which in 1883 cost 2,237,000 taels.
Meanwhile, he owed the native banks in Shanghai more than two
million taels.[62] Yeh Ch'eng-chung, a prominent comprador-merchant at Shanghai in the late nineteenth century, is known to have
accumulated eight million taels by the time of his death in 1899.[63]

At the turn of the century, two other compradors stood out in
Hong Kong and Shanghai for their wealth. The multimillionaire
comprador Ho Tung (Jardine's Hong Kong comprador, 1883–1900)
was probably the richest and most prominent Chinese merchant in
Hong Kong, where he was a "leading expert in insurance, shipping
and the import and export business." At the same time, he was a
"director of eighteen of the leading companies in Hong Kong and
Shanghai—chairman and largest shareholder of a number of
them."[64] Ho Tung's counterpart at Shanghai was Chu Ta-ch'un
(Jardine's comprador, 1890's–1900's), who was one of the wealthiest
Chinese in the first decade of the twentieth century and one of the

biggest comprador-investors in modern China. His investment in modern enterprises amounted to at least two million taels by 1910.[65]

The compradors to foreign banks were also likely to be rich. Wang Huai-shan, the first comprador to the Hongkong and Shanghai Banking Corp. at Shanghai from 1865, finally became a "very rich" man who owned a great deal of land at his native place, and his successor, Hsi Cheng-fu (late 1870's–1907), was a wealthy native banker.[66] At Hankow, Liu Hsin-sheng, comprador to the Banque de l'Indochine from the 1900's, was "one of the wealthiest and best known Chinese businessmen."[67] Another wealthy comprador-investor was Yü Hsia-ch'ing, comprador to the Russo-Chinese Bank at Shanghai in the early twentieth century, who invested two million dollars (ca. 1,400,000 taels) in steamship enterprises, and another two million in his native town to promote public welfare in the 1920's.[68] Teng Chün-hsiang, comprador to the Hongkong and Shanghai Banking Corp. at Peking from 1917, misused four million dollars of the bank's funds and absconded in 1927.[69] Wu Yao-t'ing, comprador to the Yokohama Specie Bank at Shanghai, was bailed out with one million taels in 1928.[70]

The comprador-merchant's style of life indicated his wealth as well. Hsü Jun's garden-style house at Shanghai was so beautiful that a visiting foreign lady described it as a fairyland. Attended by at least eighteen servants, it was immaculately clean: "floors and desks were as shining as glass." The house was so big that she finally became lost in it.[71] Sun Chung Ying, comprador to Handl & Co. at Tientsin from 1888, owned "a magnificent house and garden, built at a cost of over half a million dollars."[72] Yang K'un-shan, comprador to Craven & Company at Hankow in the twentieth century, was called "the millionaire" by the local people.[73] Indeed, even the comprador's staff members were rich. Jardine's F. B. Johnson wrote to W. Paterson on January 10, 1884: "Your old godown man . . . a man of means . . . could readily put in a qualified man under his guarantee."[74]

While it is thus possible to conclude that the comprador-merchants were generally rich, it would also be informative to figure out the number of the major compradors, or even the total number of compradors. The year 1854 may be used as an example. It is known that there were 120 foreign mercantile houses at Shanghai at the time, and that before the establishment of modern banks during the sixties, almost all of the foreign houses were gigantic. Each house usually employed one comprador, and accordingly, there were about 120 major compradors at Shanghai. At the same time, the total number of major compradors in other treaty ports was at least as many as those in Shanghai.[75] Therefore, there were about 250 major compradors in China in 1854.

The year 1870 may be taken as another example. There were then 550 foreign mercantile houses in China (203 at Shanghai and 202 at Hong Kong) and about 350 major compradors.[76] The case of Jardine, Matheson & Co. indicates that there were at least an equal number of former compradors who were very active in trade. Therefore, about 700 major comprador-merchants were operating in China in 1870, each of them likely to have approximately 100,000 taels. Furthermore, the number of comprador-merchants certainly increased with the passage of time. For instance, foreign firms in 1899 numbered 933.[77] Since a foreign firm would be expected to establish more branch offices and agencies at the ever-increasing open ports, with a comprador to each of them, and each office might have more than one comprador at this time, by the end of the nineteenth century there may have been over 10,000 compradors in China, not including another 10,000 or so former compradors.

It is difficult to estimate the comprador-merchants' total income. Such an estimate, though far from being exact, is nevertheless possible and useful. Based on the figures of their income calculated in nine different categories, their accumulated earnings from 1842 to 1894 were around 530 million taels.

The first category is the salary they earned as compradors. According to the number of foreign firms given in the customs reports for this period, the cumulative number of years that a comprador served in a foreign firm was about 44,000. Since the average annual salary of a comprador, as just shown, was 1,000 taels, the total salary income of the compradors in the 1842–1894 period would have been 44 million taels. But the salary constituted only a small part of the compradors' income, and their main source of profit came from commissions on import-export transactions. The total amount of China's foreign trade during the 1867–1894 period, according to the customs reports, was 4,679 million taels.[78] If one excludes from this figure the value of the imported opium, which was 798 million taels, the amount was 3,881 million taels. There were no complete trade statistics during the 1842–1866 period. Assuming that the average annual amount of foreign trade (excluding opium) during those twenty-five years was 60 million taels, the total amount was 1,500 million taels. Therefore, the total volume of China's import-export (excluding opium) during the 1842–1894 period was 5,381 million taels. Inasmuch as the compradors probably got three percent of this figure, including two percent as pure commission and one percent as shroffing fees and income resulting from the handling of drafts and bills, their total would have been 161.43 million taels.

The compradors' income from the opium trade has to be estimated separately. Based on Huang I-feng's estimate, between 1842 and 1884 there were 3.58 million piculs of opium imported to China, including the amount smuggled in.[79] Its total value was 1,600 million taels. It is certain that the comprador-merchants did not handle all of this opium. Although Sassoon's Chinkiang comprador named Sung Ts'ai sold opium worth 1.5 million taels in 1875, and Jardine's Takee and Russell's Sunkee sometimes also sold opium for their firms, the sale of opium was seldom handled by Heard's and Russell's compradors in Canton and Hong Kong, nor by Jardine's Tong King-sing in Shanghai.[80] F. B Johnson wrote in 1868: "As a rule I do nothing in Opium through Tong King-sing but on a special occasion like that of the last trip of the *Slangyle* it was necessary I should employ his services."[81] Tucksing, with whom Jardine's frequently did opium business in the sixties, was not a comprador.[82] In addition, opium trade might be handled by foreign opium brokers, as in the case of Heard's in Hong Kong in the fifties.[83] If the compradors handled half of the 1842–1894 opium trade (1,600 million taels), for which they got a commission of 1.5 percent, they would have earned 12 million taels.[84]

The foreign firms' activities became diversified with the passage of time. Many of them operated factories, and each factory probably hired a comprador.[85] According to Sun Yü-t'ang's study, the cumulative years that a comprador served in a foreign factory in China in the 1842–1894 period were about 1,892.[86] The comprador to a foreign factory was likely to have an ordinary income of 10,000 taels a year.[87] Thus, the total income of the foreign factories' compradors in this period would have been 18.9 million taels. In the same fashion, the foreign firms also managed steamship, insurance, and real estate business, and the compradors to these companies were likely to have earned 15 million taels in total.[88]

Foreign banks, however, were beyond the control of any single foreign house. There were approximately 300 cumulative years that a comprador served in a foreign bank in this period. An average bank comprador at Shanghai in the early twentieth century is known to have made 20,000 taels a year, so that the bank compradors' total income would have been 6 million taels.[89] The firearm business was surprisingly lucrative: the comprador to Mandl & Co. at Tientsin, according to the testimony of his fellow-comprador Cheng Kuan-ying, earned more than 200,000 taels in this business during the Sino-Japanese war of 1894–1895.[90] Compradors to the firms handling firearm business would have earned a total of at least 5 million taels. The Ch'ing government foreign loans before 1895 were 44 million taels, and the brokers, according to Huang I-feng's estimate, got about 7 million taels.[91] While Teng Chi-ch'ang, comprador to the Hongkong and Shanghai Banking Corp. at Hankow from 1865, "carried through many of the most important financial negotiations between Britishers and the Chinese government," Hu Kuang-yung, who negotiated much of these loans, was not a comprador.[92] If half of these foreign loans passed through the compradors' hands, they would have earned 3.5 million taels.

The total amount earned by the compradors during 1842–1894 is thus far 265.4 million taels. But at the same time, the compradors, being independent merchants in their own right, had their separate businesses, which greatly benefited from their comprador position. The case of Tong King-sing suggests that the profits the compradors received from their own businesses were as much as the amount they earned as compradors.[93] Therefore, the conclusion is that during the 1842–1894 period the compradors' total income, earned either as compradors or as independent merchants, was about 530 million taels. (See Table 7.)

What is the significance of this amount? For the sake of comparison, it is useful to cite other relevant figures. In terms of the central government's income, it is estimated that the annual revenue was 40 million taels before 1850, 89 million taels in the early 1890's, and

A Nouveau Riche

Table 7. Total income of the compradors, 1842–1894 (million taels).

Item	Amount	
As Compradors		
Salary	44.0	
Foreign trade (excluding opium)	161.0	
Opium trade	12.0	
Factories	18.9	
Steamship, insurance, real estate companies	15.0	
Banks	6.0	
Firearm companies	5.0	
Government foreign loans	3.5	
Subtotal		265.4
As Private Merchants		265.4
Total		530.8

Source: Huang I-feng, "Chiu Chung-kuo," 87: 97, 102; Sun Yü-t'ang, Chung-Jih; Yen Chung-p'ing, T'ung-chi. Calculations are mine.

103 million taels in the early 1900's.[94] Compared with the gentry's income, which according to Chang Chung-li was 645 million taels per annum, the compradors' income seemed insignificant.[95] This was not necessarily true, however, when China's foreign trade is considered. The Chinese custom trade returns indicate that the average annual value of China's exports was about 56 million taels in the 1860's, 69 million taels in the 1870's, 77 million taels in the 1880's, and 133 million taels in the 1890's.[96] As to the total foreign investment in China, no comprehensive estimates have been made for the period prior to 1895, but C. F. Remer estimated that the total amount of foreign investment in China for the year 1902 was 584 million taels (U.S. 787.9 million dollars).[97]

On the social level, the *nouveaux riches* compradors demonstrated the fluidity of the status system. They brought about a steady upward social mobility trend in late Ch'ing China at the treaty ports, which provided golden opportunities for the humble and obscure. It was in such noted compradors as Takee, Tong King-sing, Cheng Kuan-ying, Ho Tung, and Yü Hsia-ch'ing that one finds typical cases of the self-made men who established themselves "from rags to riches."[98]

VI   The Comprador and Modern China's Economic Development

The role of the comprador in affecting modern China's economic development deserves special attention. Being an employee of the foreign firm, he helped to expand its business in China. In this connection, was he a running dog of Western economic imperialism? As a commercial middleman between East and West, he played a pivotal role in China's domestic and foreign trade. In so doing, did he compete with the foreigners and have a chance of getting the upper hand? In terms of China's early industrialization, how did the *nouveau riche* comprador spend his wealth? What was his role as an investor, a manager, and an entrepreneur? All in all, these economic roles can best be explored by examining his relationship to modern China's commercial and industrial development.

Foreign Economic Intrusion

Working professionally for the foreign merchants, the comprador was inevitably involved in the issue of foreign economic intrusion—foreign trade and investment—in modern China. With the spread of modern nationalism, China's external economic confrontation with the West over the past century from 1842 to 1943 has come to be widely regarded by the Chinese as detrimental to the national economy. According to the theory of mercantilism, foreign economic intrusion drained China's economy of its wealth, as evidenced by the secularly unfavorable balance of trade. It also stifled the Chinese-owned modern enterprises because of the foreign merchants' privileged status under the so-called "treaty system," and upset China's traditionally self-sufficient economy by disrupting agriculture and ruining the handicraft industries.[1]

China was not the only country subjected to foreign economic penetration, since the effects of imperialism were felt all over the world. Some of the major theories advanced recently by scholars concerning international trade and investment echo the theories of imperialism developed by Hobson and Lenin.[2] According to the Singer-Prebisch-Myrdal "absorption" thesis, the economic intercourse between rich and poor countries has contributed greatly to the growing inequality in the distribution of their wealth. Foreign investments may have harmed the poor countries, since their export development may have absorbed their existing native entrepreneurship and domestic investments. Whatever benefit derived from export development was absorbed by the foreign investing countries.[3]

However, it has been equally emphasized that international trade and investment have contributed considerably to the economic development of the participants, including the less developed countries. Specifically, international trade and investment have brought to the developing countries not only capital and foreign exchange but also technological knowledge, managerial ability, technical personnel, entrepreneurship, administrative organization, and innovations in products and production techniques. Foreign trade has been, and still is, one of the basic factors promoting the economic well-being and increasing the national income of every participating country. The higher the level of output, the easier it has been to escape the "vicious circle of poverty." Foreign trade that raises the level of income thus concomitantly promotes economic development.[4] Meanwhile, foreign investment—a symbol of foreign invasion—has supplied the fuel for mercantile nationalism, which strives to develop national modern industry.[5] All in all, foreign trade and investment bring to the recipient countries capital, skill, and growth mentality—all of which are in short supply.

A thorough, full-scale comparative study of the processes of development, or the lack of it, in a number of less developed countries would help to clarify this controversy.[6] So far as China is concerned, there is little doubt that her economic intercourse with the West had some positive effects on her long-run development. Above all, it created "external economies," promoted a national market, and provided opportunities of training managerial personnel and channeling Chinese savings into modern investments, as was well illustrated by the comprador-merchants. Yet the fact that the Chinese economy remained underdeveloped suggests that such positive effects had their limitations. With regard to a market, since the foreign enterprise was attracted by production for export instead of for China's internal market, more emphasis was placed on the production of a few labor-intensive primary products, such as tea and silk. The increase in exports, which were based on unskilled labor, was in effect dissipated on imports. Leakages from China to foreign countries through the medium of profit remittances made it possible for some of the multiplier effects of trade and investment upon income and employment to be felt in the home countries of the foreign firms rather than in China itself. In terms of economic growth within China, the effect of the imperialistic domination of the modern sector of China's economy was positive as well as negative. In short, so far as Sino-foreign economic intercourse is concerned (without taking political imperialism into consideration), present knowledge does not permit the drawing up of a net balance sheet.

The problem here is the extent to which the comprador facilitated or hindered foreign trade and investment in modern China. There is little doubt that he played a pivotal role in keeping the business of the foreign house going—and going smoothly. For this reason, he was regarded by his fellow-countrymen, especially in the twentieth century, as the spearhead of foreign colonialism and economic imperialism. According to the "absorption" theory, he thus did great harm economically to China's national interest in connection with foreign trade and investment as a whole, not to mention his role in the opium trade. Whatever may be the truth, the question arises as to whether this was just a part of the story. Has the other side of the coin been neglected? To put the issue in its proper historical perspective, one has to examine whether the amount of foreign investment in China was large and the profit rate high.

The international capital movement assumed importance as early as the beginning of the seventeenth century, but the rate of increase of long-term foreign investments in the 1874–1914 period was the highest in the history of international investment. A closer look at the capital-receiving countries shows that the unprecedented international capital movement was quite concentrated geographically. The British capital exported before 1914 went to the so-called "regions of recent settlement" in America and Australia: the spacious, fertile, and virtually empty plains of Canada, the United States, Argentina, and Australia. Only about a quarter of British export capital went to what are known today as the low-income, often densely populated, less developed countries.[7] Being one of them, China received only a small amount of foreign investment.

Although foreign governments were intimately involved, foreign trade and investment in China (except in Manchuria) were primarily operated by individual businessmen, motivated by private profit expectations. At first they had high hopes of exploiting what they believed to be an almost unlimited market in China. For instance, immediately after the Opium War, some British merchants believed that the Chinese market for textiles would exceed that in all of Europe.[8] But a recent study of the ratio of net profit (net of all expenses and taxes) to net worth (difference between total assets and total liabilities)—the best measurement of return on investment so far as the private investor is concerned—shows that the profit-net worth ratios of foreign firms in China during 1872–1932 were mostly between 5 and 20 percent. Compared with the rate of earnings on ordinary capital of the British joint-stock companies (13 percent in 1908–1937) and the profit rates of manufacturing firms in the United States (11 percent in 1919–1928), the profit rates of foreign firms in China did not appear exceedingly high, contrary to frequent assertions.[9]

What accounts for the fact that the amount of foreign trade and investment in China was small and the profit rates of foreign firms in China were not as high as expected? China obviously could not, on the one hand, compete with the "regions of recent settlement" in attracting foreign capital. On the other hand, despite setbacks, China was by and large able to resist foreign economic penetration in the interior. Other factors included the low level of national income and the sophistication of Chinese civilization.[10] To all of these must be added another often neglected factor—the costly comprador system.

The Comprador in China

The profits earned by foreign merchants in China had to be shared with their Chinese compradors. Ho Kai, a prominent Chinese in Hong Kong, contended in the 1890's that the compradors made as much money as the foreign merchants.[11] This estimate was a conservative one for the time, since it was often maintained that a comprador actually made more money than his foreign employer: his "native cunning and business capacity sufficed in most cases to draw himself the largest share of the profits arising from mercantile transactions."[12] For instance, a foreign commissioner of the Chinese Customs reported in 1865 that the comprador "is often enriched while his employer is ruined"; and in the same vein, a foreign newspaper claimed that "the compradors as a class are all fat, whilst their foreign principles are generally lean."[13] This view was also expressed by Julean Arnold, an American commercial attaché in China, who wrote in the 1910's that he himself had "heard of many cases in which compradors made more than the firms they represented."[14] At the end of the nineteenth century, a British China expert went so far as to claim that the comprador made twice as much as his employer.[15]

At any rate, the employment of a Chinese comprador was costly to foreign merchants. A foreign commissioner of the Chinese Customs reported from Newchwang in 1865, explaining why it was so difficult for foreign merchants to make money: "Were the foreign merchants . . . to acquire a knowledge of Sycee . . . were they to dispense with the costly service of the compradore, and of the shroff, and their several staffs . . . a considerable reduction of expenditure would be effected, their gains would be infinitely augmented. . . . Now they may sell on most profitable terms, and yet submit to a loss. This, I am aware, is no new discovery."[16]

How costly was the comprador's service? A foreign eyewitness reported at Tientsin in 1866: "It will never be possible to conduct business without Chinese assistants, but it is surely not necessary that they should levy on the goods which pass through their employers' hands a charge which is equal to the cost of bringing the goods into China, and which, on the principal articles of English manufacture, is equal to the import duty required by the Tariff." In 1866, Tientsin and Chefoo received half of the cotton goods imported into Shanghai, and three-fourths of the Tientsin trade was in cotton goods and woolens. In order to save money, a great number of northern Chinese merchants sent their agents to Shanghai to purchase these textiles. In discussing the possibility of establishing a direct Sino-British trade in northern China by setting up more foreign firms at Tientsin, the same witness continued: "If direct trade should be established, the sale of the imports would, of course, come back into the hands of the foreign firms established here [Tientsin]; but since we are contemplating the reduction of expense in one direction, we must not forget that there is another charge on trade. . . . I am referring to the charge levied by the compradors, a body of middlemen who survived the state of things which brought them into existence. Their foreign employers complain of them with good reason, but take no steps to get rid of their exorbitant charges."[17]

Indeed, it was these "exorbitant charges" of the comprador that forced some of the big foreign houses to withdraw their agencies from the smaller treaty ports. A British consul reported from Tientsin in 1869: "Thus the great importing British houses at the larger ports, who had agencies at the smaller, naturally withdrew them, finding it more profitable to concentrate than to extend operations which could only be carried out by the too expensive aid of an additional staff of Chinese employees attached to a foreign agent's establishment."[18] The foreign partners were even more sensitive to the costly comprador. F. B. Johnson wrote from Shanghai to William Keswick in 1871: "The 'squeezes' placed upon the transactions in Native produce here by the Compradore & his staff & those imposed at your end render foreign competition with the Native dealers almost impossible."[19] The comprador's charges must indeed have been great, because twelve years later Johnson complained once more that such expenses had virtually driven the foreigners out of China's coastal trade: "I am not at all sure that the Compradoric system is not pushed to an extreme & very detrimental extent. . . . It looks as if the commissions & exactions of the Chinese staff about us would stifle foreign shipping interests as they have driven foreigners out of the traffic in merchandise on the Coast."[20]

When the comprador is charged by his fellow-countrymen with having collaborated in foreign economic imperialism and thus having arrested the development of Chinese capitalism, a distinction is drawn between "comprador capital" and that of the national bourgeoisie who represented genuine Chinese interests.[21] However, one can hardly make such a differentiation. First of all, the distinction between a comprador and an independent merchant was virtually blurred, for a comprador usually also did business in his own right.[22] What is more, a "national capitalist" might end up with a well-noted comprador, as typified by the Hsi family of Soochow.[23] Finally and most important, in sharp contrast to popular belief, a prominent comprador frequently became a *bona fide* merchant and competed vigorously with his foreign counterpart, as in the case of Tong King-sing and Hsü Jun. Nothing testifies so well to this rivalry as commercial and industrial developments in modern China.

Modern China's Commercial Development

Commerce linked the agrarian with the governmental sector of the late Ch'ing economy, and interregional trade partly met the needs of the general urban-rural interchange. Against this background, foreign trade may be viewed as merely a special form of interregional trade.[24] Since the activities of the comprador-merchants were by no means limited to the service of foreign houses, they thus played an important role in China's commercial development, domestically as well as internationally. As time went on, they turned out to be vigorous rivals of the foreign merchants in China's domestic and foreign trade.

Domestic Trade. In the field of domestic trade, the comprador-merchants, attracted by the high rate of return, invested to some extent in traditional Chinese forms of enterprise. One of them was the pawnshop business. It was so profitable that Takee built a new pawnshop at Shanghai in the fifties.[25] Tong King-sing, who operated two profitable pawnshops at Hong Kong in 1858, obtained a loan of 100,000 taels from Jardine's in 1866 to operate another one with Acum, a former comprador to Jardine's, which Tong estimated would yield an annual profit of 40 percent.[26] Sun Ting Huan, comprador to the Shanghai Land Investment Co. in the early twentieth century, also owned a pawnshop in his own district of Shao-hsing, Chekiang.[27]

Few compradors invested in land to any great degree. An outstanding exception was Wang Huai-shan, the first comprador to the Hongkong and Shanghai Banking Corp. at Shanghai from 1865, who bought over 7,000 *mou* (ca. 1,060 acres) of land in his native district of Yü-yao, Chekiang.[28] The traditional pattern of land investment—purchasing land and then leasing it to farmers at high rentals—was seldom adopted by his fellow-compradors. However, with the rapid development of the newly-emerged treaty ports, where according to the proverb, "ten feet of ground are more valuable than a cubic inch of pure gold," compradors began to purchase land there and build houses for rent.[29] On the advice of Dent's partner Edward Webb, Hsü Jun acquired 3,000 *mou* (ca. 455 acres) of land in and near the International Settlement at Shanghai, on which he erected 2,064 houses, the income from which amounted to 620 taels a day.[30] According to Hsü, the principal owner of landed property at Shanghai before the seventies was a comprador with the surname of Wang.[31] From the eighties, Ho Tung was a large owner of landed property at Hong Kong, Macao, and Tientsin.[32] Thus, the compradors invested in land in a form that, by solving the housing problem in the growing treaty ports, promoted modern China's urbanization.

The comprador-merchant played a more important role in interregional trade. The regionally traded commodities in which he was interested included tea, silk, and salt. As a comprador, he was instrumental in bringing tea and silk from the producing areas to the treaty ports.[33] As an independent merchant, he was attracted by the salt trade, especially in the sixties. Yakee, Jardine's former Shanghai comprador until 1859, made a handsome 60 percent profit in the salt trade in 1868, and it was under his encouragement that his fellow-comprador Tong King-sing decided to enter the trade. In a letter to F. B. Johnson dated January 5, 1869, Tong wrote: "Yakee has made 60% profit in the salt trade in 1868, he has assured me that the low exchange of copper cash & the low rate of freight at the present time has already laid foundation for a good year for 1869. And he believes present licenseholders will without any interruption enjoy the benefit of that trade for many more years to come yet."[34] With Jardine's help, Tong became a Chinese government-licensed salt merchant in 1869, shipping salt from

Yangchow to Hankow in hopes of earning 47 percent of the annual return. [35] He acted as a salt merchant for at least three years.[36] Heard's Kiukiang comprador Achow and its Hankow comprador Seating were also salt merchants in 1862.[37] In the sixties, Heard's former Foochow comprador Tong Loog-maw and one of Dent's former compradors are known to have engaged in the salt trade, which must have been profitable, since Tong Loong-maw observed from Hankow in 1862: "Everyman likes [to] do salt pigeon [business]."[38]

As an independent merchant, the comprador was also engaged in one way or another in China's coastal trade. Sugar was brought from the south and bean products were shipped from the north. His role in traditional patterns of distribution is illustrated by an abortive effort in the grain tribute system. In 1861, when the Taiping uprising was making it difficult for the tribute rice to be shipped to Peking by means of inland transportation, the Cantonese compradors stood ready to supply Peking with rice. They planned to buy rice in China and abroad on their own account and ship it to Tientsin. The Cantonese compradors were so well-known that General Ignatiev, Russian envoy to China, in a proposal to Prince Kung singled them out to share responsibility with the American merchants in handling the tribute rice transport.[39]

The comprador's private commercial activities were not limited to the coastal areas, but also extended far into the interior. For instance, Hoo Mei-ping, comprador to David Sassoon, Sons & Co. at Tientsin (1869–1884), did "a large business on his own account, having hongs in Mongolia, and shops in Peking, Tientsin and Tzuchulin, and in Shanghai a bank as well as shops."[40]

Foreign Trade. The comprador's main area of activity, however, was in foreign trade, with which he was connected professionally. In keeping the foreign trade in motion, he often played an innovating role, as illustrated in the upcountry purchase system. In the early fifties foreign houses procured tea at Foochow from the native merchants, whose undependability caused them trouble. In 1853–1854 for the first time Russell & Co.'s Foochow comprador went to the tea-growing interior districts to make purchases directly from the growers. The upcountry system thence became standard pattern at Foochow.

The compradors' role in promoting foreign trade also lay in their ability to bring China's traditional economic institutions into its service. This capacity was illustrated by means of the native banks, with which the compradors had various connections. The native bank played a vital role in China's foreign trade, in that the native bank order was one of the main forms of payment in transactions, and the comprador was the one who guaranteed the note's dependability for foreign houses.[41] The native bank's relationship with foreign trade became even closer when in the late sixties the comprador introduced the system of chop loan—a short-term loan to native banks by the foreign firms. The compradors were also connected with the native banks as partners. Takee and Hsi Cheng-fu had been prominent native bankers before they became compradors, and it was common for noted compradors to be bankers at the same time, such as Hsü Jun, Tong King-sing, and Yen Lan-ch'ing. (See Table 8.) Thus, the compradors, by acting as intermediaries in various ways between the native banks and the foreign merchants, brought the native banks into the service of China's foreign trade— a role that the native banks probably had never before played.[42]

Table 8. Noted compradors as native bankers, Shanghai, 1840's–1880's.

Comprador	Foreign employer	Year	Native bank investment (taels)
Takee	Jardine, Matheson & Co.	1840's–50's	—
Ting Chien-chang	Bedford & Co.	1850's	—
Wang Huai-shan	Hongkong & Shanghai Banking Corp.	1860's	—
Tong King-sing[a]	Jardine, Matheson & Co.	1860's	200,000
Hsü Jun	Dent & Co.	1860's	ca. 40,000
Hsü Ch'un-jung	Reiss & Co.	1860's–70's	—
Hsi Cheng-fu	Hongkong & Shanghai Banking Corp.	1870's–	ca. 50,000
Yen Lan-ch'ing	Gore-Booth & Co.	1870's–	ca. 160,000

Source: Morse, *Taipings*, pp. 41, 28; Yao Kung-ho, *Shang-hai*, p. 162; Liu Kwang-Ching, "Tong King-sing," p. 146; Hsü Jun, *Nien-p'u*, pp. 5, 21; *Shang-hai ch'ien-chuang*, pp. 743–746, 752.

a. Tong operated jointly with Ekee.

The compradors' role in China's foreign trade can also be seen in their connections with the customs banks that were established after 1842 for handling payments owed by the merchants to the customs. The compradors, knowing foreign trade better than any other group, were appointed by the officials to handle some of China's earliest customs banks. In 1884, a British merchant recalled the situation at Tientsin in 1860: "There was no Consul, no Custom House, no customs' bank on my arrival. And Chung How [Ch'unghou], Superintendent of Trade, who was quite ignorant of everything connected with foreign trade, in 1861 appointed three (3) of the compradores of the foreign hongs to manage the Customs' Bank in regard to duties on goods belonging to foreigners. . . . One of the oldest compradores who was in foreign employ here is now [1884] the chief Customs' Banker in the city."[43] Another Cantonese comprador to Russell & Co. is known to have managed the Tientsin customs bank from 1878.[44]

It is easy to understand why the compradors invested in the merchandise business connected with foreign trade. Choping and Koofunsing are known to have been eminent silk merchants. Tong King-sing was a partner in a large tea firm, operated by his fellow-Cantonese comprador-merchants Acum and Aleet, which sold tea to Jardine's as well as to other Western firms in Shanghai.[45] Hsü Jun was an important tea and silk merchant who "contracted" (pao-pan) the business of tea, silk, and cotton with foreign firms. He also traded other export produce, such as wax, tobacco leaf, and tung oil.[46] At Hankow, Tong Loong-maw of Heard's had some tea business with Russian merchants.[47]

Doing business in his own right, the comprador sometimes engaged directly in international trade. For example, compradors to Russell's and Jardine's are known to have engaged in business in Japan in the fifties and sixties. In a letter to Heard's agent at Yokohama, A. F. Heard wrote from Shanghai in 1859: "A lot of China cargo sent over by R. [Russell] & Co.'s Chinaman San Yuk lately paid a very large profit, and Kiukee [Koofunsing, also a comprador to Russell's] is to investigate the matter here."[48] In the late fifties, Koofunsing also entered into Japanese trade and tried to get a tea monopoly license from the Japanese emperor.[49] In 1859 Yakee of Jardine's purchased from China "300 packages of Chinese merchandise, shipped per *Troas* to Nagasaki on joint account [with the firm] costing Tls. 9884."[50] His fellow-comprador Takee sometimes went to Japan on his own business, and in 1860 he shipped from Shanghai to Nagasaki 800 packages of merchandise, including antique items such as "tortoise-shell, dragon's foam and jar," and a package of medicine.[51] Through Jardine's, Takee sold 140 bales of silk to England in 1851, and Yakee sold 10 bales to New York in 1859.[52] Awei, another comprador associated with Jardine's, "had a bonafide offer from the Japanese for the machinery of the oil mill" in 1870, and for this business he immediately proceeded to Yokohama.[53]

Rivalry with Foreign Merchants. Not only was the comprador's service costly to foreign merchants, but he also gradually turned into their most effective rival in China's commerce, locally as well as internationally. Through lengthy association with foreigners, he had become equally adept in the ways of modern trade operations and business transactions. In an article entitled "John Comprador" published in *Harper's New Monthly Magazine* in 1878, Thomas Knox, an American merchant engaged in trade in the Far East, observed: "The result of this association of the foreigner and the Chinese in business has been not altogether to the advantage of the foreigner. The Chinese [comprador] has learned the lesson which the foreigner has unintentionally taught him, and learned it well. He . . . is proving more than a match for his instructor. In all the Chinese ports there are Chinese banks, Chinese insurance companies, Chinese boards of trade, Chinese steamship companies, and other concerns, all in Chinese management, and supported by Chinese capital. There are Chinese importers and exporters."[54]

In their rivalry with foreign merchants in commercial activities, the compradors rapidly took over some of China's local and foreign trade, as Augustine Heard, Jr., recalled: "By 'local trade' I mean the trade between the ports on the coast of China, and with ports in neighboring countries, such as Siam, Singapore, Batavia, etc. Formerly this was all in the hands of foreigners, but as the Chinese grew to understand foreign methods, they took it themselves, and why should they not? They were as clever as other merchants; they could get advances from the Banks; they could use the telegraph, and above all, they paid no commission or brokerage in China, which a foreigner must do."[55]

The Comprador in China

By the sixties, the Chinese merchants, a great number of whom were compradors, had become increasingly active in trade between the entrepôts of Shanghai or Hong Kong and the other treaty ports. Since they could operate more economically than could the foreign firms, both the distribution of import goods and the collection of export produce came to be concentrated in their hands. The Hankow customs commissioner reported in 1864 that the Chinese, particularly the Cantonese, were competing effectively against foreign merchants: "Formidable opponents have arisen in the persons of Chinese, who forward foreign imports from Shanghai to Hankow, where, owing to their having no expensive establishments to maintain, they can undersell the foreign merchants. The facilities also offered by banks and certain commission houses, enable the Cantonese to compete with foreigners in the tea market."[56]

This trend was similarly apparent in Kiukiang, where the customs commissioner's report of 1866 gives statistics on the respective shares of Chinese and foreign merchants. (See Table 9.) He found that the foreign merchants' share in the trade of the port carried by foreign vessels was 2,457,429 taels, out of a total of 10,119,020 taels—"or roughly estimated one-fourth to the Foreign, three-fourth to the Native dealer."[57] In like manner, at Tientsin in 1867 the handling of foreign-trade goods gradually fell into the hands of the Chinese

Table 9. Major commodities shipped between Shanghai and Kiukiang on foreign vessels, 1866, with division between Chinese and foreign ownership.

Commodity	Share of foreign merchant	Share of Chinese merchant
From Shanghai to Kiukiang		
Grey shirtings (pieces)	13,500	75,640
Long ells (pieces)	900	15,143
Lean (piculs)	600	11,238
Malwa opium (chests)	650	1,765
From Kiukiang to Shanghai		
Black tea (piculs)	32,376	59,239
Green tea (piculs)	32,850	46,268

Source: IMC, *Reports on Trade, 1866,* p. 66.

118

merchants: "The trade of the port in foreign goods . . . is fast merging into the hands of the native merchants who, having learnt to avail themselves of every facility (such as steamers, etc.), at the disposal of the foreigner, are fast ousting him from a participation in the profits to be made in China."[58]

Playing such an important role in handling the foreign-trade commodities, the Chinese merchants must surely have controlled the domestic-trade commodities. While certain Western firms in Shanghai occasionally traded in these Chinese goods between the treaty ports, all but the smallest percentage of the shippers were undoubtedly Chinese. (See Table 10.)

With their knowledge of international trade, the compradors competed with the foreigners outside of China as well. According to Thomas Knox, "John Comprador" was active in Japan, and his competition was "more with Europeans than with the Japanese and . . . succeeded in making a very large inroad into the profits of the foreigner." In Indochina, "the Chinese have been steadily cutting into the trade, until they have by far the best of it, and have driv-

Table 10. Chinese produce shipped on foreign vessels between Shanghai and Chinkiang, 1866, showing division between foreign and Chinese ownership.

Commodity	Amount shipped (piculs)	Share of foreign merchant	Share of Chinese merchant
From Shanghai to Chinkiang			
Brown sugar	21,155	360	20,795
White sugar	17,828	0	17,828
Pea oil	13,569	0	13,569
Black dates	1,078	0	1,078
From Chinkiang to Shanghai			
Hemp	6,096	195	5,901
Wood oil	29,928	361	29,567
Vegetable tallow	8,389	373	8,016
Tobacco leaf	1,819	0	1,819
Prepared tobacco	2,656	0	2,656

Source: IMC, *Reports on Trade, 1866*, p. 73.

en some foreign houses out of business." In addition, the comprador traded extensively in other parts of southeast Asia, such as Bangkok, Penang, Malacca, Singapore, Java, and Manila.[59]

The Comprador as Industrial Investor

China's modern enterprises in the nineteenth century were often confronted by a problem typical of underdeveloped or premodern economies. Because of the comparative scarcity of capital and the high cost of borrowing (interest charges on short-term commercial loans amounted to 10 to 15 percent per annum at Shanghai in the 1860's), it was very difficult to secure funds for long-term investment.[60] The compradors, who had acquired considerable wealth through lengthy association with foreign merchants and realized the importance and profitability of modern enterprises, were willing to invest in them before any other class had a similar intention. Although they invested in Chinese traditional forms of enterprise as well, such investments constituted a small portion of their total investments.

The compradors' capacity and willingness to invest in modern enterprises can be seen in the history of foreign and Chinese steamship companies in the treaty ports. In the case of Tong King-sing, the time-honored traditional modes of investment did not work as well for him as expected, and they were abandoned after only a few years. From 1869, Tong devoted his attention increasingly to steamship investments.[61] He became a shareholder and member of the board of directors in two small British steamship companies— the Union and the North China. In 1870 he invested in a ship, the *Nanzing* (30,000 taels), which Jardine's managed. In the next three years, he took interest in another two ships, one of them managed by Heard's. In 1872, when Jardine's consolidated the firm's shipping interests into the China Coast Steam Navigation Co., Tong was elected a director.

Tong's interest in steamships was by no means exceptional among his fellow-compradors at the time. For as early as 1859 Heard's compradors invested $15,000 in the purchase of the steamship *Fire Dart* ($100,000), the firm's first steamship on the Yangtze.[62] In the same fashion they invested in the firm's other steamships, such as the *Shangtung* (82,000 taels), *Kiang Loong* ($20,000), *Kin Shan* ($45,000), *Tom Hunt* ($50,000), and *Suwonada*.[63] When Russell & Co. organized the Shanghai Steam Navigation Co. in 1862, the first steamship firm ever established in China and by far the largest one in the sixties and early seventies, the company's compradors subscribed about one third of its initial capital of 1,000,000 taels.[64] Choping and Koofunsing, the firm's compradors at Shanghai, invested 130,000 and 150,000 taels, respectively.[65] Futhermore, Koofunsing was the major investor in the Shanghai Steam Navigation Co.'s warehouse, Kin-lee-yuen.[66] And Choping made an investment not only in Russell and Co.'s steamship firm but also in steamships operated by Augustine Heard & Co. (See Table 11.) The compradors' total investment in the Shanghai Steam Navigation Co. reached 600,000 taels by 1874.[67]

The Union Steam Navigation Co. was organized by the British firm of Glover & Co. in 1867. Its shareholders in the late sixties included such noted compradors as Kuo Kan-chang, Tong King-sing, Li Sung-yün, and Cheng Kuan-ying.[68] Olyphant & Co. and the North China Steam Navigation Co. are known to have enlisted the compradors' financial help as well.[69] The method of raising

Table 11. Steamship investments of Choping (comprador to Russell & Co. at Shanghai), 1862–1863 (taels).

Steamship enterprise	General manager	Year	Initial capital	Choping's investment
Shanghai Steam Navigation Co.	Russell & Co.	1862	1,000,000	130,000
Fire Dart	Augustine Heard & Co.	1862	100,000	3,600[a]
Ocean Steamer	Augustine Heard & Co.	1862	145,000	5,000
Shantung	Augustine Heard & Co.	1863	82,000	69,700
Kiang Loong	Augustine Heard & Co.	1863	$175,863	7,200[b]
Total				215,000

Source: A. F. Heard (Shanghai) to Augustine Heard, Jr., April 18, 1862, HL–36; EL–1; EQ–5; HC.
a. Originally $5,000.
b. Originally $10,000.

funds by joint-stock from the local merchant community, so successfully used by Russell's partners, was later followed by Jardine's, when the firm established the China Coast Steam Navigation Co. in 1873. Compradors subscribed 60,775 taels, or 20.3 percent, of the total initial capital of 299,000 taels for the new company, the other investors being entirely foreign merchants.[70] (See Table 12.)

The comprador-merchants' capital played a decisive role in forming the China Merchants' Steam Navigation Co.—the first steamship company owned and operated by Chinese. When Tong King-sing resigned his Jardine's comprador post and, on the invitation of Governor-general Li Hung-chang, became general manager of the government-sponsored China Merchants' Steam Navigation

Table 12. Compradors' investments in the China Coast Steam Navigation Co., Shanghai, 1873 (taels).

Investor	Share[a]	Capital	Percentage
Chinese compradors			
The *Nanzing*[b]	400		
"Chinese engaged through TKS"	300		
Subscriptions organized by Awei[c]	235		
Subtotal	935	60,775	20.5
Other foreign merchants			
Sassoon, Sons & Co. (or Mr. Gubbay)	100		
Vincent & Co.	20		
Davidson & Co.	10		
Others	585		
Subtotal	715	46,475	15.3
Jardine, Matheson & Co.	2,950	191,750	64.2
Total	4,600	299,000	

Source: Liu Kwang-Ching, *Steamship Rivalry*, pp. 140–141.
a. Tls. 65 each.
b. Owned by Jardine's Tong King-sing and others.
c. Jardine's Foochow comprador.

Co. in 1873, he was confronted with the problem of raising funds. The new company was organized as a joint-stock company, since Li Hung-chang sought to have private merchants bear part of the entrepreneurial risk. Li expected Tong to obtain investment capital totaling 1,000,000 taels from the Shanghai mercantile community, and Tong made a serious effort in that direction. Between 1873 and 1874 he succeeded in raising a capital of 476,000 taels. By 1877, this total had increased to 751,000 taels.

There is little question that the bulk of the capital was subscribed by the comprador-merchants. Besides Tong himself, his friend Hsü Jun subscribed about 120,000 taels in 1873–1874. When the full stock capital of 1,000,000 taels was paid up in 1881, 240,000 taels was subscribed under the surname of Hsü. In 1882, when the paid-up stock capital was increased to 2,000,000 taels, Hsü's total subscription was increased to 480,000 taels. In a petition to the governor-general in 1897, Hsü maintained that apart from his subscription of 480,000 taels, he had "also solicited subscriptions from relatives and friends amounting to no less than 500–600,000 taels."[71] Other comprador-merchants, such as Seating, Heard's comprador at Hankow and Kiukiang in the 1860's, and Awei, Jardine's comprador at Foochow in the 1870's, are known to have taken shares.[72]

In 1872, John Samuel Swire, head of John Swire & Co. in London and Butterfield & Swire in Shanghai, was able to raise in London a fund of 360,000 pounds (the equivalent of 970,000 taels) for his new steamship company at Shanghai, the China Navigation Company. By 1873 this company was the only steamship company in China that obtained its capital abroad.[73] Thus, of the total initial paid-up capital of the six steamship companies established at Shanghai from 1862 to 1873, amounting to 3,171,000 taels, the comprador-merchants invested about 975,975 taels (30.8 percent), the rest being contributed mainly by foreigners, including the British investors in London. (See Table 13.)

The comprador-merchants continued to show an unfailing interest in the steamship business. A new steamship company, Greaves & Co. (Hung-an kung-ssu), was established by Chinese and British merchants in 1890, with a capital of probably over 200,000 taels. At least 70 percent of the capital was owned by Chinese, who were none other than the compradors to Jardine,

Table 13. Compradors' investments in steamship companies in China, Shanghai, 1862–1875 (taels).

Year	Company	Founder	Nationality	Initial paid-up capital	Compradors' capital	
					Amount	Percentage
1862	Shanghai S. N.	Russell & Co.	American	1,000,000	330,000[a]	30
1867	Union S. N.	Glover & Co.	British	170,000	51,000[a]	30
1868	North China Steamer	Traut-mann & Co.	British	194,000	58,200[a]	30
1872	China Navigation	Butterfield & Swire	British	970,000[b]	0	0
1873	China Coast S. N.	Jardine, Matheson & Co.	British	325,000	60,775	20.3
1873	China Merchants' S. N.	Govern-ment-sponsored	Chinese	612,000[c]	476,000	77.8
Total				3,171,000	975,975	30.8

Source: Liu Kwang-Ching, *Steamship Rivalry*, pp. 11, 29–30, 135, 140–141; "Two Steamship Companies," p. 138; Hsü Jun, *Nien-p'u*, pp. 37, 86–86b.

a. Estimated capital.

b. The China Navigation Co. was financed from England.

c. Figure includes the Chinese government loan of Tls. 136,000. The company was formally established in 1872.

Matheson & Co., Butterfield & Swire, and China Merchants' Steam Navigation Co.[74] From 1872 to 1893, comprador-merchants undoubtedly constituted the main investors of the steamship companies owned by Chinese. (See Table 14.) Among the new generation of compradors, Yü Hsia-ch'ing invested at least one million taels in the early twentieth century, being the biggest Chinese investor in the steamship enterprise. (See Table 15.)

Aside from steamships, the compradors invested heavily in other forms of modern enterprise. The Kaiping Mines, China's first large-scale, modern coal-mining enterprise, was a good example.[75] From 1877, Tong King-sing, who was instrumental in promoting

Table 14. Compradors' investments in Chinese-owned steamship companies, 1872–1893 (taels).

Year of establish-ment	Company	Initial paid-up capital				
		Government	Other merchants	Gentry-official	Compradors	Total
1872[a]	China Mer-chants' S. N.	136,000	—	0	476,000	612,000
1890[a]	Hung-an	0	60,000[b,c]	0	140,000	200,000[c]
1890[d]	Hsien-t'ou	0	75,000[c]	0	—	75,000
1890[d]	Ch'ao-Hsien	0	0	0	50,000	50,000
1891[e]	HK-Canton	0	250,000[c]	250,000[c]	—	500,000
1892[f]	Tai-sheng-ch'ang	0	120,000	0	0	120,000
1893[d]	Nan-chi-hang-hao	0	0	0	200,000	200,000
1893[d]	Po-ch'ang	0	0	0	201,000	201,000
Total		136,000	505,000	250,000	1,067,000	1,958,000
Percentage		6.94	25.79	12.77	54.50	

Source: Yen Chung-p'ing, *T'ung-chi*, p. 223; Liu Kwang-Ching, "Two Steamship Companies," p. 138; Hsü Jun, *Nien-p'u*, pp. 37, 86–86b.

 a. In Shanghai.
 b. Probably British merchants' capital.
 c. Estimated capital.
 d. In Swatow.
 e. In Canton.
 f. In Hangchow.

the new project and later served as its managing director, was mainly responsible for raising capital. The task was difficult, but successful. At least 200,000 taels were raised in 1878, and by 1882 the capital had grown to 1,000,000 taels. In 1889, Tong went to Shanghai to raise additional funds for the development of new coal shafts and the purchase of steamers. He was subsequently reported "on good authority" to have obtained 500,000 taels of new share capital. A

Table 15. Yü Hsia-ch'ing's investments in steamship enterprises,
Shanghai, 1909–1918 (Mexican dollars).

Year of establish-ment	Steamship company	Capital		
		Initial paid-up	Increased	
			Amount	Year
1909	Ning-shao	$1,000,000	$1,500,000	1918
1914	San-pei	200,000	2,000,000	1919
1917	Ning-hsing	ca. 100,000[a]	ca. 100,000	1917
1918	Hung-an	450,000	1,000,000	1919
Total		$1,750,000	$4,600,000	
		(ca. Tls. 1,230,000)	(ca. Tls. 3,312,000)	

Source: Yen Chung-p'ing, *T'ung-chi*, pp. 223–226; Fang T'eng, "Yü Hsia-ch'ing," 12.2: 49–51.

a. In the name of Yü Shun-en, Yü Hsia-ch'ing's son, who was also a comprador.

British newspaper described Tong's accomplishment as "an under-taking which no other Chinese director of any joint stock enterprise, mining or otherwise, has been able to achieve for the past five or six years. This speaks volumes for the reputation which Tong enjoys among the wealthy mercantile classes in Shanghai and elsewhere."[76] Tong's successful fund-raising role was noteworthy in the light of the fact that other enterprises, both foreign and Chinese, were having serious trouble in raising capital, and not even Tong's successor at Kaiping was able to secure share capital for the same enterprise.[77]

Actually, the compradors' interest in modern mining did not begin with the Kaiping Mines of 1877. It can be traced back to as early as the sixties. Since most of the big foreign houses in China operated steamships, the foreign partners tried to obtain coal locally. Heard's sent their compradors to Hunan and Hupeh in 1863 to purchase land for coal mining.[78] In 1877, when Tong King-sing was organizing the Kaiping Mines in Chihli, the Ch'ih-chou Coal-Mining Company was set up in Anhuei with a capital of 100,000 taels by Yang Teh, a Cantonese comprador of Evans, Pugh & Co.[79]

Among the modern-type mines, the compradors were particularly interested in the coal mines. From 1863 to 1886, they made an investment in coal mining of over two million dollars, almost twice the funds coming from other sources. (See Table 16.)

Aside from coal mines, the compradors were interested in other types of mining as well. Early in 1869, Tong King-sing and his friends made an effort to operate jointly with Jardine's a graphite mine near Chinkiang, but the Ch'ing government did not approve it.[80] In 1873, Augustine Heard & Co. entered into an agreement with Atai, an ex-comprador of Dent's, to operate jointly the "copper and other mines" in the Hainan Island.[81] The San-shan Silver Mining Company was set up in Ch'eng-teh, Jehol, in 1882 by another

Table 16. Compradors' investments in China's modern coal mines, 1863–1886 (Mexican dollars).

Year of operation	Company	Place	Capital		Mode of operation[a]
			Comprador	Noncomprador	
1863	—	Hunan	—	—	Merchant
1876	Chi-lung	Taiwan	0	$195,804	Official
1876	Hsing-kuo	Hupei	0	186,480	KTSP
1877	Ch'ih-chow	Anhuei	$139,860	0	KTSP
1878	K'ai-p'ing	Chihli	2,055,944	0	KTSP
1880	Chung-hsing	Shantung	0	27,972	KTSP
1882	Lin-ch'eng	Chihli	0	139,860	KTSP
1882	Li-kuo-i	Kiangsu	0	800,000	KTSP
1886	—	Kwang-tung	100,000	0	Merchant
1886	Ho-hsien	Kwangsi	0	—	KTSP
Total			$2,295,804	$1,350,116	
Percentage			62.7	37.3	

Source: HM–30, HC; *North China Herald*, April 7, 1886, p. 264; Yen Chung-p'ing, *T'ung-chi*, p. 96.

a. KTSP stands for *Kuan-tu shang-pan* (government supervision and merchant management).

Table 17. Compradors' investments in China's modern mines, 1863–1898 (taels).

| Company | Year | Place | Comprador investment | | |
			Initial paid-up capital	Name	Foreign employer
(Coal)	1863	Hunan Hupeh	—	—	Augustine Heard & Co.
(Silver)	1873	Hainan	—	Atai	Dent & Co.
Kaiping (coal)	1877	Hopeh	200,000	Tong King-sing	Jardine, Matheson & Co.
Ch'ih-chow (coal)	1877	Anhuei	100,000	Yang Te	Evans, Pugh & Co.
San-shan (silver)	1882	Jehol	—	Li Wen-yao	—
(Coal)	1886	Kwangtung	72,000[a]	Ho A-mei	—
(Iron, galena, etc.)	1886	Kwangtung	72,000[a]	Ho A-mei	—
(Silver)	1888	Kwangtung	—	Hsü Jun	Dent & Co.
Mo-ho (gold)	1892	Manchuria	—	Li Chin-yung	Jardine, Matheson & Co.
Mo-ho (gold)	1892	Manchuria	—	Hsü Jun	Dent & Co.
Yang-hsin (coal)	1896	Hupeh	233,000	Liu Hsin-sheng	Racine, Acker-man & Co.
Hsüan-ch'eng (coal)	1898	Anhuei	—	Cheng Kuan-ying	Butterfield & Swire

Source: HM–30, HC; Case 9, HC II; Carlson, *Kaiping*, pp. 34–37; Sun Yü-t'ang, *Kung-yeh*, I, 50; II, 1087, 1131, 1173; *North China Herald*, April 7, 1886, p. 364; Hsü Jun, *Nien-p'u*, p. 45b; Negishi, *Baiben seido*, p. 103; Hatano, p. 420; Chang Chih-tung, *Ch'üan-chi*, 117: 34–36; Wang Ching-yü, *Kung-yeh*, II, 979.
a. $100,000.

comprador, Li Wen-yao.[82] By 1886, Ho A-mei, a Cantonese with comprador background, was deeply interested in mining of various kinds around Canton, as described by a foreign newspaper: "Mr. Ho A-mei himself has started two mining companies, each with a capital of $100,000, and has further acquired rights with respect to an iron and galena mine at Cheng Fa [Ts'ung-hua, one of the districts of the Canton prefecture], about a day's journey from Canton, and a gold mine at Yung San [Yang-shan, a district one hundred miles northwest of Canton]."[83] The noted compradors

Hsü Jun and Cheng Kuan-ying later also invested in modern mines. (See Table 17.)

The compradors were intimately involved in China's modern textile enterprise as well. The Shanghai Cotton Cloth Mill, the first of its kind, was initiated in 1878 by P'eng Ch'i-chih, who was probably an ex-comprador to a British firm at Shanghai.[84] In his petition to Governor-general Li Hung-chang in 1878, he declared that he would be able to raise the necessary capital of 500,000 taels in shares in the same manner as that of the China Merchants' Steam Navigation Co. Li supported this project whole-heartedly and, on the request of P'eng, dispatched the "scholarly comprador" Cheng Kuan-ying to share with him in its management. After an unfortunate split among the promoters, P'eng withdrew from the project in 1879. To head the firm, the governor-general designated Cheng Kuan-ying and Kung Shou-t'u, two expectant taotai. Cheng, as head of the company's business affairs, faced the task of raising sufficient capital. Of the initial paid-up capital of 500,000 taels (five thousand shares at 100 taels each), Cheng was able to solicit 352,800 taels.[85] The history of China's cotton textile development shows that the comprador-merchants invested steadily in this field, and in 1910 Chu Ta-ch'un, comprador to Jardine's at Shanghai, organized one of China's largest cotton textile mills. Among the twenty-seven Chinese-owned textile mills in China established during 1890–1910, eight were mainly promoted and capitalized by comprador-merchants. (See Table 18.)

Table 18. Compradors' investments in China's cotton textile enterprises, 1890–1910 (Mexican dollars).

| Year of operation | Company | Capital[a] | | | | |
		Government	Gentry-official	Merchant	Comprador	Total
1890	Shanghai Cotton Cloth Mill	0	0	$204,444	$490,000	$694,444
1891	Hua-hsin	$349,650[b]	0	349,650[b]	0	699,300
1892	Hu-pei Weaving	1,342,700	0	0	0	1,342,700
1894	Hua-sheng	895,120[b]	$223,780[b]	0	0	1,118,900

Table 18—*Continued*

Year of operation	Company	Capital[a]				
		Government	Gentry-official	Merchant	Comprador	Total
1894	Yü-yüan	0	1,188,800	0	0	1,188,800
1895	Yü-chin	0	0	0	279,700	279,700
1895	Ta-ch'un	0	0	279,700	0	279,700
1896	T'ung-chiu-yüan	0	0	450,000	0	450,000
1897	Yeh-ch'in	0	335,700	0	0	335,700
1897	T'ung-i kung	0	533,300	0	0	533,300
1897	Su-lun	839,200	0	0	0	839,200
1898	Hu-pei Spinning	359,400	0	359,400	0	718,800
1898	Yü-t'ung	0	209,800	0	0	209,800
1899	Ta-sheng	0	699,300	0	0	699,300
1899	T'ung-hui-kung	0	0	559,400	0	559,400
1905	Yü-t'ai	0	0	699,300	0	699,300
1906	Chi-t'ai	0	699,300	0	0	699,300
1906	Hong-feng	0	839,200	0	0	839,200
1907	Ta-sheng	0	968,720[b]	242,180[b]	0	1,210,900
1907	Cheng-hsin	0	0	110,000	100,000	210,000
1907	Cheng-hua	0	0	0	419,600	419,600
1907	Chiu-ch'eng	0	0	0	461,500	461,500
1908	T'ung-ch'ang	0	0	0	600,000	600,000
1908	Li-yung	0	0	419,600	0	419,600
1908 (?)	—	0	0	0	500,000	500,000
1909	Kuang-i	0	419,580[b]	279,720[b]	0	699,300
1910	Kung-i	0	0	0	1,340,000	1,340,000
Total		$3,786,070	$6,117,480	$3,953,394	$4,190,800	$18,047,544
Percentage		20.98	33.89	21.90	23.23	

Source: Yen Chung-p'ing, *T'ung-chi*, pp. 98–99; *Mien-fang-chih*, pp. 152–155, 342–351; Wright, *Impressions*, p. 548.

a. It is assumed that the general price level was relatively stable during the period. Technically, if there was any big change in prices, the dollar figures ought to be "deflated."

b. Estimated capital.

As for machine manufacturing, excluding the government-operated military installations, the compradors showed great interest in this area. In 1883, when no other Chinese merchants were paying attention to this kind of enterprise, Chu Ta-ch'un single-handedly established the Yüan-ch'ang Machinery Company at Shanghai in 1883, with an initial paid-up capital of $100,000 (ca. 72,000 taels), which was quite a large amount for the time. The third and largest company of this kind was founded at Shanghai in 1902 by another comprador, Chu Chih-yao of the Banque de l'Indochine, with a capital of $699,000 (ca. 500,000 taels). The investment of compradors in the machine-manufacturing field exceeded the investment of the government and gentry-officials or other merchants in the 1883–1913 period. (See Table 19.)

Table 19. Compradors' investments in China's machine-manufacturing industries, 1883–1913 (Mexican dollars).[a]

Year of establishment	Company	Place	Capital[b]				
			Government	Gentry-official	Merchant	Comprador	Total
1883[c]	Yüan-ch'ang	Shanghai	0	0	0	$100,000	$100,000
1895[c]	Jung-ch'ang	Shanghai	0	0	$10,000	0	10,000
1902[c]	Ch'iu-hsin	Shanghai	0	0	0	699,000	699,000
1902[c]	Ta-lung	Shanghai	0	0	100,000	0	100,000
1904[c]	K'ai-ch'eng	Chinkiang	0	$140,000	0	0	140,000
—[c,d]	T'ung-i	Huai-ning, Anhuei	0	0	21,000	0	21,000
1905[c]	Tzu-sheng	Nan-t'ung, Kiangsu	0	70,000	0	0	70,000
1906[c]	Pei-yang	Tientsin	$200,000	0	0	0	200,000
1906[c]	Wan-ch'ang	Shanghai	0	0	84,000	0	84,000
1907[c]	Yang-tzu	Hankow	0	0	490,000	0	490,000
1908[c]	Jih-sheng	Yung-ting, Fukien	0	0	10,000	0	10,000

Table 19—*Continued*

Year of establishment	Company	Place	Capital[b]				
			Government	Gentry-official	Merchant	Comprador	Total
1908[c]	T'ien-chin	Tientsin	0	420,000	0	0	420,000
1909[e]	Hu-pei	Wu-ch'ang	300,000	0	0	0	300,000
1912[c]	Hsin-hsiang	Shanghai	0	0	60,000	0	60,000
1913[c]	Hou-sheng	Wu-chin, Kiangsu	0	0	15,000	0	15,000
—[c,f]	Heng-yü	Shanghai	0	168,000	0	0	168,000
Total			$500,000	$798,000	$790,000	$799,000	$2,887,000
Percentage			17.32	27.64	27.36	27.68	

Source: Wang Ching-yü, *Kung-yeh*, II, 878–879, 959–960; Yen Chung-p'ing, *T'ung-chi*, pp. 94–95.

a. Not including government-operated military installations.

b. It is assumed that the general price level was relatively stable during the period. Technically, if there was any big change in prices, the dollar figures ought to be "deflated."

c. Private enterprise.

d. Established before 1905.

e. Government enterprise.

f. Origin of capital uncertain.

When Sir MacDonald Stephenson, a distinguished engineer, arrived in China in 1864 with a view to developing railroad enterprises, the Cantonese merchants, including some compradors, responded to his project enthusiastically.[86] While it is certain that some compradors were connected with the railroad as managing directors (such as T'ang Chieh-ch'en and Wu Mao-ting), or were interested in its early period of development (such as Choping of Russell's), the amount of their investments in its growth is not known. In 1906, after the Canton-Hankow Railroad had become a private joint-stock enterprise, Cheng Kuan-ying, former comprador to Butterfield & Swire, and Ch'en Keng-yü, comprador to

Douglas Lapraik & Co., were two of the biggest shareholders.[87]

Although the exact amount of the compradors' investments in the modern banks is unknown, they certainly demonstrated continuous interest. Chinese shareholders of the Hongkong and Shanghai Banking Corp. in the eighties included Lo Shou-sung, the bank's own comprador, Wai Poo Kee, Jardine's comprador, and Woo Chee Dong, comprador to H. M. Schultz & Co.[88] The Trust and Loan Company of China, Japan and the Straits, Ltd., was established in 1890, and by 1895, 52,600 of its 100,000 shares belonged to Chinese merchants, many of them with a compradorial background.[89] They probably also invested in the National Bank of China and the Oriental Bank during the nineties.[90] Meanwhile, the compradors tried to set up modern banks owned and operated by the Chinese. An abortive plan was made by Tong King-sing as early as 1876, and Yü Hsia-ch'ing and Chu Pao-san were major promoter-investors in the founding of the Ningpo Bank in 1908, with an initial paid-up capital of 1,500,000 taels.[91]

Compradors were the first Chinese merchants to invest in the insurance business. In response to the rapidly developing steamship enterprises, maritime insurance companies were established first. Jardine's founded the Canton Insurance Office, for which some of their compradors, such as Ho Tung, Ho Fu, and Ho Kan-t'ang, subscribed considerable shares in the eighties.[92] More of their fellow compradors, like Wu Shao-ch'ing of Arnhold, Karberg & Co. and Yeh Ming-chai of the Yokohama Specie Bank, invested in fire and life insurance companies during the next decade.[93] As early as 1876, two Chinese-owned insurance companies—Pao-hsien chao-shang chü and Jen-ho, each with an initial paid-up capital of 200,000 taels—were promoted and invested in by the compradors Hsü Jun, Tong King-sing, Cheng Hsiu-shan, and others.[94]

As for public utilities, Tong King-sing planned in 1882 to invest 30,000 taels in the Tientsin Gas Co., Ltd., and through his efforts both the Kaiping Mines and the China Merchants' Steam Navigation Co. subscribed its shares.[95] When the gas company was formally founded in 1888, Wu Mao-ting, comprador to the Hongkong and Shanghai Banking Corp. at Tientsin in 1883–1905, became one of its promoter-investors, and in the nineties he held a directorship.[96] At Shanghai in 1882, Tong Mow-chee and Li Sung-yün invested heavily in the foreign-controlled Shanghai Electric Co., the first company of its kind ever established in China.[97] In the nineties, Wang I-t'ing was a director of the Shanghai Inland Electricity Works, and Chu Pao-san was a director of the Hankow Waterworks and the Canton Waterworks.[98]

In addition, compradors had interests in various other forms of light industry. The Chinese Glass Works Co., a Sino-British joint enterprise, was founded in 1882 as a result of three compradors' efforts—Tong Mow-chee, Li Sung-yün, and Ch'en K'o-liang. They subscribed 80,000 taels of the initial paid-up capital of 100,000

Table 20. Investments of the comprador Chu Ta-ch'un, 1870's–1913 (Mexican dollars).

Period	Place	Item	Capital[a]
1870's	Shanghai	Yuen Chong Trading Co.	$30,000[b]
1880's	Shanghai	Steamships	50,000[b]
1883	Shanghai	Yuen Chong Machinery Co.	100,000
1898	Shanghai	Yuen Chong Rice Mill	400,000
1900	Shanghai	Wah Shing Flour Mill	200,000
1904	Shanghai	Yuen Chong Silk Mill	500,000
1906	Shanghai	I-ho-yüan Packing Co.	280,000
1908	Soochow	Cheng-hsing Electric Light Co.	140,000
1908	Shanghai	Land and house property	50,000[b]
1908	Shanghai	Native banks	50,000[b]
1909	Wu-hsi	Yüan-k'ang Silk Mill	45,000
1910	Shanghai	Kung-yik Cotton Mill	750,000
1913	Wu-hsi	Hui-yüan Flour Mill	150,000
1913	Yang-chow	Cheng-yang Electric Light Co.	320,000
Total			$3,065,000
			(ca. Tls. 2,206,800)

Source: Sun Yü-t'ang, Kung-yeh, I, 50; II, 958–960, 979–981; Wright, Impressions, p. 548

a. It is assumed that the general price level was relatively stable during the period. Technically, if there was any big change in prices, the dollar figures ought to be "deflated."

b. Estimated capital.

taels; other comprador investors included Hsü Jun, Wei Wen-pu, and Cheng Hsiu-shan.[99] In the same year, Li Sung-yün and Ts'ao Tzu-chün, among others, invested in the China Tannery Co.[100] Wu Mao-ting established in 1886 the Tientsin Chinese Match Factory (T'ien-chin tzu-lai-ho kung-ssu), a Chinese undertaking and China's first large-scale company of this kind.[101] It was surpassed by the Hsieh-ch'ang Match Co., set up at Hankow in 1897, with a capital of $420,000, by Wu's fellow-compradors Yeh Ch'eng-chung and Sung Wei-ch'en.[102] Jardine's Chu Ta-ch'un single-handedly established China's first large-scale rice mill at Shanghai in 1898, with the sizable capital of 400,000 taels.[103] In fact, Chu was probably the biggest investor in modern enterprises among compradors at the turn of the century. He traded in coal and other minerals, ran a number of steamers between Singapore, Shanghai, and Japan, and also made considerable investments in industrial

Table 21. Investments of the comprador Chu Chih-yao, 1897–1910's (Mexican dollars).

Year	Place	Item	Capital[a]
1897	Shanghai	Ta-te Oil Mill	$210,000
1899	Shanghai	T'ung-ch'ang Oil Mill	130,000
1902	Shanghai	Ch'iu-hsin Machinery Co.	699,000
1905	Shanghai	Ta-ta S. N. Co.	70,000
1907	Peking	Fu-li Woolen Textile Co.	1,398,000
1908	Shanghai	T'ung-ch'ang Hsieh-chi Cotton Mill	600,000
1910	Shanghai	Sheng-ta Flour Mill	280,000
—	—	Ta-t'ung S. N. Co.	70,000[b]
—	Shanghai	Chung-hsi Bookstore	50,000[b]
—	—	Rice mills	150,000[b]
Total			$3,657,000 (ca. Tls. 2,633,040)

Source: Wang Ching-yü, Kung-yeh, II, 960–961, 1901.
a. It is assumed that the general price level was relatively stable during the period. Technically, if there was any big change in prices, the dollar figures ought to be "deflated."
b. Estimated capital.

undertakings such as rice, flour, silk, packing, textile, and machine factories. (See Table 20.) By 1913, he had invested about two million taels in modern enterprises. His towering position as an investor in modern enterprises was closely challenged by one of his fellow-compradors, Chu Chih-yao of the Banque de l'Indochine at Shanghai, who was among the most prominent Chinese investors by the 1910's. (See Table 21.)

Whereas high government officials like Tseng Kuo-fan, Tso Tsung-t'ang, and Li Hung-chang were preoccupied with military installations, the compradors were mainly interested in the non-military arena. They not only managed and invested heavily in China's first large-scale steamship, mining, textile, and machine-manufacturing projects, but were also among the first of their countrymen to set up other modern enterprises. (See Table 22.) It is clear that the amount of capital which the compradors are known to have invested in modern industrial enterprises in China is not the full amount. In view of the fact that some of their enterprises were registered under foreign names and that many of them made investments in foreign-controlled enterprises, the complete picture of their investment activities is still not entirely clear. For example, by the late 1890's, roughly 40 percent of the paid-up stock of Western firms in shipping, cotton spinning, and banking was held by Chinese investors, who occupied seats on the boards of directors of 18 firms during the sixties, 27 firms during the seventies, 21 during the eighties, and 64 during the nineties. By 1894 Chinese investors shared managerial responsibilities in three-fifths of the foreign firms, in which they had invested about 400 million taels. And a great number of these investors were compradors.[104] It is hard to figure out the exact amount of the compradors' capital in China's early industries as a whole, but the proportion of their capital in steamship, mining, textiles, and machine-manufacturing—crucial fields in China's early industrialization—was remarkable.

The Comprador as Industrial Manager

While the comprador-merchants' role as modern investors was significant, their managerial ability was equally crucial to China's early industrialization. Through lengthy and close association with

Table 22. China's first large-scale modern enterprises promoted and invested in by the compradors (taels).

Year of opera-tion	Place	Company	Capital[a]		Mode of opera-tion[b]	Promoter-investor
			Noncom-prador	Com-prador		
1873	Shanghai	China Mer-chants' S. N. Co.	612,000	476,000	KTSP	Tong King-sing, Hsü Jun
1878	Chihli	Kaiping Mines	—	1,490,280	KTSP	Tong King-sing, Hsü Jun
1883	Shanghai	Yüan-ch'ang Machine-ry Co.	0	138,888	Merchant	Chu Ta-ch'un
1886	Tientsin	Tientsin Chinese Match Factory	—	—	Merchant	Wu Mao-ting
1890	Shanghai	Shanghai Cotton Cloth Mill	148,000	352,000	KTSP	P'eng Ch'i-chih, Cheng Kuan-ying
1898	Shanghai	Yüan-ch'ang Mill	0	400,000	Merchant	Chu Ta-ch'un

Source: Tables 14, 15, 17, 19; Sun Yü-t'ang, Kung-yeh, I, 50; II, 959–960, 988–989.

a. It is assumed that the general price level was relatively stable during the period. Technically, if there was any big change in prices, the tael figures ought to be "deflated."

b. KTSP stands for kuan-tu shang-pan (official superivision and merchant management).

foreign merchants, they gradually learned the new techniques of handling modern enterprises. This unique expertise was invaluable, as it could hardly be acquired otherwise. Since China's early industrialization was mainly undertaken by compradors and the traditional gentry members, including high officials and traditional gentry-merchants (merchants with purchased gentry status), a contrast between them as managers may throw light on the problem of business management in modern China. In this contrast the compradors' new expertise assumes special significance. Too often the traditional gentry members proved incompetent when confronted with what were essentially management problems of an enterprise, such as making advance plans and calculations, determining the cost structure, pricing the product, and predicting its profitability of the enterprise.

Knowing more about Confucian classics than about business management, the high officials who promoted China's industrialization were not qualified as modern executives. The industrial enterprises initiated by Chang Chih-tung, for instance, seem to have been projected on impulse or sudden inspiration rather than after careful calculation or sound guidance. When Chang was at Canton in 1888, he tried to set up a cotton mill, but after being transferred to Wuchang, he could not acquire enough funds to continue the operation. The machinery ordered from London had to be stored there for four years before he could obtain funds and ready the buildings. Finally the machinery reached Wuchang and was set up for operation, but it was discovered that the subsidiary equipment was insufficient and, worst of all, that there were not enough foreign engineers to operate the machinery properly. Again operation had to be suspended.[105] Thus, it appears that Chang Chih-tung knew little about combining the various productive elements in order to achieve industrial profits and stability.

The traditional gentry-merchants do not seem to have performed any better, as illustrated by the early history of the China Merchants' Steam Navigation Co.[106] Around August 1872, Governor-general Li Hung-chang decided to set up a steamship company so as to facilitate the transport of tribute rice and to compete commercially with foreigners in China. His principal advisor was Prefect Chu Ch'i-ang, a traditional gentry-merchant in charge of the transport of tribute rice by seagoing junks.[107] As a junk owner in his private capacity and a commissioner (*tsung-pan*) of the Chekiang Bureau of Sea Transport, Chu was unusual among traditional gentry-merchants for his knowledge of the shipping business. In 1867, he received the following government commendation for his work in supervising the junk transport of tribute rice: "When disputes arose among the junks or in case of negotiations with foreign vessels, this official always took great pains to deal with the problems and give sound advice and instructions. He has therefore won the admiration and respect of the captains and helmsmen, and is indeed an official of rare qualifications."[108]

But all his knowledge of Chinese junks was of little avail when it came to judging steam vessels. Early in November 1872 he purchased through a Portuguese broker the ship *Aden*. After having paid 50,000 taels for her, he discovered that the vessel actually was worth only about 30,000 taels. His purchase of the ship *Daybreak* from England did not prove satisfactory either, for he learned after signing the contract that he was paying too high a price, whereupon he demanded a rebate of 10–15,000 taels from the broker, George Barnett & Co.[109] For the wharf he bought at Pootung, across the river from Shanghai, "he paid extravagantly."[110] In his relations with the foreign captains he employed to command the steamers, Chu again demonstrated his incompetence. For instance, in 1873 the *Aden*'s captain, James W. Connor, was summarily dismissed on grounds of recklessness in navigation and putting a "squeeze on the crew," whereupon he sued for breach of contract on a "frivolous pretense." This story suggests that Chu either did not get good men or failed to handle them properly.[111] A Heard's partner observed that "the mandarins have . . . mismanaged the [shipping] affair through ignorance."[112]

Prefect Chu was troubled not only by technical problems but also by the difficulty of raising capital. His efforts toward "inviting merchants" seem to have begun promisingly, but by January 1873 the famous banker and silk merchant Hu Kuang-yung and the tea merchant Li Chen-yü had changed their minds and refused to invest. By early May 1873 it became quite apparent that Chu and his staff could not develop the steamship project.

Chang Chien (1853–1926) was one of the unusual and distinguished gentry-officials who undertook modern enterprises. In many ways he was a better manager than his fellow gentry-officials, yet when compared with the compradors, he appears less modern-minded. For example, he did not realize the importance of the steamship business until after 1900, and he showed "particularism," such as favoritism, toward his workers. When he organized the Dah Sun Cotton Mill, he did not understand the concept of limited liability—an idea that the comprador learned from the foreign merchants at least as early as 1856.[113]

By 1873 Li Hung-chang had come to realize that Chu Ch'i-ang was not suited to the role of manager for the China Merchants' Steam Navigation Co. In May 1873, Li appointed Tong King-sing, then Jardine's chief comprador at Shanghai, to replace Chu in managing the steamship enterprise.[114] Tong's post was that of "merchant chief" (*shang-tsung*), that is, head of a group of merchants who were to undertake operation of the project jointly. The merchants were to be shareholders, and Tong was theoretically to be the managing director elected by them. At the same time, since the joint-stock organization functioned inside a government bureau, Tong also held an official title as bureau commissioner (*tsung-pan*). This new way to become an official was a departure from the traditional channel to success through the examination system, for Tong's official position was obtained solely on account of his own successful business career as a comprador at Shanghai.

Tong's capability as a businessman was well known among the foreign merchants, and they expected that the new Chinese company under his leadership would compete effectively with them. Russell's F. B. Forbes was therefore relieved when he heard in May 1873 of the alleged failure of Tong's negotiations with Governor-general Li: "I am glad to learn that Tong King-sing failed in his negotiations, and I only wish I could be a little surer that the details of the story told you were all correct."[115] The rumor proved untrue. Another American merchant in Shanghai anticipated that Tong's steamship company would be more successful than Jardine's.[116] Tong was highly regarded by his fellow Cantonese merchants as well. Having had a conversation with the firm's Chinese staff shortly before Tong took his new position, R. I. Fearon of Heard's wrote: "Numerous shareholders might be found if they saw that the [new Chinese] company were being properly managed by Tong King-sing."[117]

To Chu Ch'i-ang the steamship project had proved merely burdensome, but to Tong King-sing it offered definite advantages. Tong's qualifications to operate a modern steamship project were unusual for a Chinese at the time. Having several connections with the steamship business, he was probably the most experienced Chinese in the field. First, he owned steamships himself. Second, he was associated with a number of foreign steamship companies as a director. Third, and most significant, he served for ten years as Jardine's Shanghai comprador, whose duties included the steamship business, since Jardine, Matheson & Co. acted as agent for several other steamship companies and, under the "managing-agency" system, handled their actual management as well. Thus, Tong must have acquired considerable understanding of steamship management on the operational level. This expertise was indicated in the case of the *Nanzing*, a ship that Tong purchased. One of Jardine's partners observed: "The expenses of this boat have hitherto averaged 7,000 taels per month, while they are now about Tls. 4,500."[118]

Relying on the support of Chinese merchant guilds, particularly the Cantonese, Tong was able to develop an effective system of attracting freight from the Chinese traders in the treaty ports. What was more, his background as a comprador greatly helped him to operate the enterprise efficiently. In matters relating to navigation personnel and steamship repairs, he obtained the advice of foreign captains and engineers, particularly D. R. Spedding, who jointly owned some steamships with him. A British newspaper in Shanghai noted that Tong's foreign staff was "as capable and trustworthy" as that of any foreign steamship company in Shanghai.[119]

While it was thus possible for Tong to enlist the help of foreigners, he himself was equipped with a technical knowledge of steamships that enabled him to exercise general supervision. In August 1873, when the steamship *Laptek* arrived at Shanghai from England, Archibald Little & Co., the ship's owner, claimed that the ship had been ordered by Prefect Chu in January 1873 for the Chinese Merchants' Steam Navigation Co. Tong then made a personal inspection of the vessel and found her unsatisfactory. His testimony at court illustrates that he had considerable knowledge of steamships on the technical level: "We did not buy the *Laptek*, as her carrying capacity was not large enough for our purposes. . . . I went on board with Mr. [D. R.] Spedding to examine her. I went all over her. I do not know what her class was. If I had been a Lloyd's surveyor, I would not have classed her '90a.' "[120] Tong then refused to take the ship, on the legal grounds that although a contract had been drawn up in January, Chu had not signed it. In August 1873, Tong ordered a large new steamship named the *Hochung* from England, a vessel that later proved to be very suitable for the coastal trade in China.

Just as Tong depended on foreigners in questions of navigation and repairs, in matters relating to business operation and organization he made use of the talents of the Chinese compradors. Of the six merchant directors Tong nominated to head the company's branch offices, three can be identified as compradors—Hsü Jun, Seating (Liu Shao-tsung), and Asong (Ch'en Shu-t'ang). (See Table 23.) All of them were capable merchants. Hsü Jun, Tong's deputy at Shanghai, was the former Shanghai comprador to Dent & Co. in 1861–1868. After 1868, Hsü conducted a prosperous tea business, owning many firms in the tea districts of the Yangtze Valley. He must have been an able businessman, since Russell & Co. in 1873 tried very hard but unsuccessfully to hire him as the firm's Shanghai comprador.[121] Seating, the merchant director at Hankow, was a former comprador to Heard's at Hankow, where he had experience in promoting freight for the firm's steamers. That Seating was a capable comprador is indicated by the fact that "C. D. William [Heard's Hankow agent] always swore by him,"[122] and also that F. B. Forbes of the rival firm of Russell & Co. thought highly of him: "Augustine Heard & Co.'s comprador [at Hankow] is a very energetic and accommodating man, who mixes much with

Table 23. Social background of the merchant directors of the China Merchants' Steam Navigation Co., 1873.

Name	Title	Background
Tong King-sing	Merchant chief	Comprador
Hsü Jun	Merchant director at Shanghai	Comprador
Chu Ch'i-shun	Merchant director at Shanghai	Official
Sung Chin	Merchant director at Tientsin	Official
Seating (Liu Shao-tsung)	Merchant director at Hankow	Comprador
Asong (Ch'en Shu-t'ang)	Merchant director at Hong Kong	Comprador
Fan Shih-yao	Merchant director at Swatow	—

Source: Liu Kwang-Ching, "Two Steamship Companies," p. 122.

the freighting people."[123] In early July 1873, Seating represented Tong in negotiations with Augustine Heard & Co. for the purpose of purchasing Heard's waterfront properties in Hankow. Soon he was sent by Tong to Japan to prepare for the freighting business there.[124]

Under the able leadership of Tong King-sing and Hsü Jun, the China Merchants' Steam Navigation Co. developed rapidly until 1883, when the Sino-French crisis arrested its promising development.[125] If there had been no Sino-French war in 1883–1884, China's industrial efforts would probably have been more successful. In view of the fact that the company earned handsome profits (869,210 taels in 1878–1879) and that its capital stock increased surprisingly (2,000,000 taels in 1883),[126] one may say that comprador-merchant Tong King-sing was a better manager than Chu Ch'i-ang. That Tong was a talented manager is also indicated by a comment made after Tong had left the company in 1884 by H. B. Morse, who was associated with the China Merchants' Steam Navigation Co. in 1886–1887: "I have always thought it a pity . . . that we could not connect Tong King-sing with the Company, so as to have the advantage of his business capacity; he need not have absolute control; meeting a board of Directors twice a week would have secured that."[127]

If Tong's efficient management of this company was owing to his specific knowledge of the steamship business, then the fact that he demonstrated equal ability as an efficient manager in other enterprises must be attributed to his broader knowledge of Western practices as a whole, acquired chiefly as a comprador. His role as a manager in the Kaiping Mines, China's first large-scale coal mine, was as significant as his role in the China Merchants' Steam Navigation Co.[128] In the first place, Tong was instrumental in setting up this enterprise. Serving as an interpreter, he was sent in 1876 by Li Hung-chang to accompany an English mining engineer to inspect the site at Kaiping, Chihli. In his report to Li, Tong stated that the traditional methods of mining, which had been used in this area since Ming times, obtained poor results.[129] Only the use of modern methods in production and transport, he asserted, could bring about successful mining.

Supported by Li Hung-chang and helped by "his Cantonese

colleagues" such as Hsü Jun and Cheng Kuan-ying, Tong was responsible for organizing the company under the pattern of "official supervision and merchant management."[130] Although there was a Board of Directors, the actual responsibility for management was undertaken by Tong, who ordered most of the modern machinery and equipment from England. Boring machines were purchased for determining the depth of the coal seams and the points at which water would be encountered. Other equipment included a pumping machine for taking away water and power-driven fans for removal of gases. Modern methods permitted deeper, safer, and more efficient excavation. As in the case of the steamship company, Tong once more enlisted the help of foreigners—in this case engineers and experienced workmen. He employed three English engineers in 1878, and the company's foreign staff increased to nine the next year, and to eighteen by 1883.[131]

Under the leadership of Tong, the Kaiping Mines operated successfully. Production increased rapidly and steadily, and Kaiping coal was finally able to drive foreign coal out of the Tientsin market and to spread its market to other treaty ports.[132] The significance of the accomplishment lay not only in the fact that the company successfully applied modern technology in China, but also in the fact that Kaiping gradually became the center of a series of modern enterprises. Besides coal, which supplied the government's Northern Fleet and stimulated local industries, the Kaiping Mines produced coke, bricks, tile, and cement at T'ang-shan and was involved in gold and silver mining in the nearby Jehol province.[133] With the deepening of the shaft, a gas lighting system was provided in 1880. By 1884, the company maintained a hospital with accommodations for forty Chinese patients. In order to carry Kaiping coal to Tientsin and thence to other places, a railroad was constructed by 1883 from T'ang-shan to Hsü-ko-chuang, where coal then could be shipped through a canal to Tientsin. This was China's first successful railroad.[134] Thanks to Tong King-sing's efforts, the company acquired its own shipping line in 1889 for the transportation of coal.

Deeply convinced that China would benefit from Western technology, Tong sucessfully managed the Kaiping Mines for fifteen years until his death in 1892. He was highly regarded by Chinese and foreigners alike. Those who knew him, particularly foreigners, spoke highly of him for his "modern ideas,"[135] his "progressive spirit and large mind,"[136] and his "real desire for progressive measures."[137]

In like manner, the scholar-comprador Cheng Kuan-ying played the role of promoter-manager in China's first cotton textile enterprise. He was chiefly responsible for organizing and developing the Shanghai Cotton Cloth Mill in 1879, and when P'eng Ch'i-chih withdrew from the project in 1879, Cheng was forced to demonstrate his managerial ability as well. In addition to raising 352,800 taels of the 500,000-tael initial paid-up capital, he proceeded with establishment of the company's physical plant, purchased machinery, and ensured an adquate source of raw cotton.

In order to determine whether the foreign machinery could actually process China's cotton, Cheng wrote to Yung Wing—a fellow-Cantonese who in the fifties had served as a tea purchaser for Dent & Co., and who was then in the United States as head of the Chinese Educational Mission—asking him to engage an American technical expert to conduct a first-hand investigation of the matter in China. When the American, A. W. Danforth, arrived in Shanghai, he raised some doubts about the suitability of the shorter fibers of Chinese cotton for the machine manufacture of cloth. Cheng then sent him back to the United States with some samples of raw Chinese cotton, to be made into cloth. Fortunately, the resulting cloth was found to be equal in quality to American cloth, so Cheng decided to go ahead as planned. Danforth was then engaged to superintend construction of the factory and selection and installation of the machinery. Cheng also hired foreign technicians to install the machinery and to teach Chinese workers how to operate spindles and looms. Later he sent a Chinese to the United States to learn the cultivation and manufacture of cotton.[138]

The compradors' managerial role in China's railroad development is generally overlooked. Wu Mao-ting was appointed by Li Hung-chang in 1894 as managing director of the North China Imperial Railways while he was a comprador to the Hongkong and Shanghai Banking Corp. at Tientsin. The railroad witnessed good progress during his three years' capable leadership, and "his endeavours to stamp out corruption were extolled" by Chinese and foreign staff alike.[139] Similarly at the turn of the century, T'ang

Chieh-ch'en concurrently served as general manager of the Shang-hai-Nanking Railroad and as comprador to Jardine, Matheson & Co. at Shanghai.[140] Meanwhile, Cheng Kuan-ying was appointed by Sheng Hsüan-huai to join the Hankow-Canton Railroad, and when it became a private enterprise in 1906, Cheng was elected as general manager.[141]

Convinced that China would benefit "from a thorough grasp of Western methods," the compradors were eager to learn the latest Western technology and ideas.[142] The modern enterprises operated by them were usually equipped with the most modern Western machines. For instance, aside from the undertakings operated by Tong King-sing and Cheng Kuan-ying, Chu Ta-ch'un's Wah Shing Flour Mill was "equipped with modern machinery supplied by Turner & Co., through Jardine & Co.," in which firm he served as comprador. In the same fashion, his Kung-yik Cotton Mill acquired "modern machines through Jardine."[143] At Hankow, the bean-cake oil mill of Liu Hsin-sheng, a prominent comprador there, was likewise "equipped with the latest machinery."[144] When P'eng Ch'i-chih made the first proposal to Li Hung-chang in 1878 for setting up a cotton textile mill at Shanghai, he planned to copy from England the latest methods of weaving and spinning.[145]

Equipped with the knowledge of handling modern business, the comprador-merchants were thus the first group of people called upon to operate the government-sponsored modern enterprises. In addition to steamship, mining, and textile undertakings, they managed other less spectacular enterprises. For instance, on the recommendation of Li Hung-chang, Wu Mao-ting, comprador to the Hongkong and Shanghai Banking Corp. at Tientsin in 1883–1905, "was appointed to open up a tannery and certain government mills in the neighbourhood of Tientsin."[146] Teng Chi-ch'ang, the same bank's comprador at Hankow, was later connected with the government cotton mills at Wuchang.[147]

The Comprador as Entrepreneur

A manager is not necessarily an entrepreneur, who by definition is an innovator as well. A pioneering scholar on entrepreneurship defines it as "the purposeful activity (including an integrated sequence of decisions) of an individual or group of associated individuals, undertaken to initiate, maintain, or aggrandize a profit-oriented business unit for the production or distribution of economic goods."[148] Thus, an entrepreneur is a decision-maker whose initiative draws all factors of production together to initiate and expand the business enterprise. Schumpeter's theory of economic development assigns a central role to this kind of daring and innovative entrepreneur.[149]

How did the comprador, as entrepreneur, devise new combinations of productive factors? First of all, he was a fund supplier. He not only invested in modern enterprises himself, but also employed new ways of raising the large amounts of capital that were indispensable for the modern, usually large-scale undertakings. Hsü Jun and Cheng Kuan-ying successfully used the joint-stock system in getting funds for the China Merchants' Steam Navigation Co. and the Shanghai Cotton Cloth Mill in 1872 and 1879, respectively. Hsü later remarked: "It was by no means an easy task to have raised so huge an amount at a time when the public was yet to have confidence [in modern enterprises.]"[150]

The comprador's success as a manager was especially outstanding in light of the incompetence of other groups of people. Moreover, engaging in a profession that was unconventional in itself, the comprador was usually willing to take risks.[151] It is true that such adventurousness occasionally involved failure: some compradors lost money when investing in modern-style enterprises, and others went bankrupt by speculating.[152] But whatever the drawbacks, this venturesome trait was very significant when contrasted to the general reluctance of traditional merchants to enter new fields of business.

The comprador was quick to introduce new ideas, as illustrated by the insurance business. Trading in the treaty ports, where the modern insurance business was first introduced to China, the compradors rapidly realized the convenience and value of insurance. As a British merchant recalled from his days in Tientsin in the 1860's: "I was for sometime the only agent for Marine Insurance at this port, and several of the compradores, and especially 'Apung,' comprador for Dent & Co., regularly insured, and on a large scale, with me, in his own name and on his own account."[153] In the late sixties and early seventies, Tong King-sing and Hsü Jun jointly established marine and fire insurance companies.[154] The importance of modern insurance was shown in the history of the Shanghai Cotton Cloth Mill. Cheng Kuan-ying, the Cantonese comprador who had associated with the project since its inception, left the mill in 1883. Yang Tsung-lien, the new official manager, regarded insurance as a waste of money and thus failed to buy any for the company. Unfortunately, China's first modern textile company, which had been very profitable since its actual operations began in 1890, was completely burned down in October 1893, with a loss of more than 700,000 taels.[155]

The comprador went one step beyond simple emulation, for each entrepreneur has to consider the nature of the economic problems peculiar to his own enterprise. In other words, an entrepreneur works out new combinations of factors of production and distribution. In the industrial arena, for instance, Tong King-sing realized that the conditions in which the coal was found in China were different from those in England. Cheng Kuan-ying and Chu Ta-ch'un likewise had to consider the consequences of using native short-staple cotton, of hiring Chinese labor, and of operating in the local natural environment as a whole. As to the development of commercial capitalism, the comprador's innovative spirit was abundantly evidenced in the uprecedented upcountry purchase system and the chop loan practice.

It is generally maintained that China's slow economic modernization is, to a great extent, attributable to the lack of an entrepreneurial spirit. But the comprador, in his capacity as a supplier of funds, a competent manager, a risk-taker as well as an innovator, was an entrepreneur in the true sense of the word. Of course, not all of the compradors were entrepreneurs (especially these in the small foreign firms after the 1890's, who usually remained petty brokers), and entrepreneurs of China's early industries did not necessarily have a compradorial background (the exact proportion of modern entrepreneurs with a compradorial origin is hard to tell). But the compradors' enterpreneurial role was particularly significant in view of the fact that few traditional merchants took part in China's early industrialization (Hu Kuang-yung declined the challenge), and the role of overseas Chinese in the industrialization was negligible until the twentieth century.

However, the comprador's role as an entrepreneur was greatly inhibited by his compradorial background, as well as by the economic and institutional factors existing in the treaty ports of late Ch'ing China. He was normally shrewd, efficient, and talented, but his integrity was open to doubt. According to Cheng Kuan-ying's associate Kung Shou-t'u, the failure of the Shanghai Cotton Cloth Mill to begin production earlier was owing to the fact that Cheng tended to treat the company's funds as his own. Cheng had let out large sums in loans or as investments in other enterprises, pocketing the interest himself.[156] In the same fashion, Hsü Jun, the assistant manager to the China Merchants' Steam Navigation Co., privately took a considerable amount of money from the company to tide over his personal financial crisis in 1883–1884. He later admitted that he owed the company 155,300 taels in 1884.[157] This irregularity was a great blow to the company's development and caused Hsü's dismissal in 1884. Tong King-sing was himself dismissed from the company shortly thereafter for "heavy deficits" discovered in his accounts. Although this changing of post was related to other factors, such as provincial and personal rivalries, the financial malpractice of these compradors at least constituted the pretext for their dismissal. Their misuse of funds was related to the speculative activities that were common in their comprador years.

Thus arises the question of motivation, one of the subtle but still significant factors in business success. How was Tong King-sing motivated to establish the Kaiping Mines? While he was manager of the China Merchants' Steam Navigation Co., one important reason for Tong's interest in the development of Kaiping was his desire to provide return cargo for vessels carrying tribute rice from the south to Tientsin. The opening of mines in the north, which could produce for a coal market in Shanghai and elsewhere in the south, would make it possible for the ships of the China Merchants' Steam Navigation Co. to return from Tientsin with cargo. Thus, Kaiping not only promised to make profits in its own right but also opened possibilities for increased profits for the steamship company, which Tong and his fellow-compradors hoped to share, since they had invested in the company on a grand scale. At the same time, Tong wanted a supply of native coal for his steamers, and the Kaiping company regulations provided that the China Merchants' Steam

Navigation Co. should have the right to purchase coal before any was put on the market. It seems probable, however, that Tong was concerned more about cargo for his steamers than about the nationality of their bunker fuel.

Although the compradors were, in the main, risk-takers, it is necessary to distinguish between risk-taking in long-term investment, which is significant, and speculation for immediate profit. In contrast to the Meiji entrepreneurs in Japan, who took the long view of their undertakings,[158] the compradors, especially in the nineteenth century, paid great attention to short-term gains. Takee, Fung Heen, Sunkee, Choping, and many others were frequently engaged in speculative activities,[159] and it was for this reason that Hsü Jun lost about one-third of a million taels in 1862 when he was a comprador to Dent & Co.[160] This practice was detrimental to economic development, for not only did the compradors' "speculative disposition" frequently lead to their bankruptcy, as in the case of Fung Hien, Hsü Jun, Yang Kuei-hsüan, and Liu Hsin-sheng, but the speculative market also placed new industry in an unfavorable situation to absorb capital.[161]

Since Tong King-sing, Hsü Jun, and Cheng Kuan-ying tended to regard their posts under the *kuan-tu shang-pan* pattern as temporary ones, they lacked an all-embracing and long-term program of development. They were good at employing foreign technicians, but seem to have paid little attention to the problem of Chinese takeover. When Tong and Hsü were managers of the China Merchants' Steam Navigation Co., the firm entered into an agreement with the China Navigation Co. (of Butterfield & Swire) and the China Coast Steam Navigation Co. (of Jardine's) concerning a uniform rate. This arrangment may have been partly owing to the fact that, since the compradors also had an interest in the foreign steamship companies, they were reluctant to compete in all efforts with the foreign firms.

Yet these questions must also be considered against the background of the society within which the compradors operated. As to the issue of integrity, the compradors were not conspicuously corrupt. In the first place, they were probably no more corrupt than their contemporary businessmen, since embezzlement was a common practice in nineteenth century China, where enterprises generally lacked an adequate auditing system. Second, in discussing the comprador's integrity, one should bear in mind the difference between corruption or "squeeze," on the one hand, and the customary mercantile practices under the system of "complete responsibility," on the other.[162] Under the premodern system, little distinction was made between personal and company funds. Unfortunately, too often the compradors could not make such a distinction even when managing a joint-stock company sponsored by the government. Third, the comprador's embezzlement seems insignificant when compared with the regular "squeeze" on the part of officials. And fourth, although the comprador's specially close relationship with his relatives and fellow-townsmen encouraged corruption and illicit financial dealings, it was also chiefly responsible for his successful fund-raising for modern enterprises.

In the last analysis, the *kuan-tu shang-pan* system, whatever its merits, was probably not the proper milieu for the activities of individual entrepreneurs. If Tong, Hsü, and Cheng had worked for their own private enterprises, the problem of embezzlement would not have arisen, as was clearly demonstrated by the younger generation. In contrast to the fact that before the seventies the compradors were interested in investing either in foreign firms (as were Choping and Koofunsing) or in the *kuan-tu shang-pan* enterprises (as were Hsü Jun, Tong King-sing, and Cheng Kuan-ying), the investment pattern of their younger fellow-compradors tended to break away from both the foreigners and the Chinese officials. The younger generation gradually turned toward managing businesses privately and independently, for they were too wealthy to remain financially subordinate to foreign firms, and they disdained official supervision and interference. With the Ch'ing government's encouragement, Chu Ta-ch'un, Wu Mao-ting, Chu Chih-yao, and Yü Hsia-ch'ing gradually set up and successfully managed enterprises of their own after the 1880's. But circumstances—economic, social, and otherwise—in China during the 1870's did not permit the establishment of large-scale modern enterprises entirely owned and operated by the merchants, and the *kuan-tu shang-pan* system was thus an expedient program, particularly suited to industrial effort under these circumstances. So long as China was not able to make an institutional breakthrough, no matter how "new" the compradors were, they had to operate in many senses within the existing social context.

Business motivation must likewise be viewed against a broader social background. The compradors' interest in immediate rather than long-term profit was prompted by various social and economic factors. The fluctuating market of the treaty ports tempted them to speculation, and indeed, other traditional merchants were not free from speculation (Hu Kuang-yung, for instance). However, in one way the compradors responded to this situation more positively than did the traditional merchants, for as a rule, they at once invested in modern undertakings in a great variety of forms. Almost all major compradors, like Choping, Hsü Jun, Tong King-sing, Cheng Kuan-ying, Chu Ta-ch'un, Chu Chih-yao, and Yü Hsia-ch'ing, invested at the same time in about a dozen different kinds of modern enterprises. This diversification of investment, despite its drawbacks, was a major factor in their achieving a more balanced and stable financial position in an overly risky and uncertain environment.

The compradors' lack of a long-term program of development was also related to institutional factors. Under the *kuan-tu shang-pan* system, they knew that their posts were partly dependent on the attitude of the high officials. Tong and Hsü, for example, were forced to leave the China Merchants' Steam Navigation Co. in 1883–1884 by Governor-general Li's protégé Sheng Hsüan-huai. The officials' "squeeze," the lack of adequate legal protection through corporation, property, or contract law, and the foreigners' privileged status, all forced the compradors to turn to the foreign firms.

Modern China's slow economic development has frequently been contrasted to the more rapid development in Japan. In a sense, one may claim that their different tempos of economic growth were owing to the existence of a patriotic entrepreneurial class in Japan and the lack of one in China. But viewed in perspective, the willingness of the Meiji entrepreneurs to suffer immediate losses can be understood as arising from a confidence in the central government's unfailing support, and a conviction that in the long run they would make profits. In contrast, the Chinese compradors singularly lacked such assurances from the Ch'ing government. After all, every businessman, regardless of national origin, tends to be profit-oriented, and corruption was a serious problem in Meiji Japan as well. Furthermore, the issue as to whether any country's businessmen were motivated by profit or by national interest is itself an insignificant one in the light of that country's economic development as a whole. All in all, the compradors played a most important role in modern China's economic development, and their activities have to be considered against the broader social and institutional background.

VII   The Comprador System as a Socioeconomic Institution

So far we have discussed the economic role of the comprador mainly as an individual. He was, however, more than just an individual. Indeed, a socioeconomic institution centering around him was gradually established. Not every Chinese merchant could become a comprador at will, as several qualifications had to be taken into consideration and formal processes completed before he was employed. Since he could not handle all the foreign merchants' transactions by himself, the comprador in turn recruited his own Chinese staff. Business was then conducted through him in certain customary ways. These practices gradually became well established, and the comprador institution was formed.

The main function of the comprador institution was of course an economic one. However, since an economic institution is inseparably related to society as a whole, and the economic aspect was in fact intertwined with practically all other aspects of life, the comprador institution must be considered against a broader social and political background—in its proper historical perspective. What was the mechanism of the institution and what were its social implications? To what extent was it affected by Chinese and Western institutions and values? In short, how was the comprador—the man and the institution—related to the society within which he functioned?

The Process of Becoming a Comprador

The lucrative comprador position was not available to every

Chinese merchant. He must either be a prominent merchant in his own right or have a connection with the foreign house in one way or another, since it was usually the foreign partners who took the initiative in employing the comprador. Few Chinese merchants applied directly to foreign houses for the comprador position until the 1890's, when the method of recruiting compradors changed.[1] Before being employed as a comprador, he had to have special qualifications and meet certain formal requirements.

There were no absolute criteria for the ideal comprador. Actually, his qualifications depended on the kind of business to be done for the foreign house. A successful comprador in one particular business might fail in another.[2] However, several qualifications were usually taken into consideration when a foreign merchant was selecting a comprador. One was linguistic training. There was an international language at the treaty ports known as pidgin or business English. It was a mixture of Portuguese, Chinese, and English, with numerous local additions. Although a comprador's English need not be as good as that of Tong King-sing or Young Atong, he certainly was expected to be able to speak pidgin English.[3] Inability to do so was considered unusual.[4]

Another qualification was business-promoting ability, which depended on the comprador's wealth, social standing, and acquaintance with Chinese merchants. Since the chief aim of an agency house was to bring in more business, this qualification was as important as the ability to speak pidgin English. John Heard spoke highly of the Hong Kong comprador See Yong in 1860: "I have no doubt he is worth $50,000 at least, probably more. He does not speak much English, but as being rich and one of the old Compradores of the place, he has 'large face.' "[5]

However, the foreign house was equally concerned about the comprador's dependability. There were several ways to find a trustworthy comprador. The first was through recommendation of the former hong merchants with whom the foreign partners had been acquainted. In the fifties and sixties, Russell & Co. enjoyed successful relations with the Chinese merchants at Shanghai because of the firm's comprador Ahyue, who had been recommended by one of the richest hong merchants, Howqua.[6] The other way of finding a trustworthy comprador was through direct and frequent

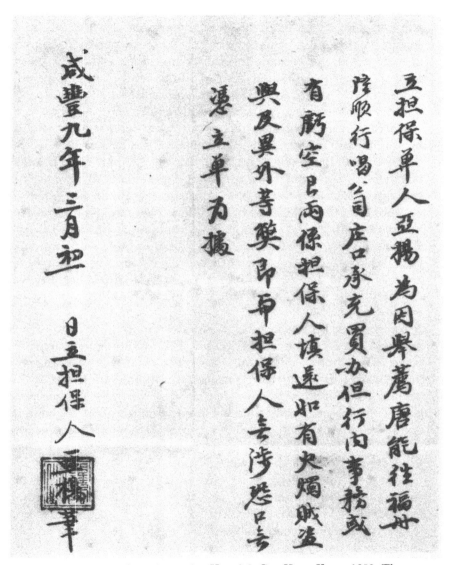

Comprador's security chop: Augustine Heard & Co., Hong Kong, 1859. The Hong Kong comprador See Yong secured the Foochow comprador T'ang Neng. *Source:* Agreements, 1846–1861, Case 9, HC II.

business contacts with Chinese merchants for a long time. Having gained the trust of the foreign partners, a Chinese merchant might thus be employed as comprador. Hsü Yü-t'ing of Dent's and Choping and Koofunsing of Russell's had all been eminent tea and silk merchants in their own right before becoming compradors. Wang Huai-shan, a clerk in a native bank who was closely connected with the newly-appointed Shanghai agent of the Hongkong and Shanghai Banking Corp., later become the bank's first Shanghai comprador in 1869.[7] Or, a comprador could start his career as a young apprentice in the comprador's office. After serving the firm for a long time, he might succeed the former comprador.[8]

All other things being equal, a man of wealth had the best chance of being employed.[9] A highly successful merchant might be invited as comprador even if he had no particularly close connection with the foreign merchants. The classic example was Hsi Cheng-fu, a successful native banker who in the seventies became comprador to the Hongkong and Shanghai Banking Corp. at Shanghai. Once a merchant was employed as a comprador, he usually brought in his family members and fellow-townsmen as staff members or recommended them as compradors to other houses.

In the period from 1842 to the late 1850's, a letter of recommendation from a well-known merchant was enough for any Chinese to become a comprador. A more sophisticated system of guarantees was developed from the late fifties. Almost every comprador had to be "secured" (financially guaranteed). His surety might guarantee him fully or partially.[10] In some cases, a guarantor might have another guarantor stand surety for him, which made a double guarantee.[11] The practice of joint guarantee was also common, whereby two to four sureties would jointly guarantee one comprador.[12] If one of them turned out to be unable to meet the responsibility, the others would share it equally.[13] A guarantor in turn would be paid by the comprador. In one instance he was offered 20 percent of the comprador's annual net profit.[14]

Once a surety agreed to guarantee a comprador, a gurantee document, or "security chop," was drawn up. It had to be signed in the proper consulate, with the foreign agent as witness.[15] It was occasionally written in English, but ordinarily in Chinese.[16] (See illustration above.) In the case of the security chop drawn in 1860 at Hong Kong for Akow, the Yokohama comprador for Heard's, a free English translation was added at the end, which reads: "Samcock's [Ch'en San-ku's] son named Yok Chu, Akow, having gone to Japan to act Comprador in the house of Heard. Somcock secures that all business placed in his hands shall be conducted properly and honestly and if he cheats his Employers or acts dishonestly Samcock holds himself responsible to make good any loss which may ensue. Chun Sam Cock (signed.)"[17] (See illustration below.) Although most of the security chops guaranteed only the comprador's honesty, in some cases specifications were added. When the native banks at Hankow were showing weakness in

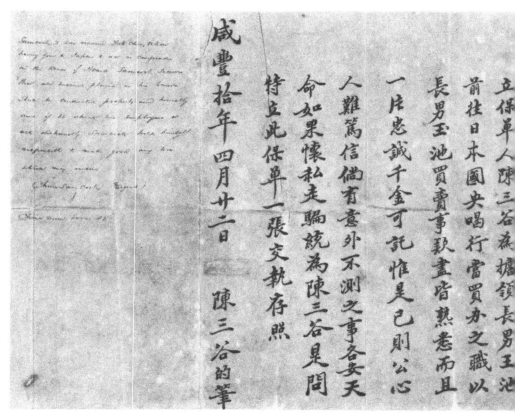

Comprador's security chop with free English translation: Augustine Heard & Co., Hong Kong, 1860. The Yokohama comprador Akow was secured by his father. *Source:* Agreements, 1846–1861, Case 9, HC II.

the sixties, some guarantee papers were "worded to fully cover all such risks" resulting from the compradors' guarantee of the native bank orders.[18] Another paper, however, excluded the surety's financial responsibility for the comprador's speculations or private business,[19] as indicated in the following English translation of a comprador's security chop at Shanghai in 1865:

On the 3rd May, 1865, Ch'eng Lan Sheng and Ch'eng Hsiu Shan enter into a Bond; signifying that they become guarantee for Ch'eng Fen native of Hsiang Shan, who has (or is to have) charge of all issues and receipts in money or bills, and all articles in the warehouses of the Firm of Preston Breuell & Co.,—that all the business of the house (or within the house) shall be completely (or satisfactorily) disposed of—

[The Securities] knowing Ch'eng Fen to be an honest and trustworthy man, for this cause [they,] Lan Sheng and Hsiu Shan, are willing to guarantee him. If there be deficits or wrong doings (tricks, frauds) we will certainly, as in justice bound, straightway make good the sum (will make restitution according to the amount). Lest there should be at some future time no proof [of our undertaking], we agree to execute this bond in witness (thereof).

But, it is further agreed, that if Ch'eng Fen does business on his own account, or does business on a grand scale, it shall be incumbent upon him to consult his employers and to obtain their permission before he engages [in the proposed scheme].

Bond executed on Tung Chih 4th year 4th moon 9th day, by the securities Ch'eng Lan Sheng and Ch'eng Hsiu Shan.[20]

To make the guarantee system more dependable, foreign firms sometimes demanded that the comprador provide "some substantial security in exchange for confidence." While examining Jardine's comprador system in various treaty ports, F. B. Johnson emphasized the importance of such security, as he wrote from Hong Kong in 1884:

My dissatisfaction with the Shanghai arrangements arises entirely out of principle & is caused by apprehension that for the large amount of money which we have at stake we have no proper security & that although today we may be all right, tomorrow we may be all wrong. Here, at Canton & at Foochow I am satisfied with Awei's guarantee. At Swatow I have insisted on being placed in possession of solid securities in the shape of title deeds of property &c to a sufficient value & it is neccessary that we be equally well assured about our native employees at Shanghai, Hankow & Tientsin. We have had warning enough in recent events & I shall be content with nothing less than some substantial security in exchange for our confidence.[21]

The Comprador in China

From the 1900's, when the relationship between the comprador and the foreign firm became more impersonal, a deposit (*ya-kuei*) of cash or of title deed (*tao-ch'i*) on the part of the comprador was always required.[22] By doing so, the foreign merchants no longer need worry about the comprador's defalcation, while at the same time obtaining the badly needed capital.[23] At the turn of the century, an ordinary foreign firm would ask a deposit of 10,000 taels,[24] and as a rule, foreign banks required more. (See Table 24.)

Although the comprador usually made money for himself, the security chop was necessary because there certainly was the chance of loss. The comprador system was based on the Chinese institution of "complete responsibility" (*pao*).[25] The comprador was fully responsible for the conduct of his staff, for the credit of the firm's Chinese constituents, and for the dependability of the native bank orders that he received and kept for the firm. As a result, the comprador always faced the risk of loss. According to Tong King-sing, he lost more money than he made in his first five years of service to Jardine's (1863–1868).[26] In the first two months of this period (September-November), he lost 9,000 taels as a result of the failure of two Chinese cotton hongs with which Jardine's traded.[27] Yang Kuei-hsüan, comprador to Butterfield & Swire at Shanghai, accumulated a debt of 100,000 taels to the firm over a three-year period (1881–1884).[28]

Table 24. Comprador's deposits required by foreign banks, Shanghai, 1907 (taels).

Russo-Chinese Bank	150,000
Chartered Bank of India, Australia & China	100,000
Hongkong and Shanghai Banking Corp.	100,000
Banque de l'Indochine	40,000
Guaranty Trust Co. of New York	40,000
International Banking Corp.	40,000
Yokohama Specie Bank	40,000
Netherland Trading Society	30,000
Sino-Belgian Bank	30,000
Deutsch-Asiatische Bank	0

Source: Tōa Dōbunkai, *Shina keizai*, II, 348.

Hsü Shu-p'ing (son of Hsü Jun), comprador to a German firm at Shanghai, "suffered to the extent of $500,000 . . . owing to the great business depression [brought on by the Boxer uprising in 1900]."[29]

After a comprador had been guaranteed, an agreement was made between him and the house. Before the seventies, the agreement was usually simple, as in the case of Augustine Heard & Co. and their Yokohama comprador Akow (who was guaranteed by his father, Chun Sam Cock; see illustration). According to this agreement, Akow would serve as their comprador "for as long a time as mutually agreeable . . . to further and assist in their business in every way in his power." He would enter into no trading transactions on his own account without previously obtaining the consent of the firm's agent. (This consent was usually given, except when the comprador's private business interfered with the firm's transactions.) He would guarantee his staff, which consisted of a shroff (a clerk), a cook, and two coolies. Heard's would pay their passages to and from Japan as well as their wages of one hundred and seventy Mexican dollars a month.[30] The agreement was written in English, signed by both the firm and Akow (in Chinese). Agreements made after the eighties, however, were much more complicated. They specified in detail the comprador's duties, deposits, salaries, commissions, and the organization of the comprador's office. They were written both in Chinese and in the appropriate foreign language in triple form, to be kept respectively by the firm, the comprador, and the appropriate consulate.[31] Having completed such an agreement, a comprador was ready to assume his duties.

Mechanism of the Institution

The first problem that a comprador faced after being employed was how to recruit and organize his staff so as to keep them trustworthy and efficient. The foreign partners also encountered this problem with regard to the comprador's trustworthiness. Although disputes sometimes arose, and resignations or even defalcations on the part of the comprador happened from time to time, the comprador institution thrived, for there were always other competent persons ready to succeed to the post.

The comprador's office (also known as the comprador's room,

Hong Kong 7th June 1860.

Mem? of agreement entered into on the date above written, between Augustine Heard &Co on the one part and Akow Chinese, on the other part, to wit.

Akow agrees to proceed at once to Yokahama in Japan and to act there, or in any other Port in Japan if required, as Compradore to the Agent of Augustine Heard &Co, for as long a time as mutually agreeable. He can not however leave them within one year from the time of his arrival here, nor without giving them at least four months notice of his intention, although they shall have the right to discharge him, if dissatisfied with his conduct, at any time, on payment of one month's extra wages.

He also agrees to further and assist in their business in every way in his power, and to enter into no trading transactions on his own account without the consent previously obtained, in each instance, of Augustine Heard &Co? Agent It is understood that such consent will not be with held except when the transaction interferes with the business of the House.

Augustine Heard &Co agree to pay his passages to and from Japan and also those of his shroff, two coolies and Cook. These men are hereby secured and guaranteed by Akow.

They also agree that his compensation, for himself and for all his men mentioned above shall be one hundred and seventy mexican dollars per month, say $170. Commencing 1 June 1860

Augustine Heard &Co

陳亞九

Comprador's agreement: Augustine Heard & Co., Hong Kong, 1860. Agreement was made with Akow, the firm's Yokohama comprador. *Source:* Agreements, 1846–1861, Case 9, HC II.

comprador's department, or Chinese office[32]) was usually located in the same large compound building as the agency house: "The first foreign buildings [in Shanghai in the sixties] were mainly godowns (warehouses) and residences combined in one large establishment within two-or-three acre compounds along the landward side of the Whangpu bund. . . . In the rear of the compound were usually four or five godowns . . . dwellings for the Chinese assistants, the residence and office of the comprador (the chief Chinese assistant or agent), and the stables."[33] This description fits Heard's physical layout as well, except that there the comprador's office was in the main building. The chief functions of the comprador are evidenced by the location of his office—next to the treasury and the tea room. (See illustration.) It was always on the first floor of the building, whereas the foreign manager's office was probably on the second.[34] On one occasion a comprador's failing health was surmised from his complaints of the "fatigue of ascending

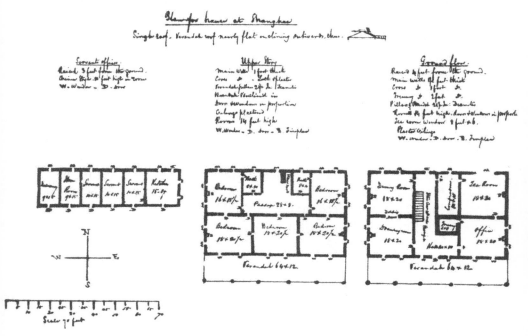

Plan for house at Shanghai: Augustine Heard & Co., 1846. Note comprador room, tea room, and treasury. *Source:* Case 30, HC II.

stairs."[35] All foreigners lived on the second floor, but the comprador and his staff lived in the "comprador's quarters"—a separate building adjacent to the main building.

Although ordinarily one comprador served only one foreign house before the eighties, gradually he began to act as the comprador for more than one firm at the same time.[36] In the firm's main office and each branch office there was one comprador who recruited and guaranteed all his staff members. In order to reduce the great risk involved in his position, the comprador sometimes worked with a partner, to whom he offered the title of vice-comprador or "second comprador" (fu-pan).[37] For example, when Ahyue became the Shanghai comprador to Russell's in 1858, he "was afraid to undertake it alone and got [his friend] Sunchong to take half the responsibility and profits."[38] Sunchong could not speak English and secured "some friend, as customary, to assist him [Ahyue] in the discharge of the business."[39] A similar case existed in Augustine Heard & Co. When the firm's Hong Kong comprador, Atchu, died in the sixties, "See Yong and Atchune went into partnership to continue his business on about equal terms. See Yong [was] apparently the head."[40] In addition, a comprador to a big house might employ an assistant comprador (pang mai-pan). They took his place in his absence but accepted no responsibility.[41] Or the comprador might ask others to act for him temporarily.[42]

Next came the different clerks (ssu-shih), who were more commonly known as "shroffs" or "comprador's men."[43] The number of shroffs depended on the size of the foreign house, with at least ten in each of Heard's branch offices.[44] (See Table 25.) A comprador's office usually consisted of the following: an office shroff or purser, a bookkeeper or accountant (the comprador's most trusted clerk), a customs shroff, a selling and purchasing shroff, and a godown shroff or gate-keeper. The comprador to a big foreign house employed other shroffs as well. A market shroff or reporter (p'ao-chieh) was responsible for market intelligence, and a liaison shroff (p'ao-lou, "he who goes up and down the different floors") maintained close contact with the foreign partners, who were probably on the second floor most of the time.[45]

Naturally, variations appeared under different circumstances. For example, since some big houses, like Russell's, also handled

Table 25. The number of comprador's clerks in foreign banks,
Shanghai, ca. 1900.

Banque de l'Indochine	12
Chartered Bank of India, Australia & China	45
Deutsch-Asiatische Bank	16
Guaranty Trust Co. of New York	9
Hongkong and Shanghai Banking Corporation	50
International Banking Corporation	11
Mercantile Bank of India	24
Netherland Trading Society (Nederlandsche Handel-Maatschappij)	9
Russo-Chinese Bank	25
Sino-Belgian Bank	8
Societa C. I. Banearia di Shanghai	10
Yokohama Specie Bank	12
Average	19

Source: Tōa Dōbunkai, Shina keizai, II, 345–346.

military equipment, they employed special clerks for the purpose
of writing elegant letters to the mandarins with whom the firms
dealt frequently.[46] In later days when agency houses made substantial loans to Chinese authorities, foreign partners became even more
concerned to employ a Chinese in dealing with officials.[47] To meet
special needs, several tea marketmen were added to the comprador's
office of Heard's at Foochow and other treaty ports on the Yangtze
in the sixties.[48] In the bank comprador's office, the customs and
selling shroffs were replaced by several silver experts and money
collectors. Below all these clerks was the "larn-pidgin," an apprentice who worked in the comprador's office for the purpose of "learning business."[49]

There were gate-keepers or porters who sat "in grim majesty in a
little pigeon hole, just within the entrance door."[50] In addition,
watchmen usually worked at night, who would "go up and down
the length of hongs every half hour, and bang monotonously on a
wooden gong."[51] In time of crisis, armed watchmen were added,
as Augustine Heard, Jr., later recalled in connection with his Hong

Kong office in 1858: "To the two regular Chinese watchmen, I added two Manila-men, who were armed and who were ordered to repeat on a gong, hung at the front door, the bells struck on board the ships in the harbor. By this means we could know in a few minutes on waking up in the night whether our watchmen were awake or asleep."[52]

The servant in charge of miscellaneous affairs for the house was usually called the "boy" (*hsi-tsai* or *p'u-ai*), whence came such names as "tea office boy" and "table boy" (the waiter in the dining room).[53] A foreign manager might have a personal "boy," whose duties ranged from bringing fresh water to driving away mosquitoes from his mosquito curtain.[54] A Bostonian who visited Canton in the late 1840's wrote of the boy-servant: "He is a gentleman, and has a cooley [coolie] under him to do the dirty work, and though he will go on errands, he would scorn to carry a bundle."[55] A cook was always attached to the comprador's office as well.[56] At the bottom in the organization were the coolies (*lao ssu-wu*), who were described by a western newspaper as "the most faithful class of servants."[57] Aside from the usual "house coolies" who worked under the clerks and the "boys," there were some "chair coolies" who carried sedans.[58] All these men, recruited and guaranteed by the comprador, formed a well-organized body separated from the agency house. Thus, the comprador's office was referred to as "a business in a business."

The independence of the comprador's office raises the question of how far the foreign partner could trust his comprador and the comprador's staff. Basically, the relationship between the house and the comprador was a symbiotic one, from which they both benefited. In the period 1842–1860, they enjoyed unusual mutual trust. This was clearly evidenced by the system of upcountry purchases, under which foreign partners entrusted their compradors with missions inland to purchase tea and silk. The amount of money involved was usually large, but Augustine Heard, Jr., remarked that he "never knew a case where every dollar was not accounted for."[59] This mutual trust was general business practice at the time, as he observed on another occasion: "It [the business] was always conducted honorably, as between gentlemen. A man's word was his bond and could be thoroughly relied on. There was no such thing as sharp practice; there were no lawyers, and no going to law."[60] This assertion is further supported by the integrity of Heard's compradors in this period, who "were frequently men of wealth and always men of character."[61] Confidence was indeed essential, for as the manager of the Oriental Bank put it, "business cannot be conducted without trusting the man [comprador]."[62]

However, the situation changed from the sixties. The rapid development of steamers and communication methods (particularly the telegraph) accelerated the change in old business patterns. The opening of the Yangtze and other new treaty ports on the northern coast shifted the commercial center to Shanghai where, observed John Heard, the old personal ties between merchants weakened: "This Shanghai is not the place for doing business which Canton formerly was, or rather, the men we deal with here are not the same sort of men. They make no scruple of breaking a bargain when it does not suit them, and the only way of holding them is by bargain money."[63] After the sixties, therefore, compradors no longer enjoyed the kind of trust that foreign partners had formerly showed to them. Reports of the "unprincipled Chinese compradores" began to appear in the press, and the comprador's function as a treasurer gradually declined.[64] Compradors for young firms were sued by their employers from time to time.[65] During the twentieth century, the comprador's former trustworthiness was much missed in business circles.[66]

The foreign partners made efforts to check the comprador's malpractices. For his upcountry purchase of tea through Shanghai in 1858, A. F. Heard asked for information from teamen so as to determine whether the comprador had "squeezed" the house.[67] In 1871, Russell's managers found it necessary to institute an "audit system" to check up on the Chinese shroffs at the Kin-lee-yuen.[68] William Keswick of Jardine's kept watch over Tong King-sing both by frequently examining the cashbook, which was updated every morning, and by removing the treasury from his care.[69] However, since the house needed the comprador's services and cooperation, the partners were loath to embarrass the comprador openly. In 1859 when A. F. Heard wished to withdraw the keys to the treasury from the comprador, John Heard at Hong Kong advised him to do it cautiously and to explain to the comprador carefully: "I . . . still dislike to show mistrust. You might tell him, if you decide to retain the keys, that the plan had been adopted in Hongkong at the time of the troubles, and that the seniors at home preferred it done everywhere."[70]

In fact, it was not easy to keep a check on the comprador. Fung Heen, comprador to the Oriental Bank at Shanghai, was discovered in 1864 to have embezzled 138,000 taels from the bank for his own use. He was in charge of the treasury, where the boxes containing the silver were piled up. Because of the amount of business, counting the boxes was the only means of examining the silver. Under these circumstances, Fung Heen privately took the contents of thirty-eight boxes of sycee from the treasury, leaving the empty containers in a corner, where they "looked like full boxes in every respect." Although extra precautions had been taken by the bank manager to protect the treasury, the comprador nevertheless was able to remove silver privately from time to time.[71]

Disputes between foreign merchants and their compradors increased as time went on, especially after the sixties when more foreign adventurer-merchants appeared in the treaty ports. August-ine Heard, Jr., observed: "The newcomer, almost without money and without the heavy establishments, had a great advantage. He had little to lose and much to gain."[72] He could immediately set up a firm, and the security money deposited by his comprador made up the total capital of the company. Under these circumstances, the compradors were easily "tricked and fleeced."[73] If the foreign manager declared bankruptcy, the comprador found it very difficult to have his deposit returned. Cheng Kuan-ying was much upset over this inequality.[74]

If the comprador suffered a great loss—as he might do under the system of "complete guarantee"—or if his embezzlement was discovered, he faced several possible consequences. He might do all in his power to honor his commitments; otherwise he would be sued in the proper consular court or in the Sino-foreign jointly administered Mixed Court, then probably put into prison.[75] A few compradors committed suicide before their cases were brought to court.[76] Losses by compradors sometimes led to defalcation by them. Whereas very few compradors of the big firms defaulted, such cases happened more frequently among the young firms' compradors, especially after the 1860's.[77] Naturally, any such news made the foreign managers uneasy.[78] The most prominent case in the nineteenth century was perhaps that of Fung Heen, comprador to the Oriental Bank at Shanghai, who absconded in 1864, owing more than 100,000 taels to Chinese and foreign merchants.[79] Fung Heen's defalcation was followed by a more spectacular one in the twentieth century. Sir Ewen Cameron, manager of the head office of the Hongkong and Shanghai Banking Corp. at Hong Kong, paid tribute to the Chinese merchants' integrity at the turn of the century by pointing out that he had never known a Chinese defaulter.[80] Two decades later, the bank's Peking office suffered perhaps the heaviest loss (four million taels and more) in the history of the compradors' defalcations.[81]

Under the guarantee system a foreign firm could hold the comprador's surety responsible. For this reason Tong King-sing remitted to Sassoon & Co. 14,000 taels in 1875, and Cheng Kuan-ying reluctantly paid to Butterfield & Swire 100,000 taels in 1884.[82] But it was not always easy for the foreign house to secure such payment, and the surety might question the meaning of the words used in the security chop. Thus, there was dispute over the word *pao-chung*, as to whether it meant "those who recommend" or "those who financially guarantee."[83]

This confusion can be best illustrated in the case of Sassoon & Co. v. Fan Teh-sheng at Shanghai in 1884. Fan, the surety of the defaulted comprador Ch'en Yin-t'ang, adopted the strategy of delaying repayment of the money that he should have made good as arranged in the Mixed Court. Sassoon's then appealed to the British consul-general at Shanghai, who communicated with Shao Yu-lien, the Shanghai taotai, and requested him to require Fan to quickly make good the sum. If this method proved unworkable, the consul-general would then appeal to the British Minister at Peking, who would communicate directly to the Tsungli Yamen. In reply, the Shanghai taotai said that "Fan, according to the surety-paper, could only be made to *li-she* (undertake to set the matter right) . . . and not to *tai p'ei* (make good the losses) . . . and [thus] the [Mixed] Court could not *chui-p'ei* (force him to pay)."[84] Accordingly, he suggested a compromise arrangement. What happened afterward is not known but one thing is certain, that it was not always easy for the house to get back the money after the comprador's defalcation.[85] Some compradors even stole the security chop from the house when they absconded.[86]

Even if the house possessed the security chop, it did not necessarily win the suit. Preston, Breuell & Co. at Shanghai provided an interesting example. A-fun, the firm's comprador, was also an opium merchant in his own right. In 1864 he issued forged opium delivery orders to Takee and then absconded. In the suit brought by Takee against the firm, a verdict was given in favor of Takee, since A-fun was trusted by other merchants as being the firm's comprador, and the firm was held responsible for the acts of its employees.[87] Having suffered this loss, the firm then sued the comprador's sureties for the money. The firm lost once again, on the ground that in this transaction A-fun had acted as an independent merchant, not as a comprador, in which capacity the sureties were not responsible.[88]

The comprador might leave the house for one reason or another. However, he could not quit his post without fulfilling the term requirement as specified in the comprador's agreement.[89] If there was no time limit for his service, he had to give the firm several months' notice before resigning. On the other hand, the firm "had the right to discharge the comprador at any time" if it found him guilty of malpractice or laziness.[90] Before the comprador's departure, his accounts with the house had to be cleared, and the "chop" (seal) and books handed to the manager. He could also make a public announcement if he chose.[91] When the new comprador assumed his duties (*chieh-p'an*, "to take over the management"), he too might publicly announce his new post, together with the names of his staff.[92] But since many compradors recommended their sons or other relatives as successors, they could leave their comprador posts more easily. A case in point was Tong King-sing, who settled the matter quickly in 1873 when his elder brother, Tong Mow-chee, succeeded him.[93]

If the comprador left the house amicably, he usually recommended or guaranteed his successor. When Heard's Foochow comprador, Tong Loong-maw, left for Hankow to trade there as an independent merchant in 1862, he recommended his brother Akit to replace him as a "comprador on trial." John Heard wrote: "The Foochow Compradore [Tong Loong-maw] will not return to Foochow, where his brother will take care of the business, and if he prove on trial incompetent, he will get us another man."[94] In cases where one of the comprador's close family members succeeded him, the successor naturally inherited his financial rights and responsibilities.

Characteristics of the Institution

The unique and special elements of Chinese society that prevented foreign merchants from having direct trade with China were the very elements on which the comprador relied for his existence and for the successful operation of the business. While the foreign house depended on the guarantee system to ensure a comprador's trustworthiness, the comprador himself, in recruiting his own staff, is known to have relied heavily on China's traditional values, especially familism and regionalism. For the purpose of assuring a successful transaction and promoting the common interest, the comprador depended on the guilds, both as a comprador per se and as an independent merchant.

The comprador's heavy reliance on China's traditional values and institutions stemmed partly from the weight of his own responsibilities. He might handle hundreds of thousands of taels annually for the house, especially when his function was mainly that of a treasurer or an upcountry purchaser, and this job required the assistance of a dependable staff. Besides financially guaranteeing them and making good all losses suffered by the house on their account, the comprador was held responsible for any personal conduct of theirs that might do harm to the house.

The "Hong Kong poisoning case" of 1856 illustrates the seriousness of the comprador's responsibility. On December 10, 1856, when the second Sino-British war was in progress, a rumor arose in Hong Kong to the effect that a bakery named E-Sing had been bribed by the Chinese authorities in Canton to supply poisoned bread to the foreigners as a maneuver against the British. Upon learning of this, Augustine Heard, Jr., "sent for the Comprador who was a most excellent man," and the following conversation ensued:

"Comprador, what's all this row? . . . Who is the cook?" "He's a good man, a connection of mine." . . . With great emphasis and indignation,

171

"He's an honest man. He could not be bought. I *secure*." "Now, Comprador, you know this is a seious matter. *You* are the responsible man here. You know if anything goes wrong, we shan't look to the cook, but to you. You are the first. . . . I give you my word, that on the first symptom of anything of this kind, we'll blow your brains out." "All right," he replied, "I understand," and it was understood. Each knew that the other was speaking in earnest.[95]

The Heard's incident ended happily when the firm learned that their bread came from a Portuguese baker, not from E-Sing. But a comprador to a British firm was pressed so severely by his employer that he even made a coolie taste the bread so as to ascertain whether or not it was really poisoned.[96]

Realizing the seriousness of his responsibilities, the comprador was impelled to recruit those whom he could trust. Augustine Heard, Jr., wrote on the comprador in 1856: "Feeling his responsibility, we were sure that the Chinese he would engage for our service were always respectable, belonging, if not to his own family, to his own clan or village—persons whom he knew thoroughly."[97] Indeed, it was among their family members and fellow-townsmen that the compradors usually recruited their staffs.

As was the foreign house at this time, the comprador institution was mainly a family concern. Actually, many compradors regarded their posts as hereditary,[98] and hardly a noted comprador can be found who was not related in some way to other compradors. The family of Hsü Jun provided a good example. Hsü Yü-t'ing, a successful merchant at Macao, was employed by T. C. Beale, a partner of Dent & Co., as the firm's Shanghai comprador in the 1840's. His younger brother, Hsü Jung-ts'un, succeeded him. Their nephews Hsü Jun and Hsü Yün-hsüan worked in the comprador office as assistant compradors, and the former was finally promoted to comprador in 1861. Hsü Jun in turn guaranteed several of his family members as compradors: one of his cousins, Hsü Wei-nan, as Dent's Kiukiang comprador; another cousin, Hsü Kuan-ta, as the Shanghai comprador to Carlowitz & Co.; and one of his sons, Hsü Shu-p'ing, as the comprador to a German firm. He later partially guaranteed (for 10,000 taels) another cousin, Yang Mei-nan, as the Chefoo comprador to Butterfield & Swire.[99]

The Tong (T'ang) family was similarly connected with Jardine,

Matheson & Co. When Tong King-sing was its chief comprador at Shanghai, he guaranteed his elder brother, Tong Mow-chee (1827–1897), as the firm's Tientsin comprador (1871–1873).[100] When he moved on to head the China Merchants' Steam Navigation Co. in 1873, Tong Mow-chee succeeded him as chief comprador at Shanghai. After the death of Tong Mow-chee, the position was held successively by his son, T'ang Chieh-ch'en (1897–1904), and by his grandson, T'ang Chi-ch'ang.[101] Thus, the Tong family held the Jardine's comprador position at Shanghai successively for about half a century.

This long history was surpassed by the Jung family of the Chartered Bank of India, Australia, and China at Hong Kong. From the seventies, the Hong Kong comprador position at the bank was held by the Jung family for four successive generations: Jung Liang (1870's–1893), Jung Hsien-pang (1893–1914), Jung Tzu-ming (1914–1931), and Jung Tz'u-yen (1931 on). [102] The history of the Ho's and the Lo's in Jardine's Hong Kong office was equally interesting.[103] After several years of service at Jardine's Hong Kong comprador's office, Ho Tung (1862–1956) was promoted to comprador (1883–1900). He then made his two brothers, Ho Fu and Ho Kant'ang, assistant compradors, and they later succeeded him. The position was then held by Ho Fu's brother-in-law, Lo Ch'ang-chao.[104] From that time on the comprador position shifted back and forth between the two families.[105] Meanwhile, several other members of the Ho family served as compradors to other foreign houses at Hong Kong as well.[106]

Without exception, compradors to the American firms were family-oriented. For example, Heard's Shanghai comprador in the fifties was See Kai. His brother, See Yong, was the firm's Hong Kong comprador, and his son, Coe Lun, was the firm's Hankow comprador.[107] The Foochow comprador Tong Loong-maw guaranteed his brother, Akit, as his successor.[108] The Canton comprador Acum and the Shanghai comprador Atchune were cousins.[109] This closeness led A. F. Heard to conclude: "It will be hard to disturb the hierarchy of compradores save by bringing in members of the same clan."[110]

The success of the comprador institution was due no less to regionalism than to familism. Besides his family members, a comprador would trust fellow-townsmen whom he knew well. This characteristic partly explains why the Cantonese constituted the great majority of compradors before the eighties. Among the Cantonese compradors, many came from Hsiang-shan district. A peninsula close to both Canton city and Hong Kong, it was also the location of Macao, one of China's early international trade centers. Since most of the natives were engaged in maritime trade,[111] it was natural that many compradors came from the district. The term "Hsiang-shan men" was even regarded as the equivalent to "the comprador class."[112]

The Hsiang-shan compradors kept their hold on the position by frequently introducing their fellow-townsmen as compradors. When Jardine's Shanghai comprador Acum resigned his post in 1863, he recommended a fellow-townsman, Tong King-sing, to replace him; in this way, the Tong family began its fifty-odd years of association with Jardine's. When the noted intellectual comprador Cheng Kuan-ying decided to join the China Merchants' Steam Navigation Co. in 1881, he financially guaranteed one of his townsmen, Yang Kuei-hsüan, to succeed him as chief comprador to Butterfield & Swire. Hsü Yü-t'ing had been a successful merchant at Macao, only fifteen miles from his native village of Ch'ien-shan-chai, where he met Dent's partner T. C. Beale, and thus began the family's long-time compradorial career. He was succeeded by his nephew, the renowned comprador-merchant Hsü Jun, who later partially guaranteed his fellow-townsman Yang Mei-nan as comprador to Butterfield & Swire (first at Chefoo and then at Shanghai), a position that Yang held for about half a century. In the same fashion, See Yong, Heard's old Hong Kong comprador, stood surety for the firm's Shanghai comprador Atchune and its Foochow comprador Tong Loong-maw, both being his fellow-townsmen.

The Hsiang-shan compradors tended to recruit fellow-townsmen for their staff as well. A contemporary author observed: "Almost all the compradors in the employ of foreign merchants are natives of the District [of Hsiang-shan], servants recommended by these men will naturally be from their own part of the country."[113] Cantonese servants were numerous in the treaty ports and were so popular that they were paid much higher than were the natives employed at the different treaty ports.[114]

The compradors of Chekiang first challenged the supreme position of the Cantonese compradors in the treaty ports. Takee, a native of Ningpo, refused in 1851 to appoint a Cantonese as his vice-comprador when he was negotiating to be the comprador of Jardine's at Shanghai. In a letter dated April 4, 1851, A. G. Dallas reported to David Jardine from Shanghai: "If I have Takee in the house, it will to a great extent supercede the necessity of having such a Comprador as Affo [a Cantonese]. I sounded Takee as to the feasibility of co-operating with Affo, but he is against it, saying in the first place that he & all his friends being Ningpo men would not get on well with a Canton man, & that Affo has neither connexion—money or influence in this part of China."[115] Takee finally became Jardine's comprador on his own terms. Other noted compradors from Cheki-ang included Mu Ping-yüan, one of the first compradors at Shang-hai; Choping of Russell's, a very rich silk merchant; Wang Huai-shan, the first comprador to the Hongkong and Shanghai Banking Corp. at Shanghai; and Yü Hsia-ch'ing, the biggest investor in steamships in modern China. By the Republican period, the com-pradors of Chekiang overshadowed their fellow-compradors from all other provinces.

The natives of both Canton and Ningpo were noted for their commercial talent and maritime trade achievements. Ningpo merchants were particularly active in the Yangtze ports, where the Ningpo compradors consequently had much influence.[116] One of Heard's agents in the Yangtze ports claimed that it would be advantageous to have a comprador who could speak English, but more important was to have a comprador of good health (especially not an opium-smoker) who would be able to "make friends with the northern men."[117] Feeling the need of employing a Ningpo com-prador, this agent later wrote in 1866: "What would best suit the house requirements here [Hankow] is a Ning Po Compradore, who would possess a decided advantage both in procuring freight and selling imports. The trading people here are . . . from Ning Po or from districts much better inclined towards Ning Po men than Cantonese, and the ease and success with which the only two Ning Po Compradores in the place have made has been very marked, and with a Ning Po Compradore it would be much easier to do business in wax, tobacco, etc."[118]

After the 1870's, a group of compradors emerged from Kiangsu. This was mainly due to the rise of the Hsi family (of Soochow) which had been noted for their commercial activities from the early seventeenth century.[119] In order to escape from the Taipings, Hsi Cheng-fu and his three brothers fled to Shanghai in the early sixties, where they entered into partnership and in a very short time found employment with native banks. This led to the appointment of Hsi as comprador to the Hongkong and Shanghai Banking Corp. at Shanghai shortly after its establishment, probably during the late seventies.[120] Through his recommendation, many of his family members, relatives, and fellow-townsmen became compradors to the foreign banks at Shanghai. (See Table 26.) Just as most of the Kwangtung compradors came from Canton prefecture (for example, Tong King-sing, Hsü Jun, and Cheng Kuan-ying), and most of the Chekiang compradors came from Ningpo prefecture (Takee, Mu Ping-yüan, Yü Hsia-ch'ing), so most of the Kiangsu compradors came from Soochow prefecture.

An interesting question arises here. Why was Fukien, alone

Table 26. Noted bank compradors from Soochow, Kiangsu, in Shanghai, 1870's–1920's.

Comprador	Foreign bank	Period
Hsi Cheng-fu	Hongkong and Shanghai Banking Corp.	1870's–1907
Hsi Li-kung	Hongkong and Shanghai Banking Corp.	1908–
Hsi Lu-sheng	Hongkong and Shanghai Banking Corp.	1910's
Hsi Hsi-fan	Chartered Bank of India, Australia & China	ca. 1910's
	Russo-Chinese Bank	ca. 1920's
Wang Hsien-ch'en	Chartered Bank of India, Australia & China	—
Hsi Chin-hua	Mercantile Bank of India	ca. 1880's
	Russo-Chinese Bank	–1908–
Yeh Ming-chai	Yokohama Specie Bank	ca. 1900's
Wang Chun-ch'en	International Banking Corp.	ca. 1900's
Hsi Chü-hsing	Mercantile Bank of India	ca. 1900's
Hsi Te-hui	Guaranty Trust Co. of New York	—
Hsi Te-mao	Sino-Italian Bank	ca. 1920's

Source: Shang-hai ch'ien-chuang, pp. 37–38; Wright, *Impressions*, p. 540; Tōa Dōbunkai, *Shina keizai*, II, 384–385.

among the southeastern coastal provinces of China that were famous for their compradors, so singularly unproductive of compradors? Among the compradors discussed so far, only one was Fukienese— Ts'ai Hsing-nan, who around 1880 was Jardine's comprador at Hong Kong.[121] In 1908, out of sixty-three noted compradors in the treaty ports, only one was Fukienese.[122] Although the Cohong history shows that at Canton there were as many Fukienese hong merchants as there were Cantonese, and that in the early eighteenth century most of the linguists and ship compradors were Fukienese, their role in China's foreign trade had gradually decreased.[123] Apparently, after the abolition of the Cohong system in 1842, the Fukienese, unlike the Cantonese, failed to respond successfully to the new situation.

One of the main reasons for this failure was probably that, unlike the Cantonese who emigrated to other big Chinese cities and to America, the Fukienese emigrated mainly to Taiwan and Southeast Asia. It was difficult for a comprador to conduct business in a place where his fellow-provincials were few in number. Thus, a Fukienese comprador who could easily bring business to a foreign firm in Taiwan was hardly a successful comprador in Hong Kong.[124] Ts'ai Hsing-nan's term at Hong Kong was short, since he could not do much business with the local natives, most of whom were Cantonese. He was finally forced to give up his post to a Cantonese, Ho Tung, who began that family's long compradorial history.[125]

The Fukienese could not become good compradors even in their own province, because of the commercial specialization on a regional basis. Just as the Chekiang people specialized in silk and the Kiangsu people were noted for banking, the Cantonese were particularly good at the tea business. Since Fukien was one of China's main tea-producing areas, the Cantonese were usually employed there as compradors to conduct the tea business. The Cantonese expertise in the tea business was one reason that there were so many Cantonese compradors in Japan as well.

There seems to have been no formal organization among the compradors until the 1890's, when they established their own guilds. Nevertheless the compradors did participate in, and even led, other guilds of the period. Generally, there were two kinds of guilds in late Ch'ing China. Those based on geographical connections were called *hui-kuan,* and those centering on commercial connections were named *kung-so.* The former were "concerned with individuals," whereas the latter were "concerned with merchandise."[126] Hsü Jun and Tong King-sing were recognized leaders of the Cantonese guild in Shanghai, and at the same time were directors of the silk and tea guilds in Shanghai.[127] Because the ordinary guild could effectively boycott foreign merchants (whence came the verb *koong-so,* deriving from *kung-so* and meaning "boycott"[128]), the compradors were protected by it without necessarily having to form a separate guild of their own. In other words, they were able fully to utilize the existing guilds for their own purposes.[129]

Another reason that the formation of a formal comprador's organization came comparatively late in the history of the comprador institution was probably that the compradors, having a symbiotic relationship with the foreign house, did not like to provoke foreign merchants by organizing a guild. Chinese guilds were strong, and the foreign merchants resented them intensely.[130] A foreign merchant observed in 1879: "The name 'guild' had been a word which had created a feeling of loathing whenever and wherever it had been mentioned."[131] A Heard's partner later recalled the general situation in the late nineteenth century: "The Co-hong was abolished, but there was another Chinese system with which we had to count sometimes . . . and that was the Guild which controlled the native merchants. All the dealers in each article formed a guild. . . . The guild, as a body, imposed its laws on its members. No one dared to go contrast to its orders, and it constituted a most effectual system for boycotting that has never been imagined."[132]

Although there seems to have been no formal comprador organization before the nineties, the compradors did maintain informal close contacts among themselves. In 1864, the foreign merchants' Shanghai General Chamber of Commerce received "a letter . . . [having] reference to the relations between the compradors and their employers," which was jointly signed by fifty-two compradors.[133] Again, among the prizes for the horse races in the treaty ports, there were "compradors' gifts" at Hankow and "compradors' cups . . . presented by the compradors" at Shanghai.[134] But not until the nineties, when the comprador institution faced final abolition, did some of the compradors begin to strengthen their ties and to form their own special organizations so as to prolong their existence.[135]

A British wrote in the 1890's: "Like every other calling in China, the compradors have their guild or society, corresponding to our own trade unions, which looks after the interests of its members, and frames regulations for their government. So powerful are the majority of these guilds, that it is practically impossible to counteract their influence."[136] When many native banks at Shanghai went bankrupt in 1911, a bank compradors' association was formed for the purpose of getting back the chop loans, totaling 1,820,000 taels. The association was later called Chi-i hui (Benefit-promoting association).[137] In the 1920's, the steamship compradors on the Yangtze organized a guild called Kung-p'iao chü (Common ticket bureau), with a view to avoiding competition among themselves.[138] There was also a compradors' association at Hong Kong in the twentieth century.[139]

The newly-formed comprador's organizations made every effort to hinder direct contact between Chinese and foreign merchants. Although the Yokohama Specie Bank abolished the position of comprador in 1918, both the subsequent inconvenience and the boycott staged by other compradors forced the bank partially to restore its comprador system in 1924.[140] Later, when the foreign banks at Shanghai attempted to make direct contact with Chinese banks, the bank compradors' association vigorously objected. Consequently, such contact was postponed for some time.[141] Actually, this kind of pressure was not new, for early in the 1900's when certain Chinese and foreign merchants had tried to carry on direct trade, both parties suffered reprisals from compradors and thus incurred "unexpected losses."[142]

VIII   Beyond a Purchaser: Noneconomic Activities of the Comprador

The comprador's important role in modern China was by no means limited to the economic arena, which was the springboard for his other activities. The areas of his influence ranged from the living style to China's intellectual response to the West. Being comparatively rich, the comprador was able to buy gentry status and thus become a social leader. At the same time, he was politically active, playing a role in China's reform and revolutionary movements. Through his expertise in pidgin English and his knowledge of the West, he became a middleman between East and West, not only economically but also socially, politically, and culturally.

Style of Life

The treaty port constituted a hybrid culture, which in many ways was exemplified by the compradors. On the one hand, being the first group in China with professionally constant and intimate association with Westerners, they readily came under the Western influence. This contact affected their way of life, as in clothing, housing, entertainment, beliefs, and social relations—in a word, their style of life. On the other hand, they were strongly influenced by Chinese culture, having been raised in a Chinese society. In essence, therefore, they were cultural hybrids, in whom Chinese and Western cultures mingled.

This hybridization was indicated by the lack of uniformity in the kind of clothes that they normally wore. Many of them liked the Chinese style, such as "the long gown of blue silk and the closely fitting black cap on the shaven head."[1] As shown by their personal portraits, Hsü Jun, Cheng Kuan-ying, and Ho Tung wore typical Chinese clothes.[2] Wu T'ing-sheng, comprador to the British-American Tobacco Co., made a worldwide tour in 1907 and "retained his national costume throughout the whole journey."[3] Others preferred the Western style of dress. Chu Ta-ch'un's portrait shows that he wore a tuxedo.[4] On certain occasions, however, probably all of them found it advantageous to put on Western dress. For example, one of the international problems in the newly-opened treaty ports was the question of dual nationality, and Britain's Straits-Chinese subjects from Singapore identified themselves in China by wearing Western dress. This practice inspired the Cantonese—many of them compradors—at other ports "to adopt that garb whenever evil was afoot or when they were on the business of their foreign employers in the interior."[5]

That the comprador was a bicultural product was also illustrated by his home. He ordinarily had a Western-style building as his private residence, which was supplied with Western furnishings. At the turn of the century, for example, Ch'en K'o-liang (comprador to China Navigation Co., 1880's–1900's) lived at Shanghai "in a large English house erected in 1903," and Sun Chung-ying (comprador to Handl & Co. at Tientsin from 1888) owned "a magnificent house and garden, built at a cost of over half a million dollars and furnished with specially imported European furniture."[6] Yet such a house was usually decorated with fine Chinese porcelains and surrounded by Chinese-style gardens.[7] Its setting, too, confirmed the comprador's hybrid style of life, since the house was generally situated in a foreign settlement,[8] which in turn was surrounded by areas populated with Chinese and governed by the Chinese treaty port authorities.

Even the language spoken by the comprador with the foreigners was a multicultural product, being a mixture of Chinese, Indian, English, and Portuguese, with numerous local additions. Pidgin English followed the Chinese word order and included duplicatives in the Chinese fashion, like *chop-chop* (quickly). Other words were adopted from Chinese dialects, such as *junk* (a sailing ship) and *taipan* (the big manager). From the Anglo-Indian culture derived words like *shroff* (a money-dealer), *godown* (a warehouse), and *lac* (one hundred thousand). From the Portuguese came words like *joss* (idol), *amah* (a native nurse), and of course *comprador* (the purchaser). Some purely English words were used with a special meaning: *country ship* referred to the merchant trading in Far Eastern waters, notably between India and China, and *boy* meant the foreigner's Chinese servant, valet and butler combined, whose age might range from a callow youth of seventeen to a grandfather of seventy.[9] The word *pidgin* (or *pigeon*) was a corruption of the word *business*, so that the term *pidgin English* was itself pidgin English. Being mainly spoken and not written, pidgin English changed rapidly. Augustine Heard, Jr., gave a sample of it from 1856 during the Hong Kong poisoning incident, when he sent for the comprador to ask: "Comprador, what's all this row?" The comprador replied, "My no savey. Talkee that blead got spilum. My savey this house blead all light. [I don't know. They say the bread is spoiled. I only know the bread we have in this house is all right.]"[10]

The compradors' social life was similarly bicultural. On the one hand, they were influenced by traditional Chinese values and customs, such as Buddhism, Confucianism, familism, and geographical guilds. They were proud of their filial piety, celebrated Confucius' birthday, and few, if any, violated the rules of mourning.[11] Wang I-t'ing was a gifted calligrapher and one of the celebrated Chinese-style painters at the end of the Ch'ing. He was also a devout Buddhist and an active national Buddhist leader, having once served as president of the Chinese Buddhist Association.[12] Hsü Jung-ts'un (Hsü Jun's uncle) spent more than 100,000 taels in three years on geomancy, changing the sites of his ancestors' tombs with a view to bringing his family good luck.[13]

In contrast, although the compradors' intimate circle of friends did not include Westerners, they were probably the most Western-oriented Chinese in the nineteenth century in terms of social life. Western influences ranged from names and hobbies to social organizations. It was not common practice for a Chinese to have a Western given name even in the early years of the twentieth century, yet among the compradors there was a "Julian" T. A. Zi at Shanghai in the 1890's, "Robert" Ho Tung at Hong Kong in the 1880's, and even

"William" Affo at Shanghai in the 1850's.[14] A number of the compradors took up Western hobbies and entertainments. Some of them smoked cigarettes or pipes,[15] and many showed an early interest in the horse races that were sponsored and participated in mainly by foreigners in the treaty ports. For example, the compradors at Hankow sent gifts to the Hankow spring race meeting in 1865, and a "compradors' cup" was "presented by the compradors of Shanghai" to the Shanghai race of 1869.[16]

The Western orientation of the compradors' social life was also illustrated by their deep interest in social clubs, their great confidence in the regenerative power of athletics, and their active participation in Western-style socio-religious organizations such as the Y.M.C.A. Ho Tung was the first Chinese in Hong Kong to organize a Chinese club in the 1890's.[17] In the early twentieth century, Kuo Tsan was football secretary of the Chinese Athletic Association, and Yang Mei-nan (1872–1941) was the founder and first president of the Y.M.C.A. at Chefoo.[18]

Most of the compradors were probably dominated by Chinese ideas and values, but some of them changed their beliefs to become Christians. Compradors to French firms were likely to become Catholics, whereas compradors to Anglo-American firms were usually converted to Protestantism. The comprador-investor Chu Chih-yao (comprador to the Banque de l'Indochine at Shanghai from 1907) was a Catholic and operated a bookstore in the French Settlement of Shanghai for selling French and Catholic books at the turn of the century.[19] Wu T'ing-sheng (comprador to the British-American Tobacco Co. at Shanghai), son of Wu Hsiang-chun who had "for thirty-two years served as a pastor of the Baptist Mission in Northern and Southern China," was himself president of a small chapel at Hongkew, with his brother as secretary.[20] Li Ch'iu-p'ing, a wealthy comprador at Shanghai in the seventies and eighties, donated land for the missionary hospital of St. Luke's in 1880 and then "helped to raise money to build two wards, with an office and operating room."[21] Despite these facts, their Christian belief was perhaps somewhat superficial. Yang Mei-nan (comprador to Butterfield & Swire, 1895–1939), though interested in Christian organizations and missionary activities for years, formally became a Christian only on his deathbed.[22]

These manifestations of the Westernization of the compradors went side by side with their departure from Chinese tradition. Takee rejected Chinese customs by refusing to have his daughter's feet bound, although that was the usual practice in a well-to-do or rich family. At a time when interracial marriage was extremely rare in the treaty ports, she was later married (probably in the late 1850's) to the first commander of the Ever-Victorious Army, Frederick Townsend Ward of Salem, Massachusetts.[23] The compradors' further departure from Chinese tradition was most clearly evidenced by the way in which they educated their sons. Since the compradorship was by and large a family affair, they usually encouraged one son to become their successor. Their other sons would either attend the Western-style schools in the treaty ports or receive an education in American or European universities, with a view to assuming a career in *yang-wu* (foreign matters).[24] Very few compradors encouraged their sons to study Confucian classics so as to pass the time-honored civil service examination. This was in sharp contrast to the traditional way of achieving success which was usually adopted by both the gentry members and the traditional merchants.

Sociopolitical Activities

Being comparatively rich, the compradors gradually emerged in a position of social leadership. Their wealth was of particular advantage in securing this role because, like other rich merchants in the late Ch'ing, it purchased them examination degrees and official titles and thus entry to gentry status.[25] Many of them purchased the title of taotai, and hardly a noted comprador can be found who did not at the same time hold an honorary title. Men like Takee, Yakee, Hsü Yü-t'ing (see illustration), Hsü Jun, Tong King-sing, Cheng Kuan-ying, to name only a few, all held the taotai title. Among the forty noted compradors at Shanghai around 1900, at least fifteen were expectant taotai.[26] Some compradors purchased even higher titles. Hsü Jun, for example, obtained in 1872 the title of honorary department director of the Board of War (*ping-pu lang-chung*).[27] Like their fellow-merchants, the compradors cherished their honorary titles.[28]

The compradors purchased examination degrees and official

十六世德球公遺像

Comprador portrayed as a mandarin: Hsü Yü-t'ing (1793–1859), comprador to Dent & Co., Shanghai, 1840's. He purchased the taotai title. *Source:* Hsü Jun et al., *Hsiang-shan Hsü-shih tsung-p'u*, 7:17.

titles for two reasons. On the one hand, they were persuaded to do so by the officials so as to improve the government's poor financial situation. On the other, they were thereby obtaining a higher social standing, which was in itself desirable.[29] A closer look shows that this high social standing (referred to in the foreign partners' correspondence as "big face") was directly connected with their economic pursuits. Not only was it valuable when conducting business with other merchants, but it also was essential in dealing with officials on behalf of the foreign house, because only merchants with official titles could talk to mandarins on a socially equal basis.

Although a purchased degree or title was not as highly respected as a regular one, which was acquired through the civil service examination system, the compradors nevertheless performed many gentry functions and assumed responsibility for many of their activities. They raised funds for and supervised public works, such as canals, roads, and bridges, as demonstrated by Hsü Jun in his native distict of Hsiang-shan.[30] They compiled and published local histories or gazetteers, as in the case of Takee.[31] Choping and Ho Tung were famous as philanthropists.[32] As was the case with other gentry members, the compradors were interested in the promotion of education. They set up and supported local schools and academies. Tong King-sing was an active promoter for establishing the Anglo-Chinese School at Shanghai in the 1870's, and Ho Tung donated one million Hong Kong dollars to the University of Hong Kong.[33] In the nineties, Yeh Ch'eng-chung single-handedly established and maintained a successful private school named after himself at Shanghai, on which he spent at least 200,000 taels.[34] The compradors were equally interested in public health. For instance, Wei Yü was instrumental in establishing the Hong Kong Sanitary Board and was most helpful during the plague epidemic of 1894.[35] Compradors at Shanghai also helped to organize the Red Cross and the Shanghai Rescue Society.[36]

In times of disaster, the compradors, together with other gentry members, led relief activities. For this reason, Hsü Jun was honored by the government with an "honorific arch" (*p'ai-fang;* see illustration), and Cheng Kuan-ying and his father were particularly mentioned in the local history of Hsiang-shan.[37] Actually, this kind of gentry activity was a turning point of Cheng Kuan-ying's career,

The honorific arch with which the Ch'ing government honored
Hsü Jun (1838–1911), comprador to Dent & Co. (1861–1868),
for his efforts in famine relief in the 1860's. *Source:* Hsü Jun et al.,
Hsiang-shan Hsü-shih tsung-p'u, 9:1.

because as a result of his activities in raising funds for flood and famine relief in Shansi in 1878–1879, Cheng, a comprador to Butter-field & Swire at the time, first came to the attention of Governor-general Li Hung-chang, who later appointed him to manage various *kuan-tu shang-pan* enterprises. The compradors also shared the responsibility for maintaining order. Besides generally mediating controversies,[38] they organized and led the local militia as defense corps. For instance, early in the 1850's, Hsü Yü-t'ing helped the Shanghai taotai, Wu Hsü, to organize a local militia in order to protect themselves from the Taipings.[39] Later, Yü Hsia-ch'ing and his fellow-compradors raised a fund of over 300,000 taels to form a Chinese merchant corps (*shang-t'uan*), which in 1907 formally joined the foreigners' Shanghai Volunteer Corps and became its "Chinese company."[40]

Hsü Jun's social activities clearly illustrate the role of the compradors as members of the gentry. At Shanghai in the sixties, he was a leading figure in the silk, tea, opium, and Cantonese guilds. He held a directorship in a hospital and a school, and was active in the Chihli famine relief in 1876. In his Hsiang-shan home, he spent at least 28,000 taels for promoting local public affairs and compiling his clan history. He entered a fraternal association with such high officials as Liu Ming-ch'uan, and was regarded by a foreign lady (who had been deeply impressed by his magnificent home) as an Oriental nobleman.[41] The compradors' various social activities were vividly described by Tong Mow-chee of Jardine's in a letter dated September 22, 1877, explaining why he could not always attend to the comprador's office: "There are great many things which occupy some of my time, that I hate to have any thing to do with, but in some I cannot possibly avoid. As chairman of the Canton Guild, I have always some cases in hand for inquiry, arrangement or decision. Many officials and litteraties pass up and down through this port, they pay me their formal visits and I have to return them. [If] I forget to do so they take for impoliteness on my part. I have to make friends all around."[42] Some of the younger compradors tried hard to modernize their native towns. Yü Hsia-ch'ing spent about one million taels—a surprising amount for the time—in his native district of Chen-hai, Ningpo, for building modern schools, parks, wharfs, highways, railroads, and telegraph lines.[43]

In addition to such activities, the ordinary gentry promoted the Confucian doctrine and public morals, maintaining the local Confucian temple as well as proper social behavior among the masses. In contrast, the compradors seem to have cared little about the Confucian doctrine, for their rise to power was based precisely on a departure from orthodox Confucianism—a special concern for barbarian affairs and, more important, wealth. Realizing that the advancement of Confucianism would avail them little, they were interested instead in the development of commerce and industry. Indeed, their important role in China's modern history was to be played in the commercial world at the treaty ports. At Shanghai, they were leaders among their fellow merchant townsmen. For instance, Tong King-sing, Tong Mow-chee, Hsü Jung-ts'un, Hsü Jun, and Ch'en K'o-liang are known to have played a leading role in the Cantonese guild, which maintained its own school, hospital, and cemetery.[44] Takee, Yeh Ch'eng-chung, and Yü Hsia-ch'ing were leaders of the Ningpo guild (*Ssu-ming kung-so*).[45] Compradors were often the leaders of their particular trade as well. This was unmistakably evidenced by Tong King-sing and Hsü Jun who were prominent figures in the silk and tea guilds at Shanghai.[46] Sheng Heng-shan, Dent's Hankow comprador, established and presided over the tea guild at Hankow in 1868.[47] In 1898, Wu T'ing-sheng, comprador to the British-American Tobacco Co., was instrumental in organizing the Shanghai tobacco guild.[48]

Compradors continued to play a leading role in the new social organizations, such as the chamber of commerce. With the assistance of prominent compradors such as Feng Hua-ch'uan, Ho Tung, Ho Fu, Lo Ch'ang-chao, and Ch'en Keng-yü, the Chinese Chamber of Commerce at Hong Kong was established in 1900, with Feng as the first president.[49] Their fellow-compradors at Shanghai refused to fall behind, and four years later, when the Chinese Chamber of Commerce at Shanghai was formed, Hsü Jun and Chu Pao-san were elected as vice-presidents, and Chu Ta-ch'un and Yü Hsia-ch'ing played important roles.[50] By 1911 among its twenty-one directors were seven compradors, who represented seven different kinds of trade.[51] Compradors in other minor treaty ports followed these examples, such as Ch'en Lien-po in Canton, Yang Mei-nan in Chefoo, and Liu Hsin-sheng and Teng Chi-ch'ang in Hankow.[52]

For these activities, the compradors were honored by the Chinese and foreign governments and by the local authorities. Chang Tzu-piao was knighted by the king of Portugal, and Wei Yü and Ho Tung were knighted by the British king.[53] Hsü Jun and Cheng Kuan-ying were granted "honorific arches" by the Chinese emperor.[54] Several roads in the treaty ports were named after them. At Shanghai, there was a Yü Hsia-ch'ing Road and a Chu Pao-san Road; at Hankow, there was a Liu Hsin-sheng Road.[55] There is still a Ho Tung Road in Kowloon, Hong Kong.[56]

The compradors' role as social leaders was by no means limited to their native towns or to the treaty ports. With their expertise, their ever-growing economic power, and the rising influence of the merchant class as a whole, they became involved in China's politics on the national level. Having frequent contact with foreigners and thus being able to communicate with them and being familiar with their customs, the compradors were enlisted by the Chinese government to help in its dealings with foreigners. They were involved in each of China's major wars with foreign powers. Actually, their connections with politics can be traced back to the Cohong period. At that time compradors were supposed to keep a close watch on the foreign merchants' conduct and political intentions.[57] Later, in connection with the Opium War, Pao P'eng (comprador to Dent & Co., 1838–1840) played a pivotal role in the Sino-British negotiations of 1840–1841.[58] He had been a degree-holder and by 1841 was an eighth grade official. Trusted by Imperial Commissioner Ch'i-shan and knowing English himself, Pao carried on the actual negotiations with George Elliot, the British commissioner to China. He carried official documents back and forth between Ch'i-shan and Elliot, and frequently held long "private talks" with Elliot.[59] When in 1841 the Emperor determined to fight, both Pao P'eng and Ch'i-shan were punished for giving in too readily to the British demands.[60]

When the Ch'ing government was fighting against the Anglo-French allied forces in 1860, Hsüeh Huan, the Kiangsu governor, and Wu Hsü, the Shanghai taotai, asked the compradors Takee and Hsü Yü-t'ing for help in negotiating.[61] In the Sino-French war of 1884, Cheng Kuan-ying, a prominent comprador, was sent to Hong Kong by General P'eng Yü-lin to purchase weapons for the Chinese army. He was also dispatched to Annam and Siam to persuade the authorities there not to assist the French during the war.[62] Next came the Sino-Japanese war of 1894–1895. After China's defeat, the Ch'ing government faced the problem of the foreigners' setting up factories in the treaty ports. To cope with this situation, Governor-general Chang Chih-tung ordered the Shanghai hsien magistrate to solicit advice from nine "big merchants" (ta-shang) in Shanghai, five of them being compradors. Chang particularly mentioned the Cantonese merchants in Shanghai, whose opinions should be sought by T'ang Jung-chün, a Cantonese who was then a comprador to Jardine, Matheson & Co.[63]

The Ch'ing government enlisted the compradors' help not only in negotiating with foreign powers but also in dealing with internal crises. In order to fight against the Taipings, a foreign-officered mercenary force was formed in the sixties at Shanghai, which was led by Frederick Townsend Ward and supervised by the Kiangsu governor. Hsü Yü-t'ing, Dent's Shanghai comprador in the forties, helped raise funds for this Ever-Victorious Army, and Takee, comprador to Jardine, Matheson & Co. from 1849 to 1851, was instrumental in organizing it. Speaking English well and being one of the prominent merchants at Shanghai, Takee was responsible for its supplies for three years and worked closely with its commanders Ward and H. A. Burgevine. His opinion was sought frequently by the Kiangsu governor, Hsüeh Huan, and the Shanghai taotai, Wu Hsü. He held a second rank taotai title, one of the highest ranks that a comprador ever attained.[64] Meanwhile, Ting Kienchang, former comprador to Bedford & Co., served first as a scoutmaster and captain in the Ever-Victorious Army and later as the interpreter-in-chief to its commanders Ward and Charles George Gordon. A more remarkable figure was Wu Chien-chang, who was probably a former comprador to Russell & Co. He purchased the taotai title and finally became the Shanghai taotai in the fifties. He was the first Ch'ing official who tried (as early as 1853) to hire foreign troops and vessels to fight against the Taipings.[65]

Valuing the compradors' expertise, foreigners tried to get their help as well. In the Opium War, when the British occupied the Ting-hai Islands, Chekiang, they employed a young native named Mu Ping-yüan as comprador and brought him north with them. When they captured Shanghai, the Ch'ing officials fled. Mu then became responsible for maintaining order and thus was able to prevent the British troops from committing more crimes against the Shanghai residents.[66] The compradors' services were sought by Americans as well. When Colonel Humphrey Marshall, the American commissioner to China, first arrived at Shanghai in 1853, he engaged the services of a Cantonese comprador who had been in Shanghai for years in an effort to present his credentials to the Viceroy of the Liangkiang and, if possible, to go to Nanking, the capital of the Taipings. At the turn of the century, most of Shanghai was governed by the foreign Municipal Council. With constant pressure from the Chinese residents, it occasionally sought advice from distinguished Chinese, and for this purpose a Chinese consultative council was finally elected. In 1906, this council consisted of seven prominent merchants, three of them being compradors. The chairman was Wu Shao-ch'ing, the chief comprador of the German firm of Arnhold Karberg & Co. and president of the Chinese silk guild.[67]

In addition, the compradors actively participated in modern China's reform and revolutionary movements. Noted compradors are known to have participated directly in the 1898 reform movement. In that year Cheng Kuan-ying was active in Shanghai.[68] In the same year Wu Mao-ting, a former comprador to the Hongkong and Shanghai Banking Corp. at Tientsin, was assigned by Emperor Kuang-hsü as one of the three directors of the newly established Bureau of Agriculture, Industry, and Commerce in Peking. It was he who first proposed to the emperor that a new social organization—the chamber of commerce—be established.[69] After the coup d'etat, K'ang Yü-wei, leader of the reform movement, fled to Hong Kong, where Ho Tung, the most noted comprador at Hong Kong, personally welcomed him at the port on September 29, 1898. He then lived at Ho's home for two weeks before leaving for Japan.[70] After the reform movement was crushed by the Empress Dowager, some reformers in 1900 led a revolt at Hankow in which Jung Hsing-ch'iao (Yung Wing's nephew), a comprador to a Russian firm at Hankow, played a leading part.[71]

Other compradors were not contented with the reform program and went so far as to turn against the existing political order. Many of them are known to have participated in the revolutionary movement led by Sun Yat-sen, who came from Canton, as did most of the compradors. The main ideas, even sentence patterns, in Sun's proposal to Li Hung-chang, which Sun drafted at Shanghai in 1894, are reminiscent of those of the scholar-comprador Cheng Kuan-ying with whom Sun had been associated.[72] When Sun formed the Hsing-Chung hui, the first revolutionary organization, at Honolulu in 1894, quite a few compradors participated. Its first meeting was held in the home of Ho K'uan, a native of Hsiang-shan and at the time comprador to an American bank at Honolulu. He was elected vice-president of the organization.[73] Yang Ch'ü-yün, one of Sun's followers at Hong Kong and the moving spirit of the uprising against the Ch'ing at Canton in 1895, was a comprador to E.D. Sassoon & Co.; and Hsieh Tsan-t'ai, another of Sun's followers, was a comprador to the *South China Morning Post*, a foreign newspaper at Hong Kong.[74] When Sun's uprisings failed, some of the revolutionaries temporarily became compradors to foreign firms, for the special privilege of being employed by a foreign house made it difficult for the Ch'ing government to proceed against them. Thus, after failure of the 1895 uprising at Canton, Liu Hsiang, president of the Hsing-Chung hui, went to Hong Kong and served as comprador to an American steamship company.[75] In the same fashion, Yang Hsin-ju went to Taiwan and became comprador to the German firm of Melchers & Co., and Jung Hsing-ch'iao served as a Russian firm's comprador at Hankow.[76]

Some noted compradors at Shanghai took part in the 1911 Republican revolutionary movement. When the Shanghai revolutionary government was set up that year, many prominent compradors, such as Yü Hsia-ch'ing, Wang I-t'ing, and Chu Pao-san, played remarkable roles.[77] Among them, Yü Hsia-ch'ing was the most active. He not only gave financial support to the revolutionary government, but also bribed (with one million dollars) Ch'eng Te-ch'üan, governor of Kiangsu, to surrender.[78] When his similar effort failed in the case of Chang Jen-chün, governor-general of Liangkiang, he and Wang I-t'ing helped the revolutionaries to capture Nanking by military force.[79] Since the compradors had been particularly active in the local Shanghai government from 1905 to 1911, their participation in the revolutionary government had substantial influence on their fellow-merchants' political attitudes.[80]

In the Republican period, many compradors retained their interest in politics. For example, Ho Tung, contemplating the ceaseless civil war in China, suggested in the 1920's that China's future well-being should be sought through peaceful means, not war, to which end a conference of all warlords should be held.[81] The most noted comprador of the period was probably Ch'en Lien-po, who clashed with Sun Yat-sen's forces at Canton in 1924.[82] Another equally interesting figure was Yü Hsia-ch'ing, a leading magnate in modern China's steamship enterprise. He was active at Shanghai in the May Thirtieth incident of 1925. He was also a staunch supporter of Chiang Kai-shek (both came from Chekiang), and his important role in the split between the Nationalists and the Communists in 1927 remains to be explored.[83]

Since the comprador has often been regarded as a traitor and a running dog of imperialism, it is necessary to discuss the issue of comprador patriotism — or the lack of it. Since the comprador's role in foreign economic intrusion has already been discussed,[84] only his political activities will be explored here. It is true that a comprador sometimes identified his interests with those of the foreigners, but at the same time he was often most sensitive to foreign imperialism, for in his business dealings with foreigners, especially when disputes were involved, he saw the need of a strong Chinese government to back him up. While many compradors actively participated in modern China's reform and revolutionary movements, some of them (such as Tong King-sing and Hsü Jun) were engaged in modern enterprises with a view to competing with the foreigners. In concert with China's first large-scale boycott, which was directed against the United States, some compradors to American business firms resigned their posts in 1905.[85] On the intellectual level, the scholarly comprador Cheng Kuan-ying was a strong advocate of nationalism.[86]

This does not mean, however, that all of the compradors were patriotic. On the contrary, some of them were traitors in the true sense of the word. Certain facts indicate that Pao P'eng, who played a vital role in the Sino-British negotiations during the Opium War, was probably a traitor working secretly for George Elliot.[87] Another traitor during that war was also a Cantonese comprador named Pu Ting-pang, who must have greatly helped the British fleet, for after his arrest by Chinese authorities, the British troops encountered a serious problem in getting fresh water and consequently many became sick.[88] When Emperor Tao-kwang decided to fight, I-shan, the newly appointed imperial commissioner, determined to cut the supplies of the British troops at Hong Kong. But Lu Ya-ching, who had been comprador to the British ships, escaped to Hong Kong and continued to supply them with necessities. In order to attract Lu back to Canton, I-shan offered him an official position of sixth grade. Lu accepted.[89] In the same vein, Mu Ping-yüan is condemned by Chinese historians as a traitor for his activities with the British in the Opium War.

The most notorious collaborator among the compradors was probably Ch'en Lien-po in the twentieth century. Ch'en, a Cantonese and in the early 1920's comprador to the Hongkong and Shanghai Banking Corp. at Canton, led the Canton merchants' corps to oppose Sun Yat-sen's forces at Canton in 1924. Because of the facts that modern nationalism was on the rise in China, that Ch'en was evidently supported by an imperialist British government, and that Sun's government was able to make effective propaganda, this incident seriously hurt the ever-deteriorating image of the comprador in the minds of the Chinese people.[90]

But at the same time, one must keep in mind the fact that modern nationalism was generally weak in nineteenth century China and that noncomprador collaborators were not uncommon in the coastal provinces during China's wars with the foreign powers. At any rate, the compradors, quite contrary to the generally accepted contention, probably were not the most unpatriotic group of people in China. On the contrary, many of them were very nationalistic.

Intellectual Response to the West

The way in which a modern Chinese responded to the Western impact depended to a great extent on his knowledge of the West. This knowledge was usually acquired through either personal contact with, or close observation of, foreigners. It was such experiences that played a decisive role in the change of attitude toward foreigners on the part of the leaders of the "self-strengthening" movement—men such as Prince Kung, Tseng Ku-fan, and Li

Hung-chang.[91] Such experiences, too, made it possible for the compradors to respond realistically to the Western impact.

In this context, it would be significant to examine the formative years of several of the distinguished compradors. Historical sources permit discussion in detail of only two, Tong King-sing and Cheng Kuan-ying, though neither of them was necessarily a typical comprador. Tong King-sing (1832–1892), a native of Hsiang-shan, Canton, was exposed to foreigners and foreign influence from his childhood. Beginning in 1842 when Tong was only ten, he studied at Hong Kong in one of the earliest missionary schools in East Asia, that of the Robert Morrison Society (a Protestant institution) of Macao and Hong Kong. After completing his study at the Morrison school and another missionary institution, he served as an interpreter in courts of the colonial government in Hong Kong between 1851 and 1857.

In 1858, Tong became as an assistant secretary at the customhouse at Shanghai, and from 1859 to 1861 worked as its chief secretary and interpreter. Tong resigned from his customs post in 1861 when he joined Jardine, Matheson & Co. at Shanghai, first as a salesman of import goods at the newly opened Yangtze ports, and finally as the firm's chief comprador from September 1863. He held the comprador post until July 1873, when Governor-general Li Hung-chang invited him to manage the China Merchants' Steam Navigation Co. and other modern enterprises.[92]

Thus, before Tong entered into the service of government-sponsored enterprises, he had for thirty-one years (1842–1873)—from the age of ten to the age of forty-one—been associated with nearly all of the most important Western institutions in China: the missionary school, colonial government, foreign-managed maritime customs, and the foreign commercial house.[93] With this background that he himself described as a "thorough Anglo-Chinese education,"[94] Tong could respond effectively to the West as both a substantial investor and a competent manager.

Cheng Kuan-ying (1842–1923) had a similar early connection with foreigners.[95] Like so many other prominent compradors at the time, Cheng was a native of Hsiang-shan, Canton. His father was a school teacher, and he probably came from a lower middle-class family. His elder brother, Cheng Chi-tung, was a comprador first to Dent & Co. (1860–1867) and then to Russell & Co.[96] The younger brother's failure to pass the preliminary examination or to obtain the *hsiu-ts'ai* degree led him to abandon the traditional education and go to Shanghai to enter trade when he was seventeen years old. There he learned some English from his uncle Cheng Hsiu-shan, a comprador to Overweg & Co., who invested actively in Shanghai in the seventies and eighties,[97] and more English from John Fryer (1839–1928), one of the most influential missionaries in China.[98] After two years' apprenticeship, Cheng worked from 1860 to 1867 at the British firm of Dent & Co. in charge of freighting and warehouses, under the direction of the noted comprador Hsü Jun and his uncle Hsü Jung-ts'un.[99]

After serving as an interpreter in a Shanghai tea hong for several years, Cheng was employed at Shanghai from 1873 to 1881 as the comprador to the China Navigation Co., founded by the British firm of Butterfield & Swire in 1872.[100] Before 1882, while Cheng was connected mainly with foreign firms, he was naturally exposed to a great deal of foreign influence. He read Western newspapers and talked widely with foreigners, including some Japanese.[101] During the nineties he became an enthusiastic reader of the *Wan-kuo kung-pao* (The Globe Magazine), an influential journal sponsored by foreign missionaries which contained articles on religion, science, history, and world news.[102] According to Timothy Richard, a missionary whose writings greatly influenced Cheng, Cheng was so fascinated by the Western idea of progress that he once bought a hundred copies of the translation of Robert Mackenzie's *Nineteenth Century—A History* (*T'ai-hsi hsin-shih lan-yao*) and distributed them to his Peking friends.[103]

The compradors' background of missionary education was noteworthy. The experiences of Tong King-sing and Cheng Kuan-ying were by no means exceptional, for compradors had ordinarily known foreigners in one way or another before they became compradors. For one thing, they had to learn English. Although some might learn English from private Chinese and foreign tutors or in the Chinese government schools, a great number were brought up by the missionary schools.[104] In 1865, the Church Missionary Society established the Anglo-Chinese School (Ying-Hua shu-kuan) at Shanghai, as an institution suited "chiefly to the children of the mercantile class," at which the "English language shall be taught carefully." John Fryer, formerly of St. Paul's College at Hong Kong, was employed as headmaster. Among those who "kindly consented to be referred to concerning the institution" were William Keswick, Jardine's Shanghai partner, and Choping, comprador to Russell & Co.[105] Other compradors who were educated by the foreign missionaries included Liu Hsin-sheng, "one of the wealthiest and best known Chinese businessmen in Hankow," and Wu T'ing-sheng, an active comprador in Shanghai.[106] With the opening of the interior, especially after the Chefoo Convention of 1876, the missionaries' influence increased as they began to move inland in large numbers.[107]

The missionaries generally put heavy emphasis on education. From the late seventies, an organization was established at Shanghai for the primary purpose of educating prospective compradors. It was called the Anglo-Chinese Department of St. John's College.[108] A report of 1883 reads: "The pupils are mostly the sons of compradores and the higher class of Chinese in the [Shanghai] Settlements. . . . The course includes reading, spelling, writing, composition, grammar, arithmetic, natural physics, geography, etc. . . . The boys appear to be thoroughly well taught and well prepared for clerical or other duties in foreign hongs."[109]

With such backgrounds, the compradors were fully exposed to the Western influence and readily acquired new ideas and attitudes. This influence in many ways helped China to respond realistically to the West. First, the compradors became interested not only in promoting education in the treaty ports but also in helping the Chinese students to study abroad. The Chinese educational mission to the United States in 1872–1881 — China's first project for training students abroad—was promoted by Yung Wing (1828–1912), the first Chinese graduated from an American university (Yale, 1854), who was in 1859 an agent of Dent & Co. for tea purchase in Kiangsi.[110] The noted comprador Hsü Jun, who was Yung's fellow-townsman from Hsiang-shan, Canton, was appointed in 1873 by Tseng Kuo-fan to assist in this project.[111]

Besides, some of the compradors were interested in newspaper and printing enterprises. Partly for the purpose of keeping Chinese in the treaty ports well informed, and partly to compete with the foreign-owned *Shen pao*, the leading Chinese newspaper in Shanghai established by the British merchants in 1872, Tong King-sing and Yung Wing established at Shanghai in 1874 the newspaper *Hui pao*, one of the earliest newspapers owned by Chinese.[112] An abortive effort was later made by Cheng Kuan-ying to set up an English newspaper named *Chiao-she pao* (the negotiation newspaper) in Shanghai.[113] Lo Ho-p'eng, comprador to the Hongkong and Shanghai Banking Corp. at Hong Kong, single-handedly established the newspaper *Yüeh pao* at Hong Kong in 1885, with his own capital of 21,600 taels ($30,000).[114] T'ao Mei-sheng, a Shanghai investor who was the comprador to the British Consulate at Shanghai for more than twenty years, founded sometime before 1907 the newspaper *Sze-sze pao*.[115] Meanwhile, *Shen pao* was purchased in 1906 for $75,000 by its Chinese comprador, Hsi Yü-fu, who was also its manager.[116] The T'ung-wen shu-chü, a printing factory established by the Cantonese comprador Hsü Jun in 1882, was one of China's first lithographic printing enterprises.[117]

Finally, living in the treaty ports, the compradors were easily influenced by the Western legal ideas and institutions that underlay modern business—such as the laws of contract and limited liability. In dealing with foreigners, they seem to have realized the importance of the worded contract, for they generally concluded contracts with their foreign employers. The legal decisiveness of the contract was demonstrated clearly in a lawsuit, the case of Holliday, Wise & Co. v. Chow-gin-kwei, comprador to the Commercial Bank of India, on December 30, 1856: "The said company bought Bills from the comprador and claimed under the arrangement for four days grace. The comprador denied. Since there was no stipulations for time inserted in the contract, the comprador won the case."[118] Not only did the compradors enter into contracts with foreign firms, but they also made written agreements with their comprador partners.[119]

The compradors learned the concept of limited liability from the foreign merchants as well. It had been the practice in the treaty ports, according to Chinese custom, that the comprador was held entirely responsible for the conduct of his staff, as Augustine Heard, Jr., recalled: "The principle of responsibility is essentially Chinese, and is seen through the whole system of Chinese polity. On it we relied with entire confidence."[120] But the Hong Kong poisoning incident of 1856 somewhat changed the Chinese "principle of responsibility," as properly understood by the comprador.

As explained earlier, the poisoning incident occurred on December 10, 1856, during the second Sino-British war. It started with rumor that a bakery had been bribed by the Chinese authorities to supply poisoned bread to the foreigners. Before the plot was discovered, some foreigners were affected and several of them died, including the wife of Sir John Bowring, governor of Hong Kong. Alum, the proprietor of the E-Sing Bakery involved, was arrested in Macao and brought over to Hong Kong, where he was put in jail to await trial. Augustine Heard, Jr., later commented: "Alum was tried in an English Court with the advantages of English technicality, and, as was feared would be the case, he could not be proved to have mixed the arsenic with the bread, and was acquitted."[121]

This court decision, contrary to the Chinese "principle of responsibility," brought about a change of attitude in the Chinese in general and the compradors in particular, as Augustine Heard, Jr., further observed: "This was a great blow to the sense of all right-thinking and respectable Chinamen. They were disposed to believe that Alum had not personally taken an active part in the crime . . . but by all Chinese law and custom, he, as Head and owner of the establishment, was responsible for the acts of his workmen and merited all the punishment—even unto death—which might belong to them. It is easy to see what a vast change was made by this decision in our relations with our Chinese employees. Before it we were under as complete a safeguard from their possible hostility as could be devised. After it we had no protection whatever."[122]

The effect of this incident is illustrated by the changed attitude of Heard's comprador toward the "principle of responsibility." Before the trial, he had looked upon Alum as probably innocent but, as "Head" of the establishment, deserving of death nonetheless. This attitude is evidenced by the following conversation between Augustine Heard, Jr., who had just learned of the poisoning, and his comprador:

[Heard:] "There's no danger of his [the cook's] doing what has been done today, putting poison in the food?"
[Comprador:] "No. He's an honest man. He could not be bought, I *secure*."

[Heard:] "Now, Comprador, you know this is a serious matter. *You* are the responsible man here. You know if anything goes wrong, we shan't look to the cook, but to you. You are the first."

[Comprador:] "All right, I understand."[123]

But some weeks later, after Alum had been acquitted, Heard noticed a difference. He remarked one morning that the breakfast was late. Upon learning that this was owing to the change of cooks, he asked the comprador to "secure" the new cook. However, having learned of the concept of limited liability from the case of Alum, the comprador now "showed his consciousness" of it and refused, as Heard continued:

[Heard:] "Comprador, it is something more than a cook that we want. We must have in these times an absolutely honest man, a man we can trust. Who is this man? Where does he come from? Do you know all about him?"

[Comprador:] "Oh, I think he's all right. He comes from Gibb Livingston's House. Mr. Gibb's Comprador says he is a good man."

[Heard:] "Yes, that is all very well. But do you *secure* him? You know it is *your* business."

"No," he replied with a smile, which showed his consciousness that we had changed all that, "I can't secure him, but I think he's all right." And I was obliged to put up with that.[124]

The ideas of the scholar-comprador Cheng Kuan-ying most vividly illustrate the way in which the compradors responded to the West. Although the compradors were consulted occasionally by high officials and sometimes proposed reforms themselves, Cheng Kuan-ying provided a systematic reform program that made him famous. Intellectually, Cheng may not have been a typical comprador, in that he was one of the most progressive reformers of his time, but his ideas in a way exemplified the compradors' response to the West. As a scholar-comprador with wide contact among foreigners and an acquaintance with missionary writings, especially those of Timothy Richard, as well as with contemporary Chinese literature, Cheng was in a position to further his ideas.

In 1862, after two years of service in Dent & Co.'s comprador office and at the age of only twenty, Cheng published a book on reform under the title *Chiu-shih chieh-yao* (Important suggestions for the salvation of the time), which was later reprinted in Japan. In

1870–1871, after he had left Dent's and before he had assumed his comprador post with Butterfield & Swire, he was able to revise and enlarge it. This new edition, under the title *I-yen* (Easy words), appeared in 1871 and was circulated in Japan and Korea.[125] The last version, *Sheng-shih wei-yen* (Warnings to the prosperous age), which came out in 1893, had a much greater influence. Eventually this book was presented to the Emperor Kwang-hsü, who ordered the Tsungli Yamen to publish and distribute it to officials. It was popularly read in the decade after its publication and had a vogue before the 1898 reform movement.[126] It was also one of the books Mao Tse-tung liked to read in his boyhood.[127] Cheng published other works afterward, including his poems and two sequels to the *Sheng-shih wei-yen.*[128]

A perusal of Cheng Kuan-ying's writings evokes the image of a man who was acutely alive to the critical issues of his day and wrote prolifically about them. Both *I-yen* and *Sheng-shih wei-yen* were full of humanitarian sentiments, describing vividly the social abuses of the time. In particular, Cheng mentioned foot-binding, illiteracy, the inhumanity of penal practices and prison conditions, and the general misery in the countryside. His reform programs included relief of the poor, industrialization, and agricultural and legal improvements.

Yet Cheng's significance in modern China's intellectual history lay not so much in these humanitarian sentiments as in the way in which he responded to the West, in his capacity as a comprador-reformer. Cheng's realistic response to the Western impact was revealed by his comment that, in his own period, Chinese history had undergone a really significant change. To illustrate this point, he outlined three broad periods of Chinese history. History from ancient times to the end of Chou (third century B.C.) was feudalistic (*feng-chien*), from Ch'in to the treaty system of 1842 was centralistic (*chün-hsien*, literally, "prefecture and district"), and from the treaty system onward was internationalistic (*Hua-i lien-shu* or "Sino-barbarian interrelationship").[129] Of all the turning points in Chinese history, Cheng singled out the treaty system as an unprecedented big change (*ta pien-chü*), for unlike China's traditional barbarian neighbors, the Westerners were the first foreigners seriously to challenge Chinese civilization.[130]

But the Western impact, though unprecedented in scope and intensity, was not, according to Cheng, unnatural.[131] What concerned him was the direction of change, not change itself, for he regarded change as not only natural but also inevitable in the course of history. Since the Westerners' arrival in China was therefore natural and unavoidable, the crucial point was to respond to it wisely. The "wealth and power" (*fu-ch'iang*) of the West stemmed from its civilization, which was a complex of centuries-long accumulation, to which an indiscriminate response would be ineffective and undesirable.[132] Cheng's idea of a selective response—an idea shared by his contemporary scholar-reformer Kuo Sung-t'ao—made him outstanding among the early reformers.[133] But what reform program did Cheng regard as of primary importance?

Basically, Cheng was an institutional reformer. The salient features of his reform programs included the parliamentary system and a strong emphasis on commerce and industry. Working for two British business firms for at least fifteen years, Cheng was an admirer of British political life. He saw the need of introducing the parliamentary system to bring together the ruler and the ruled. This idea was first vaguely mentioned by Cheng in one of his early books, *I-yen*, and when China was defeated by France in 1884, he clearly and directly proposed to the government that the parliamentary system be instituted.[134] Thus, he was probably the first among modern China's reformers to propose the establishment of a parliament, for it was not until 1890 that T'ang Chen and Ch'en Ch'iu made a similar suggestion.[135] Cheng was not a true democrat, but he had a deeper understanding of political reform than most of his contemporary reformers. For instance, in contrast to both T'ang and Ch'en, who would have limited the parliament to include only officials, Cheng conceived of parliament as representing the common people as well.

A corollary of China's internal political reform, according to Cheng, was a change in its traditional attitude toward foreign countries. He discovered the efficacy of international law—a Western device of considerable value for defense against the West. But China could benefit from it only when she abandoned the traditional Confucian concept of universal empire (*t'ien-hsia*) and came to regard herself as a member of the family of nations.[136] As to China's foreign policy, Cheng advocated caution. He vigorously criticized the Ch'ing-liu Tang (Purification party), a group of scholar-officials who were generally against the self-strengthening movement and yet advocated a more belligerent foreign policy.[137]

In Cheng's view, China would ultimately benefit from a cautious foreign policy, which would promote her own commerce and industry. If she could compete successfully with foreign goods, the foreign merchants would be forced to lose money and would naturally go home. If China were wealthy, she would also be strong. Even if China then challenged foreign countries to war, they would seek ways to avoid it.[138] As Cheng saw it, China had been suffering foreign incursion because of an inability to make herself strong. To support his argument, Cheng cited Japan's modern history. At first, Japan, like China, suffered from foreign exploitation. But since Japan had "emulated Western manufacture and revitalized her commerce," among other matters, she was able not only to avoid the harmful aspects of the treaty system but in fact to benefit from it.[139]

Cheng Kuan-ying's economic reform program was even more significant, for in this field he was most competent. Being a comprador, he saw more clearly than anyone before him the dynamic function of industry (*kung*) and commerce (*shang*) in Western society. While the high officials were preoccupied with military self-strengthening, Cheng ascribed to commerce and industry a comparable role in bringing about a strong nation. He argued that since wealth and power were interrelated and mutually dependent, they deserved equal attention. As time went on, he put more and more emphasis on "national wealth."[140]

To achieve such wealth, Cheng asserted that China had to catch up with the West in three key areas. In order to acquire true talents, it was essential to reform the civil service examination system and to establish technological and professional schools. To utilize natural resources, the importance of mining and the modernization of agriculture was stressed. To promote commerce, the government must reform the tax system and abolish the likin. At the operational level, there were two ways to augment national wealth—increase Chinese exports and decrease Chinese imports. In both cases, Cheng realized the economic role of the government.[141]

Having asserted that the strength of the West stemmed from

wealth, and that wealth in turn came from commerce and industry, Cheng argued that it would be more significant for China to learn to wage "commercial warfare" (*shang-chan*) than "military warfare" (*ping-chan*). The world of his time, as Cheng saw it, was a world of commercial rivalry.[142] Cheng was in fact one of the first reformers in modern China to advance mercantile nationalism. His strong emphasis on commerce and industry distinguished his reform program most sharply from the ideas of other contemporary non-comprador reformers, such as Feng Kuei-fen, Kuo Sung-t'ao, and Wang T'ao. All in all, the significance of Cheng's response to the West seems to lie in his economic interpretation of world history in general and of Western society in particular.

Without consciously deserting orthodox Confucianism, Cheng Kuan-ying nevertheless challenged some of China's traditional values. As a modern-minded comprador, he questioned the validity of the existing social stratification, according to which the merchant was at the bottom. He argued that since the role of the modern merchant (an entrepreneur) was much more important in function and scope than that of his predecessor (a trader), he deserved a higher social status. That is, he should be treated as a member of the gentry and have access to the officials. With this view in mind, Cheng severely criticized bureaucratism, especially the system of *kuan-tu shang-pan* (government supervision and merchant operation), which curbed a merchant's entrepreneurship.[143] The merchant, in his pursuit of a profit that was justified and desirable, should have a sense of pride instead of shame.[144] Indeed, Cheng was the first merchant in modern China to provide an ideological rationalization of his own class.

Other ideological changes advocated by Cheng included a stress on nationalism. He regarded China as one member of the family of nations, an understanding that was prerequisite to the rise of modern nationalism. In fact, he was one of the first reformers in modern China not only to view nationalism in terms of relationships between nations, but also to see it against the background of China's internal factors, such as familism. He remarked, "The reason why China is poor and weak whereas the West is rich and strong lies in their different social customs (*li-chiao*)—the familism (*chia-tsu chu-i*) of China and the nationalism (*kuo-chia chu-i*) of the West."[145] Cheng later played a leading part in China's first large-scale boycott, which was directed against the United States in 1905, in connection with a dispute over American immigration policy and abuse of the Chinese in America.[146]

Criticizing China's familism, Cheng questioned concomitant Confucian values as well. As to the Confucian ideal of the omnicompetent scholar-official who entrusted technical matters to his assistants, Cheng contended that the functional differentiation of officials was necessary in modern times.[147] In comparing Chinese merchants with those of the West, Cheng asserted that China's custom of ancestor worship and reluctance to leave the home town inhibited the development of commerce.[148] Indeed, Cheng had never been a pure Confucian scholar, and as time went on, he took further steps away from orthodox positions. According to his own account, he had become interested in various Chinese schools of thought when he was young, and with the passage of time, he showed an increasing interest in popular Taoism.[149] His nonaffiliation with Confucianism is further demonstrated by the fact that he advocated a theory of "common-origin" (*t'ung-liu*), which maintains that Taoism, Buddhism, and Confucianism originated from the same source and were not really different. Accordingly, they should be treated equally.[150] This constituted an obvious protest against the predominant position of Confucianism.

All in all, Cheng Kuan-ying's reform programs reflected the views of the newly emerged merchants in the treaty ports, and his intellectual outlook was markedly influenced by his comprador background. This fact was illustrated by several of his more important ideas, such as his interpretation of the impact of the West, his proposal for a parliamentary system, his advocacy of a strong nationalism combined with a prudent foreign policy, his emphasis on the dynamic role of commerce and industry, and his rationalization of the new merchants' status. Finally, he challenged some of China's traditional values, such as familism and functional universalism. Such knowledge was not acquired through a reading of the Confucian classics; rather, it resulted from his association with the foreigners as a comprador.

IX Conclusion: Significance of the Comprador as a Middleman between East and West

For China until about the mid-nineteenth century, the Pacific Ocean had always been a barrier, an end. After the establishment of the "treaty system" in 1842 it became a bridge, a starting place. The treaty ports, where China met the West, remade Chinese life. Against this background, the significance of the comprador becomes more clear. Acting as a middleman between two worlds, he played a strategically important role in modern China's economic growth, social change, and general acculturation.[1]

The comprador's uniqueness—both its strengths and weaknesses—lay in the fact that he was a middleman. This characteristic was clearly manifested by his amorphous economic status, according to which he performed a multifunctional role. Hired under contract by a firm and receiving a salary for his services, he was an employee. Receiving a commission from a transaction made through him, he was a broker. Entrusted by foreign merchants with the sale and purchase of goods as well as the collection of business information, usually at remote places, he was an agent. Using his own name in all transactions and responsible both for native bank orders and for the goods purchased from, and sold to, Chinese, he was a contractor in charge of transactions "farmed out" to him. Finally, besides performing the ordinary comprador functions, in most cases he operated his own business and was thus an independent merchant. Engaged in several professions at once, he belonged in particular to none of them. He was, in short, a middleman.

Yet the significance of the comprador for China's response to the West lies not so much in his function as an ordinary medium, but rather in his role as a bicultural middleman between East and West. An examination of his relationship with the foreign merchant throws light on this role. A salient feature of the relationship was its symbiotic character. For his part, the comprador depended too heavily on the foreign merchant. First, not having started out as an independent merchant, he fastened his hopes for success on his connections with the foreigner and thus on China's unstable foreign relations. Second, the comprador occupied a still more passive position in that the foreign merchant took the initiative in employing him. Finally, a comprador's functions, which generally reflected those of his employer, were mainly determined by the needs of the foreign house.

On the other hand, the foreign merchant equally relied on the comprador for operating his business smoothly. As a middleman, the comprador performed three major functions in a foreign house. He was at once the head of servants, the Chinese manager, and the agent in the interior. However, his diverse functions were greatly limited by local factors. Although he had general functions, the importance of each function differed from place to place. Thus, while the comprador's functions were many-faceted, his role was nowhere the same, and all of the compradors had to adapt themselves to existing local circumstances.

Adjustment to the indigenous conditions was also the key to success in China for the foreign merchants. It is clear that their entrepreneurship on the local scene was essential to achieving a better connection with the Chinese merchants, including the compradors. At the times when an agency house enjoyed successful relations with able compradors, its business was carried on smoothly and profitably. In contrast, a deteriorating relationship brought the loss of business. Thus, the foreign partners exerted themselves to woo compradors and to cultivate Chinese connections. Furthermore, a foreign house often developed its business according to the background and ability of the comprador. Tong King-sing, for instance, who could fulfill Jardine, Matheson & Co.'s general needs, was also instrumental in developing the firm's shipping business. He contributed more to Jardine's as an entrepreneur than as an upcountry purchaser, just as Tong Loong-maw was more valuable to Heard's as a produce purchaser than as a freight broker.

Because the success of the foreign firm and the comprador were mutually dependent on the whole, closer cooperation was more profitable for both. A comprador of high social standing or "big face" was desirable to the foreign partners, since he could bring more business to the house. By the same token, a large foreign firm was more attractive to the comprador than a small one, since it would enhance his social standing and thus promote his private business. Their relationship was such that neither the foreign merchant nor the Chinese comprador was in a position of absolute control. Indeed, although foreigners dominated the scene, Chinese and Western merchants met halfway in the common pursuit of profit.

This symbiotic relationship, apart from its economic consequences, had noteworthy implications for China's response to the West. In the history of modern Sino-foreign contact, two of the major forces having an impact on China were the Western merchants and the missionaries, and to both of them China responded differently. The reasons for the gentry's hostility toward the missionaries were manifold and deep-rooted. Aside from the Christian doctrines of original sin and the virgin birth, for instance, which the Confucian gentry criticized as superstitious and heterodox, the gentry, as the responsible local elite throughout the country, were disturbed by the missionaries' emergence as would-be rivals in the role of social leaders, especially in the fields of education and social welfare. In the last analysis, by associating closely with the lower classes and the discontented and conveying the Christian message of spiritual salvation, the missionaries posed a natural threat to the social order of which the gentry were the local protagonists.[2]

The case was entirely different for the foreign merchants. Their aim of making money was much less ambitious than the goal of the missionaries to save souls, and they offered little ideological challenge to the social order. Rivalry with the foreign merchants seems to have come less from the Chinese compradors and merchants, to say nothing of the gentry, than from one another. This did not mean, however, that the officials and gentry were free of hostility toward Western merchants; indeed, some of the keenest competition encountered by foreign firms came from the China Merchants' Steam

Navigation Co. But the point is that, compared with the missionaries, the foreign merchants received less resistance from Chinese society, and their symbiotic relationship with the compradors and more friendly relations with the gentry provided an easy avenue for introducing modern technology and ideas to China.

Since the comprador was an intermediary between Chinese and foreign merchants, his role in modern China was mainly economic. Yet in one sense the effect of his economic activities on China was peripheral, for neither foreign trade nor the treaty ports, with which he was inseparably connected, played a pivotal role in the country's economic development as a whole. Prior to the Opium War, China's foreign trade had been regarded as merely a special and unimportant form of interregional trade, and its growth had been contained within the traditional social order. Furthermore, its volume was small when compared with China's size, population, and produce. More impotant, the new growth of the economy encouraged by foreign trade radiated out only slightly into the traditional economy; it remained largely bottled up in the treaty ports, which in many respects became foreign-influenced enclaves. Thus, the modern sector of the Chinese economy was isolated, located on the periphery of the old economy—or in Tawney's description, a modern fringe that was stitched along the hem of an ancient garment.[3]

Along the same lines, it might be maintained that neither was the comprador a thoroughly modern economic man. Although alive to new ideas and liberated to some extent from tradition, he was still moved by many traditional institutions and values. He had likewise inherited a number of drawbacks. For instance, while he was ordinarily shrewd and talented, his integrity was open to doubt. He was sometimes attracted by the traditional investment pattern, emphasizing properties such as pawnshops and land, and a considerable portion of his resources was never put into productive use. Trying to exploit fully the wildly fluctuating markets in the treaty ports, many compradors engaged in risky speculations aimed at immediate profit. Consequently, while a great deal of wealth undoubtedly passed through their hands, quite a few went bankrupt and did not remain wealthy for long. In short, their investment activities and entrepreneurial endeavors were inhibited as much by their professional experience as by the economic and institutional context. If the compradors had been financially more successful, their influence on the Chinese economy and society as a whole might have been greater.

But viewed perspectively, it is abundantly clear that in many respects the comprador played a significant role in modern China's economic development—a role that stemmed from his position as an economic middleman between East and West. He was particularly active in China's commercial development, especially in the field of foreign trade. His role in promoting foreign trade lay not only in his direct participation as the foreign merchants' indispensable employee, but also in his ability to bring indirectly to its service some of China's traditional economic institutions. A case in point was the native bank. As an independent merchant, the comprador was often one of its partners; and as a comprador, he always guaranteed its drafts and credit bills. He thus provided the first link between the native banks and China's foreign trade. This new trade, stimulated by an age of oceanic communications, reoriented China. For one thing, the coastal provinces, which enjoyed natural advantages over the interior, became dominant. For another, foreign trade appears to have been the most important disequilibrating force in Chinese economy in the nineteenth century, in that it provided the impetus for economic change and performed the role of a "leading sector," generating a process of cumulative economic growth.

The comprador's role as a bicultural middleman had significant consequences for China's early industrialization. Modern industrial enterprises require large amounts of capital, and this the compradors could provide. They were able to accumulate wealth more easily than the noncomprador merchants for several reasons. In contrast to the ordinary merchant, a comprador profited in multiple ways from a single transaction—through salary, commission, and squeeze. Indirectly, his own private business benefited from his compradorial position. Because of his bicultural status, he was also in general free from the mandarins' exaction, a privilege denied to the ordinary Chinese merchant. Whereas large contributions had been collected by the Ch'ing government from his predecessors, the Liang-Huai salt merchants and the hong merchants, he was largely spared this expense. In fact, while some facets of Chinese economic history remain unknown, it is likely that the compradors were the first group of merchants in Chinese history to accumulate great wealth through a business career free in theory and practice from official squeeze. Unlike the typical practice in Chinese society, the comprador acquired wealth neither by official means nor by resorting to gentry cooperation or official patronage, but instead by various economic activities on his own initiative.

The comprador's bicultural background as a middleman contributed in still another way to wealth accumulation. Although the treaty ports embodied imperialism in many ways, they nevertheless provided a social and cultural environment favorable to business expectations. This setting was particularly conducive to capital formation. How the gentry and the compradors allocated or spent their income is not yet entirely known, but the compradors, living in unorthodox social surroundings, became more convinced than any other group in China that money was reputable and desirable for its own sake. They thus spent less than did the traditional merchant princes in emulating the gentry class. Such emulation had proved a serious drain on the resources of their predecessors who, in order to maintain their elite status in Chinese society, had to spend extravagantly on conspicuous consumption. They had found it necessary to cultivate scholarly hobbies and to live in a grand style, maintaining a large number of domestic servants and having constant and lavish entertainments. It is true that the compradors emulated the gentry class in certain ways, but their spending for this purpose was small in terms of their total wealth. Furthermore, in contrast to the traditional merchant princes, whose dilution of wealth accelerated the downward social mobility, few compradors, if any, were connoisseurs or bibliophiles.[4] Indeed, they did not belong to the leisure class.

It was owing partly to the pecuniary milieu in the treaty ports that the compradors maintained their profession as a family business and thus were further enabled to accumulate wealth. Such was not the case for either the ordinary gentry or the traditional merchants. Although the gentry as a rule made arrangements for their sons to follow in their careers, the effort too often ended in failure, owing largely to the competitive examination system. Accordingly, when a successful gentry member divided his wealth equally among his

Conclusion

sons, it was usually squandered by the next generation. As for the traditional merchants, the richer they became, the more they encouraged their sons to pass the civil examinations. Consequently, the success of a merchant was proportional to the degree to which his family was able to depart from its business undertakings. In contrast to both the gentry and traditional merchants, the compradors generally arranged successfully for their sons to continue in their profession. That the comprador position was a family affair was clearly illustrated by the family history of Jung Liang, Hsi Cheng-fu, Hsü Jun, and Tong King-sing.

As a result, the comprador accumulated considerable wealth in a surprisingly short period of time, finally becoming a nouveau riche in modern China. My estimate is that in the 1842–1894 period, the compradors' total income was approximately 530 million taels. Compared with the gentry's income, estimated at 645 million taels per annum by Chang Chung-li,[5] this amount seems insignificant. But in terms of economic development, the important factor was not just the amount of wealth, but the way it was spent. An observation that was true for eighteenth century England was also true for nineteenth century China: "What was inadequate was not the quantity of stored-up wealth, but its behaviour. The reservoirs of savings were full enough, but conduits to connect them with the wheels of industry were few and meagre."[6]

The comprador provided a valuable link between savings and industry, for his significance as middleman in the crucial period of China's early industrialization lay not only in his being rich, but also in his willingness to invest in modern enterprises. Through intimate contact with foreign merchants, he realized the importance and desirability of modern enterprises and was thus eager to invest in them before any other groups formed a similar intention. His willingness was important when viewed against the background of China's financial situation. Its early industrialization was often confronted by a problem typical of underdeveloped or premodern economies—the great difficulty of securing funds for long-term investment because of the relative scarcity of capital and the high cost of borrowing (interest charges on short-term commercial loans amounted to 10 to 15 percent annually at Shanghai in the 1860's).

The comprador-merchants' capacity and willingness to invest

in modern enterprises are made abundantly clear by the history of foreign and Chinese steamship companies in the treaty ports. They subscribed one-third (about half a million taels) of the total initial paid-up capital of the first three foreign steamship companies established at Shanghai in 1862–1868. Their capital played a decisive role (476,000 taels, or 78 percent of the initial paid-up capital) in 1873–1874 in the forming of the China Merchants' Steam Navigation Co. In the early twentieth century, Yü Hsia-ch'ing invested at least one million taels in steamships, becoming the biggest investor in this field in modern China. They also invested heavily in other forms of modern enterprise, such as China's first large-scale mining (the Kaiping Mines, 1878), machine manufacturing (the Yüan-ch'ang Machinery Co., 1883), and textiles (the Shanghai Cotton Cloth Mill, 1890). By 1913, Jardine's comprador Chu Ta-ch'un had invested at least two million taels in modern enterprises, being one of the richest Chinese investors at the time. Chu's towering position was soon challenged by one of his fellow-compradors, Chu Chih-yao, who was among the most prominent Chinese investors by the 1910's.

It is hard to determine the exact ratio of the compradors' capital invested in China's early industries as a whole, but the proportion of their capital in steamships, mining, textiles, and machine manufacturing—crucial fields in China's early industrialization—was remarkable. In view of the fact that some of their enterprises were registered under foreign names and many of them made investments in foreign-controlled undertakings, the amount of capital that they invested in modern industrial projects in China as indicated here is the minimum.

The comprador-merchants' managerial ability was equally crucial to China's early industrialization. Through lengthy and close association with foreign merchants as middlemen, they became adept in the ways of new business operations. Their enterprises were usually equipped with the latest Western machines, and the most advanced techniques were utilized. They used successfully the joint-stock system and grasped the concepts of insurance, laws of contract, and limited liability—all of which were new to China. This expertise was essential to China's early industrialization, yet other groups had almost no means to acquire it.

Conclusion

Schumpeter's theory of economic development assigns a central role to the daring and innovative entrepreneur. An entrepreneur is conceived of as "a decision-maker whose creative initiative draws all factors of production together to initiate, maintain, and expand the business enterprises."[7] Compared with the typical person in an agrarian society, the compradors were more like entrepreneurs— efficient, aggressive, calculating, commercial-minded, market-oriented, and above all, adventurous. Although these qualities were not entirely new to the traditional merchant, they did bring a new dimension to entrepreneurship. It is generally maintained that one of the major reasons for China's slow economic modernization was the lack of an entrepreneurial spirit. But in examining modern China's commercial and industrial developments, one finds that the comprador-merchant, by being an innovator, a risk-taker, a supplier of funds, as well as a competent manager, was a Schumpeterian entrepreneur *par excellence*.[8]

It is true that not all of the compradors were entrepreneurs and that entrepreneurs of China's early industries did not necessarily have a compradorial background; the exact proportion of modern entrepreneurs with a social origin as compradors is in fact hard to tell. But the compradors' successes as entrepreneurs in China's first large-scale steamship, mining, and textile enterprises were outstanding in the light of the unresponsiveness of other groups. For instance, few traditional merchants took part in China's early industrialization. They tended to have a great reluctance to enter a new field, as indicated by the fact that the former hong merchants seem to have disappeared quickly from the scene once the business pattern had changed. In the same vein, the salt merchants seldom participated in the financing and operation of modern enterprises, nor could the traditional Shansi bankers meet the new economic situation, as did the Japanese Zaibatzu. As for the traditional gentry members who tried to promote modern enterprises, too often they were incompetent when confronted with what were essentially management problems, such as planning, analyzing the cost structure, pricing the product, and determining the profitability of the enterprise. Finally, the role of the overseas Chinese in China's early industrialization was negligible until the twentieth century.

As middlemen between Chinese and foreign merchants, the

215

compradors were among the first Chinese to have direct and extensive contact with the Westerners. More than any other group of people, they saw the promise in engaging in modern enterprises and had the capacity and expertise to follow through. In short, the significance of the comprador in China's early industrialization lies in the fact that he constituted a new type, who combined the roles of investor and manager, thus becoming one of the leading forces in pioneering China's new industrial enterprises. This unique combination was invaluable, since at the time it could hardly have been achieved otherwise.

Any discussion of the compradors' economic role between East and West raises the issue of imperialism. After the rise of modern nationalism, the compradors, by rendering services to the foreign merchants, were naturally regarded by Chinese patriots as spearheads of foreign colonialism and economic imperialism. It is certain that China's external economic confrontation with the West during the past century was detrimental in many respects to her national economy. According to mercantilism, foreign economic intrusion drained China's economy of its wealth (as evidenced by the secularly unfavorable balance of trade), stifled Chinese-owned modern enterprises, and upset China's traditionally self-sufficient economy. Seen in the long view, however, this contact also had a number of positive effects on her economic development. Above all, it created "external economies," promoted a national market, stimulated mercantile nationalism, and provided opportunities for training managerial personnel and channeling Chinese savings into modern investments. In short, with respect to economic growth in China, the effect of imperialist domination of the modern sector of the economy was positive as well as negative. As for evaluating the Sino-foreign economic intercourse alone, without consideration of political imperialism, it seems that the present state of knowledge does not permit the preparation of a net balance sheet.

The problem at hand is the extent to which the compradors facilitated or hindered foreign economic intrusion—that is, foreign trade and investment—in modern China. There is no doubt that, by acting as housekeeping stewards, business assistants, and upcountry purchasers, they did play a pivotal role in keeping the business of foreign houses going, and going smoothly—including the sale of opium. But this was only a part of the story, and another part was often neglected. To put the issue in its proper historical perspective, one has to examine the quantity of foreign investment in China and its profit rate. As for the quantity, the international capital movement in the nineteenth century was concentrated geographically, with most of the foreign investment going to the so-called "regions of recent settlement" in America and Australia, while China received only a very small amount. And the profit rate of investment in China, compared with those in England and the United States, was not exceedingly high, as has often been asserted.

One reason for the ordinary profit rate and the small amount of foreign investment in China was the costly comprador system, for the profits earned by foreign merchants in China had to be shared with their Chinese compradors. The compradors' "exorbitant charges," as a foreigner put it,[9] forced some of the big foreign houses to withdraw their agencies from the smaller treaty ports and at the same time "rendered foreign competition with the Native dealers almost impossible."[10] Moreover, in sharp contrast to popular belief, the comprador-merchants turned out, in time, to be the foreign merchants' most effective rivals in commercial and industrial activities both in China and in Asia as a whole. In other words, the comprador-merchants in a sense curbed foreign economic intrusion —indirectly by limiting its scope and intensity, and directly by competing with the foreign merchants. Thus, one can scarcely make a valid distinction between the so-called "comprador capital" and that of the national bourgeoisie; any distinction is virtually blurred.

The comprador was more than just an economic man. In fact, his economic function as a middleman was the springboard for his other roles, because his economic pursuits promoted his social activities. Being comparatively rich, many compradors purchased rank or degree status from the government and thus became members of the gentry. By so doing, they obtained a higher social standing, which in itself was desirable. It was also directly useful to their economic pursuits, for not only was a high social standing beneficial when conducting business with officials or other merchants, but it was helpful to minimize the mandarin's squeeze. By and large, compradors could easily obtain the wealth that was necessary to buy status. Status, in turn, brought them more wealth. Wealth and status were closely allied because the purchase of rank was permitted. In terms of social mobility, the nouveaux riches compradors demonstrated the fluidity of the status system. They brought about a steady upward trend in social mobility in the late Ch'ing China treaty ports, which provided ready opportunities for the humble and obscure. In such noted compradors as Takee, Tong King-sing, Cheng Kuan-ying, Ho Tung, and Yü Hsia-ch'ing may be found typical representatives of the self-made men who raised themselves "from rags to riches."

As a member of the gentry and therefore a social leader, the comprador performed many gentry functions such as social relief, and assumed responsibility for maintaining order. As a result, he was honored by the Chinese and foreign governments and by the local authorities. But being chiefly an economic middleman, he also differed from the ordinary gentry in several respects. In the last analysis, he was not a genuine member of the gentry, for his status resulted merely from economic, not scholarly, achievements. And his role as a member of the gentry was played not in the rural community, as was usual, but in the commercial world of the treaty ports. Furthermore, the social functions he performed went beyond those of the ordinary gentry, particularly in the fields of commerce and "barbarian" affairs, both of which were beneath their attention. In short, he was both a businessman and a member of the gentry, but belonged fully to neither category. Rather, he belonged to the category of, as it were, the "commercial gentry," an amorphous status that symbolized his role as a middleman.

The compradors' function as middlemen was primarily economic, but because of the fact that they learned pidgin English and acquired knowledge of the West, they often played a role in China's politics on the national level. Their help was enlisted by the Chinese government not only in its dealings with foreigners (they were involved in practically all of modern China's major wars with foreign powers) but in handling internal crises as well (the Taipings, for instance). They are also known to have participated in China's reform movements. Cheng Kuan-ying was a celebrated reformer whose book had a vogue in the nineties, and other noted compradors took part directly in the 1898 reform movement. Still others were not content with the reform program and went so far as to turn against the

Conclusion

existing political order by joining the revolutionary forces led by Sun Yat-sen.

Politically, since a comprador has been regarded from the rise of modern nationalism in China as a traitor and a tool of imperialism, the issue of his patriotism demands attention. Although a comprador sometimes identified his interests with those of the foreigners, he was often most sensitive to foreign imperialism. In his business dealings with foreigners, for instance, especially when disputes were involved, he recognized the need of a strong Chinese government to back him up. This partly explains why many compradors actively participated in modern China's reform and revolutionary movements, and some even resigned their comprador posts in protest against foreign imperialism. On the intellectual level, the scholarly comprador Cheng Kuan-ying was a strong advocate of nationalism.

This does not mean, however, that all of the compradors were patriotic. Far from it, for some of them, such as Pao P'eng, Pu Ting-pang, Lu Ya-ching, Mu Ping-yüan, and Ch'en Lien-po, were traitors in the true sense of the word. But at the same time, one must keep in mind that modern nationalism was generally weak in nineteenth century China and that other noncomprador collaborators were by no means rare. At any rate, contrary to the generally accepted contention, the compradors were probably not the most unpatriotic group in China. On the contrary, many of them were very nationalistic.

The comprador played a prominent role in Sino-Western acculturation as well. It is true that, in a sense, he worked at the ragged edges of two cultures and was thus not in position to mediate in a full and adequate way. But in the process of cultural diffusion, people who serve the intermediary functions are often "inadequate" groups, for the "adequate" people either hesitate to act or lack the opportunity to do so. Indeed, his importance in the process of cultural interaction should by no means be underestimated on the ground of his heterodox social position and more prosaic role. On the contrary, acculturation is composed of a variety of "situational circumstances" rather than fundamental interchanges between big "systems." Cultural interaction is usually effected piecemeal in the workaday world of human affairs, rather than by wholesale abandonment and adoption of fundamental social structures. Yet fragments merge into larger themes, and a process of great cultural change is seen to have arisen, in the last analysis, from the everyday activities of quite ordinary men.

The comprador's role as a middleman between two cultures was vividly expressed by the kind of building named after him. One foreigner recalled the days after Shanghai had been opened for foreign trade in 1843: "Within a few years bricks began to arrive from England, and the brick work prominently displayed in verandah arches fencing the [Whangpu] Bund. . . . No foreign architects were available, and the plans were drawn by the [foreign] merchants and modified by Chinese builders to fit local materials and Chinese techniques. . . This architectural style, common to all the nineteenth century treaty ports in Central and South China, was wittily and fittingly christened the 'Compradoric,' for it was a necessary blend of Chinese with foreign methods."[11]

As a bicultural middleman, the comprador in many ways exemplified the hybrid treaty port culture. Having professionally constant and intimate association with Westerners, he was easily exposed to Western influences. These influences ranged from his style of life to his intellectual outlook. But he was likewise certainly affected by Chinese culture in which he had been raised. Thus, although affected by both Chinese and Western elements, he was dominated by neither. He embodied both, but through a process of adjustment and modification. On the one hand, for instance, he utilized the Chinese institutions of "complete responsibility" and "personal guarantee" and was moved by familism and regionalism. On the other, he was obviously influenced by the concepts of contract and limited liability, which were mainly Western in nature.

His style of life, including his clothing, housing, entertainment, beliefs, and social activities, also gave eloquent testimony to his bicultural role. There was no uniformity to the kind of clothes he normally wore, and his residence was supplied with Oriental and Western furnishings. Even the language he usually spoke, pidgin English, was a multicultural product. In terms of beliefs and social life, he was, on the one hand, influenced by traditional Chinese values and customs, such as Confucianism, Buddhism, and geographical guilds. On the other hand, although his intimate circle of friends did not include Westerners, he was certainly among the most Western-oriented Chinese of the time. Western influences ranged from names, hobbies, and new social organizations to intellectual outlook and religious beliefs.

In terms of values and beliefs, the comprador's new social attitude and intellectual outlook deserve more attention. With unique knowledge and experience, acquired mainly as a middleman, he held a different view from his contemporaries and exemplified social deviation. He was among the first in modern China to emphasize the importance of commercial and industrial development as opposed to military equipment and the Confucian social order. He broke with tradition in many respects. He could reject Chinese customs, especially in a well-to-do family, by refusing to have his daughter's feet bound, or encourage interracial marriage when such a practice was extremely rare in mid-nineteenth century China. More significantly, he not only combined the roles of passive owner and active manager of capital, but also showed a readiness to take risks in a new field.

The comprador's further departure from Chinese tradition was abundantly evidenced by the way in which he educated his children. Since the compradorship was by and large a family affair, he usually encouraged one of his sons to succeed him. His other children often attended the Western-style schools in the treaty ports or abroad, with a view to assuming a career in the *yang-wu* (foreign affairs). He seldom encouraged his sons to study Confucian classics so as to pass the civil service examination. This was in sharp contrast to the traditional way of achieving success that was usually adopted by both the gentry members and the traditional merchants. Indeed, in contrast to the ordinary gentry, he seems to have cared little about the Confucian doctrine, for his rise to power was based precisely on a departure from orthodox Confucianism—a special concern for "barbarian" affairs and, more important, for wealth. Realizing that the advancement of Confucianism would avail him little, he interested himself instead in economic development.

Yet new cultural elements introduced or represented by the compradors could immediately acquire undesirable associations from the compradors' initially low social status or the stereotyped accusation of unpatriotism, which might outweigh their intrinsic advantages. According to Hsiao San, the scholarly comprador Cheng Kuan-ying's celebrated work on reform (*Sheng-shih wei-yen*) was one of the books Mao Tse-tung liked to read in his boyhood;[12] but Mao in his own writings mentions Yen Fu and K'ang Yu-wei as the favorite authors of his youth, not Cheng. Perhaps this reluctance on the part of modern Chinese to admit their intellectual indebtedness to the compradors obscures the fact that the compradors exerted a greater influence than is usually realized.

Because the comprador's activities involved an interaction between two cultures at a variety of levels, he serves as an example of the "marginal man." The marginal man is a personality type that arises at a time and place where, through the conflict of races and cultures, new societies, new peoples, and new cultures are coming into existence. The expansion of the West in modern times brought about an unprecedented degree of international contact and fusion of cultures, and the treaty ports in late Ch'ing China, where different cultures met, constituted a typical hybrid society. The situation that compelled the comprador to live simultaneously in two different societies and even in two antagonistic cultures also caused him "to assume, in relation to the worlds in which he lives, the role of a cosmopolitan and a stranger. Inevitably he becomes, relatively to his cultural milieu, the individual with the wider horizon, the keener intelligence, the more detached and rational viewpoint."[13]

All in all, the comprador constituted a new type of merchant who, acting between China and the West, played a prominent and strategically important role in modern China. Economically, the *nouveau riche* comprador uniquely combined wealth with expertise and thus became one of the leading forces in China's early industrialization. His sociopolitical role belonged to that of the commercial gentry, acting as a social leader in the treaty ports. Intellectually, inasmuch as new ideas and attitudes underlay the modern enterprises, he became a promoter of new ideas and, consequently, a challenger of some of China's traditional values. His response to the West was based on his understanding of the world outside the Middle Kingdom. It was not that he liked Chinese tradition any the less; he merely knew the West better. Therefore, he was a typical "marginal man," influenced by, and in turn exerting influence on, different cultures, while belonging to neither. He was, in essence,

Conclusion

a cultural hybrid, in whom Chinese and Western cultures met and mixed. A middleman usually is not a central figure, but given the particular circumstances of nineteenth century China, the comprador's special significance lay precisely in his role as a middleman between East and West.

Appendices   Bibliography   Notes   Glossary   Index

Appendix A Augustine Heard & Co.'s Compradors, 1850's–1860's.

Unless otherwise noted, the source is the Heard Collection.

Name	Place of work	Period	Native place	Source
Achen	Canton	1850's	Canton	EG–2
Atchu	Canton	–1857	Canton	HL–15
Acum	Canton	–1860	Canton	HL–15
Atow	Hong Kong	1850's	Canton	HL–15
Atchu	Hong Kong	1857	Canton	HL–15
See Yong	Hong Kong	1850's–1860's	Canton	HL–15, HL–16, HM–5. Case 3, HC II.
Atchune	Hong Kong	1860's	Canton	HL–15, HM–5
See Kai	Shanghai	–1853	Canton	HM–23
Chu-u-teng	Shanghai	1850's–1860's	Canton	HL–14, HL–15, HM–4
Tong Loong-maw	Foochow	1850's– April 1862	Canton	HM–28, HM–30. Case 9, HC II.
Akit	Foochow	April 1862–	Canton	FL–6, HM–49
Aming	Kiukiang	1860's	Canton	HM–23
Agunn (Leang Nan Chi)	Kiukiang	–1862	Canton	HM–23
Ahee	Kiukiang	1862	—	HL–19
Atong	Kiukiang	1860's	Canton	HL–14, HM–23
Achow	Kiukiang	–1862–	Canton	HQ–1
Atsing	Kiukiang	1863–	—	HM–30

Appendix A

Name	Place of work	Period	Native place	Source
Soyseng	Hankow	Early 1860's	—	HM–23
Coe Lun	Hankow	1865	Canton	HM–23
Seating	Hankow	1866	Canton	HM–23
Akow	Yokohama, Japan	June 1860– July 1865	Canton	HL–23, HM–55. Case 9, HC II.
Sow-no	Yokohama, Japan	–1866–	Canton	HM–55
Leong A Tien	Saigon, Annam	May 1860–	Canton	Case 9, HC II.
One A Cheong	Saigon, Annam	May 1860–	Canton	Case 9, HC II.

Appendix B Russell & Co.'s Compradors, 1830's–1870's.

The sources include Frank Blackwell Forbes' Letter Books; Forbes' Collection; Heard Collection; Nieh Pao-chang, "Mei-shang"; and *North China Herald.*

Name	Place of work	Period	Native place	Source
Ayow (Ayaow)	Canton	1831–	Canton	E–2, FC. *NCH,* Mar. 12, 1859, p. 126.
San Yuk	—	1859	—	Aug. 17, 1859, HL–14, HC.
Ahyue	Shanghai	1858–1865	Canton	May 14, 1868; June 4, 1868; Case 26, RA.
Sunchong	Shanghai	1858–1861	Canton	*Ibid.*
Choping	Shanghai	1865–1874	Chekiang	April 18, 1862, HL–36, HC. June 14, 1873, FBFLB.
Koofunsing	Shanghai	1860's	Canton	*Ibid.*
Chongfat	Shanghai	1860's	Canton	*Ibid.*
Chu-han	Shanghai	1868–1876	—	*NCH,* July 29, 1876.
Sunkee	Tientsin	1861–1873	Shanghai	Jan. 6, 1873, HM–43, HC. Dec. 22, 1874, FBFLB. *NCH,* Aug. 28, 1875

Appendix B

Name	Place of work	Period	Native place	Source
Dasing	Chinkiang	–1873	Tientsin	*NCH,* Aug. 28, 1875, p. 213.
Dasing	Tientsin	1873–	Tientsin	Oct. 7, 1875, Dec. 22, 1874, FBFLB.
Chen Cho Ching	Kiukiang	–1863–	—	EM–13, HC.
Achai	Kiukiang	–1874–	—	Mar. 13, 1873, FBFLB.
Apun	Hankow	–1865	Canton	June 20, 1866, HM–23, HC. Dec. 22, 1874, FBFLB.
Coe Lun	Hankow	1865–	Canton	June 20, 1866, HM–23, HC.
Cheng Chi-tung	—	1867–	Canton	Nieh, p. 100.

Appendix C Jardine, Matheson & Co.'s Compradors, 1850's–1900's.

Sources include the Heard Collection; *Ch'ou-pan i-wu shih-mo;* Jardine, Matheson & Co. Archives; *North China Herald;* Wang Ching-yü, *Kung-yeh;* and Wright, *Impressions.*

Name	Place of work	Period	Native place	Source
Asam	Shanghai	1845–1846	Canton	JMA
Atow	Shanghai	1846–1851	Canton	JMA
William Affo	Shanghai	1851	Canton	JMA
Takee	Shanghai	1851–	Ningpo	JMA
Yakee	Shanghai	–1859	Canton	JMA
Aleet	Shanghai	1850's	Canton	JMA
Acum	Shanghai	–1863	Canton	JMA
Tong King-sing	Shanghai	1863–1873	Canton	JMA
Tong Mow-chee	Shanghai	1873–1897	Canton	JMA; *NCH,* Aug. 28, 1875.
Allum	Shanghai	1883–	Canton	JMA
T'ang Chieh-ch'en	Shanghai	1897–1904	Canton	Wang Ching-yü, II, 979.
T'ang Yü-t'ien	Shanghai	1890's?	Canton	*Ibid.*
T'ang Jung-chün	Shanghai	1890's	Canton	*Ibid.*
T'ang Chi-ch'ang	Shanghai	1904–	Canton	*Hua-tzu jih-pao,* March 7, 1904.
Chu Ta-ch'un	Shanghai	1900's	Kiangsu	Wang Ching-yü, II, 958–960.

Appendix C

Name	Place of work	Period	Native place	Source
Achook	Hong Kong	1859	—	JMA
Ch'en Chao	Hong Kong	1865	—	Case 1, HC II.
Lo Kum Woon	Hong Kong	1873	—	JMA
Ts'ai Hsing-nan	Hong Kong	1870's	Fukien	My interview with Ho Tung's family, 1963.
Ho Tung	Hong Kong	1883–1900	Canton	*Ibid.*
Ng Chuck	Hong Kong	1862	—	JMA
Acum	Foochow	1860	Canton	FM–13, HC. *NCH*, Oct. 13, 1860.
Awei	Foochow	1870's	—	Wright, p. 138.
Allum	Foochow	–1883	Canton	JMA
Yowloong	Hankow	1860's	Canton	JMA
Ting Seag-sing	Hankow	1867	—	JMA
Sow Moey	Hankow	–1885	—	JMA
Wun Hing	Hankow	1885–	—	JMA
Ahsing	Kiukiang	1872	—	JMA
Tong Mow-chee	Tientsin	1871–1873	Canton	JMA; *NCH*, Aug. 28, 1875.
Ahsan	Amoy	1869	—	JMA
Achow	Swatow	1874	—	JMA

Appendix D Dent & Co.'s Compradors, 1830's–1860's

The sources include Hsü Jun, *Nien-p'u;* Hsü Jun et al., *Tsung-p'u; IWSM;* Jardine, Matheson & Co. Archives; and *North China Herald*.

Name	Place of work	Period	Native place	Source
Pao Jen-kuan	Canton	–1838	Canton	IWSM: TK, 29: 13, 30: 28b.
Pao P'eng	Canton	1838–1840	Canton	*Ibid.*
Hsü Yü-t'ing	Shanghai	1840's	Canton	Hsü et al., 7: 64–66b.
Coekeye	Shanghai	–1851–	—	Shanghai, 510, JMA
Yungkee (Hsü Jung-ts'un)	Shanghai	1850's–1861	Canton	Hsü et al., 7: 72–73b.
Tseng Chi-fu	Shanghai	1850's–1861	—	Hsü, 3: 7b.
Amew	—	–1859–	—	*NCH*, Oct. 15, 1859, 42.
Hsü Jun	Shanghai	1861–1868	Canton	Hsü, 7b, 16
Ya San	Hong Kong	–1861–	Canton	Hsü, 8.
Ya Ti (Atai)	Hong Kong	–1861–	Canton	Hsü, 8.
Ya P'ei	Tientsin	–1861–	—	Hsü, 8.
Apung	Tientsin	1860's	—	*NCH*, Nov. 19, 1884.
Hsü Tzu-jung	Tientsin	–1861	Canton	Hsü, 8.
Ch'en Lo-ming	Tientsin	–1861–	—	Hsü, 8.
Liang Chih	Chefoo	–1861–	—	Hsü, 8.
Huang Mo-yen	Chinkiang	–1861–	—	Hsü, 8.

Appendix D

Name	Place of work	Period	Native place	Source
Tou Yen-shan	Wu-hu	–1861–	—	Hsü, 8.
Hsü Wei-nan	Kiukiang	–1861–	Canton	Hsü, 8.
Cheng Chi-tung	Kiukiang	–1861–	Canton	Hsü, 8.
Sheng Heng-shan	Hankow	–1861–	Canton	Hsü, 8.
Yang Hui-shan	Hankow	–1861–	Canton	Hsü, 8.

Bibliography

Adachi Ikutsune 安達生恒. "Baiben" 買辦 (The comprador), Tōkō 東光 (Eastern light), 9:26–38 (1949).

Agarwala, A. N., & S. P. Singh, eds. *The Economics of Underdevelopment*. London, 1958; 510 pp.

Allen, G. C., and A. G. Donnithorne. *Western Economic Enterprise in Far Eastern Economic Development*. New York, 1954; 292 pp.

Arnold, Julean. *Commercial Handbook of China*. 2 vols. Washington, D.C., 1919, 1920.

Augustine Heard & Co. Archives, Heard Collection; Heard Collection II. Baker Library, Harvard Business School.

BPP: British Parliamentary Papers, published.

"Returns of Trade in China." Vol. 39, 1849.

"Reports from Her Majesty's Consuls in China, 1864." Vol. 71, 1866.

"Reports from the Foreign Commissioners at the Various Ports in China for the Year 1865." Vol. 68, 1867.

"Commercial Reports from Her Majesty's Consuls in China, Japan, and Siam, 1865–1866." Vol. 68, 1867.

"Reports on Trade by the Foreign Commissioners at the Ports in China for the Year 1866." Vol. 69, 1867–1868.

"Commercial Reports from Her Majesty's Consuls in China and Siam, 1869." Vol. 65, 1870.

"Commercial Reports from Her Majesty's Consuls in Japan, 1869–1870." Vol. 65, 1870.

Basu, Dilip K. "The American Entrepreneurs and Howqua: A Study in Sino-American Trade During 1829–1834." Seminar paper, Harvard University, January 1965.

Bourne, F. S. A., et al. *Report of the Mission to China of the Blackburn Chamber of Commerce: 1896–1897*. London, 1898.

Carlson, Ellsworth C. *The Kaiping Mines, 1877–1912*. Cambridge, Mass., 1957; 174 pp.

Chang Chih-tung 張之洞. *Chang Wen-hsiang-kung ch'üan-chi* 張文襄公全集 (The complete works of Chang Chih-tung). 229 *chüan*. Peking, 1928.

Chang Chung-li. *The Chinese Gentry: Studies on Their Role in Nineteenth-Century Chinese Society*. Seattle, 1955; 250 pp.

———. *The Income of the Chinese Gentry*. Seattle, 1962; 369 pp.

Chang Kuo-hui 張國輝. "Shih-chiu shih-chi hou-pan-ch'i Chung-kuo ch'ien-chuang ti mai-pan hua" 十九世紀後半期中國錢庄的買辦化 (The comprador-ialization of China's native banks in the late nineteenth century), *Li-shih yen-chiu* 歷史研究 (Historical study), 6:85–98 (1963).

Chang Ts'un-wu 張存武. *Kuang-hsü san-shih-i nien Chung-Mei kung-yüeh feng-ch'ao* 光緒三十一年中美工約風潮 (The crisis of Sino-American dispute over labor agreement in 1905). Taipei, 1965; 269 pp.

Change and the Entrepreneur: Postulates and Patterns for Entrepreneurial History, prepared by the Research Center in Entrepreneurial History, Harvard University. Cambridge, Mass., 1949; 200 pp.

Ch'en Chin-miao 陳金淼. "T'ien-chin chih mai-pan chih-tu" 天津之買辦制度 (The comprador system in Tientsin), *Ching-chi hsüeh-pao* 經濟學報 (Journal of economics), 1: 27–69 (1940).

Ch'en Ch'iu 陳虯. *Tung-yu t'iao-i* 東遊條議 (Proposals made during a trip to the east). Shanghai, 1890.

Ch'en Shao-po 陳少白. *Hsing-Chung hui ko-ming shih-yao* 興中會革命史要 (A brief history of the revolutionary activities of the Hsing-Chung hui). Taipei, 1956; 64 pp.

Cheng Kuan-ying 鄭觀應. *I-yen* 易言 (Easy words). Shanghai, 1881.

———. *Sheng-shih wei-yen* 盛世危言 (Warnings to a prosperous age). 6 *chüan*. 1893. Preface dated 1892.

———. *Tseng-ting Sheng-shih wei-yen* 增訂盛世危言 (Warnings to a prosperous age, revised). 8 *ts'e*. Preface dated 1892.

———. *Lo-fu ch'ih-ho shan-jen shih-ts'ao* 羅浮侍鶴山人詩草 (Poems of Cheng Kuan-ying). 2 *ts'e*. Shanghai, 1897.

———. *Sheng-shih wei-yen hsü-p'ien* 盛世危言續篇 (Warnings to a prosperous age, continued). 1909.

———. *Sheng-shih wei-yen hou-p'ien* 盛世危言後篇 (Warnings to a prosperous age, second part). 15 *chüan*. Shanghai, 1920. Preface dated 1910.

———. *T'ang-jen chien-hsia chuan* 唐人劍俠傳 (T'ang knight-errant stories). Shanghai, 1937; 164 pp.

———. *Nan-yu jih-chi* 南遊日記 (Diary of a trip to the south). N.d. Preface dated 1884, reprinted in Taipei, 1967; 150 pp.

Chin hsien chih 鄞縣志 (The gazetteer of the district of Chin), comp. Chang Shu 張恕. 64 *chüan*. 1891.

China, Imperial Maritime Customs. See IMC.

Ching Wu 靜吾 and Chung Ting 仲丁, eds. *Wu Hsü tang-an chung ti T'ai-p'ing t'en-kuo shih-liao hsüan chi* 吳煦檔案中的太平天國史料選輯 (Selected papers from the Wu Hsü archives concerning the Taipings). Peking, 1958; 300 pp.

Ch'ou-pan i-wu shih-mo. See IWSM.

Chronicles and Directory for China, Japan and the Philippines. Hong Kong, Hong Kong

Bibliography

Daily Press, 1870, 1879.

Chu, Samuel C. *Reformer in Modern China: Chang Chien, 1853–1926.* New York, 1965; 256 pp.

Ch'ü T'ung-tsu. *Local Government in China under the Ch'ing.* Cambridge, Mass., 1962; 360 pp.

Cohen, Paul A. *China and Christianity: The Missionary Movement and the Growth of Chinese Antiforeignism, 1860–1870.* Cambridge, Mass., 1963; 392 pp.

Cowan, C. D., ed. *The Economic Development of China and Japan.* London, 1964; 255 pp.

Cunningham, Edward. *Our Political and Commercial Relations with China.* Washington, D.C., 1855.

DP: F. G. Dexter Papers. Massachusetts Historical Society, Boston, Mass.

Dexter, F. G. Papers. See DP.

Downing, C. T. *The Stranger in China: or, the Fan-Qui's Visit to the Celestial Empire in 1836–1837.* 2 vols. London, 1838.

Dyce, Charles M. *Personal Reminiscences of Thirty Years' Residence in the Model Settlement, Shanghai, 1870–1900.* London, 1906; 238 pp.

Elvin, Mark. "The Mixed Court of the International Settlement at Shanghai (Until 1911)," *Papers on China,* 17:131–159 (1963). Harvard University, East Asian Research Center.

FBF. See Forbes, Frank B.

FC. See Forbes Collection.

Fairbank, John King. *Trade and Diplomacy on the China Coast: The Opening of the Treaty Ports, 1842–1854.* 2 vols. Cambridge, Mass., 1953.

Fairbank, John K., Alexander Eckstein, and Lien-sheng Yang. "Economic Change in Early Modern China: An Analytic Framework," *Economic Development and Cultural Change,* 9.1:1–26 (October 1960).

Fairbank, John K., Edwin O. Reischauer, and Albert M. Craig. *East Asia: The Modern Transformation.* Boston, 1965; 955 pp.

Fang T'eng 方騰. "Yü Hsia-ch'ing lun" 虞洽卿論 (On Yü Hsia-ch'ing), *Tsa-chih yüeh-k'an* 雜誌月刊 (Monthly miscellany), 12.2:46–51 (November 1943); 12.3:62–67 (December 1943); 12.4:59–64 (January 1944).

Feng Tzu-yu 馮自由. *Ko-ming i-shih* 革命逸史 (Reminiscences of the revolution). 5 vols. Chungking and Shanghai, 1934–1947.

———. *Hua-ch'iao ko-ming tsu-chih shih-hua* 華僑革命組織史話 (A history of revolutionary organizations of overseas Chinese). Taipei, 1954; 150 pp.

Feuerwerker, Albert. *China's Early Industrialization: Sheng Hsüan-huai (1844–1916) and Mandarin Enterprise.* Cambridge, Mass., 1958; 311 pp.

Fieldhouse, D. K. "Imperialism: An Historiographical Revision," *Economic History Review,* 14.2:187–209 (December 1961).

Forbes, Frank B. Letter Books. Baker Library, Harvard Business School.

Forbes, Robert B. *Personal Reminiscences,* 2nd ed. rev. Boston, 1892; 374 pp.

Forbes Collection. Baker Library, Harvard Business School.

Gaimushō Tsūshōkyoku 外務省通商局 (Foreign Office, Bureau of Commercial Affairs), comp. *Shinkoku jijō* 清國事情 (Conditions in the Ch'ing Empire). 2 vols.

Bibliography

Tokyo, 1904.

Giles, Herbert A. *A Chinese Biographical Dictionary.* Shanghai, 1898; 715 pp.

Greenberg, Michael. *British Trade and the Opening of China, 1800–1842.* Cambridge, Eng. 1951; 221 pp.

Griffin, Eldon. *Clippers and Consuls: American Consular and Commercial Relations with Eastern Asia, 1845–1860.* Ann Arbor, Mich. 1938; 533 pp.

HC: Heard Collection. Baker Library, Harvard Business School.

HC II: Heard Collection, Second Part. Baker Library, Harvard Business School.

Hall, Robert A. "Chinese Pidgin English Grammar and Texts," *Journal of the American Oriental Society,* 64.63:95–113 (July-September 1944).

Hao Yen-p'ing 郝延平. "Yu shou-chiu tao ko-hsin" 由守舊到革新 (From conservatism to reform), *Ta-lu tsa-chih* 大陸雜誌 (Continental magazine), 20.7: 26–27 (April 1960).

————. "The Abortive Cooperation between Reformers and Revolutionaries, 1895–1900," *Papers on China,* 15: 91–114 (1961). Harvard University, East Asian Research Center.

————. "A Study of the Ch'ing-liu Tang: The 'Disinterested' Scholar-official Group, 1875–1884," *Papers on China,* 16: 40–65 (1962). Harvard University, East Asian Research Center.

Harrison, Brian, ed. *University of Hong Kong: The First 50 Years, 1911–1961.* Hong Kong, 1962; 247 pp.

Hatano Yoshihiro 波多野善大. *Chūgoku kindai kōgyōshi no kenkyū* 中國近代工業史の研究 (Studies on the early industrialization in China). Kyoto, 1961; 556 pp.

Hauser, Ernest O. *Shanghai: City for Sale.* 1940; 323 pp.

Heard, Augustine, Jr. "Diary," FP-4, Heard Collection.

————. "Old China and new," GQ-2, Heard Collection.

————. "The Poisoning in Hongkong," GQ-2, Heard Collection.

Heard Collection. See HC.

Hirschman, Albert O. *The Strategy of Economic Development.* New Haven, 1958; 210 pp.

Hirschmeier, Johannes. *The Origins of Entrepreneurship in Meiji Japan.* Cambridge, Mass., 1964; 347 pp.

Ho Ping-ti 何炳棣. *The Ladder of Success in Imperial China: Aspects of Social Mobility, 1368–1911.* New York, 1962; 385 pp.

————. *Chung-kuo hui-kuan shih-lun* 中國會舘史論 (A historical survey of landsmannschaften in China). Taipei, 1966; 149 pp.

Hong Kong Daily Press. Available at the Hong Kong High Court Library, Hong Kong.

Hong Kong Telegraph. Available at the Hong Kong High Court Library, Hong Kong.

Hou Chi-ming. *Foreign Investment and Economic Development in China, 1840–1937.* Cambridge, Mass., 1965; 306 pp.

Hsiao San 蕭三. *Mao Tse-tung t'ung-chih ti ch'ing-shao-nien shih-tai* 毛澤東同志的青少年時代 (The childhood and boyhood of comrade Mao Tse-tung). Peking, 1949; 109 pp.

Hsi Yü-fu 席裕福. *Huang-ch'ao cheng-tien lei-ts'uan* 皇朝政典類纂 (Political encyclopedia of the Ch'ing). 500 *chüan*, 1903.

Hsiang-kang Hua-tzu jih-pao 香港華字日報 (Chinese mail). Available at the Feng P'ing-shan Library, University of Hong Kong, Hong Kong.

Hsü Jun 徐潤. *Hsü Yü-chai tzu-hsü nien-p'u* 徐愚齋自敍年譜 (Chronological autobiography of Hsü Jun). 1 *ts'e*, 1927.

——— et al. *Hsiang-shan Hsü-shih tsung-p'u* 香山徐氏宗譜 (The history of the Hsü clan in the Hsiang-shan hsien). 8 *ts'e*. Shanghai, 1844.

Hsü K'o 徐珂. *Ch'ing pai lei-ch'ao* 清稗類鈔 (A classified collection of Ch'ing dynasty anecdotes). 48 *t'se*. Shanghai, 1928.

Hsü Ti-hsin 許滌新. *Kuan-liao tzu-pen lun* 官僚資本論 (On official capital). Shanghai, 1958; 148 pp.

Hsü Yü-shu 徐玉書, comp. *Shang-hai chin-jung chi-kuan i-lan* 上海金融機關一覽 (A list of the financial institutes in Shanghai). Shanghai, 1920; 108 pp.

Hu Ch'iu-yüan 胡秋原. "Cheng Kuan-ying chi ch'i Sheng-shih wei-yen" 鄭觀應及其盛世危言 (Cheng Kuan-ying and his book *Warnings to a Prosperous Age*), *San-min chu-i pan-yüeh-k'an* 三民主義半月刊 (The three people's principles fortnightly), 3: 11 (Chungking, June 1, 1944). Available at the Fu Ssu-nien Library, Academia Sinica, Taipei.

Hua-tzu jih-pao. See *Hsiang-kang Hua-tzu jih-pao.*

Huang I-feng 黃逸峯. "Kuan-yü chiu Chung-kuo mai-pan chieh-chi ti yen-chiu" 關於舊中國買辦階級的研究 (A study of the comprador class in old China), *Li-shih yen-chiu*, 87:89–116 (June 15, 1964).

———. "Ti-kuo chu-i ch'ing-lüeh Chung-kuo ti i-ko chung-yao chih-chu: mai-pan chieh-chi" 帝國主義侵略中國的一個重要支柱—買辦階級 (One important pillar of imperialism's incursion on China: The comprador class), *Li-shih yen-chiu*, 91: 55–70 (February 1965).

Huang Wei 黃葦. *Shang-hai k'ai-fu ch'u-ch'i tui-wai mao-i yen-chiu* 上海開埠初期對外貿易研究 (A study of Shanghai's foreign trade during the initial period of its opening). Shanghai, 1961; 150 pp.

Hummel, Arthur W., ed. *Eminent Chinese of the Ch'ing Period, 1644–1912*. 2 vols. Washington, D.C., 1943–1944.

Hung Jen-kan 洪仁玕. *Tzu-cheng hsin-p'ien* 資政新篇 (A new work for aid in administration). 1859.

Hunter, William C. *The "Fan Kwae" at Canton before Treaty Days, 1825–1844*. London, 1882; 158 pp.

Hyatt, Irwin T., Jr. "Protestant Missions in China, 1877–1890: The Institutionalization of Good Works," *Papers on China*, 17: 67–100 (1963). Harvard University, East Asian Research Center.

IMC: China, Imperial Maritime Customs. *Reports on Trade, 1864*. Shanghai, 1865.

———. *Reports on Trade, 1866*. Shanghai, 1867.

———. *Returns of Trade at the Treaty Ports of China*. Shanghai, 1870–1912, annually.

———. *Reports on the Haikwan Banking System and Local Currency at the Treaty Ports*. Shanghai, 1879.

———. *Returns of Trade and Trade Reports*. Shanghai, 1882.

———. *Decennial Report, 1882–1891*. Shanghai, 1892.

Bibliography

————. *Treaties, Conventions, etc. between China and Foreign States,* 2nd ed. 2 vols. Shanghai, 1917.

IWSM: *Ch'ou-pan i-wu shih-mo* 籌辦夷務始末 (A complete account of the management of barbarian affairs). 260 *chüan.* Peiping, 1929–1931.

Inoue Nobumasa 井上陳政. *Uiki tsūsan* 禹域通纂 (A general compendium on China). 2 vols. Tokyo, 1888.

JMA: Jardine, Matheson & Co. Archives. The University Library, Cambridge, England.

Jardine, Matheson & Co. *An Outline of the History of a China House for a Hundred Years, 1832–1932.* Hong Kong, privately printed, 1934; 87 pp.

Jardine, Matheson & Company Archives. See JMA.

Jardines and the Ewo Interests. Shanghai, 1947.

Kent, Percy Horace. *Railway Enterprise in China: An Account of Its Origin and Development.* London, 1907; 304 pp.

Ketels, M. *Le role du comprador dans les relations commerciales en Chine.* Chine et Belgique, 1906.

King, Frank H. H. *Money and Monetary Policy in China, 1845–1895.* Cambridge, Mass., 1965; 330 pp.

————, ed., and Prescott Clarke. *A Research Guide to China-Coast Newspapers, 1822–1911.* Cambridge, Mass., 1965; 235 pp.

Kipling, Rudyard. *The Works of Rudyard Kipling.* 10 vols. New York, 1909.

Knight, Frank H. *Risk, Uncertainty and Profit.* Boston, 1921; 381 pp.

Knox, Thomas. "John Comprador," *Harper's New Monthly Magazine,* 57: 427–434 (1878).

Ko Kung-chen 戈公振. *Chung-kuo pao-hsüeh shih* 中國報學史 (History of Chinese journalism). Shanghai, 1927; 385 pp.

Ko Yüan-hsü 葛元煦. *Hu yu tsa-chi* 滬游雜記 (Miscellaneous records of a sojourn in Shanghai). 4 *chüan.* Shanghai, 1876.

Koh Sung Jae. *Stages of Industrial Development in Asia: A Comparative History of the Cotton Industry in Japan, India, China and Korea.* Philadelphia, 1966; 461 pp.

Krausse, Alexis. *China in Decay: A Handbook to the Far Eastern Question.* London, 1898.

Kuang Shih-nan 鄺勢南. "Hsiang-kang ti mai-pan chih-tu" 香港的買辦制度 (The comprador system in Hong Kong), in Li Chin-wei 黎晉偉, ed. *Hsiang-kang pai-nien shih* 香港百年史 (A history of Hong Kong, 1848–1948). Hong Kong, 1949, p. 13.

Kuang-tung k'ou chieh ch'ao 廣東扣械潮 (The Kwangtung weapon-impounding crisis). Comp. *Hsiang-kang Hua-tzu jih-pao* 香港華字日報. Hong Kong, 1924; 150 pp.

LaFargue, Thomas E. *China's First Hundred.* Pullman, Wash., 1942; 176 pp.

LeFevour, Edward. *Western Enterprise in Late Ch'ing China: A Selective Survey of Jardine, Matheson & Company's Operations, 1842–1895.* Cambridge, Mass., 1968; 215 pp.

Levy, Marion J., and Shih Kuo-heng. *The Rise of the Modern Chinese Business Class: Two Introductory Essays.* New York, 1949; 64 pp.

Li Chin-wei 黎晉偉, ed. *Hsiang-kang pai-nien shih* 香港百年史 (A history of Hong

Bibliography

Kong, 1848–1948). Hong Kong, 1949; 110 pp.

Li Chung-chüeh 李鐘珏. *Ch'ieh-wan lao-jen ch'i-shih tzu-hsü* 且頑老人七十自敍 (The autobiography of Li Chung-chüeh at seventy), 6 *ts'e*. Shanghai, 1922.

Liang Chia-pin 梁嘉彬. *Kuang-tung shih-san hang k'ao* 廣東十三行考 (A study of the Canton thirteen hongs), rev. ed. T'ai-chung, Taiwan, 1960; 341 pp.

Liang T'ing-nan 梁廷枬. *Yüeh hai-kuan chih* 粵海關志 (Gazetteer of the maritime customs of Kwangtung). 30 *chüan*. Postface, 1839. *Ts'e* 1, 7, and 8 reprinted in *Kuo-hsüeh wen-k'u* 國學文庫, Nos. 18, 21, and 33, Peiping, 1935 *et seq.*

Lin Ch'ung-yung 林崇墉. *Lin Tse-hsü chuan* 林則徐傳 (A biography of Lin Tse-hsü). Taipei, 1967; 732 pp.

Linton, Ralph. *The study of Man: An Introduction.* New York, 1936; 250 pp.

Liu Kwang-Ching 劉廣京. "Two Steamship Companies in China, 1862–1877." Ph.D. thesis. Harvard University, 1956.

———. "Steamship Enterprise in Nineteenth-Century China," *Journal of Asian Studies*, 18.4:435–455 (August 1959).

———. "T'ang T'ing-shu chih mai-pan shih-tai" 唐廷樞之買辦時代 (Tong King-sing: His comprador years), *Ch'ing-hua hsüeh-pao* 清華學報 (Tsing Hua journal of Chinese studies), n.s. 2.2: 143–183 (June 1961).

———. *Anglo-American Steamship Rivalry in China, 1862–1874.* Cambridge, Mass., 1962; 211 pp.

———. "British-Chinese Steamship Rivalry in China, 1873–1885," in C. D. Cowan, ed., *The Economic Development of China and Japan.* London, 1864.

Lo Chia-lun 羅家倫, ed. *Kuo-fu nien-p'u* 國父年譜 (Chronological biography of Sun Yat-sen). 2 vols. Taipei, 1958.

———. *Ko-ming wen-hsien* 革命文獻 (Documents of revolution). 30 vols. Taipei, 1958–1963.

Lockwood, Stephen C. "Augustine Heard & Co.: American Merchants in China on the Eve of the Opening of the Yangtze, 1858–1862." Undergraduate honors thesis, Harvard University, 1963.

Lu Ch'i-yün 魯奇雲. *I-pai ming-jen chia-cheng shih* 一百名人家政史 (The family history of one hundred prominent Chinese). Shanghai, 1922; 85 pp.

MLB: Letter Books of H. B. Morse Containing Copies of His Correspondence While Commissioner with the Chinese Maritime Customs, 1886–1907. 5 vols. The Houghton Library, Harvard University.

Ma Yin-ch'u 馬寅初. "Chung-kuo chih mai-pan chih" 中國之買辦制 (The comprador institution in China), *Tung-fang tsa-chih* 東方雜誌 (The eastern miscellany), 20.6:130–131 (Mar. 25, 1923).

———. *Ma Yin-ch'u yen-chiang chi* 馬寅初演講集 (The collected lectures of Ma Yin-ch'u). 4 vols. Shanghai, 1929.

Mayers, William F., N. B. Dennys, and Charles King. *The Treaty Ports of China and Japan.* London, 1867; 650 pp.

Medhurst, W. H. *China: Its State and Prospects, with Especial Reference to the Spread of the Gospel.* London, 1840; 592 pp.

Meier, Gerald M. *Leading Issues in Development Economics.* New York, 1964; 572 pp.

Morse, Hosea Ballou. *Currency, Weights, and Measures in China.* Shanghai, 1906; 91 pp.

Bibliography

————. *The International Relations of the Chinese Empire.* 3 vols. Shanghai and London, 1910–1918.

————. *The Chronicles of the East India Company Trading to China, 1635–1843.* 4 vols. Oxford, 1926. Vol. 5 for 1742–1774, Oxford, 1929.

————. *The Trade and Administration of China,* 3rd ed. New York, 1921; 505 pp.

————. *In the Days of the Taipings.* Salem, Mass., 1927; 434 pp.

Myers, Ramon H. "Entrepreneurship in Modern China: An Interpretative Study." Ms., 1967.

NCH. See *North China Herald.*

Nan-yang hsiung-ti yen-ts'ao kung-ssu shih-liao 南洋兄弟煙草公司史料 (Historical materials concerning the Nanyang Brothers Tobacco Co.), comp. Chinese Academy of Sciences and Shanghai Academy of Social Sciences. Shanghai, 1958; 756 pp.

Negishi Tadashi 根岸佶, ed. *Shinkoku shōgyō sōran* 清國商業綜覽 (General survey of Chinese commerce and industry). 5 vols. Tokyo, 1906–1908.

————. *Baiben seido no kenkyū* 買辦制度の研究 (A study of the comprador system). Tokyo, 1948; 392 pp.

Nieh Pao-chang 聶寶璋. "Ts'ung Mei-shang Ch'i-ch'ang lun-ch'uan kung-ssu ti ch'uang-pan yü fa-chan k'an mai-pan ti tso-yung" 從美商旗昌輪船公司的創辦與發展看買辦的作用 (The function of the comprador as viewed from the history of the American firm of Shanghai Steam Navigation Company), *Li-shih yen-chiu,* 2.91–110 (1964).

North China Herald. Weekly, Shanghai, 1850—.

Okun, Bernard, and Richard W. Richardson, eds. *Studies in Economic Development.* New York, 1961; 315 pp.

Pao Kuang Yung (Pao P'ei-chih 包培之). "The Comprador: His Position in the Foreign Trade of China," *Economic Journal,* 21.84: 636–641 (December, 1911).

Papers Relating to the Foreign Relations of the United States. Washington, D.C.: Government Printing Office, 1878.

Parsons, Talcott, et al., eds. *Theories of Society.* 2 vols. New York, 1961.

P'eng Yü-hsin 彭雨新. "K'ang-Jih chan-cheng ch'ien Han-k'ou ti yang-hang ho mai-pan" 抗日戰爭前漢口的洋行和買辦 (The foreign firms and compradors at Hankow before the resistant war against Japan), *Li-lun chan-hsien* 理論戰線 (Theoretical warfront), 11: 28 (February 1959).

Postan, M.M. "Recent Trends in the Accumulation of Capital," *Economic History Review,* vol. 6, no. 1 (October 1935).

Pott, F. L. Hawks. *A Short History of Shanghai.* Shanghai, 1928; 336 pp.

RA: Russell & Co. Archives. Baker Library, Harvard Business School.

Saeki Tomi 佐伯富. *Shindai ensei no kenkyū* 清代鹽政の研究 (The salt administration under the Ch'ing). Kyoto, 1956; 400 pp.

Sakakida, Evelyn T. "Cheng Kuan-ying: Comprador-reformer." Seminar paper, Harvard University, January 1963.

Sayer, Geoffrey R. *Hong Kong: Birth, Adolescence, and Coming of Age.* London, 1937; 232 pp.

Scarth, J. *Twelve Years in China.* Edinburgh, 1860; 328 pp.

Bibliography

Schumpeter, Joseph A. *The Theory of Economic Development.* Cambridge, Mass., 1934; 255 pp.

————. *Capitalism, Socialism and Democracy,* 3rd ed. New York, 1950; 434 pp.

Schwartz, Benjamin. "The Intellectual History of China: Preliminary Reflections," in John K. Fairbank, ed. *Chinese Thought and Institutions.* Chicago, 1957; pp. 15–30.

Sha Wei-k'ai 沙爲楷. *Chung-kuo chih mai-pan chih* 中國之買辦制 (The comprador institution in China). Shanghai, 1927; 55 pp.

Shang-hai ch'ien-chuang shih-liao 上海錢庄史料 (Historical materials of the native banks in Shanghai), comp. Chung-kuo jen-min yin-hang Shang-hai-shih fen-hang 中國人民銀行上海市分行 (The Chinese Peoples' Bank, Shanghai). Shanghai, 1960; 854 pp.

Shanghai gazetteer, continued. See *Shang-hai hsien hsü chih.*

Shang-hai hsien hsü chih 上海縣續志 (Gazetteer of the Shanghai District, continued). 30 *chüan.* Shanghai, 1918.

Shang-hai t'ung-chih kuan ch'i-k'an 上海通志館期刊 (Journal of the Gazetteer Bureau of Shanghai).

Shang-hai yen-chiu tzu-liao 上海研究資料 (Materials for research on Shanghai), ed. Shang-hai t'ung-she 上海通社. Shanghai, 1936.

Shang-hai yen-chiu tzu-liao hsü-chi 上海研究資料續集 (Materials for research on Shanghai, second part), ed. Shang-hai t'ung-she 上海通社. Shanghai, 1936.

Shen pao 申報. Shanghai, 1872—.

Shen-pao-kuan 申報舘, comp. *Tsui-chin chih wu-shih-nien: Shen-pao kuan wu-shih chou-nien chi-nien* 最近之五十年，申報舘五十週年紀念 (The past fifty years: in commemoration of the Shen pao's Golden Jubilee, 1872–1922), a special supplement published by the *Shen pao.* Shanghai 1923.

Stanley, C. John. *Late Ch'ing Finance: Hu Kuang-yung as an Innovator.* Cambridge, Mass., 1961; 117 pp.

Sun Yat-sen. *Chung-shan ch'üan-shu* 中山全書 (Complete works of Sun Yat-sen). 4 vols. Shanghai, 1927.

Sun Yü-t'ang 孫毓棠. *Chung Jih chia-wu chan-cheng ch'ien wai-kuo tzu-pen tsai Chung-kuo ching-ying ti chin-tai kung-yeh* 中日甲午戰爭前外國資本在中國經營的近代工業 (Modern enterprises in China financed by foreign capitals before 1894). Shanghai, 1955; 91 pp.

————, comp. *Chung-kuo chin-tai kung-yeh shih tzu-liao chi-yao: ti i chi* 中國近代工業史資料輯要，第一集 (Selected materials for China's modern industrial history, first series). 2 vols. Peking, 1957.

Suzuki Sōichirō 鈴木總一郎. "Baiben seido" 買辦制度 (The comprador institution), *Tōa keizai ronsō* 東亞經濟論叢 (East Asian economic journal), 1.1:179–198 (February 1941).

————. "Baiben hassei no shakaiteki konkyo" 買辦發生の社會的根據 (Social causes of compradors), *Tōa keizai ronsō,* 1.3: 177–193 (September 1941).

Tawney, R. H. *Land and Labour in China.* London, 1832; 207 pp.

T'ang Chen 湯震. *Wei-yen* (Warnings). 4 *chüan.* Shanghai, 1890.

Teng Ssu-yü and John K. Fairbank. *China's Response to the West: A Documentary Survey, 1839–1923.* Cambridge, Mass., 1954; 296 pp.

Bibliography

Terada Takanobu 寺田隆信. "So-Shō chihō ni okeru toshi no mengyō shōnin ni tsuite" 蘇松地方における都市の棉業商人に就いて (On the cotton merchants of cities in Su [Soochow] and Sung [Sungkiang], *Shirin* 史林 (Historical studies), 41.6:52–69 (Nov. 1, 1958).

Tiffany, Osmond, Jr. *The Canton Chinese; or the American's Sojourn in the Celestial Empire*. Boston, 1849; 250 pp.

Ting Wen-chiang (V. K. Ting) 丁文江, comp. *Liang Jen-kung nien-p'u ch'ang-pien ch'u-kao* 梁任公年譜長編初稿 (First draft of the chronological biography of Liang Ch'i-ch'ao). 2 vols. Taipei, 1959.

Tōa Dōbunkai 東亞同文會. *Shina keizai zensho* 支那經濟全書 (Chinese economy series). 12 vols. Vols. 1–4, Osaka, 1907; vols. 5–12, Tokyo, 1908.

Toyama Gunji 外山軍治. "Shanhai no shinshō Yō Bō" 上海の紳商楊坊 (The Shanghai gentry-merchant Yang Fang), *Tōyōshi kenkyū* 東洋史研究 (Studies on Oriental history), n.s. 1.4: 17–34 (November 1945).

Tso Tsung-t'ang 左宗棠. *Tso Wen-hsiang-kung ch'üan chi* 左文襄公全集 (The complete works of Tso Tsung-t'ang). 100 *chüan*. Changsha, 1888.

Tsuchiya Keizayū 土屋計左右. *Baiben seido* 買辦制度 (The comprador institution). Tokyo, 1940; 104 pp.

Tzu yüeh ts'ung-k'an 子曰叢刊 (Confucius' saying magazine), 3: 6 (Shanghai, 1925).

Uchida Naosaku 內田直作. "Baiben seido no kenkyū" 買辦制度の研究 (A study of the comprador system), *Shina kenkyū* 支那研究 (Studies on China), 47: 19–36 (July 1938); 48:1–28 (December 1938); 49:1–24 (January 1939).

———. "Yōkō seido no kenkyū 洋行制度の研究 (A study of the foreign firm system), *Shina kenkyū*, 50:187–211 (March 1939).

———. "Zai-Shi Eikoku shōsha I-wa [I-ho, Ewo] yōkō no hatten shi-teki bunseki" 在支英國商社怡和洋行の發展史的分析 (An historical analysis of the development of the British firm of Jardine, Matheson & Co. in China), *Shina kenkyū*, 51:213–240 (June 1939); 52:151–192 (November 1939).

Wang Ching-yü 汪敬虞, comp. *Chung-kuo chin-tai kung-yeh shih tzu-liao chi-yao: ti erh chi* 中國近代工業史資料輯要，第二集 (Selected materials for China's modern industrial history, second series). 2 vols. Peking, 1960.

———. "Shih-chiu shih-chi wai-kuo ch'in-Hua shih-yeh chung ti Hua-shang fu-ku huo-tung" 十九世紀外國侵華事業中的華商附股活動 (The activities of Chinese merchants to buy capital shares in the aggressive foreign enterprises in China during the late nineteenth century), *Li-shih yen-chiu*, 4:39–74 (1965).

Wang Shu-huai 王樹槐. *Wai-jen yü wu-hsü pien-fa* 外人與戊戌變法 (The foreigners and the 1898 reform movement). Taipei, 1965; 304 pp.

Who's Who in China. Shanghai, 1926.

Williams, S. Wells. *The Chinese Commercial Guide*, 5th ed. Hong Kong, 1863; 266 pp.

Wright, Arnold, ed. *Twentieth Century Impressions of Hongkong, Shanghai, and Other Treaty Ports of China: Their History, People, Commerce, Industries, and Resources*. London, 1908; 848 pp.

Wu Hsing-lien 吳醒濂. *Hsiang-kang Hua-jen ming-jen shih-lüeh* 香港華人名人史略 (The prominent Chinese in Hong Kong). 2 vols. Hong Kong, 1937.

Yang kung Mei-nan ai-ssu-lu 楊公梅南哀思錄 (Memorial records of Yang Mei-nan).

Bibliography

Ca. 1941; 123 pp.

Yang Lien-sheng 楊聯陞. *Money and Credit in China: A Short History*. Cambridge, Mass., 1952; 143 pp.

————. *Les aspects economiques des travaux publics dans la Chine imperiale*. College de France, 1964; 83 pp.

Yang-wu yün-tung 洋務運動 (The "foreign matters" movement), ed. Chung-kuo shih-hsüeh hui 中國史學會 (Historical Association of China). 8 vols. Shanghai, 1958.

Yao Chih-ho 姚之鶴. *Hua-Yang su-sung li-an hui-pien* 華洋訴訟例案彙編 (Collected lawsuit cases between Chinese and foreigners). 2 vols. Shanghai, 1915; 796 pp.

Yao Kung-ho 姚公鶴. *Shang-hai hsien-hua* 上海閑話 (Shanghai gossip). 2 vols. Shanghai, 1917.

Yen Chung-p'ing 嚴中平. *Chung-kuo mien-yeh chih fa-chan* 中國棉業之發展 (The development of the Chinese cotton industry). Chungking, 1943; 305 pp.

————. *Chung-kuo mien-fang-chih shih kao, 1289–1937* 中國棉紡織史稿 (A draft history of Chinese cotton spinning and weaving). Peking, 1955; 384 pp. Rev. ed. of the preceding item.

———— et al., comp. *Chung-kuo chin-tai ching-chi shih t'ung-chi tzu-liao hsüan-chi* 中國近代經濟史統計資料選輯 (Selected statistical materials for China's modern economic history). Shanghai, 1961; 374 pp.

Yüan Lang 阮朗 et al. *Nan-hsing chi* 南星集 (Southern star collection). Hong Kong, 1962; 318 pp.

Yung Wing (Jung Hung 容閎). *My Life in China and America*. New York, 1909; 286 pp.

Notes

BPP	British Parliamentary Papers
DP	F. G. Dexter Papers
FBF	Frank Blackwell Forbes's Letter Books
FC	Forbes Collection
HC	Heard Collection
HC II	Heard Collection, Second Part
IMC	China, Imperial Maritime Customs
IWSM	*Ch'ou-pan i-wu shih-mo*
JMA	Jardine, Matheson & Co. Archives
MLB	Letter Books of Hosea Ballou Morse
NCH	*North China Herald*
RA	Russell & Co. Archives

I. INTRODUCTION: THE COMPRADOR IN CHINESE SOCIETY

1. "Oh, East is East, and West is West, and never the twain shall meet,/Till Earth and Sky stand presently at God's great Judgment Seat." Rudyard Kipling, "The Ballad of East and West," *The Works of Rudyard Kipling* (New York, 1909), X, 11.

2. Of particular importance was the Liang-Huai area and its zone of distribution, covering roughly the whole of the rich Yangtze basin and the eastern seaboard. See Saeki Tomi, *Shindai ensei no kenkyū* (The salt administration under the Ch'ing; Kyoto, 1956).

3. For the history of the hong merchants, see Liang Chia-pin, *Kuang-tung shih-san hang k'ao* (A study of the Canton thirteen hongs), rev. ed. (T'ai-chung, 1960).

4. *Change and the Entrepreneur: Postulates and Patterns for Entrepreneurial History*, prepared by the Research Center in Entrepreneurial History, Harvard University (Cambridge, Mass., 1949), p. 99.

5. For Hu's activity, see C. John Stanley, *Late Ch'ing Finance: Hu Kuang-yung as an Innovator* (Cambridge, Mass., 1961), pp. 1–44.

6. Liu Kwang-Ching, "Two Steamship Companies in China, 1862–1877," Ph. D. thesis (Harvard University, 1956), pp. 99–192.

7. See, for example, Marion J. Levy and Shih Kuo-heng, *The Rise of the Modern Chinese Business Class, Two Introductory Essays* (New York, 1949).

8. For the social status of merchants in traditional China, see Ho Ping-ti, *The Ladder of Success in Imperial China: Aspects of Social Mobility, 1368–1911* (New York, 1962), pp. 41–42, 256–257.

9. For the functions of the gentry, see Ch'ü T'ung-tsu, *Local Government in China under the Ch'ing* (Cambridge, Mass., 1962), p. 180.

10. Liu Kwang-Ching, "Two Steamship Companies," pp. 186–192.

11. By "elite" is meant persons whose position was socially recognized. It therefore implies no value judgment. The term *shen-tung* also has a specific meaning and is not necessarily equivalent to "gentry merchant."

12. Talcott Parsons et al., eds., *Theories of Society* (New York, 1961), II, 944–946. See also Robert E. Park's "Introduction" to E. V. Stonequist, *The Marginal Man* (New York, 1937), pp. xiii–xviii.

13. For the treaty port mandarin, see John King Fairbank, *Trade and Diplomacy on the China Coast: The Opening of the Treaty Ports, 1842–1854* (Cambridge, Mass., 1953), I, 195.

14. Ralph Linton, *The Study of Man: An Introduction* (New York, 1936), pp. 324–346. Reprinted in Parsons, II, 1371–1380.

15. A comprador as a rule had several names. The name by which he was generally known in the treaty ports is used in this study. Unfortunately, not all of the compradors' Chinese names can be identified.

16. Parsons, II, 1380. For Yung Wing, see his *My Life in China and America* (New York, 1909), ch. 8.

17. *Yang-wu yün-tung* (The "foreign matters" movement; Shanghai, 1958), ed. Chung-kuo shih-hsüeh hui (Historical Association of China), I, 1, 2.

18. See Benjamin Schwartz, "The Intellectual History of China: Preliminary Reflections," in John K. Fairbank, ed., *Chinese Thought and Institutions* (Chicago, 1957), pp. 15–30, esp. pp. 20–21.

19. Hsü Ti-hsin, *Kuan-liao tzu-pen lun* (On official capital; Shanghai, 1958), pp. 8–12.

20. Julean Arnold, *Commercial Handbook of China* (Washington, D.C., 1920), II, 254.

21. For example, one can find hardly any information concerning the comprador in *Ch'ing-shih kao* (Draft history of the Ch'ing dynasty; 1942 photolithographic ed.), *Ta-Ch'ing hui-tien* (Collected statutes of the Ch'ing dynasty), and *Ch'ing-shih lieh-chuan* (Biographies of the Ch'ing history).

22. Augustine Heard & Co. archives (Heard Collection, Heard Collection II), Russell & Co. Archives, Forbes Collection, and Frank B. Forbes Letter Books are all at the Baker Library, Harvard Business School. Jardine, Matheson & Co. Archives are at the University Library, Cambridge University, England.

II. THE WESTERN MERCHANT AND HIS CHINESE COMPRADOR

1. Augustine Heard & Co. was organized "for the purpose of transacting

commission business." Partnership Agreement, April 28, 1842, EA-1, HC. For commission scale in 1863, see Case 19, HC II.

2. See various partnership agreements of Heard's, EA-1, HC.

3. Decentralization in a foreign house was illustrated by an abortive proposal for the transport of tribute rice to Peking by Heard's and Russell's in 1861. For details, see Stephen C. Lockwood, "Augustine Heard & Co.: American Merchants in China on the Eve of the Opening of the Yangtze, 1858–1862," undergraduate honors thesis, Harvard University, 1963, pp. 92–104.

4. When J. Parker became a partner in Olyphant & Co., bringing with him many constituents, John Heard expressed the wish that Heard's had taken him. Augustine Heard to John Heard, Aug. 15, 1859, BL–4, HC. Augustine Heard commented on the partnership of J. B. Dixwell: "He is not much of a businessman [but will] carry with him the business of a number of friends." Augustine Heard to John Heard, Aug. 15, 1860, BL–4, HC.

5. William Cole (Shanghai) to F. G. Dexter (Boston), 1860, DP.

6. Thomas Walsh (Shanghai) to F. G. Dexter (Foochow), Dec. 21, 1860, DP.

7. Thomas Larken (Foochow) to Joseph Jardine (Hong Kong), Aug. 29, 1856, JMA.

8. Memorandum for season 1870–1871, JMA. The Japanese tea prepared at Shanghai suffered the same fate in England: "The Japan oolongs you complain of were made up here from the unfired Japan leaf, but as it was ascertained at once from the valuation that they would not answer, no more were made. Mr. Keswick has been advised not to purchase any more of the article unless at very low rates as it's out of favor in England." James Whittall (Shanghai) to Jardine, Matheson & Co. (Hong Kong), Oct. 5, 1861, JMA.

9. Memorandum for season 1870 and 1871, JMA.

10. EA-1, HC.

11. Edward Cunningham to P. S. Forbes, June 4, 1861, FC.

12. A. G. Dallas (Shanghai) to Donald Matheson (Hong Kong), July 5, 1849, JMA.

13. Fairbank, *Trade and Diplomacy*, I, 61.

14. IMC, *Decennial Report, 1882–1891*, p. 322.

15. *NCH* (June 26, 1873), p. 75.

16. Memorandum for season 1870–1871, Mar. 10, 1870, JMA.

17. Edward Cunningham to P. S. Forbes, June 4, 1861, FC.

18. Albert P. Heard to Augustine Heard, Jr., Oct. 22, 1961, HL–36, HC.

19. F. B. Forbes (Shanghai) to M. Cordier (Paris), Aug. 17, 1872, FBF. For Russell's connection with the steamship enterprise, see Liu Kwang-Ching, *Anglo-American Steamship Rivalry in China, 1862–1874* (Cambridge, Mass., 1962), pp. 9–111.

20. *Ibid.*

21. *Ibid.*, pp. 31–32.

22. *Ibid.*, pp. 112–113.

23. For complete list, see Case 9, HC II.

24. Uchida Naosaku, "Yōkō seido no kenkyū" (A study of the foreign firm system); *Shina kenkyū*, 50: 187–211 (March 1939); Uchida Naosaku, "Zai-Shi Eikoku shōsha I-wa [I-ho, Ewo] yōkō no hatten shi-teki banseki" (An historical analysis of the development of the British firm of Jardine, Matheson & Co. in China); *Shina kenkyū*, 51: 213–240 (June 1939); 52: 151–192 (November 1939).

25. Quoted in Pao Kuang Yung, "The Comprador: His Position in the Foreign

Trade of China," *Economic Journal*, 21.84: 636 (December 1911).

26. George F. Weller to Albert F. Heard, Sept. 11, 1862, HM–49, HC.

27. The comprehensive list of taels included in H. B. Morse, *Currency, Weights, and Measures in China* (Shanghai, 1906), shows the number of taels in the larger commercial centers.

28. For different foreign silver dollars circulated in nineteenth century China, see Frank H. H. King, *Money and Monetary Policy in China, 1845–1895* (Cambridge, Mass., 1965), p. 179.

29. James Whittall (Shanghai) to Jardine, Matheson & Co. (Hong Kong), July 2, 1861, JMA.

30. For the inaccuracy of measurement in late Ch'ing, see King, pp. 190–191.

31. *NCH* (Nov. 19, 1884), p. 578.

32. For example, if the price quoted was one tael, the amount of sycee to be paid would depend upon the custom of the market. Thus, in Canton, if cotton were quoted at one tael, only 0.97 liang of current sycee would be paid to the cotton merchants; in retail shops, 0.974 liang. To pay foreign customs duties, however, one tael required payment of 1.07 liang of current sycee. See King, p. 77.

33. Edward Cunningham was a clerk with Russell & Co. (1845–1849), and a partner (1850–1857, 1861–1863, and 1867–1877). See his letters to P. S. Forbes in FC, and letters of John Murray Forbes, 1840–1867 (typewritten, Baker Library). See also Liu Kwang-Ching, *Steamship Rivalry*.

34. *Ibid.*, pp. 9–24.

35. Fairbank, *Trade and Diplomacy*, I, ch. 22. See also Edward Cunningham, *Our Political and Commercial Relations with China* (Washington, D.C., 1855), available at the Massachusetts Historical Society, Boston.

36. Edward Cunningham to P. S. Forbes, Nov. 10, 1865, FC. See also Liu Kwang-Ching, *Steamship Rivalry*, pp. 27–28.

37. *Ibid.*, p. 25.

38. Robert B. Forbes, *Personal Reminiscences*, 2d ed., rev. (Boston, 1892), pp. 364–366; Liu Kwang-Ching, *Steamship Rivalry*, p. 26. An article of the *NCH* described the Kin-lee-yuen site: "The premises of the [Shanghai Steam Navigation] Company are upon the French Concession, and under the walls of the native city, so that they are very favorably situated for every description of merchandise." *NCH* (Mar. 29, 1862), p. 50.

39. F. B. Forbes to Edward Cunningham, April 10, 1870, FBF. See also Liu Kwang-Ching, *Steamship Rivalry*, p. 90.

40. *Ibid.*, p. 92.

41. Edward Cunningham to P. S. Forbes, Sept. 19, 1871, FC. See also Liu Kwang-Ching, *Steamship Rivalry*, p. 196.

42. Dilip K. Basu, "The American Entrepreneurs and Howqua: A Study in Sino-American Trade During 1829–1834," seminar paper, Harvard University, January 1965.

43. Arthur W. Hummel, ed., *Eminent Chinese of the Ch'ing Period, 1644–1912* (Washington, D. C., 1943, 1944), II, 867–868.

44. Russell & Co. (per John M. Forbes, Jr.) to E. M. King, U.S. Consul, Canton, May 2, 1868, Case 26, RA; Edward Cunningham (Shanghai) to John M. Forbes, Jr. (Canton), June 4, 1868, Case 26, RA.

45. A. F. Heard (Shanghai) to Augustine Heard, Jr., April 18, 1862, HL–36, HC.

46. Liu Kwang-Ching, *Steamship Rivalry*, p. 48.

47. George Tyson (Shanghai) to P. S. Forbes (Boston), March 24, 1865, FC. See also Liu Kwang-Ching, *Steamship Rivalry*, p. 48.

48. A. F. Heard (Shanghai) to Augustine Heard, Jr., April 18, 1862, HL–36, HC.

49. "His [Koofunsing's] reputation and standing are too important for him to risk them." A. F. Heard (Shanghai) to John Heard, Feb. 26, 1858, HL–13, HC.

50. "Sunkee's ability is undoubted; if one could only depend on his honesty." F. B. Forbes (Shanghai) to T. Moore (Tientsin), Mar. 18, 1873, FBF.

51. F. B. Johnson (Shanghai) to William Keswick, June 18, 1872, JMA.

52. F. B. Forbes (Shanghai) to P. S. Forbes (Boston), June 14, 1873, N–8, p. 104, FBF.

53. F. B. Forbes (Shanghai) to Edward Cunningham, June 11, 1872, FBF.

54. F. B. Forbes (Shanghai) to P. S. Forbes, June 14, 1873, FBF.

55. F. B. Forbes (Shanghai) to Edward Cunningham, Dec. 22, 1874, FBF.

56. *Ibid.*

57. F. B. Forbes (Shanghai) to S. C. Rose, July 22, 1873, FBF.

58. A. F. Heard to John Heard, Feb. 28, 1858, HL–13, HC.

59. FL–7, p. 197, HC. See also Liu Kwang-Ching, *Steamship Rivalry*, p. 25.

60. FL–7, p. 210, HC. See also Liu Kwang-Ching; *Steamship Rivalry*, p. 25.

61. John Heard to A. F. Heard (Shanghai), Apr. 4, 1862, FL–6, p. 136, HC.

62. A. F. Heard (Shanghai) to Augustine Heard, Jr., Apr. 18, 1862, HL–36, p. 368, HC.

63. *Ibid.*

64. A. G. Dallas (Shanghai) to Donald Matheson (Hong Kong), Mar. 21, 1846, JMA.

65. Liu Kwang-Ching, "T'ang T'ing-shu chih mai-pan shih-tai" (Tong King-sing: His comprador years), *Ch'ing-hua hsüeh-pao*, New Ser., 2.2: 172–176 (June 1961).

66. "They [Ekee and Yakee] will be able to do some good in the country. I have arranged with both these native friends to purchase through them in the country." William Keswick (Shanghai) to James Whittall, May 21, 1864, JMA. "Before giving definite limits to Yowloong and our other Native friends about the prices at which to go to the country, I will await later home intelligence." William Keswick to James Whittall, Mar. 21, 1866, JMA.

67. A. F. Heard (Shanghai) to Augustine Heard, Jr., Apr. 18, 1862, HL–36, p. 368, HC. "Ahone, the Native with whom I had some silk business last year is offering to contract with me for the delivery of two chops finest Ningchow at 30 taels." F. B. Johnson to William Keswick, May 18, 1868, JMA.

68. "[To Ekee] I yesterday made an advance of Tls. 40,000 to send into the interior." William Keswick to James Whittall, May 21, 1864, JMA. "I have instructed Ekee to buy [silk] for us if he can do so." Edward Whittall to James Whittall, Nov. 24, 1866, JMA. Ekee went bankrupt speculating in 1867. See E. Whittall to J. Whittall, Jan. 3, 1867, JMA.

69. "There has been business doing in Tea from day to day & about 45,000 chests have been settled of which . . . Dent & Co.'s late compradore has taken about one half. . . . Dent & Co.'s compradore has been purchasing on the market & not merely shipping chops in which he is interested." F. B. Johnson to William Keswick, July 1, 1869, JMA.

70. "My principal object however is to keep Tucksing about our Hong as he is the best informed Native I know, on all matters connected with local business." F. B. Johnson to James Whittall, May 6, 1867, JMA. "I now return you many thanks for your past favours which you have kindly favoured me for about 15 years and which I trust you will continue the same." Tucksing (Shanghai) to James Whittall (Hong Kong), Jan. 15, 1867, JMA.

71. F. B. Johnson (Shanghai) to James Whittall (Hong Kong), Nov. 16, 1867, JMA. See also Liu Kwang-Ching, "Tong King-sing," p. 155.

72. F. B. Johnson to William Keswick, Dec. 29, 1868, JMA. See also Liu Kwang-Ching, "Tong King-sing," p. 156.

73. F. B. Johnson to James Whittall, Oct. 2, 1871, JMA. See also Liu Kwang-Ching, *Steamship Rivalry*, p. 143.

74. F. B. Johnson (Shanghai) to William Keswick (Hong Kong), June 22, 1871, JMA. See also Liu Kwang-Ching, "Tong King-sing," p. 168.

75. F. B. Johnson (Shanghai) to William Keswick, Sept. 27, 1871, JMA.

76. H. G. Bridges (Hankow) to A. F. Heard (Shanghai), June 20, 1866, HM–23, HC.

77. *Ibid.*

78. John M. Forbes (Canton) to Edward Cunningham (Shanghai), May 27, 1868, Case 26, RA.

79. *Ibid.*

80. *NCH* (Oct. 7, 1875), p. 358.

81. George F. Heard to John Heard and Augustine Heard, Jr., FM–9, HC.

82. F. B. Forbes to Edward Cunningham, June 11, 1872, FBF.

83. F. B. Forbes to P. S. Forbes, Sept. 27, 1873, FBF. See also Liu Kwang-Ching, *Steamship Rivalry*, p. 131.

84. F. B. Forbes (Shanghai) to W. S. Fitz (Hankow), Apr. 10, 1873, FBF.

85. Cheng Kuan-ying, *Sheng-shih wei-yen* (Warnings to a prosperous age), 1900 edition, 5: 34. Liu Kwang-Ching's translation. See also Liu Kwang-Ching, *Steamship Rivalry*, p. 131.

86. William Keswick (Shanghai) to James Whittall (Hong Kong), Dec. 18, 1865, JMA.

87. William Keswick (Shanghai) to James Whittall (Hong Kong), Feb. 4, 1866, JMA.

88. F. B. Johnson (Shanghai) to William Keswick, Feb. 2, 1869; Nov. 17, 1870; JMA.

89. F. B. Johnson (Shanghai) to James Whittall, May 3, 1867, JMA.

90. F. B. Johnson (Shanghai) to William Keswick, Apr. 11, 1870, JMA.

91. B. A. Clarke (Hankow) to J. J. Keswick (Shanghai), May 6, 1885, JMA.

92. E. H. Kenney (Hankow) to J. J. Keswick (Shanghai), May 27, 1885, JMA.

93. A. S. Akkeb (Kiukiang) to J. J. Keswick (Shanghai), Oct. 20, 1886, JMA.

94. B. A. Clarke (Hankow) to J. J. Keswick (Shanghai), Dec. 24, 1885, JMA.

95. "Captain Russell tells me that when he ran the *Corea*, a broker named Chongfat at Canton was the most influential shipper." F. B. Johnson (Shanghai) to William Keswick, Apr. 11, 1870, JMA.

96. John M. Forbes, Jr. (Canton) to Edward Cunningham (Shanghai), May 27, 1868, Case 26, RA.

97. John Heard to A. F. Heard, Apr. 4, 1862, FL–6, p. 137, HC.

98. One of Tong Loong-maw's letters to Dixwell will serve as an example:

"Your letter . . . is received and its contents fully noted. The sugar market at present is lower. . . . As to tea—the spring rains have been excessive. During the third month there were more than twenty rainy days and this is the month for gathering the leaves. The leaves which had been gathered early in the month could not be dried for want of sun . . . and I do not therefore see any chance of a good business in early teas. . . . Opium has gone down . . . inferior is very difficult of sale." Tong Loong-maw (Hankow) to G. B. Dixwell (Shanghai), May 19, 1863, HM–30, HC.

99. Tong Loong-maw (Hankow) to G. B. Dixwell (Shanghai), Feb. 23, 1863, HM–30, HC.

100. James Whittall (Shanghai) to Joseph Jardine (Hong Kong), Dec. 21, 1859, JMA.

101. William Keswick (Shanghai) to James Whittall, Sept. 6, 1864, JMA. See also Liu Kwang-Ching, "Tong King-sing," p. 173. Jardine's advanced Yakee 86,000 taels in 1861 for tea and silk. James Whittall (Shanghai) to Jardine, Matheson & Co. (Hong Kong), Oct. 5, 1861, JMA.

102. F. B. Johnson (Shanghai) to James Whittall, May 20, 1867, JMA. "Acum left yesterday for the silk district with $100,000 and I have enjoined him to be exceeding cautious." F. B. Johnson (Shanghai) to William Keswick, May 20, 1868, JMA.

103. James Whittall (Shanghai) to Jardine, Matheson & Co. (Hong Kong), July 30, 1861, JMA.

104. *NCH* (Apr. 16, 1864), p. 62.

105. Mr. Stubbendorff's comprador "on one occasion bought a large quantity [of cotton] from Liu-chow-fan, which he resold to his employers." *NCH* (Apr. 16, 1864), p. 62. "He [Acum, comprador to Jardine, Matheson & Co.] does sell to other hongs, but the majority of his dealings are with the E-ho hong [Jardine, Matheson & Co.]: in the same manner as the man in Messrs. Dent & Co.'s employment, who deals with other parties, at the same time that the majority of his dealings are with his own hong." *NCH* (Oct. 13, 1860), p. 50.

106. For some joint accounts of Heard's, see EA–1 and EJ–2, HC. "The *Peihp* left last night for Chinkiang to load Rice for Canton. . . . Canny & Co. will forward you a B/lading [Bill of lading] & Invoice for about 10,000 piculs [of rice] shipped by Tongkingsing on j/a [joint account] with ourselves. . . . Tongkingsing has only a small interest in the venture." F. B. Johnson to William Keswick, Oct. 4, 1871, JMA.

107. Edward Whittall to William Keswick, Oct. 6, 1865, JMA. However, it is not certain whether or not Ekee was a comprador to Jardine's at this time.

108. According to an agreement reached between Heard's and Atai on Feb. 6, 1873, Heard's was to pay the travel expenses for Atai to Hainan Island to "obtain the consent of the authorities and the inhabitants near and in Cheong-fa-hien to his working sundry copper and other mines in that vicinity." If this succeeded, "he [Atai] then is to offer to Mr. A. F. Heard the privilege of working these mines with him either as owning half share therein or with such other parties as they select to own the privilege with them." See Agreements, Case 9, HC II.

109. Augustine Heard, Jr. (Canton) to C. A. Fearon (Shanghai), June 10, 1853, GL–2, HC.

110. *Ibid.*, June 19, 1853. In another letter, Augustine Heard, Jr., wrote: "but I am sorry we can get almost nothing more out of the comprador." *Ibid.*,

June 25, 1853.

111. Case 9, HC II.

112. Augustine Heard, Jr. (Hong Kong) to C. A. Fearon (Shanghai), Mar. 12, 1854, GL–2, HC.

113. A. F. Heard (Hong Kong) to John Heard, Feb. 28, 1863, FM–4, HC.

114. A. F. Heard (Shanghai) to John Heard (Hong Kong), Jan. 21, 1861, EA–1, HC. See also John Heard (Hong Kong) to A. F. Heard (Shanghai), Feb. 8, 1861, EA–1, HC.

115. G. B. Dixwell (Shanghai) to Augustine Heard, Jr. (Hong Kong), Mar. 29, 1870, EM–14, HC.

116. *NCH* (Feb. 19, 1880), p. 147.

117. John Heard to A. F. Heard, Sept. 6, 1859, HM–4, HC.

118. See Arnold Wright, ed., *Twentieth Century Impressions of Hongkong, Shanghai, and Other Treaty Ports of China: Their History, People, Commerce, Industries, and Resources* (London, 1908), p. 550.

119. Cheng Kuan-ying, *Sheng-shih wei-yen hou-p'ien* (Warnings to a prosperous age, second part; Shanghai, 1920).

120. Negishi Tadashi, ed., *Shinkoku shōgyō sōran* (General survey of Chinese commerce and industry; Tokyo, 1906–1908), I, 37–40.

121. Tōa Dōbunkai, *Shina keizai zensho* (Chinese economy series; Osaka, 1907; Tokyo, 1908), II, 144.

122. Negishi, *Sōran*, I, 41–44.

123. *Ibid.*, I, 43; Tōa Dōbunkai, *Keizai zensho*, II, 144.

III. THE RISE AND FALL OF THE COMPRADOR

1. *NCH* (Mar. 10, 1855), p. 241. Russell & Co. denied that they had a special arrangement with Ah Yen & Co., comprador at Hong Kong, to work for the Union Line Steamers. July 29, 1881, vol. 25, RA.

2. Wright, p. 568.

3. In Shanghai the comprador was also called *chiang-pei-ta* or *k'ang-pai-tu*. Ko Yüan-hsü, *Hu yu tsa-chi* (Miscellaneous records of a sojourn in Shanghai; Shanghai, 1876), 2: 6. See also Hsü K'o, *Ch'ing pai lei-ch'ao* (A classified collection of Ch'ing dynasty anecdotes; Shanghai, 1928), 44: 85. For Hong Kong, see *Hsiang-kang Hua-tzu jih-pao* (Chinese mail; Feb. 2, 1895), available at the Feng P'ing-shan Library, University of Hong Kong. For Tientsin, see Negishi, *Sōran*, I, 45–49.

4. For the term "shang-huo," see Tso Tsung-t'ang, *Tso Wen-hsiang-kung ch'üan-chi* (The complete works of Tso Tsung-t'ang; Changsha, 1889), 26: 15b; for the term "tsung-li," see Cheng Kuan-ying, *Hou-p'ien*, 8: 31–32.

5. Negishi Tadashi, *Baiben seido no kenkyū* (A study of the comprador system; Tokyo, 1948), p. 35. W. C. Hunter, *The "Fan Kwae" at Canton before Treaty Days, 1825–1844* (London, 1882), p. 37.

6. Hatano Yoshihiro, *Chūgoku kindai kōgyōshi no kenkyū* (Studies on the early industrialization in China; Kyoto, 1961), p. 150; Negishi, *Baiben seido*, p. 34.

7. Liang Chia-pin, p. 96; Liang T'ing-nan, *Yüeh hai-kuan chih* (Gazetteer of the maritime customs of Kwangtung), 28: 94.

8. Liang T'ing-nan, vol. 1, ch. 2. For the maritime trade history of Canton, see Fairbank, *Trade and Diplomacy*, I, 46–47.

9. For the ship comprador, see S. Wells Williams, *The Chinese Commercial Guide*,

5th ed. (Hong Kong, 1863), p. 153. For a single ship, "the comprador's supplies on board of the ship Packet laying at Whampoa from the 26 December 1824 to January 10th 1825 [are]: beef, 1378 pounds; vegetables, 483 pounds; hide, 1 piece; pepper, 1 3/4 pounds; eggs, 18 dozens; fish, 15 3/4 pounds; capons, 17 1/2 pounds; pork, 22 1/4 pounds." BJ–21, HC. For the selection of a ship comprador, see Liang T'ing-nan, 26: 94–95.

10. Hosea Ballou Morse, *The Chronicles of the East India Company Trading to China, 1635–1843* (Oxford, 1926), I, 205; III, 355.

11. *Ibid.*, I, 179.

12. *Ibid.*, IV, 128, 254; *Chinese Repository*, V, 426.

13. Augustine Heard, Jr. See FP–4, p. 33, HC.

14. W. H. Medhurst, *China: Its State and Prospects, with Especial Reference to the Spread of the Gospel* . . . (London, 1840), p. 284.

15. Liang T'ing-nan, 29: 127.

16. Liang Chia-pin, p. 144. "If prostitutes go into the Hongs, and there be sufficient evidence, then the said prostitutes, together with the Comprador (house steward like a Calcutta 'Cresumer') of the Hong in question, shall be handed over to the Government and be vigorously dealt with." John Heard to A. Charley, Dec. 2, 1844, FL–1, HC.

17. Hunter, p. 54.

18. Liang T'ing-nan, 28: 82–83.

19. Liang Chia-pin, pp. 70, 96.

20. *Ibid.*, p. 96.

21. Medhurst, p. 284. "Every time that he [comprador] pays one a handful of dollars, he lays them flat on the stones, and stamps each one with his own mark, which is cut on the end of an iron chisel, and hammered into the Spaniard. So every dealer inflicts his brand on every piece that passes through his hands, until the silver is frittered into bits." Osmond Tiffany, Jr., *The Canton Chinese; or the American's Sojourn in the Celestial Empire* (Boston, 1849), p. 215.

22. C. T. Downing, *The Stranger in China; or, the Fan-Qui's Visit to the Celestial Empire in 1836–1837* (London, 1838), I, 106, 107.

23. G. F. Weller to Albert F. Heard, Apr. 4, 1862, HM–23, HC. However, it is not certain that Aming, the Kiukiang comprador, was the same Aming who had been a hong merchant. The name was common, and they could have been two persons.

24. IMC, *Treaties, Conventions, etc. between China and Foreign States*, 2nd ed. (Shanghai, 1917), I, 353. See also *NCH* (Dec. 3, 1853), p. 70.

25. Liang Chia-pin, p. 11; Fairbank, *Trade and Diplomacy*, I, 248.

26. Negishi, *Baiben seido*, p. 9.

27. For the hong merchants and Hoppo under the treaties, see Fairbank, *Trade and Diplomacy*, I, 248–251.

28. Letter from John Heard, 3rd, FP–4, p. 47, HC.

29. Fairbank, *Trade and Diplomacy*, I, 47.

30. Hatano, p. 152.

31. Augustine Heard, Jr., "Old China and New," p.26.

32. After the war, "a new settlement formed, separated from the mainland by a deep, broad canal for safety. Fine houses were built, streets laid out, trees planted, and Shameen [Sha-mien] has become one of the prettiest residences in China." Augustine Heard, Jr., "Old China and New," p. 12, GQ–2, HC.

33. The export of tea from Canton fell from 263,000 piculs in 1860 to 109,742 piculs in 1865, a decline that was mainly attributable to the opening of Hankow. The progressive decline of the import of cotton piece goods from 1860 to 1865 was also clear:

Year	Cotton, dyed, figured, & plain	Grey sheetings	T-Cloth
1860	45,000	358,000	136,000
1861	27,000	352,000	74,000
1862	21,000	133,000	38,000
1863	20,000	48,000	28,000
1864	14,000	44,000	22,000
1865	9,000	80,000	29,000

William F. Mayers, N. B. Dennys, and Charles King, *Treaty Ports of China and Japan* (London, 1867), p. 199.

34. *NCH* (Oct. 13, 1868), p. 489.

35. John Heard to A. F. Heard, Hong Kong, Sept. 6, 1859, HM–4, HC.

36. HM–28, HM–30, HC; Case 9, Case 30, HC II.

37. For Akit's activities, see George F. Weller to John Heard, Dec. 16, 1861, FM–13; John Heard to Albert F. Heard, Apr. 4, 1862, FL–6; John Heard to George F. Weller, May 2, 1862, FL–6; HC.

38. John Heard to A. F. Heard, Shanghai, Mar. 23, 1860, HL–15, HC.

39. Aug. 17, 1859, HL–14, HC; Albert F. Heard to John Heard, Shanghai, Mar. 23, 1860, HL–15, HC.

40. *NCH* (Mar. 12, 1859), p. 126. See also E–2, FC.

41. Case 26, RA.

42. Edward Cuningham to John M. Forbes, Jr., May 14, 1868, Case 26, RA.

43. *Ibid.*

44. "I am up and down every week to Woosung, & will be glad to get an assistant, as I cannot depend upon a simple letter being copied correctly, after several attempts, by anyone in the [S.S.] Folkestone. I keep my mess and servants there still, and have agreed to share expenses here with Empson." A. G. Dallas (Shanghai) to Donald Matheson (Hong Kong), Aug. 16, 1844, JMA.

45. A. G. Dallas (Shanghai) to Donald Matheson (Hong Kong), Mar. 21, 1846, JMA.

46. "I have not seen Atow yet, but he has come just in time, as the godown requires a careful and constant superintendence." A. G. Dallas (Shanghai) to Donald Matheson (Hong Kong), May 9, 1846, JMA.

47. A foreign tea-taster was usually called a *ch'a-shih*. See *NCH* (Apr. 15, 1868), p. 173.

48. M. A. Daly (Foochow) to A. F. Heard (Hong Kong), Apr. 7, 1863. HM–25, HC.

49. A. F. Heard (Shanghai) to Augustine Heard, Jr., Apr. 18, 1862, HL–36, HC.

50. *Shang-hai ch'ien-chuang shih-liao* (Historical materials of the native banks in Shanghai), comp. Chung-kuo jen min yin-hang Shang-hai-shih feng hang (The Chinese People's Bank, Shanghai; Shanghai, 1960), p. 482.

51. For Wang Huai-shan, see *ibid.*, p. 29. For Yü Hsia-ch'ing, see Wright, p. 538.
52. Ko Yüan-hsü, 2: 6b.
53. For the compradors at Hong Kong, see Negishi, *Baiben seido*, pp. 242–247; for the compradors at Shanghai, see *ibid.*, pp. 234–241.
54. In 1879, a comprador at Chinkiang came from Nanking. *NCH* (Sept. 23, 1879), p. 301. Some natives of Shanghai also served as compradors, but none of them became prominent. Huang Wei, *Shang-hai kai-fu ch'u-chi tui wai mao-i yen-chiu* (A study of Shanghai's foreign trade during the initial period of its opening; Shanghai, 1961), p. 108.
55. Wright, p. 548.
56. *Shang-hai ch'ien-chuang*, pp. 37–38.
57. See ch. VII.
58. Thomas Knox, "John Comprador," *Harper's New Monthly Magazine*, 57: 427–437 (1878).
59. Agreement, Hong Kong, May 12, 1860, Case 9, HC II.
60. Agreement, Hong Kong, 1866, Case 9, HC II.
61. B. A. Clarke (Seoul) to William Patterson (Shanghai), June 23, 1883, JMA.
62. B. A. Clarke (Jenchuan) to J. J. Keswick (Shanghai), July 27, 1884, JMA.
63. B. A. Clarke (Jenchuan) to William Patterson (Shanghai), September 16, 1884, JMA.
64. B. A. Clarke (Jenchuan) to W. G. Astor, Sept. 20, 1884, JMA.
65. *NCH*, market intelligence, 1860–1870.
66. For Hsü Jun, see Wright, p. 566; for Loo, see *NCH* (Sept. 17, 1859), p. 27; (Jan. 14, 1860), p. 6.
67. E. M. Dorr (Kanagawa) to John Heard, Nov. 11, 1859, FM–15, HC.
68. Comprador Agreement, June 7, 1860, Case 9, HC II.
69. A. O. Gay (Yokohama) to A. F. Heard (Hong Kong), May 27, 1866, HM–55, HC.
70. Comprador Agreement, June 7, 1860, Case 9, HC II.
71. G. S. Fisher, United States consul at Kanagawa, claimed that his boy had "usually been kept in waiting" at Heard's Yokohama office for consulate fees. A. O. Gay, Heard's agent, denied the charge: "Upon strict enquiry, I am most confidently assured by my Compradore and shroff, that your servant has never been kept in waiting as you assert, and I believe that such detention should never have occurred from my knowlege of their constant attendance at their office for the purpose of answering my orders." A. O. Gay (Yokohama) to G. S. Fisher (Kanagawa), Dec. 2, 1865, HM–55, HC.
72. A. O. Gay (Yokohama) to A. F. Heard (Hong Kong), May 27, 1866, HM–55, HC.
73. A. O. Gay (Yokohama) to A. F. Heard (Hong Kong), Apr. 13, 1866, HM–55, HC. "I was disappointed with him [Van Reed] in that capacity [English-Japanese interpreter] last winter, and felt, after he went away, that I got on better with the Compradore in getting information from the natives." A. O. Gay (Yokohama) to A. F. Heard (Hong Kong), Mar. 29, 1866, HM–55, HC.
74. Jardine, Matheson & Co. (Shanghai) to William Keswick (Kanagawa), Dec. 22, 1859, JMA.
75. Jardine, Matheson & Co. (Shanghai) to William Keswick (Kanagawa), May 28, 1861, JMA.
76. B 3/12–18 (1863–1871), JMA.

77. Edward Whittall (Yokohama) to James Whittall (Hong Kong), May 26, 1871, JMA.
78. Edward Whittall (Yokohama) to James Whittall (Hong Kong), Jan. 12, 1871, JMA.
79. BPP, 1870, LXV, "Commercial Reports from Her Majesty's Consuls in Japan, 1869–1870," Japan, No. 4 (1870), p. 60.
80. "I regret the unfavorable report you give on our Sugar from Swatow. There are about 2,000 pk. more which were originally intended for Japan." William Keswick (Hong Kong) to F. B. Johnson (Shanghai), Aug. 29, 1871, JMA. "Newchwang produce: In peas there has been of late a fairly active demand, 15,000 piculs having changed hands at $1.92-1/2 to $2.05 per picul. The demand for oil has been exceedingly limited." Herbert Smith (Yokohama) to Jardine, Matheson & Co. (Hong Kong), Aug. 1, 1870, JMA. For Japan's tea, see James Whittall (Shanghai) to Jardine, Matheson & Co. (Hong Kong), Oct. 5, 1861, JMA.
81. B. A. Clarke (Jenchuan) to J. J. Keswick (Shanghai), Sept. 25, 1884, JMA.
82. A. O. Gay (Yokohama) to A. F. Heard (Shanghai), Mar. 29, 1866, HM–55, HC.
83. *Ibid.*
84. "As regard for your order for firing pans and coloring matter we have only been able to obtain a small quantity which will serve as musters, and it will be necessary that you send a detailed list of *exactly what you want* in Chinese, with an English translation, as some of the articles are not obtainable here, but have to be sent for from other districts." Jardine, Matheson & Co. (Shanghai) to William Keswick (Yokohama), Feb. 5, 1862, JMA.
85. A. F. Heard (Shanghai) to Frederick Field (Yokohama), Aug. 17, 1859, HL–14, HC.
86. A. O. Gay (Yokohama) to A. F. Heard (Hong Kong), Feb. 25, 1866, HM–55, HC; Agreement, Augustine Heard & Co. and Francis Law, Case 9, 1870–1874, HC II.
87. A. F. Heard, memo., July 23, 1862, FL–19, HC; Invoice, vol. 166 (1871–1873), HC II.
88. A. O. Gay (Yokohama) to A. F. Heard (Hong Kong), Mar. 29, 1866, HM–55, HC.
89. The first two newspapers are available at the Hong Kong High Court Library, Hong Kong.
90. BPP, 1867, LXVIII, "Commercial Reports from Her Majesty's Consuls in China, Japan, and Siam, 1865–1866," p. 68.
91. G. C. Allen and A. G. Donnithorne, *Western Economic Enterprise in Far Eastern Economic Development* (New York, 1954), p. 47.
92. In 1915, foreign merchants at Hong Kong either wound up their business or tried to find agents. Some of them formed a joint concern to take care of their declining business. See *Hua-tzu jih-pao* (Feb. 15, 1915).
93. C. G. Lin & Co. (Amoy) to Jardine, Matheson & Co. (Hong Kong), Aug. 26, Sept. 4 and 16, 1890, JMA. By 1908, there were prominent Chinese export firms in the treaty ports. See Wright, p. 570.
94. For the Mitsui Company, see Negishi, *Baiben seido*, p. 2. For the Yokohama Specie Bank, see Tsuchiya Keizayū, *Baiben seido* (The comprador institution; Tokyo, 1940), p. 3.
95. Ch'en Chin-miao, "T'ien-chin chih mai-pan chih-tu" (The comprador

system in Tientsin), *Ching-chi hsüeh-pao*, 1: 27–69 (1940), p. 33.

96. For the upcountry purchase, see ch. IV.

IV. FUNCTIONS OF THE COMPRADOR IN THE FOREIGN FIRM

1. Augustine Heard, Jr., "The Poisoning in Hong Kong," p. 9, GQ–2, HC.
2. *Ibid.*
3. Augustine Heard, Jr., "Diary," p. 33, FP–4, HC.
4. Tiffany, p. 215.
5. *NCH* (Oct. 13, 1860), p. 62; (Aug. 28, 1875), p. 215.
6. Tiffany, p. 215.
7. Augustine Heard, Jr., "Poisoning," p. 9.
8. John Heard to A. Charlly, Dec. 2, 1844, FL–1, HC; Cases 27, 48, HC II; *NCH* (July 23, 1864), p. 119. "As soon as I get the keys I shall set Comprador about this [house cleaning]." John Heard to his parents, Jan. 23, 1846, FL–2, HC. "The comprador has been unable to effect any settlement [regarding the purchase of land]." H. G. Bridges (Kiukiang) to A. F. Heard (Shanghai), April 4, 1862, HM–23, HC. See also *NCH* (May 15, 1861), p. 83; (Feb. 2, 1877), p. 189.
9. H. G. Bridges (Hankow) to A. F. Heard (Shanghai), May 9, 1866, HM–23, HC.
10. Mayers et al., p. 135.
11. Vols. 267–271, 1861–1873, HC II.
12. See ch. VII.
13. Tiffany, p. 215.
14. Augustine Heard, Jr., FP–4, p. 114, HC.
15. Augustine Heard, Jr., FP–4, pp. 64–65, HC.
16. "Ku Mei-foo, the Compradore (Chinese manager) of the [Hongkew] wharves . . . has been very friendly to me." H. B. Morse (Shanghai) to Gustav Detring (Peking), Aug. 10, 1887, MLB. See also Mayers et al., p. 135.
17. H. G. Bridges (Hankow) to A. F. Heard (Shanghai), June 28, 1866, HM–23, HC.
18. *Ibid.*
19. H. G. Bridges (Kiukiang) to A. F. Heard (Shanghai), June 29, 1862, HM–23, HC.
20. *Ibid.*
21. Hsü Jun, *Hsü Yü-chai tzu-hsü nien-p'u* (Chronological autobiography of Hsü Jun; 1927), p. 8.
22. Augustine Heard, Jr., FP–4, p. 9, HC.
23. Vols. 55–56, 1870–1871, HC II.
24. Concerning the 100,000 Mexican dollars just shipped to Russell's in 1857, William Cole wrote: "Early in October, having some business with the Comprador who had charge of their Treasury, I mentioned to him that the packages of Specie from the 'Nobob' were not to be opened unless I was present." William Cole to G. Dexter, 1860, DP.
25. William Keswick (Shanghai) to James Whittall (Hong Kong), Sept. 27, 1864, JMA.
26. Tiffany, p. 215.
27. Case 9, HC II.
28. For the chit system, see King, p. 113.

29. Augustine Heard, Jr., FP–4, p. 9, HC.
30. "We thank you for the Compradore Order Books which came to hand pr. 'Glenorchy.'" Jardine, Matheson & Co. (Shanghai), to Jardine, Matheson & Co. (Hong Kong), Feb. 11, 1878, JMA. "We beg to hand you enclosed a cheque on our Comprador for $4,246.57 being balance at credit of our account with the ship 'Witch of the Seas.'" Dent & Co. (Hong Kong) to Jardine, Matheson & Co. (Hong Kong), Oct. 3, 1860, JMA.
31. Case 106, HC II.
32. A typical comprador's order at three days' sight, from Augustine Heard & Co., Hong Kong, April 1866, read: "Comprador, Three days after sight, pay to the order of Achuan Two Thousand Dollars $2,000.00 [signed] AH & Co." Case 2, HC II.
33. Case 5, HC II.
34. "My native staff is very busy at the Bank at present, shroffing the sycee for Peking, as has to be prepared for the order to forward some." Edward Cousins (Tientsin) to J. W. Keswick (Swatow), June 16, 1885, JMA. The term "shroff," meaning "banker" or "money exchanger," came from India. During the mid-nineteenth century, it referred to an expert on the intricacies of Chinese money, but gradually all comprador's business assistants were called shroffs. See Tōa Dōbunkai, *Keizai zensho*, II, 343.
35. "I have settled thro the Comprador 30,000 Foochow Dollars at 5 1/2, deliverable in two weeks—payment in drafts on Hongkong—and I shall probably have to draw for *$10,000* on Monday." T. S. Odelly (Canton) to Alexander Perceval (Hong Kong), June 8, 1861, JMA.
36. William Keswick (Shanghai) to Robert Watmore (Hankow), Sept.24, 1863, JMA.
37. William Keswick (Shanghai) to Alexander Perceval (Hong Kong), Nov. 24, 1863, JMA.
38. B. A. Clarke (Hankow) to J. J. Keswick (Shanghai), May 28, 1885, JMA.
39. Ma Yin-ch'u, "Chung-kuo chih mai-pan chih" (The comprador institution in China), *Tung-fang tsa-chih* (The eastern miscellany), 20.6: 130–131 (Mar. 25, 1923), p. 130.
40. John Heard (Hong Kong) to A. F. Heard, Oct. 8, 1860, HM–6, HC.
41. EA–1, HC. Following is a comprador's translation of market information for Augustine Heard & Co., Hong Kong, 1861:

[*Mandarin pronunciation*]	[*Cantonese pronunciation*]	[*English translation*]
[*chiu-mi*]	kow mi	Old rice
[*lao-mi*]	lao mi	Old rice
[*hsin-mi*]	sun mi	New rice
[*po-mi*]	pak mi	White rice
[*p'u-mi*]	pok mi	Cargo or trulled [sic] rice
[*ku*]	kook	Paddy

EA–1, HC.
42. M. A. Daly (Foochow) to Albert F. Heard, Mar. 24, 1865, HM–26, HC. "The Foochow compradore has been to Canton to investigate about Rice. He says it is Tls. 8 in Pekin." John Heard to Albert F. Heard, Apr. 13, 1861, FL–5, HC.
43. *NCH* (Oct. 7, 1875), p. 260.

44. H. G. Bridges (Kiukiang) to A. F. Heard (Shanghai), June 29, 1862, HM–23, HC.

45. H. G. Bridges (Kiukiang) to A. F. Heard (Shanghai), June 20, 1862, HM–23, HC.

46. *NCH* (Sept. 17, 1859), p. 27.

47. "I shall send you by mail . . . the Chinese letters and your compradore can translate to you." Albert F. Heard (Shanghai) to John Heard (Hong Kong), Sept. 17, 1859, HL–14, HC.

48. Case 30, HC II; Fairbank, *Trade and Diplomacy*, I, 396; Hsü Jun, *Nien-p'u*, p. 8.

49. Dealing with Chinese authorities was one of the duties of Hu Erh-mei (Hoo Erh Mai), comprador to Mandl & Co. Wright, p. 556. For the comprador's selling of arms, see Fairbank, *Trade and Diplomacy*, I, 221; *NCH* (Oct. 8, 1874), p. 354.

50. "If a Chinaman brings anything to the [foreign] hong to sell, he [comprador] never lets him go away without squeezing him, he is in fact a broker, and earns a fat commission for every transaction." Tiffany, p. 215.

51. Tōa Dōbunkai, *Keizai zensho*, II, 365–369.

52. Tong Loong-maw to G. B. Dixwell, Aug. 26, 1863, HM–30, HC; Ahow to G. B. Dixwell, July 3, 1864, HM–30, HC.

53. Case 1, HC II.

54. Agreement, Hong Kong, Feb. 1873, Case 9, HC II.

55. Robert B. Forbes to Joshua Bates, Feb. 24, 1850, Case 1, FC.

56. J. Scarth, *Twelve Years in China* (Edinburgh, 1860), pp. 110–111.

57. "The system adopted at Canton has been commenced at Shanghai, of sending parties under agreement with our merchants into the tea districts with ready cash to purchase certain descriptions of teas, and this will be one of the surest means of securing a fair portion of the best qualities for the Shanghai market, the great desideration hitherto." BPP, 1849, XXXIX, "Returns of Trade in China," p. 61.

58. BPP, 1867, LXVIII, "Commercial Reports from Her Majesty's Consuls in China, Japan, and Siam, 1865–1866," p. 68.

59. BPP, 1867–1868, LXIX, "Reports on Trade by the Foreign Commissioners at the Ports in China Open by Treaty to Foreign Trade for the Year 1866," p. 10.

60. Augustine Heard, Jr., "Diary," FP–4, p. 34, HC.

61. Cash Account, vol. 60, HC II. The establishment of a new office was owing to the sudden "opening" of Foochow to tea export in 1854, previously forbidden by the Chinese government.

62. This account was prepared by William Comstock, Jr. EJ–2, HC.

63. Augustine Heard, Jr., "Old China and New," p. 38.

64. *Ibid.*, p. 21.

65. May 7, 1859, FM–14, HC.

66. George F. Weller (Foochow) to Albert F. Heard, June 18, 1859, HM–49, HC.

67. M. A. Daly (Foochow) to Albert F. Heard, May 27, 1863, HM–25, HC.

68. John Heard to George F. Weller, Mar. 28, 1861, FL–5, HC.

69. George F. Weller (Foochow) to Albert F. Heard, June 18, 1859, FM–49, HC.

70. John Heard to Albert F. Heard, Apr. 4, 1862, FL–6, HC.

71. *Ibid.*
72. George F. Weller (Foochow) to John Heard, Mar. 26, 1859, FM–13, HC. For a more detailed comprador report from upcountry concerning tea purchases, see George F. Weller (Foochow) to John Heard, May 28, 1859, FM–13, HC.
73. Albert F. Heard to John Heard, Apr. 1, 1863, HL–38, HC.
74. Augustine Heard, Jr., "Old China and New," p. 31.
75. George F. Weller (Foochow) to John Heard, Apr. 20, 1862, FM–13, HC.
76. For the compradors, see *NCH* (Oct. 13, 1860), Supplement; (Dec. 1, 1860), Supplement; for the teamen, see M. A. MacLeod (Foochow) to Alexander Perceval (Hong Kong), April 8, 1861, JMA.
77. George V. W. Fisher (Foochow) to Joseph Jardine (Hong Kong), May 1, 1856, JMA.
78. "Foochow has been opened in 1843. Russell & Co. opened up (ca. 1854) connections with the black tea districts around Foochow and shipped direct to America the teas which had formerly been carried over the mountains for shipment from Canton to Shanghai. . . . They sent Chinese into the interior with large sums of money." *Shanghai Mercury* (June 4, 1891). See Folder, p. 20, RA.
79. "Ahone, Russell & Co. man, who did all their business for them last year, arrived down in the *Antelope*, but have not heard yet what his movements are likely to be." George V. W. Fisher (Foochow) to Joseph Jardine (Hong Kong), Mar. 30, 1856, JMA.
80. George V. W. Fisher (Foochow) to Joseph Jardine (Hong Kong), May 1, 1856, JMA.
81. Agreement, Shanghai, July 28, 1847, Case 2, HC II.
82. G. F. Weller (Foochow) to A. F. Heard, May 15, 1862, HM–49, HC; John Heard to A. F. Heard, May 2, 1860, HM–5, HC; A. F. Heard (Shanghai) to Charles A. Fearon, May 16, 1861, HL–36, HC.
83. A. F. Heard (Shanghai) to John Heard (Hong Kong), Sept. 17, 1859, HL–14, HC.
84. A. G. Dallas (Shanghai) to David Jardine (Hong Kong), May 3, 1851, JMA.
85. A. G. Dallas (Shanghai) to David Jardine (Hong Kong), Apr. 4, 1851, JMA.
86. *Ibid.*
87. A. G. Dallas (Shanghai) to David Jardine (Hong Kong), Sept. 27, 1852, JMA.
88. A. G. Dallas (Shanghai) to David Jardine (Hong Kong), Aug. 31, 1852, JMA.
89. James Whittall (Shanghai) to Jardine, Matheson & Co. (Hong Kong), Feb. 19. 1859, JMA.
90. William Keswick (Shanghai) to Alexander Perceval (Hong Kong), Nov. 24, 1863, JMA.
91. Wright, pp. 554, 568.
92. Liu Kwang-Ching, "Tong King-sing," p. 152. Hsü had recommended the appointment of these "north compradors." Hsü Jun, *Nien-p'u*, p. 8. Inasmuch as the disputes between Sunkee, Russell's Tientsin comprador, and the firm "must be settled with the Shanghai taipan," Choping clearly played an important role. *NCH* (Aug. 28, 1875), p. 213.
93. "Your Comprador will be in Canton tomorrow and I shall send him off by the first ship." Augustine Heard, Jr. (Canton) to C. A. Fearon (Shanghai), July

14, 1854, GL–2, HC. Also see *ibid.*, July 18, 1854.

94. Albert F. Heard (Shanghai) to John Heard (Hong Kong), Feb. 26, 1858, HL–13, HC.

95. Albert F. Heard (Shanghai) to the Captain of the *Fire Dart*, Aug. 4, 1862, FL–1, HC.

96. Liu Kwang-Ching, "Tong King-sing," p. 144.

97. "Tong King-sing has just returned from that port [Foochow] and reports very favourably of the chances of at least one of the new steamers paying well on that line." F. B. Johnson (Shanghai) to William Keswick (Hong Kong), July 1, 1869, JMA. "I have sent Tong King-sing to Chinkiang two days ago to look after an interest." F. B. Johnson (Shanghai) to William Keswick (Hong Kong), Oct. 4, 1871, JMA.

98. "In order to have Nue Hoo property investigated, I am sending Murray up [to Kiukiang] tomorrow accompanied by Tong King-sing." William Keswick (Hong Kong) to James Whittall, Feb. 4, 1871, JMA.

99. R. I. Fearon to Albert F. Heard, Jan. 6, 1873, HM–43, HC. "I [Wang Sunkee, contractor] produce two memorandums written in English at Jardine's, and translated by defendent's [F. B. Johnson, Jardine's Shanghai manager] comprador into Chinese." *NCH* (July 12, 1873), p. 30.

100. Hsü Jun, *Nien p'u*, p. 17.

101. F. B. Johnson (Shanghai) to William Keswick (Hong Kong), Feb. 21, 1870, JMA. See also Liu Kwang-Ching, "Tong King-sing," p. 167.

102. F. B. Johnson (Shanghai) to W. Keswick (Hong Kong), Aug. 30, 1871, JMA.

103. F. B. Johnson (Shanghai) to R. Anderson (Hankow), June 22, 1871, JMA. See also Liu Kwang-Ching, "Tong King-sing," p. 163.

104. F. B. Johnson (Shanghai) to William Keswick (Hong Kong), Aug. 30, 1871, JMA. See also Liu Kwang-Ching, "Tong King-sing," p. 168.

105. F. B. Johnson (Shanghai) to James Whittall (Hong Kong), Nov. 16, 1867, JMA. See also Liu Kwang-Ching, "Tong King-sing," p. 155.

106. William Keswick (Shanghai) to James Whittall (Hong Kong), Sept. 27, 1864, JMA. See also Liu Kwang-Ching, "Tong King-sing," p. 145.

107. "I have requested Tong King-sing to secure a quantity of copper cash & ship it to you by the first opportunity." Herbert Magniac (Shanghai) to Robert Watmore (Hankow), Apr. 9, 1863, JMA. "I inform you that we have a considerable quantity of copper cash going to you from Chin-keang [Chinkiang] and that I wish you to be very firm with it." William Keswick (Shanghai) to Robert Watmore (Hankow), Nov. 28, 1863, JMA.

108. F. B. Johnson (Shanghai) to Jardine, Matheson & Co. (Hong Kong), May 6, 1869, JMA.

109. The "chop loan" was reminiscent of the fact that Indian silver had been brought to Canton in the 1830's to earn high interest.

110. *Shang-hai ch'ien-chuang*, pp. 28–29.

111. F. B. Johnson (Shanghai) to William Keswick (Hong Kong), May 20, 1868, JMA.

112. "I am inclined to believe that with caution and good judgment there is a good business to be done in these local transactions, especially in Banking business with the Chinese in which we shall probably find a better account than in the hard driven competition for the export and Tea and Silk." F. B. Johnson (Shanghai) to

William Keswick (Hong Kong), Feb. 1, 1869, JMA.

113. Tong King-sing (Shanghai) to Jardine, Matheson & Co. (Shanghai), Aug. 22, 1868, JMA.

114. F. B. Johnson (Shanghai) to William Keswick (Hong Kong), June 18, 1872, JMA. See also Liu Kwang-Ching, "Tong King-sing," pp. 152–153.

115. *Ibid.*, pp. 172–176.

116. "I heard from the Native friends that greens [green teas] are likely to open at very moderate prices in the Fychow district." William Keswick to James Whittall, Apr. 26, 1866, JMA.

117. "Tong King-sing's statement of the [sugar] cost *here* is not to be depended on in our calculation as I see it is not correct & I don't know what charges he has included." F. B. Johnson (Shanghai) to William Keswick (Hong Kong), Feb. 9, 1869, JMA. "Tong King-sing tells me that he distinctly told Singham the sugar was not worth Tls. 27 here and advised him to have nothing to do with it." F. B. Johnson (Shanghai) to William Keswick (Hong Kong), Sept. 27, 1871, JMA. "The quotations for wood oil transmitted to you were given to us by our Compradore." William Keswick (Shanghai) to Robert Watmore (Hankow), Apr. 6, 1864, JMA. "I have sent Tong King-sing to Chinkiang two days ago . . . to take care that the qualities [of rice] contracted for shall be delivered equal to muster." F. B. Johnson to William Keswick, Oct. 4, 1871, JMA. "Tong King-sing has a telegram to-night to state the rice is again lower at Canton and I fear the cargo will react a bad market." F. B. Johnson (Shanghai) to William Keswick (Hong Kong), Oct. 25, 1871, JMA.

118. F. B. Johnson (Shanghai) to William Keswick (Hong Kong), Sept. 11, 1868, JMA.

119. F. B. Johnson (Shanghai) to William Keswick (Hong Kong), Mar. 14, 1869, JMA.

120. Memorandum, 1869, JMA.

121. F. B. Johnson (Shanghai) to James Whittall (Hong Kong), Jan. 16, 1867, JMA.

V. THE COMPRADOR AS A NOUVEAU RICHE

1. *Shen pao* (Nov. 21, 1878), p. 3; Negishi, *Sōren*, pp. 46–47.

2. *NCH* (Aug. 28, 1875), p. 215.

3. William Keswick (Shanghai) to James Whittall (Hong Kong), Dec. 2, 1865, JMA. At the end of 1865, F. B. Johnson promised to give 2,000 additional taels for the expenses of the comprador's office. Liu Kwang-Ching, "Tong King-sing," p. 147.

4. *NCH* (Aug. 28, 1875), p. 215.

5. *Ibid.* For Sunkee's salary, T. E. Moore, Russell & Co.'s Tientsin agent in the 1860's, testified in court: "Sometimes they [Sunkee's wages] were paid monthly, and sometimes quarterly; sometimes in the cash accounts, and occasionally his salary was credited in the journal. Some years the whole amount of his salary was passed to his account in the December cash. This was done by comprador order." *NCH* (Aug. 25, 1875), p. 215.

6. Agreement, 1846–1861, Case 9, HC II.

7. William Keswick (Shanghai) to James Whittall (Hong Kong), Dec. 19, 1865, JMA.

8. *NCH* (Aug. 28, 1875).

9. The comprador ordinarily received two percent commission on transactions, including one percent from the foreign firms and one percent from their Chinese constituents. H. G. Bridges (Hankow) to A. F. Heard (Shanghai), June 20 and 29, 1866, HM–23, HC.

10. BPP, 1867–1868, LXIX, "Reports on Trade by the Foreign Commissioners at the Ports in China for the Year 1866," p. 110.

11. Augustine Heard, Jr., "Poisoning," p. 9. See also Tiffany, p. 215.

12. G. F. Weller (Foochow) to A. F. Heard (Shanghai), Aug. 14, 1862, HM–49, HC.

13. "It was beyond the province of the Chamber to give an authoritative sanction to the practice of charging commissions, nor could it even recommend it." Annual report of the Committee of the Shanghai Chamber of Commerce, NCH (Aug. 26, 1865), p. 135. See also NCH (Oct. 1, 1864).

14. William Keswick (Shanghai) to James Whittall (Hong Kong), Dec. 2, 1865, JMA. See also Liu Kwang-Chung, "Tong King-sing," p. 148.

15. NCH (Oct. 1, 1864), p. 158.

16. For the "chop loan" system, see ch. IV. See also Shang-hai ch'ien-chuang, pp. 8–10, 36, 38, 60, 90, 490. The commission for the "chop loan" was small, but since the loan was short-term (two to seven days) and thus was more frequently used, the comprador obtained some money from it. The total amount of all chop loans in Shanghai in 1878 was 3,000,000 taels. Shen pao (Aug. 25, 1878), quoted in Shang-hai ch'ien-chuang, p. 44.

17. NCH (Aug. 28, 1875), p. 215.

18. Tong Mow-chee testified in the case of Liu Sun-kee v. Russell & Co. before the U. S. Consular Court on July 2, 1875: "The commission allowed to compradores on piece goods is one per cent for his guarantee on sales, besides brokerage, 10 cash per piece, and difference of scale 1/2 per cent. The one per cent is clear. The allowance on general merchandise is 2 per cent, but out of that he would pay about 1/2 per cent to the broker, while difference of scale would leave about one per cent net to him." NCH (Aug. 28, 1875), p. 215.

19. NCH (Aug. 28, 1875), pp. 213, 215.

20. NCH (Aug. 28, 1875), pp. 212–217; (Oct. 7, 1875), pp. 357–360; (Jan. 6, 1876), pp. 13–15.

21. H. G. Bridges (Hankow) to A. F. Heard (Shanghai), June 29, 1866, HM–23, HC.

22. H. G. Bridges (Hankow) to A. F. Heard (Shanghai), June 20, 1866, HM–23, HC. Bridges' suggestion was adopted, as he later wrote: "I note your instructions regarding steamer business. On Hong Kong cargo I have allowed the shipper 3% return in addition to the 2% the compradore gets on everything." June 29, 1866, HM–23, HC.

23. B. A. Clarke (Hankow) to J. J. Keswick (Shanghai), Dec. 24, 1885, JMA.

24. John M. Forbes, Jr. (Canton) to Edward Cunningham (Shanghai), May 27, 1868, Case 26, RA.

25. Tiffany, p. 215. Although the practice of receiving commissions from Chinese merchants was followed in the late 1840's, it is not known how common it was in later days.

26. Tōa Dōbunkai, Keizai zensho, II, 268. See also Arnold, p. 257.

27. NCH (Sept. 23, 1882), p. 315.

28. A. F. Heard to John Heard, Sept. 17, 1859, HL–14, HC.

29.   Tong King-sing (Shanghai) to William Keswick (Hong Kong), Oct. 8, 1868, JMA. See also Liu Kwang-Ching, "Tong King-sing," p. 165.

30.   Mayers et al., p. 451.

31.   When F. B. Johnson of Jardine's contemplated taking the North China Company's agency away from Trautmann & Co., he reported to James Whittall that one-third of the company's shares were held by "Chinese whom Tongkingsing can influence." Liu Kwang-Ching, *Steamship Rivalry*, p. 143.

32.   Tong King-sing, comprador to Jardine's, wrote to the firm's Shanghai manager in 1868: "Whenever I have a few minutes to spare, I always work for my native friends who all make me as [*sic*] their representative in business connected with Foreign houses. To watch their interest, I have been requested by them to accept a directorship in the Union S. N. Co. and the North China Steam[er] Co., and by doing so I don't only get an income of about Tls. 1,000 per annum, which is a great help to my family, but gives me a full knowledge of what is going on outside." Tong King-sing (Shanghai) to William Keswick (Shanghai), Oct. 8, 1863, JMA. See also Liu Kwang-Ching, *Steamship Rivalry*, p. 142.
A visit by Tong King-sing to Robert Fearon of Augustine Heard & Co. in 1873 also illustrates Tong's position as spokesman for Chinese merchants. Tong represented the shareholders of the *Suwonada*, who had been asked by the managing agent, Augustine Heard & Co., to pay additional funds in order to make up the loss in managing the ship. "On Saturday, old Yuechang, Guan Sung, and Tongking-sing (JM & Co.'s compradore, present owner of Echow's share) came to talk about the *Suwonada* a/cs. Tongkingsing, who speaks English like a Briton, was spokesman and he said that he had been requested by the others to express their views on the subject." R. I. Fearon (Shanghai) to A. F. Heard (Hong Kong), Jan. 6, 1873, HM–43, HC.

33.   "Tong King-sing applied to me for assistance & on investigating his accounts, I found to my surprise & dissatisfaction that though the small Cash balance in the Treasury was available, of the Bank orders *not due*, which he had collected to the extent of Tls. 95,000, about Tls. 80,000 had been discounted & were not forthcoming." F. B. Johnson (Shanghai) to W. Keswick (Hong Kong), June 1, 1871, JMA. See also Liu Kwang-Ching, "Tong King-sing," pp. 149–151.

34.   For example, a comprador could use the godown of the foreign house for storing his own tea. *NCH* (Jan. 7, 1854).

35.   British minister, Rutherford Alcock (Peking) to British consul, C. A. Winchester (Shanghai), *NCH* (May 23, 1867), p. 74; C. A. Winchester to Shanghai taotai, *NCH* (Feb. 8, 1867), pp. 367–368. Winchester continued: "Unfortunately the servants or compradores of the foreign hong have sometimes been permitted by their employers to act as general and special brokers and even as independent merchants in addition to the discharge of their proper duties as mercantile servants, —this too at the imminent risk of being held responsible for their acts in the two former capacities." *Ibid.*

36.   *NCH* (Oct. 20, 1860), Supplement. For the whole case, see also *NCH* (Oct. 13, 1860), Supplement; (Nov. 17, 1860), Supplement. It is not certain whether this Acum and the Acum who was Jardine's comprador at Shanghai in 1863 are the same person.

37.   Opinion of John Henderson, Assessor, in the case of David Sassoon, Sons & Co. v. Wong Gan-ying. Henderson continued: "I have never known or heard of a compradore in foreign employ using a separate stamp or seal from that of his

foreign employers, even for his own business." *NCH* (Nov. 19, 1884), p. 578.

38. The same kind of dispute arose between Chinese and foreign merchants when Teng Chün-hsiang, comprador to the Hongkong and Shanghai Banking Corp., Peking office, absconded in 1927, owing more than 4,000,000 taels. For details, see *Hua-tzu jih-pao* (May 4, 5, 9, and June 23, 1927).

39. *NCH* (May 23, 1867), pp. 73–74.

40. In 1864, a Chinese cotton merchant named Liu Chow brought suit against H. Stubbendorff. Liu had sold 1,000 bales of cotton to Stubbendorff's comprador, who later absconded. Liu claimed that the transaction was made "not with the defendant . . . but with his comprador . . . but still, it should be considered as done in the name of the defendant through his comprador." Stubbendorff asserted, however, that he had "closed the transaction in question with his comprador Weng Kwai only." *NCH* (Apr. 16, 1864), p. 62.

41. C. A. Winchester continued: "This was the principle which ruled in a case recently decided in the Supreme court wherein the Chinese plaintiffs obtained judgment." *NCH* (Feb. 8, 1867), p. 367.

42. Edward Cunningham (Shanghai) to John M. Forbes, Jr. (Canton), June 4, 1868, Case 26, RA.

43. *NCH* (Aug. 28, 1875), p. 216. See also *NCH* (Oct. 7, 1875), p. 360. Sunkee actually had "three hongs at Tientsin—one of them being a brokerage business and the other two merchants'." *NCH* (Aug. 28, 1875), p. 213.

44. The testimony of Ts'un Chen-san in the case of Liu Sunkee v. Russell & Co. before U. S. Consular Court, July 2, 1875. *NCH* (Aug. 28, 1875), p. 214. Sunkee himself testified in court: "When it became known that I was discharged, all the cargo was taken out of my place, and my hong was ruined." *NCH* (Aug. 28, 1875), p. 213.

45. F. B. Johnson (Shanghai) to William Keswick (Hong Kong), June 1, 1871, JMA. See also Liu Kwang-Ching, "Tong King-sing," p. 149.

46. This point is advanced by Chang Chung-li, *The Chinese Gentry: Studies on Their Role in Nineteenth-Century Chinese Society* (Seattle, 1955).

47. Ho Ping-ti, *Ladder,* pp. 82, 228, 300.

48. F. L. Hawks Pott, *A Short History of Shanghai* (Shanghai, 1928), p. 67.

49. Fairbank, *Trade and Diplomacy,* I, 221.

50. In 1854, the Shanghai taotai's police secretly carried off from the foreign factories the comprador of a British Indian for selling powder to the Taipings. The British subject petitioned the consul, and two armed boats were dispatched to the taotai's war vessels, where the comprador was supposed to be confined. The comprador was not there, but two mandarins were seized instead. The comprador was released soon. See Fairbank, *Trade and Diplomacy,* I, 221.

51. Hatano, pp. 334–335. See also *NCH* (Nov. 15, 1882), p. 537. For a similar case in 1910, see *Shang-hai ch'ien-chuang,* pp. 37–38, 78.

52. Yao Chih-ho, *Hua-Yang su-sung li-an hui-pien* (Collected law-suit cases between Chinese and foreigners; Shanghai, 1915), II, 508–513.

53. *NCH* (Sept. 16, 1865), p. 146.

54. *NCH* (Oct. 17, 1879), p. 388. D. M. David, a British merchant in Chinkiang, notified the commissioner of customs at that port that he operated the following firms: An Chee (An Chi, established Feb. 29, 1876), Sin-ee-ho (Hsin I-ho, established May 28, 1877), and Quang-ho (established Nov. 26, 1877). *NCH* (Oct. 17, 1879), p. 388.

55. A. F. Heard to John Heard, Aug. 16, 1860, HL–16, HC.
56. For the China Merchants' Steam Navigation Co., see Wang Ching-yü, "Shih-chiu shih-chi wai-kuo ch'in Hua shih-yeh chung ti Hua-shang fu-ku huo-tung" (The activities of Chinese merchants to buy capital shares in the aggressive foreign enterprises in China during the late nineteenth century), *Li-shih yen-chiu* (Historical study), 4: 39–74 (1965), p. 73. For a similar case in the field of insurance, see *ibid.*, p. 51. As to Jardine, Matheson & Co., F. B. Johnson wrote in 1870: "I have made a verbal agreement with the owners of the *Dragon* to run her under our flag. . . . The nominal owners are Holmes & Co. but the real owners are a Chinese hong of some standing in Chefoo and Tientsin." F. B. Johnson (Shanghai) to William Keswick, Feb. 16, 1870, JMA.
57. *NCH* (May 11, 1883), p. 525.
58. Toyama Gunji, "Shanhai no shinshō Yō Bō" (The Shanghai gentry-merchant Yang Fang), *Tōyōshi kenkyū* (Studies on Oriental history), new ser., 1.4: 17–34 (November 1945).
59. A. F. Heard (Shanghai) to Augustine Heard, Jr., Apr. 18, 1862, HL–36, HC. I am indebted to Professor Liu Kwang-Ching for this information.
60. Cheng Kuan-ying, *Hou-p'ien*, 10: 118b–119; 11: 1, 16–17, 25b.
61. See Ellsworth C. Carlson, *The Kaiping Mines, 1877–1912* (Cambridge, Mass., 1957).
62. Hsü Jun, *Nien-p'u*, pp. 34–37, 81–82.
63. Huang I-feng, "Kuan yü chiu Chung-kuo mai-pan chieh ti yen-chiu" (A study of the comprador class in old China), *Li-shih yen-chiu*, 87: 89–116 (June 15, 1964), p. 97. See also Wang Ching-yü, comp., *Chung-kuo chin-tai kung-yeh shih tze-liao chi-yao: ti erh chi* (Selected materials for China's modern industrial history, second series; Peking, 1960), II, 955.
64. Wu Hsing-lien, *Hsiang-kang Hua-jen ming-jen shih-lüeh* (The prominent Chinese in Hong Kong; Hong Kong, 1937), I, 3.
65. Wright, p. 548; Wang Ching-yü, *Kung-yeh*, II, 958–960.
66. *Shang-hai ch'ien-chuang*, p. 29; Wright, p. 540.
67. Wang Ching-yü, *Kung-yeh*, II, 962–963.
68. Fang T'eng, "Yü Hsia-ch'ing lun" (On Yü Hsia-ch'ing), *Tsa-chih yüeh-k'an* (Monthly miscellany), 12.2: 47 (November 1943).
69. *Hua-tzu jih-pao* (May 4, 6, 7, 9, 11, 1927).
70. *Hua-tzu jih-pao* (Aug. 8, 1927).
71. For a detailed description of the house, see Hsü Jun, *Nien-p'u*, p. 116.
72. Wright, p. 752.
73. P'eng Yü-hsin, "K'ang Jih chan-cheng ch'ien Han-k'ou ti yang-hang ho mai-pan" (The foreign firms and compradors at Hankow before the resistant war against Japan), *Li-lun chan-hsien* (Theoretical front), 11: 28 (February 1959).
74. F. B. Johnson (Hong Kong) to William Paterson (Shanghai), Jan. 10, 1884, JMA.
75. *Jardines and the Ewo Interests*, p. 48.
76. *The Chronicles and Directory for China, Japan and the Philippines* (Hong Kong Daily Press, Hong Kong, 1870), p. 221.
77. Huang I-feng, "Chiu Chung-kuo," p. 95.
78. The unit used in the customs reports was the Haikuan tael.
79. Huang I-feng, "Chiu Chung-kuo," pp. 97, 102.
80. For Sung Ts'ai, see *Shen pao* (May 5, 1876), p. 3. For Takee, see ch. IV. For

Sunkee, see *NCH* (August 28, 1875), p. 213. In the early years of the treaty system, each Jardine receiving ship had an opium comprador or an interpreter and a shroff. By the mid-fifties there were compradors at Woosung, one of whom specialized in opium and supervised payment for and delivery of large monthly sales. Edward LeFevour, *Western Enterprise in Late Ch'ing China: A Selective Survey of Jardine, Matheson & Company's Operations, 1842–1895* (Cambridge, Mass., 1968), p. 22.

81. F. B. Johnson (Shanghai) to William Keswick (Hong Kong), July 1, 1868, JMA.

82. In a letter to William Keswick, Tucksing wrote in 1867: "By this opportunity, my Inspector of opium (Ah Chie) is proceeding down to your port per str. [steamer] 'Ganges,' who will reside in Ho Lee Hong for the purpose of purchasing opium there; now I will therefore respectfully beg you to advance him money against shipment on opium, which is to be shipped in your own Steamer for Shanghai, also the same to be insured in your respective Firm; by so doing I shall feel grately obliged." Tucksing (Shanghai) to William Keswick (Hong Kong), Dec. 24, 1867, JMA.

83. Charles Jameson, an opium broker, assessed, inspected, and sold opium for Heard's at Hong Kong. In 1858, he sold at least 200 chests of opium, worth 120,000 taels. Case 19, HC II.

84. It is difficult to determine the exact percentage of the opium trade handled by the compradors. However, the comprador usually received 1–2% commission for selling opium. *NCH* (August 28, 1875), p. 23. Huang I-feng's estimate of 10% commission ("Chiu Chung-kuo," p. 97) is therefore too high.

85. Negishi, *Baiben seido*, p. 40.

86. Sun Yü-t'ang, *Chung-Jih chia-wu chan-cheng ch'ien wai-kuo tzu-pen tsai Chung-kuo ching-ying ti chin-ta kung-yeh* (Modern enterprises in China financed by foreign capitals before 1894; Shanghai, 1955)'.

87. Tōa Dōbunkai, *Keizai zensho*, II, 339–342.

88. Huang I-feng, "Chiu Chung-kuo," 87: 97.

89. *Ibid.* The figure for the average income is cited from primary sources.

90. Cheng Kuan-ying, *Tseng-ting Sheng-shih wei-yen* (Warnings to a prosperous age, revised; 1892), 2: 18b. Hu Erh-mei, comprador to Mandl & Co. at Shanghai, was an active merchant at Tientsin. Wright, p. 556.

91. Huang I-feng, "Chiu Chung-kuo," p. 97.

92. For Teng, see Wright, p. 700.

93. This estimate is conservative, since some compradors, including Jardine's Acum, resigned their comprador position in order to devote full time to private business. Liu Kwang-Ching, "Tong King-sing," *passim*.

94. John K. Fairbank, E. O. Reischauer, and A. M. Craig, *East Asia: The Modern Transformation* (Boston, 1965), pp. 326–327.

95. Chang Chung-li, *The Income of the Chinese Gentry* (Seattle, 1962), p. 197.

96. Computed from Hou Chi-ming, *Foreign Investment and Economic Development in China, 1840–1937* (Cambridge, Mass., 1965), pp. 231–232.

97. C. F. Remer defines foreign investment as a source of income owned by a foreigner or a non-Chinese who may live either in or outside China. *Ibid.*, pp. 11–13.

98. For more details, see ch. VIII. For social mobility in Ming-Ch'ing China, see Ho Ping-ti, *Ladder*, esp. pp. 53–125.

VI. THE COMPRADOR AND MODERN CHINA'S ECONOMIC DEVELOPMENT

1. For a detailed discussion of these arguments, see Hou Chi-ming, pp. 1–4, 94.

2. Hobson argued that expansion of the capitalist countries was a way to solve the domestic problem of surplus capital, and that the indigenous people of their colonies were exploited. Lenin went further in maintaining that the export of capital was a necessary device to save capitalism and that imperialism was the highest stage of capitalism. For an evaluation of Hobson and Lenin, see D. K. Fieldhouse, "Imperialism: An Historiographical Revision," *Economic History Review*, 14.2: 187–209 (December 1961).

3. For the Singer-Prebisch-Myrdal "absorption" thesis, see Hou Chi-ming, pp. 4–5.

4. For the consequences of international trade and investment, see Albert 0. Hirschman, *The Strategy of Economic Development* (New Haven, 1958), p. 39. See also Bernard Okun and Richard W. Richardson, eds., *Studies in Economic Development* (New York, 1961), pt. 3, esp. pp. 157–180.

5. Hou Chi-ming, pp. 5–6, 134.

6. For the different viewpoints in the controversy, see Gerald M. Meier, *Leading Issues in Development Economics* (New York, 1964), esp. pp. 151–153, 338, 353.

7. Long-term foreign investments of the United Kingdom, France, and Germany increased from US$6 billion to US$33 billion during 1874–1914, a rate of increase never surpassed in the history of international investment. Hou Chi-ming, pp. 120–121.

8. Yen Chung-p'ing, *Chung-kuo mien-fang-chih shih-kao, 1289–1937* (A draft history of Chinese cotton spinning and weaving; Peking, 1955), p. 63.

9. Hou Chi-ming, pp. 112–118

10. *Ibid.*, pp. 119–120, 122–124, 214–216.

11. F. S. A. Bourne et al., *Report of the Mission to China of the Blackburn Chamber of Commerce, 1896–1897* (London, 1898), p. 144.

12. Tiffany, p. 451.

13. BPP, 1867, LXVIII, "Reports from the Foreign Commissioners at the Various Ports in China for the Year 1865," p. 12; Pao Kuang Yung, "The Comprador: His Position in the Foreign Trade of China," *Economic Journal*, 21.84: 637 (December 1911).

14. Arnold, II, 258.

15. Bourne, p. 144.

16. BPP, 1867, LXVIII, "Reports from the Foreign Commissioners at the Various Ports in China for the year 1865," p. 12.

17. BPP, 1867–1868, LXIX, "Reports on Trade by the Foreign Commissioners at the Ports in China for the Year 1866," pp. 110, 111.

18. BPP, 1870, LXV, "Commercial Reports from Her Majesty's Consuls in China and Siam, 1869," p. 14.

19. F. B. Johnson (Shanghai) to W. Keswick (Hong Kong), Aug. 17, 1871, JMA.

20. F. B. Johnson (Hong Kong) to William Paterson (Shanghai), June 11, 1883, JMA.

21. Hou Chi-ming, p. 2; Wang Ching-yü, *Kung-yeh*, II, 958.

22. See ch. V.

23. See ch. VII.

24. For the commercial level of China's traditional economy, see John K. Fairbank, Alexander Eckstein, and Lien-sheng Yang, "Economic Change in Early Modern China: An Analytic Frame-work," *Economic Development and Cultural Change,* 9.1: 1–26 (October 1960), pp. 7–8.

25. "When Takee built the new pawnshop, he intended to take goods in pawn for one year only." Tong King-sing (Shanghai) to William Keswick (Shanghai), Jan. 4, 1866, JMA. See also Liu Kwang-Ching, "Tong King-sing," p. 157.

26. In a letter to William Keswick asking for loans to operate a pawnshop at Shanghai, Tong King-sing wrote: "I was owner of two pawnshops at Hongkong for four years and got every year 25 to 45 per cent for my money—there being then 8 to 10 pawnshops in the colony. . . . A business of 300,000 Tls. at an interest of 3% per month will give 96,000 Tls. [*sic*]—allowing 16,000 taels for expenses & insurance will show a net return of 80,000 taels or 40% for the money laid out." Tong King-sing (Shanghai) to W. Keswick (Shanghai), Jan. 4, 1866, JMA. See also Liu Kwang-Ching, "Tong King-sing," p. 157.

27. Wright, p. 566.

28. Huang I-feng, "Ti-kuo chu-i ch'in-lüeh Chung-kuo ti i-ko chung-yao chih-chu: mai-pan chieh-chi" (One important pillar of imperialism's incursion on China: The comprador class), *Li-shih yen-chiu* (Historical study), 91: 55–70 (February 1965), p. 107.

29. This proverb was reported in Hankow in 1864. BPP, 1866, LXXI, "Reports from Her Majesty's Consuls in China, 1864," p. 122.

30. Hsü Jun, *Nien-p'u,* pp. 12, 115b; Wright, p. 566.

31. Wang Yüan-tse-t'ang, comprador to the foreign firm of Li-ch'üan; Hsü Jun, *Nien-p'u,* pp. 26–27.

32. Wright, pp. 176, 752.

33. See ch. IV.

34. Tong King-sing (Shanghai) to F. B. Johnson (Shanghai), Jan. 5, 1869, JMA.

35. In a letter to F. B. Johnson, Jardine's Shanghai partner, Tong King-sing estimated the salt business in 1869: "To lay the 4,000 bags salt down at Hankow, an old license holder can do it for Tls. 5,500. The Govt. duty on the 4,000 bags payable on delivery of the salt is Tls. 4,500—making in all Tls. 10,000. The fixed price on salt at Hankow is Tls. 3 1/2 per picul—or 3,600 piculs 12,600 giving thereby a net profit of Tls. 2,600 or 47% on the outlay." Tong King-sing (Shanghai) to F. B. Johnson (Shanghai), Jan. 5, 1865, JMA. See also Liu Kwang-Ching, "Tong King-sing," pp. 160–161; W. Keswick (Shanghai) to James Whittall (Hong Kong), Jan. 6, 1866, JMA.

36. F. B. Johnson (Shanghai) to William Keswick (Hong Kong), Sept. 27, 1871, JMA.

37. Of the salt trade at Hankow, Achow wrote in 1862: "Salt is allowed to be imported (by a license granted by the viceroy) from no other place but Taechow [T'ai-chow] where it can be obtained from one Hong *only* . . . and shipped in Chinese vessels to the Yangtsze Kiang. . . . The usual loss of weight is about 10%. Market price here 5 T. [taels] 3 M. [mace] per picul, estimated net profit 1 T. 7 M. per picul. . . . The salt must be here within 4 months from the date of the license, otherwise to lose the privilege. . . . The salt is allowed to be brought up only by Chinese vessels." Memo of Achow, Mar. 21, 1862, HQ–1, HC.

38. Tong Loong-maw (Hankow) to G. B. Dixwell (Shanghai), Apr. 30, May 2, 1862, HQ–1, HC.

39. This proposal represented a Russian attempt to curry favor with the Ch'ing government. General Ignatiev proposed to Prince Kung in 1860 that foreign and Formosan rice be purchased by American and Cantonese merchants and sent under the protection of the American and Russian flags to Peking or Tientsin. Lockwood, pp. 93–94.

40. *NCH* (Nov. 19, 1884), p. 579.

41. At Shanghai, the role of the native bank order in foreign trade can be traced back as early as 1846. Chang Kuo-hui, "Shih-chiu shih-chi hou-pan-ch'i Chung-kuo ch'ien-chuang ti mai-pan hua" (The compradorialization of China's native banks in the late nineteenth century), *Li-shih yen-chiu*, 6: 90 (1963). From the 1850's, it became one of the main forms of payment in transactions. *NCH* (June 12, 1858), p. 182; (Sept. 17, 1859), p. 27; (Oct. 29, 1859), p. 50; (Mar. 1, 1862), p. 34.

42. See Chang Kuo-hui, 6: 85–98.

43. Opinion of J. Henderson, Assessor, in the case of Messrs. David Sassoon, Sons and Co. v. Wong Gan-ying before British Supreme Court for China and Japan, Shanghai, Nov. 14, 1884, *NCH* (Nov. 19, 1884), p. 578.

44. IMC, *Reports on the Haikwan Banking System and Local Currency at the Treaty Ports* (Shanghai, 1879), p. 7.

45. "Aleet, Acum & Tong King-sing . . . by means of Aleet & Acum's partnership in the old established Tea Hong, known as Hsin Sun On have been doing a large business in the purchase of Tea up country. This season they have 7 Hongs each producing at least 2 chops." F. B. Johnson (Shanghai) to William Keswick (Hong Kong), June 1, 1871, JMA. See also Liu Kwang-Ching, "Tong King-sing," p. 150.

46. Hsü Jun *Nien-p'u*, pp. 5–16. Hsü Jun was particularly active in the tea business from 1859 to 1868.

47. G. F. Weller (Foochow) to R. I. Fearon (Shanghai), Sept. 11, 1860, EM–2, HC.

48. A. F. Heard (Shanghai) to Frederick Field (Yokohama), Aug. 17, 1859, HL–14, HC.

49. *Ibid.*

50. James Whittall (Shanghai) to Jardine, Matheson & Co. (Hong Kong), May 11, 1859, JMA.

51. Jardine, Matheson & Co. (Shanghai) to K. R. Mackenzie (Nagasaki), Aug. 15, 27, 1860, JMA.

52. For Takee, see A. G. Dallas (Shanghai) to David Jardine (Hong Kong), Apr. 7, 1851, JMA; for Yakee, see James Whittall (Shanghai) to Jardine, Matheson & Co. (Hong Kong), Mar. 5, 1859, JMA.

53. F. B. Johnson (Shanghai) to Herbert Smith (Yokohama), June 10, 1870, JMA.

54. Knox, p. 431.

55. Augustine Heard, Jr., "Old China and New."

56. IMC, *Reports on Trade, 1864* (Shanghai, 1865), Hankow, p. 12. See also Liu Kwang-Ching, *Steamship Rivalry*, p. 64.

57. IMC, *Reports on Trade, 1866* (Shanghai, 1867), p. 66. Unfortunately, it was not clear exactly how much of the Chinese share belonged to compradors.

58. Mayers et al., p. 476.

59. Knox, pp. 433–434. During 1876, the Chinese shipped nine-tenths of the Indochinese rice crop, amounting to nearly 6,000,000 piculs. Knox, p. 433.

60. For the problem of high interest, see Yang Lien-sheng, *Money and Credit in China* (Cambridge, Mass., 1952), pp. 92–103.

61. Liu Kwang-Ching, "Tong King-sing," pp. 165–169.

62. Augustine Heard & Co. (Shanghai) to Augustine Heard & Co. (Hong Kong), Mar. 21, 1863, EL–1, HC. The amount of $10,000 recorded in *American Neptune* was not reliable. See *American Neptune*, Jan. 1957, p. 43.

63. Augustine Heard & Co. (Shanghai) to Augustine Heard & Co. (Hong Kong), Mar. 21, 1863, EL–1, HC. See also *American Neptune*, Jan. 1957, pp. 45–50.

64. Liu Kwang-Ching, *Steamship Rivalry*, pp. 29–30.

65. A. F. Heard (Shanghai) to Augustine Heard, Jr., Apr. 18, 1862, HL–36, HC.

66. Wang Ching-yü, "Fu-ku," p. 41.

67. *Shen pao* (Apr. 10, 1874); Hsü Jun, *Nien-p'u*, p. 24.

68. *NCH* (Dec. 22, 1868), pp. 623, 625–626. See also Wang Ching-yü, "Fu-ku," pp. 42–43.

69. Wang Ching-yü, "Fu-ku," p. 43.

70. Liu Kwang-Ching, *Steamship Rivalry*, pp. 140–141.

71. Hsü Jun, *Nien-p'u*, pp. 37, 86–86b.

72. Liu Kwang-Ching, "Two companies," p. 138. "Thanks for your information about Awei. . . . I also knew that he had shares in the Chinese [Merchants' S. N.] Company, and that the Hankow agency had been offered to him." F. B. Forbes to Walter Scott Fits, July 31, 1873, FBF.

73. Liu Kwang-Ching, "Steamship Enterprise," p. 439.

74. Tōa Dōbunkai, *Keizai zensho*, II, 495–500.

75. Carlson, pp. 34–37.

76. *NCH* (Sept. 21, 1889), p. 356.

77. In 1862 Augustine Heard & Co. tried to organize a steamship company but could not find the necessary capital. Two other foreign projects likewise failed. Liu Kwang-Ching, *Steamship Rivalry*, p. 25. On the Chinese side, the Kuei-ch'ih coal and iron mines, which had been encouraged by Li Hung-chang, closed in 1883 because of inadequate capital. Hsü Jun, *Nien p'u*, p. 31. For Tong's successor, see Carlson, p. 36.

78. Tong Loong-maw (Hankow) to G. B. Dixwell (Shanghai), Aug. 26, 1863, HM–30, HC. It is not certain whether they started work on the mine or not.

79. IMC, *Decennial Report, 1882–1891*, Wuhu, pp. 268–270.

80. "Sometime ago, when Mr. Canny was down here, he asked me to advance the requisite funds to secure the control of the ground on which the Graphite mineral was found & I consented to do so, provided our risk should be very small. Tong King-sing's friends had already been buying some portion of it & therefore through the two parties the control of the district would come into our hands." F. B. Johnson (Shanghai) to William Keswick (Hong Kong), Jan. 25, 1869, JMA. See also Liu Kwang-Ching, "Tong King-sing," p. 162.

81. An agreement was reached on Feb. 6, 1873, according to which Atai "is to proceed to the Island of Hainan and there obtain the consent of the authorities and the inhabitants near and in Cheong fa hsien to his working sundry copper and mines in that vicinity. . . . He then is to offer to Mr. A. F. Heard the privilege of working these mines with him either as owning half share therein or with such other partners

as they select to own the privilege with them." The firm advanced Atai $600. Case 9, HC II. Atai's Chinese name was Ya-ti, who according to Hsü Jun was once Dent's comprador. Hsü Jun, *Nien-p'u*, p. 8.

82. The silver company lost money, and Li absconded the next year. Sun Yü-t'ang, comp., *Chung-kuo chin-tai kung-yeh shih tzu-liao chi-yao: ti i chi* (Selected materials for China's modern industrial history, first series; Peking, 1957), I, 50; II, 1087.

83. *NCH* (Apr. 7, 1886), p. 364. Ho A-mei, or Ho K'un-shan, must have been a man of high social standing, since the *NCH* continued: "The formal opening of the Tai Yu Shan [Ta-yü shan] silver-lead mines, one of Mr. Ho A-mei's enterprises, took place on the 28th of March, in the presence of a fair gathering of English and Chinese residents of Hongkong. The most roseate predictions were hazarded as to the future of the mine, the engineer stating that a discovery had already been made at the shaft which placed its success beyond all doubt." *NCH* (Apr. 7, 1886), p. 34. Ho was a wealthy merchant in Hong Kong who was particularly interested in modern enterprises. He founded a telegraph company (the Hong Kong-Canton Wa Hop Telegraph Co.) at Hong Kong in 1891, which was purchased two years later by Sheng Hsüan-huai, director-general of the Imperial Chinese Telegraph Administration at Shanghai. Wright, p. 134.

84. Sun Yü-t'ang, *Kung-yeh*, II, 1144; Yen Chung-p'ing, *Mien-fang-chih*, p. 98.

85. *Ibid.*, p. 103.

86. Percy H. Kent, *Railway Enterprise in China: An Account of Its Origin and Development* (London, 1907), pp. 3, 5.

87. *Hua-tzu jih-pao* (May 6, 1906).

88. *NCH* (Sept. 5, 1898), p. 452.

89. *NCH* (Jan. 18, 1895), p. 84; Wang Ching-yü, "Fu-ku," pp. 53–54.

90. Wang Ching-yü, "Fu-ku," p. 53.

91. Tong King-sing tried to set up a large modern Chinese-owned bank, with branches in Tokyo and London. He discussed it with Ting Jih-ch'ang at Foochow in 1876 but the plan never materialized. *Shen pao* (Mar. 18, 1876), p. 1. For the Ningpo Bank, see Fang T'eng, 12.3: 62.

92. Wang Ching-yü, "Fu-ku," pp. 48–49.

93. Wright, pp. 540, 554.

94. *Shen pao* (Nov. 4, 1875), p. 5; (July 13, 1876), p. 6.

95. *NCH* (Feb. 15, 1882), p. 188.

96. Wang Ching-yü, "Fu-ku," p. 63.

97. Li Sung-yün, comprador to the British-owned Union Steam Navigation Co. in the 1860's was a director of the Shanghai Electric Co. during 1882–1885. *Shen pao* (Apr. 20, 1885), p. 5. Tong Mow-chee, Jardine's comprador, was a representative of the shareholders. *NCH* (May 1, 1885), p. 506.

98. For Wang, see Wright, p. 536; for Chu, see *ibid.*, p. 530.

99. Wang Ching-yü, "Fu-ku," p. 66.

100. *NCH* (Nov. 15, 1882), p. 519.

101. For the history of the Tientsin Chinese Match Co., see Sun Yü-t'ang, *Kung-yeh*, II, 988–989, 992.

102. Wang Ching-yü, II, 888–889.

103. Sun Yü-t'ang, *Kung-yeh*, II, 959–960.

104. Wang Ching-yü, "Fu-ku," pp. 69–70. Wang's article, based on extensive research on Chinese and foreign newspapers in China in the nineteenth century, is

well-documented and reliable. See also Ramon H. Myers, "Entrepreneurship in Modern China: An Interpretative Study," ms., 1967.

105. Yen Chung-p'ing, *Mien-fang-chih*, pp. 108–110. See also Yen's earlier work, *Chung-kuo mien-yeh chih fa-chan* (The development of the Chinese cotton industry; Chungking, 1943), pp. 76–79.

106. For the China Merchants' Steam Navigation Co., see Liu Kwang-Ching, "Two Steamship Companies"; Albert Feuerwerker, *China's Early Industrialization: Sheng Hsüan-huai (1844–1916) and Mandarin Enterprise* (Cambridge, Mass, 1958), pp. 96–188.

107. Chu Ch'i-ang was a native of Pao-shan, Kiangsu. According to an official biography, he participated in the war against the Taipings in the 1860's and first acquired the official title of Prefect through money contributions to the government. In 1865 he was a "candidate for sub-prefect" (*hou-pu t'ung-chih*) and a commissioner of the Chekiang Bureau of Sea Transport at Shanghai. Liu, "Two Steamship Companies," pp. 155–156.

108. *Chekiang Sea-transport Documents*, 3rd ser., 8: 22; quoted in Liu Kwang-Ching, "Two Steamship Companies," p. 156.

109. *Ibid.*, pp. 109–110.

110. *NCH* (June 14, 1873), pp. 529, 532.

111. Walter Connor v. Chu I-fu, *NCH* (July 5, 1873), p. 15.

112. R. I. Fearon, Shanghai partner of Heard's, commented on Chu's new steamers purchased from England: "All the boats coming out are said to be guaranteed to carry 18,000 piculs on 14 feet draft, and to go 10 knots on a small consumption of coal—none of which conditions except the capacity are likely to be fulfilled and the mandarins have generally so mismanaged the affair through ignorance that the universal impression outside appears to be that the [China Merchants' Steam Navigation] Company will have to resell their steamers." R. I. Fearon (Shanghai) to A. F. Heard, Feb. 13, 1873, HM–43, HC.

113. Samuel C. Chu, *Reformer in Modern China: Chang Chien, 1853–1926* (New York, 1965), pp. 38, 49. For the comprador, see ch. VIII.

114. It was probably Sun Chu-t'ang, an official of the Tsungli Yamen, who persuaded Li Hung-chang that the Cantonese compradors were best qualified to undertake the steamship enterprise. Sometime in May 1873, Lin Shih-chih, an official of the Tientsin native customs, and Prefect Chu held conversations at Shanghai with two Cantonese compradors, Tong King-sing and Hsü Jun. Tong went to Tientsin to see Governor-general Li in June and returned to Shanghai to resign his comprador post in July. Prefect Chu relinquished the management of the steamships but continued to handle the tribute rice business. Liu Kwang-Ching, "Two Steamship Companies," p. 112; Liu Kwang-Ching, "Tong King-sing," p. 169.

115. F. B. Forbes (Shanghai) to M. G. Moore (Tientsin), May 27, 1873, FBF.

116. F. B. Forbes to E. Cunningham, June 27, 1873, FBF.

117. Robert I. Fearon to A. F. Heard, June 2, 1873, HM–43, HC.

118. F. B. Johnson (Shanghai) to James Whittall, July 11, Sept. 1, 1870, JMA; quoted in Liu Kwang-Ching, "Two Steamship Companies," p. 116. See also F. B. Johnson to William Keswick, June 1, Sept. 27, 1871, JMA.

119. *NCH* (Oct. 7, 1880), p. 316.

120. *NCH* (Mar. 18, 1875), p. 257.

121. F. B. Forbes (Shanghai) to S. C. Rose, July 22, 1873, FBF.

122. R. I. Fearon to A. F. Heard, June 27, 1873, HM–43, HC.

123. F. B. Forbes to George Tyson, Sept. 20, 1866, FBF.

124. R. I. Fearon to A. F. Heard, July 12, Aug. 2, Aug. 26, 1873, HM–43, HC; Liu Kwang-Ching, "Two Steamship Companies," p. 171.

125. Liu Kwang-Ching, "British-Chinese Steamship Rivalry in China, 1873–1885," in C. D. Cowan, ed., *The Economic Development of China and Japan* (London, 1864), pp. 55–57, 67, 69–70. Li Sung-yün played an important role in the China Merchants' Steam Navigation Co. in the 1880's. Wang Ching-yü, "Fu-ku," pp. 42, 61.

126. Liu Kwang-Ching, "Steamship Rivalry," pp. 67, 70.

127. H. B. Morse to Gustav Detring, Oct. 19, 1886, MLB.

128. For Tong King-sing's role in the Kaiping Mines, see Carlson, pp. 4–7, 23–42; Sun Yü-t'ang, *Kung-yeh*, II, 1171.

129. The coal seam had never been reached. Miners told Tong that they eventually encountered water and the pits became flooded and had to be abandoned. Besides, as Tong's report indicates, "the sides of the pit fall in; foul air accumulates, or the workings catch fire, all of which possibilities render mining a dangerous employment. Profits, too, are very small." *Papers Relating to the Foreign Relations of the United States* (Washington, 1878), pp. 123–124; quoted in Carlson, p. 9.

130. *NCH* (Apr. 17, 1886), p. 396; Hsü Jun, *Nien-p'u*, pp. 27, 89.

131. The most important of Tong's foreign staff were R. R. Burnett and Claude W. Kinder. As chief engineer, Burnett supervised the original excavations. Kinder, who had previous experience in Japan, succeeded Burnett as chief engineer by 1883. Carlson, p. 12.

132. Production at the Kaiping Mines was 3,613 tons in 1881 and rose to 38,383 tons in 1882 and 75,317 tons in 1883. Thereafter production increased rapidly and steadily. Kaiping coal not only captured the Tientsin market but also had influence in other treaty ports, especially the northern ports such as Newchwang and Chefoo. Carlson, pp. 12, 25, 27.

133. Kaiping's coal went to the arsenals at Tientsin and was used at brick and lime kilns, potteries, and distilleries. One important result of the opening of the colliery, according to the British consul, was "the revival of several industries which were languishing or extinct on account of the surface coal of the district being mostly worked out." IMC, *Returns of Trade and Trade Reports* (1882), 2: 17.

134. China's first railroad was built by the British in 1876 from Woosung to Shanghai. It was shortly purchased by the Chinese and destroyed. Kent, pp. 9–15. For the Kaiping railroad, see Kent, pp. 22–35.

135. In a dispatch to the Department of State, the United States consul at Tientsin stated in 1879 that Tong was a man who considered it "of the greatest importance to the welfare of his country that she should adopt the modern ideas of civilization." Dispatch No. 34 of Oct. 31, 1879, from Consul Denny (Tientsin), to the Department of State, National Archives (quoted in Carlson, pp. 5, 117).

136. Kent, p. 22.

137. Herbert A. Giles, *A Chinese Biographical Dictionary* (Shanghai, 1898), p. 715. See also *NCH* (Oct. 14, 1892), pp. 562, 568.

138. Yen Chung-p'ing, *Mien-fang-chih*, pp. 87–88.

139. Wright, p. 754. Wu was with the North China Imperial Railways at different times but could not stay long enough for political reasons. For his efforts to control the railroad, see *NCH* (June 29, 1894), p. 1004; (May 22, 1896), p. 787; (July 12, 1897), p. 420.

140. T'ang Chieh-ch'en succeeded his father, T'ang Mao-chih, as Jardine's Shanghai comprador in 1897 until his death in 1904. *Hua-tzu jih-pao* (Mar. 7, 1904).

141. Cheng Kuan-ying, *Hou-p'ien*, 8: 31–32; *Hua-tzu jih-pao* (May 6, 1906).

142. Ho Fu, comprador to Jardine, Matheson & Co. at Hong Kong, "recognizes the advantages which, in a British colony, naturally follow from a thorough grasp of Western methods." Wright, p. 178.

143. Wright, p. 178.

144. *Ibid.*, p. 723.

145. Yen Chung-p'ing, *Mien-fang-chih*, p. 99; *NCH* (Feb. 21, 1879), pp. 168–171.

146. Wu Mao-ting (Wu Jim Pah) served the Hongkong and Shanghai Banking Corp. for thirty-nine years, first as an assistant comprador at Shanghai (1866–1883), then as a comprador at Tientsin (1883–1905). Wright, p. 754.

147. Teng Chi-ch'ang (Tang Kee Shang) joined the Hongkong and Shanghai Banking Corp. when its Hankow branch opened in 1865. Wright, p. 723.

148. A. H. Cole's definition. See *Change and the Entrepreneur*, p. 88.

149. Joseph A. Schumpeter, *Capitalism, Socialism and Democracy* (New York, 1950), *passim*, esp. pp. 131–134.

150. Hsü Jun, *Nien-p'u*, pp. 37, 86–86b.

151. For the entrepreneur's ability to bear risk and uncertainty, see Frank H. Knight, *Risk, Uncertainty and Profit* (Boston, 1921).

152. Yang Hai Tsar, for example, comprador to Ward, Probst & Co. at Shanghai, "joined others in the establishment of several cotton mills and silk filatures, but lost a lot of money in this way." Wright, p. 570. For bankruptcy, a case in point is Fung Heen, comprador to the Oriental Banking Corp., Shanghai. See *NCH* (June 4, 1864), p. 91.

153. Opinion of John Henderson, Assessor, in the case of Messrs. David Sassoon, Sons and Co. v. Wong Gan-ying before British Supreme Court for China and Japan, Shanghai, Nov. 14, 1884, *NCH* (Nov. 19, 1884), p. 578.

154. The companies were the Jen-ho Marine Insurance Co. and Chi-ho Fire Insurance Co. Lu Ch'i-yün, *I-pai ming-jen chia-cheng shih* (The family history of one hundred prominent Chinese; Shanghai, 1922), pp. 27–28. Later, Jung I-t'ing, comprador to the Chartered Bank of India, Australia and China at Hong Kong, tried to organize the China Marine Insurance Co., Ltd. For advertisement, see *Hua-tze jih-pao* (July 15, 1895).

155. Yen Chung-p'ing, *Mien-fang-chih*, p. 105; Sun Yü-t'ang, *Kung-yeh*, II, 1070.

156. Yen Chung-p'ing, *Mien-fang-chih*, p. 104.

157. Hsü Jun, *Nien-p'u*, pp. 39b–40.

158. Johannes Hirschmeier, *The Origins of Entrepreneurship in Meiji Japan* (Cambridge, Mass., 1964), pp. 196–210, 287–291.

159. For Jardine's Takee, see *NCH* (May 16, 1857), p. 166. For Fung Heen, comprador to the Oriental Bank, see *NCH* (June 4, 1864), p. 91. For Russell's Sunkee (Liu Sen-chi), see *Shen pao* (May 8, 1875), p. 3; *NCH* (Aug. 28, 1875), p. 212. In 1867, Jardine's Hankow comprador privately used the firm's fund of 74,000 taels for his own speculative endeavor. S. I. Gower (Hankow) to Jardine, Matheson & Co. (Shanghai), Sept. 3, 1867, JMA.

160. Hsü Jun, *Nien-p'u*, p. 10.

161. A contemporary newspaper observed that the comprador had "a speculative disposition . . . and his transactions were, to a great extent, fabulous. That is to

say, he sold where he had not bought, and bought without money to pay, according to his anticipations of a rise or fall in the market." *NCH* (Apr. 16, 1864), p. 62. For Hsü Jun, see his *Nien-p'u*, p. 36. For Yang Kuei-hsüan, see *NCH* (Oct. 29, 1884), p. 473. For Liu Jen-hsiang, see Wang Ching-yü, *Kung-yeh*, II, 961–963.

    162. For the system of "complete responsibility," see ch. VII.

VII. THE COMPRADOR SYSTEM AS A SOCIOECONOMIC INSTITUTION

    1. Interview with Chou Hung-chi in Taiwan, Mar. 10, 1963. At Hong Kong in 1870–1871, there was only one advertisement in the *Hong Kong Daily Press* for a man seeking the comprador position in a foreign house. *Hong Kong Daily Press* (Feb. 9, 1870), available at the Hong Kong Supreme Court Library, Hong Kong. So far as I know, among the compradors to Heard's, Dent's, Russell's, and Jardine's, only Sunkee, the Tientsin comprador to Russell's, took the initiative to become a comprador. He testified in court in 1875: "I went to Russell & Co. at Shanghai . . . [on] 18th February, 1862, to arrange to become their comprador at Tientsin. I spoke to Mr. [Edward] Cunningham about it. I was engaged." *NCH* (Aug. 28, 1875), p. 213. In the early twentieth century, foreign houses still took the initiative in employing trustworthy merchants as compradors, but they frequently advertised in the newspapers, as in Hong Kong. Considerable deposits were required. *Hua-tze jih-pao* (Mar. 15 and May 14, 1904). Besides making deposits, some Chinese at Hankow even bribed foreign managers so as to become compradors. P'eng Yü-hsin, "K'ang-Jih," p. 28.

    2. At Tientsin, Sunkee's successor had been a good comprador to David Sassoon & Co. for sale of goods, but was not able to manage the ship business smoothly for Russell's. F. B. Forbes to E. Cunningham, Dec. 22, 1874, FBF.

    3. For example, in 1875 Sunkee spoke at the U.S. Consular Court at Shanghai in pidgin English. *NCH* (Oct. 7, 1875), p. 358. In contrast, according to Robert I. Fearon of Heard's, Tong King-sing "speaks English like a Briton." R. I. Fearon (Shanghai) to A. F. Heard (Hong Kong), Jan. 6, 1873, HM–43, HC. A. F. Heard, interested in employing Young Atong as Kiukiang comprador in 1862, asked the opinion of H. G. Bridges, the firm's Kiukiang agent. Bridges replied: "I had a half hour conversation with him, and was very favorably impressed. [He] . . . looks intelligent, speaks English very well." H. G. Bridges (Kiukiang) to A. F. Heard (Shanghai), Aug. 6, 1862, HM–23, HC.

    4. In the case of He Fukee v. F. A. Groom, a witness named "Way King-kee deposed—'I am comprador at Messrs. Russell & Co. I cannot speak English.' His Honour considered it strange that, holding that position, he could not speak English and directed [Yang] Heding [the interpreter] to question him again. Witness now said he was a clerk in the comprador's office at Messrs. Russell & Co.'s." *NCH* (Feb. 22, 1877), p. 189.

    5. John Heard (Hong Kong) to A. F. Heard (Shanghai), May 2, 1860, HM–5, HC.

    6. Case 26, RA.

    7. *Shang-hai ch'ien-chuang*, p. 29; Yao Kung-ho, *Shang-hai hsien-hua* (Shanghai gossip; Shanghai, 1917), pp. 66–69.

    8. For example, Lo King Fee, comprador to Reiss & Co., Shanghai, "entered the service of the firm at fourteen, and his present appointment [as chief comprador

on May 1, 1905] was a result of a special recommendation from the manager, J. Sterm." When Mok Se On in 1908 became chief comprador to Butterfield & Swire, Hong Kong, he had been serving the firm for thirty-three years. Wright, pp. 548, 182.

9. At Hankow in the 1860's, men were usually taken on as compradors who had neither the necessary personal standing nor adequate resources. A British consular report from that city in 1865 refers to "the dangerous facilities afforded to the Chinese compradores and servants for trading on their employers' credit and capital." *British Consular Trade Report,* Hankow, 1865, p. 135; quoted in Allen and Donnithorne, p. 48.

10. See Yong of Heard's fully secured the firm's Foochow comprador, Tong Loong-maw, in 1859. However, he would not be responsible for losses resulting from "fire, theft, and other unexpected accidents" befalling the firm. Agreements, 1846–1861, Case 9, HC II. On the other hand, Yu Tze-hsiang, comprador to Lane, Crawford & Co. (1868–1870), was guaranteed for 2,500 taels only. *NCH* (Sept. 22, 1870), p. 228. In 1899, Hsü Jun guaranteed a comprador, limiting his maximum responsibility to 10,000 taels. See his *Nien-p'u,* p. 97b.

11. Cheng Kuan-ying, *Hou-p'ien,* 15: 11b–12. In the case of R. S. Raphael v. Ch'en Yuh-shao (the comprador) and his surety, Wei-yuen-chang, the judgment stated: "Wei-yuen-chang, on his part, holds a security paper from one Chang-liu-chiaou, who will be called upon to indemnify the former in the full amount paid by him in his quality of guarantor. These two guarantors will not be allowed to decline their responsibility in this matter." *NCH* (Dec. 13, 1870) pp. 432–433.

12. Ts'ai Kwei P'ei, comprador to Barnes & Co., Shanghai, embezzled 15,000 taels in 1870. His three guarantors paid back "in equal proportions, in accordance with the tenor of the security paper." *NCH* (Dec. 6, 1870), p. 416. When Cheng Kuan-ying resigned the position of comprador from Butterfield & Swire in 1882, he and two other friends jointly guaranteed his successor, Yang Kuei-hsüan. Yang went bankrupt three years later, owing 100,000 taels to the firm, which the three guarantors had to repay. Cheng Kuan-ying, *Hou-p'ien,* 15: 11–12, 39b.

13. Cheng Kuan-ying, *Hou-p'ien,* 15: 11.

14. This was a written arrangement between the guarantor Cheng Kuan-ying and the comprador Yang Kuei-hsüan. Cheng Kuan-ying, *Hou-p'ien,* 15:39.

15. Hsü Jun, *Nien-p'u,* p. 97b; testimony of James Webster, agent of the Oriental Bank Corp., Shanghai, in the Oriental Bank Corp. v. Yen Choong and Wye Kee, guarantors of the bank's comprador, *NCH* (June 4, 1864), p. 91.

16. The sureties of the comprador to the Oriental Bank Corp., Shanghai, signed an English security chop. "Securities translated orally in pidgin English by the manager [L. Lamond] to the sureties; the sureties assented to this. The agent of the Bank [James Webster] witnessed the signature of the sureties and then gave it to the manager." *NCH* (June 4, 1864), p. 91.

17. Agreement, 1846–1861, Case 9, HC II.

18. On the question of whether a comprador should be responsible for the native bank orders at Hankow, H. G. Bridges of Heard's reported: "The comprador is entirely responsible, and Taytnabb & Co. and Sassoons say their compradors' security papers are worded to fully cover all such risks." H. G. Bridges (Hankow) to A. F. Heard (Shanghai), June 29, 1866, HM–23, HC.

19. The last paragraph of the guarantee paper (drawn in 1865) for Shangfun (Ch'eng Fen), comprador to Preston, Breuell & Co., reads: "It is further agreed

that Shanfun shall not do business on his own account or have a joint interest in speculations with others, unless with the knowledge and consent of his employers, and that if he do so, the securities will not arrange the consequences." This was one version of the original English translation of the guarantee paper, which was actually written in Chinese. *NCH* (Jan. 8, 1867), p. 349.

20. *NCH* (Jan. 8, 1867), p. 349.

21. F. B. Johnson (Hong Kong) to W. Paterson (Shanghai), Jan. 10, 1884, JMA.

22. For deposit, see Ma Yin-ch'u, "Mai-pan," p. 131. The *tao-ch'i* was a title to real estate in the foreign settlements of the treaty ports. Ma Yin-ch'u, *Ma Yin-ch'u yen-chiang chi* (The collected lectures of Ma Yin-ch'u; Shanghai, 1929), III, 88–89. It became a common form of deposit after 1900. *Shang-hai ch'ien-chuang*, p. 37. It was also used as a form of deposit in Hong Kong. *Hua-tze jih-pao* (July 5, 1897).

23. Allen and Donnithorne, p. 47. For a lawsuit brought by a comprador against his foreign employer concerning the deposited money, see *NCH* (June 10, 1910), pp. 593, 644–646.

24. Tōa Dōbunkai, *Keizai zensho*, II, 367.

25. For the concept of *pao*, see Yang Lien-sheng, *Les aspects economiques des travaux publics dans la Chine imperiale* (College de France, 1964), p. 80; H. B. Morse, *The International Relations of the Chinese Empire* (Shanghai and London, 1910–1918), I, 114–117.

26. In a letter to a Jardine's partner, the firm's comprador Tong King-sing wrote: "During the last 3 years . . . you know very well that . . . there was not the slightest chance for me to save money. I have now filled my present [comprador] office for five years (the worst times at Shanghai) and have lost more money than I have made." Tong King-sing (Shanghai) to William Keswick (Hong Kong), Oct. 8, 1868, JMA.

27. Liu Kwang-Ching, "Tong King-sing," p. 164.

28. Cheng Kuan-ying, *Hou-p'ien*, 10: 119. The debt represented Yang's losses as a comprador as well as in his own speculations.

29. Wright, p. 566.

30. Agreements, 1846–1861, Case 9, HC II.

31. For the compradors' agreements around 1900, see Tōa Dōbunkai, *Keizai zensho*, II, 408–449; Uchida Naosaku, "Baiben seido no kenkyū" (A study of the comprador system), *Shina kenkyū*, 48: 1–28 (December 1938).

32. Case 26, RA; *NCH* (June 4, 1864), p. 91; (Oct. 13, 1860), Supplement, p. 6.

33. Charles M. Dyce, *Personal Reminiscences of Thirty Years' Residence in the Model Settlement, Shanghai, 1870–1900* (London, 1906), p. 50.

34. *NCH* (June 4, 1864), p. 91; *Shen pao* (Mar. 9, 1875), p. 2. Hsü Jun referred to the foreign managers of Dent's as *lou-shang* (the upstair-men). In speaking of a new proposal, he wrote: "*Lou-shang wei-pi ta-ying*" (The upstair-men [foreign managers] may not consent). Hsü Jun, *Nien-p'u*, p. 11.

35. F. B. Forbes to Edward Cunningham, June 11, 1872, FBF. See also Liu Kwang-Ching, *Steamship Rivalry*, p. 92.

36. *NCH* (Nov. 19, 1884); Negishi, *Baiben seido*, p. 104; Wright, pp. 548–570.

37. Negishi, *Sōran*, I, 46. The Oriental Bank at Shanghai had a "second comprador." *NCH* (June 4, 1864), p. 91. Ho Kam Tong (Ho Kan-t'ang) was the "second comprador" to Jardine's at Hong Kong in 1908. Wright, p. 174.

38. Edward Cunningham (Shanghai) to John M. Forbes (Canton), May 14,

1868, Case 26, RA.

39. Sunchong secured his cousin, Ho Hew Lam, "to represent him in the office of the comprador who took charge of the cash and valuables usually entrusted to the care of the Comprador, keeping the keys of the safe and rendering an account of disbursements and receipts to Leen Yau Tong [Ahyue]." Russell & Co. (per John M. Forbes, Jr., Canton) to E. M. King, U.S. consul at Canton, May 2, 1868, Case 26, RA.

40. A. F. Heard (Shanghai) to John Heard (Hong Kong), March 23, 1860, HL–15, HC.

41. Julian T. A. Zi was the "assistant comprador" in the machinery department of Jardine's in 1908. Wright, p. 548; *Hua-tzu jih-pao* (May 1, 1905).

42. "I have granted Tong King-sing three weeks leave of absence to visit Canton on family affairs. Acum will act for him the while." F. B. Johnson (Shanghai) to W. Keswick, Jan. 31, 1868, JMA.

43. Cheng Kuan-ying, *Hou-p'ien,* 15: 39; A. F. Heard (Shanghai) to John Heard (Hong Kong), Sept. 17, 1859, HL–14, HC.

44. There were "more than thirty" comprador's shroffs in Heard's head office at Canton in the late 1840's. Augustine Heard, Jr., "Diary," p. 114.

45. Tōa Dōbunkai, *Keizai zensho,* II, 365. Atchune, the purser of Heard's Hong Kong comprador Atchu, later became the firm's Hong Kong comprador. A. F. Heard (Shanghai) to John Heard (Hong Kong), Mar. 23, 1860, HL–15, HC. Sunkee, Russell's Tientsin comprador, had a very capable purser at that port in the 1860's. *NCH* (Aug. 28, 1875), p. 214. See Yong, Heard's Hong Kong comprador in the 1860's, was for a time the bookkeeper of the firm's old comprador Atchu. A. F. Heard (Shanghai) to John Heard (Hong Kong), Mar. 23, 1860, HL–15, HC. The accountant was the comprador's "most entrusted man" (*hsin-fu*). Cheng Kuan-ying, *Hou-p'ien,* 15: 30. For the gate-keeper, see *NCH* (May 3, 1873), p. 388. For the market shroff, see Cheng Kuan-ying, *Hou-p'ien,* 8: 2. The information of the liaison shroff is based on my interview with Huang Ying-chou (a comprador at Shanghai in the 1920's), Taipei, Taiwan, Mar. 15, 1963.

46. Lu Ch'i-yün, p. 35.

47. For China's early loans from foreigners (1861–1893), see Stanley, pp. 45–60. Russell's F. B. Forbes observed in 1872: "We ought to have some one accustomed to deal with mandarins. I think before long we shall have loans and other money business to be cared for." F. B. Forbes (Shanghai) to Edward Cunningham, June 11, 1872, FBF.

48. H. G. Bridges (Hankow) to A. F. Heard (Shanghai), June 20, 1866, HM–23, HC.

49. Arnold, pp. 256–257; Mayers et al., p. 135.

50. Tiffany, p. 216. In Heard's Hankow comprador's office, there was a "porter for front gate" and a "porter for street gate," each earning 5 taels a month. H. G. Bridges (Hankow) to A. F. Heard (Shanghai), June 14, 1866, HM–13, HC.

51. Tiffany, p. 216.

52. Augustine Heard, Jr., "Poisoning," pp. 12–13. The watchmen were described as "a quiet, useless class." *NCH* (Mar. 28, 1883), p. 353.

53. For the house boys as a "class," see *NCH* (Mar. 28, 1883), p. 352. For the term "hsi-tsai," see Ko Yüan-hsü, 2: 6b. The information of "p'u-ai" is based on my interview with ex-comprador Huang Ying-chou, Taipei, Taiwan, Mar. 15, 1963. For the various "boys," see H. G. Bridges (Hankow) to A. F. Heard (Shanghai),

June 14, 1866, EM–13, HC.

54. Augustine Heard, Jr., "Diary," p. 114.

55. Tiffany, p. 216. The author continued: "The varlet thinks it no degradation to bring fresh water and make up your bed, but he would consider it humiliating in the last degree to be forced to sweep the room out."

56. At Hankow in 1866, the salary of the cook (15 taels per month) was three times more than the coolie's. H. G. Bridges (Hankow) to A. F. Heard (Shanghai), June 14, 1866, EM–13, HC.

57. Interview with ex-comprador Huang Ying-chou, Taipei, Taiwan, Mar. 15, 1963. For a description of the coolies, see *NCH* (Mar. 28, 1883), p. 353.

58. H. G. Bridges (Hankow) to A. F. Heard (Shanghai), June 14, 1866, EM–13, HC.

59. Augustine Heard, Jr., "Diary," p. 34.

60. Augustine Heard, Jr., "Old China and New," p. 30.

61. Augustine Heard, Jr., "Poisoning," p. 9.

62. *NCH* (June 4, 1864), p. 91.

63. John Heard to Augustine Heard, Jr., May 10, 1858, EM–6, HC.

64. *NCH* (Dec. 17, 1864), p. 203. Jardine's partners trusted the new comprador Tong King-sing (1863–1873) less than their former comprador Acum. Liu Kwang-Ching, "Tong King-sing," pp. 145–146.

65. "The compradores who have come before the court criminally have generally been those of young firms." *NCH* (Mar. 28, 1883), p. 352.

66. *NCH* (June 10, 1910), p. 593.

67. A. F. Heard (Shanghai) to P. L. Everett, Jan. 21, 1858, HL–13, HC.

68. Liu Kwang-Ching, *Steamship Rivalry*, p. 93.

69. William Keswick (Shanghai) to James Whittall (Hong Kong), Sept. 27, 1864, JMA. Since several compradors defaulted at Shanghai in 1865, Keswick decided not to trust Tong King-sing fully. "I am quietly taking as much from under his control as possible." William Keswick to James Whittall, July 9, 1865, JMA. See also Liu Kwang-Ching, "Tong King-sing," p. 145.

70. John Heard (Hong Kong) to A. F. Heard (Shanghai), Sept. 6, 1859, HM–4, HC.

71. James Webster, manager of the Oriental Bank, testified in court: "I never inspect the contents of every box. . . . I know that it is not the practice for Bank managers to look at the boxes of silver. The Chartered Mercantile Bank and Commercial Bank don't do so." According to the accountant, "it would have taken two days to take all the money out and put it back again." Webster further testified: "There were two keys and one crank for the treasury. The manager had one key, accountant one, the comprador had the crank. One cannot enter without the other two. . . . I can't tell how the fraud has been committed." *NCH* (June 4, 1864), p. 91. With the passage of time, bank compradors were checked more frequently. One article of the comprador's agreement in the early Republican period read: "The comprador, at the close of each day or at such other times as the manager of the bank . . . may require, shall render an account of or pay over to said manager all such moneys, coins, gold and silver bullion, bank notes or orders, and other security for money, sycee, and treasure as he may, or ought to, have received as said comprador." Arnold, p. 259.

72. Augustine Heard, Jr., "Old China and New," p. 39.

73. Pao Kuang Yung, p. 639; Arnold, p. 258; P'eng Yü-hsin, p. 28.

74. Cheng Kuan-ying, *I-yen* (Easy words; Shanghai, 1881), 2: 6b.

75. For history of the Mixed Court at Shanghai, see Mark Elvin, "The Mixed Court of the International Settlement at Shanghai (Until 1911)," *Papers on China*, vol. 17 (Cambridge, Mass., 1963), pp. 131–159. Compradors sometimes died in prison. "Wong Shan-yen, Mr. J. H. Mackie's late comprador, who was sentenced to two years' imprisonment for embezzling the funds entrusted to him, died [in the prison of the Mixed Court] the other day." *NCH* (Oct. 22, 1874), p. 404. The comprador to Arnhold Karberg & Co. at Hankow also died in prison. P'eng Yü-hsin, 11: 28.

76. *NCH* (Mar. 28, 1883), p. 352. In the Republican period, the compradors to Melchers & Co. and to Carlowitz & Co. at Hankow committed suicide. P'eng Yü-hsin, 1: 28.

77. *NCH* (Mar. 28, 1883), p. 352. The earliest known case was the absconding of Alee, comprador to James Bowman & Co. at Shanghai, in 1859. *NCH* (Oct. 15, 1859), p. 42.

78. The fact that Jardine's partners did not fully trust Tong King-sing was partly attributable to the absconding of Afun, comprador to Preston, Breuell & Co. at Shanghai in 1866. Liu Kwang-Ching, "Tong King-sing," p. 145; *NCH* (Jan. 28, 1887), p. 348. F. B. Johnson particularly mentioned to Keswick in 1869 that "Gibb Livingston & Co.'s comprador failed." F. B. Johnson (Shanghai) to William Keswick (Hong Kong), Apr. 24, 1869, JMA.

79. *NCH* (June 4, 1864), p. 91. Yang Kuei-hsüan, comprador to Butterfield & Swire at Shanghai, absconded in 1884, owing 100,000 taels to his Chinese and foreign creditors. *NCH* (Oct. 29, 1884), p. 473; Cheng Kuan-ying, *Hou-p'ien*, 15: 11.

80. Arnold, p. 254.

81. Teng Chün-hsiang, comprador to the Hongkong and Shanghai Banking Corp., Peking (1917–1927), defaulted in 1927, leaving a debt of more than four million taels. *Hua-tzu jih-pao* (May 4, 6, and 11, 1927).

82. Tong King-sing had guaranteed Sassoon's Tientsin comprador, a certain Sung, who lost money in his capacity as a comprador. *Shen pao* (May 27, 1875), p. 3. Cheng Kuan-ying was one of the sureties of his successor comprador Yang Kuei-hsüan, who lost 100,000 taels in 1882–1884. As the other sureties could not afford to pay their shares, Cheng was forced to make up the entire sum. See his *Hou-p'ien*, 15: 11.

83. *NCH* (Aug. 28, 1868), pp. 414, 417.

84. *NCH* (July 11, 1884), p. 43. This English translation appeared in the *North China Herald*. However, *li-she* probably means *li-ying she-chi* [*chih-jen*] ([the person] who is logically involved).

85. A-yuk, comprador to Hogg & Co., Hankow, absconded in July 1865. His sureties had not made good the money by April 1868. *NCH* (Apr. 15, 1868), p. 173.

86. Yu Tze-hsiang, comprador to Lane, Crawford & Co. in 1868–1870 and guaranteed for 2,500 taels, stole the security chop when he absconded. *NCH* (Sept. 22, 1870), p. 228.

87. *NCH* (Jan. 8, 1867), p. 348.

88. *NCH* (Mar. 25, 1867), pp. 398–400.

89. For example, Cheng Kuan-ying had a three-year contract (1874–1877) with Butterfield & Swire, which was followed by another for five years. Only after the expiration of the second contract was he free to join the China Merchants' Steam Navigation Co. See his *Hou-p'ien*, 10: 1b.

90. According to his agreement with Heard's, Akow, the firm's Yokohama comprador, was to "act . . . as compradore . . . for as long a time as mutually agreeable. He cannot, however, leave them within one year from the time of his arrival here, nor without giving them at least four months' notice of his intention." If discharged on grounds of malpractice or laziness, he would receive "payment of one month's extra wages." Agreements, 1846–1861, Case 9, HC II. For a bank comprador, a six months' notice was required. Tōa Dōbunkai, *Keizai zensho*, II, 351.

91. The following advertisement appeared in a Hong Kong newspaper in 1885: "NOTICE: The undersigned begs to notify that he left the Firm of Messrs. Cawasjee, Pallanjee & Co., on the 10th February, 1885, when his Responsibilities Ceased. All the accounts were examined by Mr. H. C. Setna, the Manager of the said Firm, and the Chop (Seal) and Books were handed to him, at the same time. Woo A Poo, late Compradore, Messrs. Cawasjee, Pallanjee & Co., Hongkong, 19th February, 1885." *Hong Kong Daily Press* (Feb. 25, 1885), available at the Hong Kong Supreme Court Library.

92. *Hua-tzu jih-pao* (June 4, 1897; May 14, 1902).

93. Tong went to Tientsin in May 1873 to see Li Hung-chang, who had invited him to become the new manager of the China Merchants' Steam Navigation Co. Tong resigned his comprador post after returning to Shanghai. In June his brother Tong Mow-chee, then Jardine's Tientsin comprador, succeeded his as Jardine's chief comprador at Shanghai. Liu Kwang-Ching, "Tong King-sing," p. 169.

94. John Heard to A. F. Heard, Apr. 4, 1862, FL–6, p. 136, HC.

95. Augustine Heard, Jr., "Poisoning," pp. 4, 10.

96. *Ibid.*, p. 4.

97. *Ibid.*, p. 9.

98. The hereditary nature of the comprador position was illustrated by the case of Hsi Cheng-fu, comprador to the Hongkong and Shanghai Banking Corp. at Shanghai. See *NCH* (Feb. 8, 1913), pp. 418–420.

99. Hsü Jun, *Nien-p'u*, pp. 1–8; Hsü Jun et al., *Hsiang-shan Hsü-shih tsung-p'u* (The history of the Hsü clan in the Hsiang-shan hsien; Shanghai, 1844), 5: 57–59, 7: 64–79b; Wright, p. 566. For Hsü Jun's guarantee of Yang Mei-nan, see Hsü Jun, *Nien-p'u*, p. 97b.

100. Hsü Jun, *Nien-p'u*, 85b; *NCH* (Sept. 23, 1879), p. 309; (Oct. 17, 1879), p. 386; (Aug. 27, 1886), p. 235.

101. For T'ang Chieh-ch'en (1871–1904), see Hsü Jun, *Nien-p'u*, p. 106; Wang Ching-yü, *Kung-yeh*, II, 97b; Tōa Dōbunkai, *Keizai zensho*, II, 372. For T'ang Chi-ch'ang, see *Hua-tzu jih pao* (Mar. 7,1904).

102. Wright, p. 178; interview with ex-comprador Kuo Tsan, Hong Kong, Aug. 25, 1963.

103. Interview with one of Ho Tung's sons, Hong Kong, Aug. 22, 1963.

104. Wright, pp. 176, 178; Wu Hsing-lien, *Hsiang-kang Hua-jen ming-jen shih lüeh* (The prominent Chinese in Hong Kong; Shanghai, 1915), pp. 17–19.

105. Lo Ch'ang-cho was succeeded by Ho Liang, who in turn gave his position to one of Lo Ch'ang-cho's sons, Lo Wen-hsien. Interview with members of Ho Tung's family, Hong Kong, Aug. 22, 1963.

106. One of Ho Tung's sons, Ho Shih-jung, has served as comprador to the Hongkong and Shanghai Banking Corp. at Hong Kong for more than thirty years. In 1963 he was still the bank's "Chinese manager."

107. H. G. Bridges (Hankow) to A. F. Heard (Shanghai), June 20, 1866,

HM–23, HC; A. F. Heard (Shanghai) to John Heard (Hong Kong), Mar. 23, 1860, HL–15, HC.

108. John Heard to A. F. Heard, April 4, 1862, FL–6, p. 136, HC.

109. A. F. Heard (Shanghai) to John Heard (Hong Kong), March 23, 1860, HL–15, HC.

110. *Ibid.*

111. Liang T'ing-nan, 22: 47; 26: 1; Hsü Jun, *Tsung-p'u,* 7: 79.

112. *NCH* (Feb. 12, 1874), p. 129.

113. Mayers et al., p. 135.

114. Ko Yüan-hsü, 2: 6b. For example, a Cantonese watchman in Heard's Hankow comprador's office was paid 8 taels monthly, whereas a Hankow watchman was paid only 3.9 taels. H. G. Bridges (Hankow) to A. F. Heard (Shanghai), June 14, 1866, FM–13, HC. At Newchwang in the 1860's, "here as elsewhere, the natives of Canton are preferred as domestic servants by Europeans, but can only be had on payment of high wages. A Cantonese 'boy' claims from $15 to $20 per month, natives of the place being obtainable in the like capacity at from $6 to $8." At Chefoo, "servants of Canton and Ningpo are preferable." Mayers et al., pp. 542, 460.

115. A. G. Dallas (Shanghai) to David Jardine (Hong Kong), Apr. 4, 1851, JMA.

116. At Chinkiang in the 1860's, "the servants employed. by foreigners are Cantonese or natives of Ningpo." At Hankow, "foreign merchants were entirely dependent upon the assistance of their Cantonese or Ningpo compradores." Mayers et al., pp. 424, 451.

117. H. G. Bridges (Kiukiang) to A. F. Heard (Shanghai), Aug. 27, 1862, HM–23, HC. "It is a great pity Agunn will smoke so much opium." *Ibid.* "Agunn is here, it is useless for him to stay here any longer, and he is desirous to go to Canton for medical advice." H. G. Bridges (Kiukiang) to A. F. Heard (Hong Kong), Oct. 16, 1863, HM–23, HC. For the "northern men," see H. G. Bridges (Kiukiang) to A. F. Heard (Shanghai), June 29, 1862, HM–23, HC.

118. H. G. Bridges (Hankow) to A. F. Heard (Shanghai), Apr. 11, 1866, HM–23, HC.

119. Terada Takanobu, "So-Shō chihō ni okeru toshi no mengyō shōnin ni tsuite" (On the cotton merchants of cities in Su [Soochow] and Sung [Sunkiang]), *Shirin,* 41.6: 52–69 (Nov. 1, 1958).

120. Wright, p. 540.

121. Interview with members of Ho Tung's family, Hong Kong, Aug. 22, 1963.

122. Wright, pp. 174–184, 525–572.

123. Liang Chia-pin, pp. 42, 49. The Cohong merchants came mainly from Anhuei, Fukien, and Kwangtung.

124. Ch'en Shao-po, *Hsing-Chung hui ko-ming shih-yao* (A brief history of the revolutionary activities of the Hsing-Chung hui; Taipei, 1956), p. 32.

125. Interview with members of Ho Tung's family, Hong Kong, Aug. 22, 1963.

126. *NCH* (Oct. 15, 1885), p. 448. This was a general distinction. The two names could be used alternatively. For a more detailed discussion of the guilds, see Ho Ping-ti, *Chung-kuo hui-kuan shih-lun* (A historical survey of landsmannschaften in China; Taipei, 1966).

127. Hsü Jun, *Nien p'u,* p. 25.

128. "But even Tong Mow-chee himself was once *koong-soed* by the Swatow

284

Guild." *NCH* (Sept. 23, 1879), p. 309.

129.   The Shanghai General Chamber of Commerce (a foreign merchants' organization) complained: "The former [foreign merchants], acting with individual exclusiveness, and in a spirit of accustomed competition, have hitherto been unable to oppose successfully a system of irresponsible agency which is supported by a combination between the mercantile guilds and a class of middlemen (many of whom are nominally the servants [compradors] of foreigners), in the interests of illegitimate exactions and undue regulation of prices." *NCH* (Mar. 8, 1867), p. 387.

130.   A foreign newspaper at Shanghai complained in 1867 that the Western way of doing business was competition whereas the Chinese way was "combination." *NCH* (Feb. 22, 1867), p. 337. One of its editorials in 1876 reads: "The Guild system is the outward expression of the spirit of combination." *NCH* (May 6, 1876), p. 426.

131.   *NCH* (Oct. 17, 1879), p. 389.

132.   Augustine Heard, Jr., "Old China and New," p. 19.

133.   *NCH* (Oct. 1, 1864), p. 158.

134.   For Hankow, see *NCH* (Mar. 25, 1865), p. 46. The "compradors' cup" (200 taels) was the highest prize in the Shanghai races of 1872. *NCH* (Nov. 7, 1872), p. 394.

135.   Huang I-feng claims that the compradors had their own guild as early as the 1860's, but he does not give reference sources. See his "Chiu Chung-kuo," p. 98.

136.   Alexis Krausse, *China in Decay: A Handbook to the Far Eastern Question* (London, 1898), pp. 238–239, quoted in Koh Sung Jae, *Stages of Industrial Development in Asia: A Comparative History of the Cotton Industry in Japan, India, China and Korea* (Philadelphia, 1966), p. 207.

137.   *Shang-hai ch'ien-chuang*, p. 90; Negishi, *Baiben seido*, p. 250.

138.   Sha Wei-k'ai, *Chung-kuo chih mai-pan chih* (The comprador institution in China; Shanghai, 1927), p. 33.

139.   Wu Hsing-lien, p. 49.

140.   Sha Wei-k'ai, pp. 53, 58.

141.   Uchida, "Baiben seido," 49: 5.

142.   Tōa Dōbunkai, *Keizai zensho*, II, 339.

VIII.   BEYOND A PURCHASER: NONECONOMIC ACTIVITIES OF THE COMPRADOR

1.   Ernest O. Hauser, *Shanghai, City for Sale* (1940), p. 116.

2.   Wright, p. 566; Cheng Kuan-ying, *Hou-p'ien*, 1: 1; Wu Hsing-lien, p. 1.

3.   Wright, p. 544.

4.   *Who's Who in China* (Shanghai, 1926), p. 233.

5.   Fairbank, *Trade and Diplomacy*, I, 217.

6.   Wright, pp. 530, 548, 752.

7.   Tōa Dōbunkai, *Keizai zensho*, II, 339; Wright, p. 752.

8.   Wright, pp. 570, 723. The compradors were encouraged by foreigners to live in the foreign settlements. The British, French, and American consuls wrote to the Shanghai taotai in 1855: "It has been fully agreed that all whose residence is not so sanctioned and made legal shall be removed from within the settlement. . . . At the same time many Chinese connected with foreign trade of responsible character . . . are at present located within the boundaries, and in many instances

their continued residence may be . . . [of] manifest benefit both to the Foreign and Chinese merchants." *NCH* (Mar. 24, 1855), p. 137. Hsü Jun's home, for instance, was in the British Settlement at Shanghai. See his *Nien-p'u,* p. 118b.

9. For pidgin English, see Fairbank, *Trade and Diplomacy,* I, 13–14; Robert A. Hall, Jr., "Chinese Pidgin English Grammar and Texts," *Journal of the American Oriental Society,* 64.63: 95–113 (July-September 1944); Hunter, p. 62; Geoffrey R. Sayer, *Hong Kong: Birth, Adolescence and Coming of Age* (London, 1937), pp. 20–21.

10. Augustine Heard, Jr., "Poisoning," p. 2. Conversation in "pidgin" was usually a question-and-answer dialogue between the taipan and the comprador. Carl Crow gives an example of pidgin English in the early twentieth century:

Taipan: "How fashion that chow-chow (miscellaneous) cargo he just now stop godown inside?"

Comprador: "'Lat (that) cargo he no can walkee just now. 'Lat man Kong Tai (the purchaser) he no got ploper sclew (security)."

Taipan: "How come you talkee sclew noploper? My have got sclew paper safe inside."

Comprador: "Aiyah! 'Lat sclew paper he no can do. 'Lat sclew man he have no Ningpo more far (i. e., absconded into the hinterland)."

Quoted in Fairbank, *Trade and Diplomacy,* I, 13.

11. Wright, *passim; Hua-tzu jih-pao* (Sept. 29, Oct. 29, 1911).

12. Li Chung-chüeh, *Ch'ieh-wan lao-jen ch'i-shih tzu-hsü* (The autobiography of Li Chung-chüeh at seventy; Shanghai, 1922), 4: 234b. See also Tsuchiya, pp. 60–62.

13. Hsü Jun, *Nien-p'u,* p. 10.

14. Julian T. A. Zi was assistant comprador to Jardine's machinery department at Shanghai. See Wright, p. 548; Robert Ho Tung was Jardine's Hong Kong comprador from 1883 to 1900. Wu Hsing-lien, p. 1; Affo was Jardine's comprador in the early 1850's. "You are no doubt aware that William Affo has been up here for some time. . . . I would like to have him [as a comprador], as I believe him to be trustworthy." A. G. Dallas (Shanghai) to David Jardine (Hong Kong), Jan. 13, 1852, JMA.

15. *Who's Who in China* (Shanghai, 1926), p. 233.

16. *NCH* (Mar. 25, 1865), p. 46; (Nov. 9, 1869), p. 588.

17. Wright, p. 176.

18. Wu Hsing-lien, p. 62; *Yang kung Mei-nan ai-ssu-lu* (Memorial records of Yang Mei-nan; ca. 1941), p. 6.

19. Wang Ching-yü, *Kung-yeh,* II, 96:.

20. Wright, p. 543–544.

21. St. Luke's Hospital at Shanghai was founded in 1866 under the auspices of the American Episcopal Church Mission. Because of its original location, it was at first known as the "Hongkew Hospital." The name "St. Luke's" was adopted when it was moved to a new site in 1880. Pott, p. 92. For Li Ch'iu-p'ing as a comprador, see *Shen pao* (Sept. 27, 1879).

22. *Yang Mei-nan,* pp. 7, 92.

23. Frederick T. Ward bequeathed his wife, Yang Chang-mei, 50,000 taels after his death in 1862. Toyama, pp. 29, 34; Morse, *International Relations,* II, 82.

24. Wright, *passim.* Hsü Jun, for instance, sent one son to an American university in 1900 and another to Oxford the next year. They started to learn English at

the age of seven. See his *Nien-p'u*, pp. 97–118.

25. Authority over the right to purchase degrees was one means by which Ch'ing officials could control the comprador. In 1858, when the second Sino-British War was in progress, Ch'ing officials ordered that all compradors should give up their jobs and return home; otherwise they, together with their descendants, would be excluded from purchasing degrees. *NCH* (Aug. 7, 1858), p. 2.

26. Wright, pp. 525–572.

27. Hsü Jun, *Nien-p'u*, p. 16b.

28. When Cheng Kuan-ying, comprador to Butterfield & Swire, refused to pay a debt, his creditor brought this fact to the attention of the officials, who in a memorial suggested that Cheng's honorary taotai rank be canceled. Cheng promptly repaid the debt, and his rank was restored. Sun Yü-t'ang, *Kung-yeh*, II, 1055.

29. When Hsü Jun and others arrived at Shanghai from Tientsin in 1873 in connection with the China Merchants' Steam Navigation Co., the *North China Herald* read: "They have the rank of Taotais, so must consider themselves 'swells.'" *NCH* (Nov. 6, 1873), p. 387.

30. Hsü Jun, *Nien-p'u*, pp. 14b-16b, 29b, 83.

31. Toyama, p. 33.

32. For Choping, see Lu Ch'i-yün, p. 36; *NCH* (Nov. 29, 1870), p. 395. For Ho Tung, see Wu Hsing-lien, pp. 1–2.

33. For Tong, see *Shen pao* (June 18 and Sept. 4, 1874); for Ho, see Brian Harrison, ed., *University of Hong Kong: The First 50 Years, 1911–1961* (Hong Kong, 1962), p. 154.

34. The Ch'eng-chung hsüeh-t'ang (Ch'eng-chung school) consisted of a primary school and a junior high school. See *Shang-hai hsien hsü chih* (Gazetteer of the Shanghai hsien, continued; Shanghai, 1918), 10: 14.

35. Wu Hsing-lien, II, 4.

36. Wright, p. 538; Cheng Kuan-ying, *Hou-p'ien*, 14: 50.

37. Hsü Jun, *Tsung-p'u*, 9: 1. For the Chihli famine, Cheng contributed 1,000 taels in 1878, and the next year he and his friends raised 244,596 taels. See his *Hou-p'ien*, 14: 22–23.

38. Tōa Dōbunkai, *Keizai zensho*, VI, 579.

39. This local militia was called *Yang-ch'iang tui* (foreign-weapon corps). Hsü Jun, *Tsung-p'u*, 7: 79b.

40. The foreigners' Shanghai Volunteer Corps was formed in 1853. Pott, p. 26; *NCH* (Mar. 18, 1865), p. 42. The Chinese merchant corps was organized in 1905, and "to give the organization a harmless appearance, it was called 'The Chinese Physical Recreation Association.'" About five hundred merchants joined. Wright, p. 413. Noted compradors like Yü Hsia-ch'ing and Hu Chi-mei were its chief promoters. When the corps applied in 1907 to join the Shanghai Volunteer Corps, the application read: "and in the event of any trouble in the Settlement we shall be glad to do our share of the duty of protecting the Settlement under the directions of the Commanding Officer of the S. [Shanghai] V. [Volunteer] C. [Corps]." *Shanghai yen-chiu tzu-liao hsü-chi* (Materials for research on Shanghai, second part), pp. 191, 201; *Shang-hai hsien hsü chih*, 13: 11b.

41. Hsü Jun, *Nien-p'u*, pp. 14b-16b, 29b, 33b–34, 83, 116. See also *Yang-wu yün-tung*, VIII, 87; Lu Ch'i-yün, p. 27.

42. Tong Mow-chee (Shanghai) to F. B. Johnson (Shanghai), Sept. 27, 1877, JMA.

43. Fang T'eng, 12.2: 48.
44. Hsü Jun, *Nien-p'u*, p. 16. See also Wright, p. 548.
45. *Shang-hai hsien hsü chih*, 3: 4; Tōa Dōbunkai, *Keizai zensho*, II, 589; Wright, p. 560; *NCH* (May 16, 1874).
46. Hsü Jun, *Nien-p'u*, p. 14b.
47. *Ibid.*, p. 15.
48. Wright, pp. 543–544, 662.
49. Cheng Kuan-ying, *Hou-p'ien*, 11: 28; Wu Hsing-lien, p. 17; *Hua-tzu jih-pao* (Apr. 19, 1901); (June 27, 1905).
50. Huang I-feng, "Chiu Chung-kuo," p. 98. Huang's article was based on archives of the Shanghai Chamber of Commerce. *Shang-hai hsien hsü chih*, 2: 51b. *Shang-hai t'ung-chih kuan ch'i-k'an* (Journal of the gazetteer Bureau of Shanghai), 2.4: 930–1088 (1934).
51. Huang I-feng, "Chiu Chung-kuo," p. 98.
52. Ch'en was an active member of the General Chamber of Commerce in Canton and served as its president 1920–1922. See *Nan-yang hsiung-ti yen-ts'ao kung-ssu shih-liao* (Historical materials concerning the Nanyang Brothers Tobacco Co.; Shanghai, 1958), p. 139. For Yang, see *Yang Mei-nan*, p. 3. Both Liu and Teng were instrumental in organizing the Chinese Chamber of Commerce in Hankow, and Liu was elected its vice-president in the 1900's. Wright, p. 723.
53. Chang Tzu-piao (Cheong Chi Pio), "for his munificence, he was made a Knight Commendor of the Civil Royal Order of Industrial Merit by the King of Portugal on December 24, 1904." Wright, p. 532. For Wei and Ho, see Wu Hsing-lien, I, 3; II, 4.
54. Hsü Jun, *Tsung-p'u*, 9: 1; Cheng Kuan-ying, *Hou-p'ien*, 14: 22.
55. *Shang-hai yen-chiu hsü-chi*, p. 303; *Shang-hai yen-chiu tzu-liao* (Materials for research on Shanghai; Shanghai, 1936), pp. 152, 344; Hsü Yü-shu, *Shang-hai chin-jung chi-kuan i-lan* (A list of the financial institutes in Shanghai; Shanghai, 1920), p. 16.
56. The Ho Tung Road is a compraratively small street in north Kowloon, not far from the Boundary Street.
57. Hatano, pp. 153–155.
58. Pao P'eng, also known as Pao Ts'ung or Pao Ya-ts'ung, succeeded his father, Pao Jen-kuan, as the comprador to Dent & Co. at Canton in 1838. In 1840, he committed the crime of selling opium and was liable to arrest by Chinese officials. He escaped to Shantung and lived with one of his relatives, Chao Tzu-yung, who was then the wei hsien magistrate. *IWSM*: Tao-kuang period, 29: 13; 30: 28b.
59. In one of these "secret talks" (*mi-t'an*), Pao P'eng once offered Elliott an indemnity of four million taels, but was refused. (Elliot later accepted the amount of six million taels in the Chuenpi Convention signed on January 20, 1841.) On one occasion Ch'i-shan and Elliot conferred over peace terms on a small boat. Pao was the only one participating, while other eminent officials and hong merchants (including Howqua or Wu Tun-yüan) waited on shore. *IWSM*: TK, 28: 3.
60. Pao P'eng was banished to Ili, Sinkiang. *IWSM*: TK, 30: 41b.
61. *IWSM*: TK, 38: 11–13b.
62. Cheng Kuan-ying, *Hou-p'ien*, 8: 42–43.
63. The nine merchants were Cheng Kuan-ying, Yeh Ch'eng-chung, Hsü Ch'un-jung, Yang Chao-ao (Yang Hsin-chih), Chu P'ei-chen (Chu Pao-san), Hsü Ti-shan, Huang Tsung-hsien, T'ang Sung-yen, and Chu Chien. The first five were

compradors. Chang Chih-tung, *Chang Wen-hsiang-kung ch'üan-chi* (The complete works of Chang Chih-tung; Peking, 1928), 26: 2a–b.

64.   *Chin hsien chih* (The gazetteer of the district of Chin; 1891), 44: 37b–38. See also Toyama, pp. 17–34. Yang Fang's role in the Ever-Victorious Army appears in his letters to Wu Hsü, the Shanghai taotai. Ching Wu and Chung Ting, eds., *Wu Hsü tang-an chung ti T'ai-p'ing t'ien-kuo shih-liao hsüan-chi* (Selected papers from the Wu Hsü archives concerning the T'ai-p'ing t'ien-kuo; Peking, 1958), pp. 172–188. One source indicates that Yang was the joint commander with Ward. *IWSM*: T'ung-chih period, 4: 40–43, 10: 31–49b, 12:4–8, 53–54, 14: 18–27. For Hsü Yü-t'ing, see Hsü Jun, *Tsung-p'u*, 7: 64; *IWSM*: Hsien-feng period, 48: 11b.

65.   For Ting Kienchang, see H. B. Morse, *In the Days of the Taipings* (Salem, Mass., 1927), p. 28. For Wu Chien-chang, see Huang Wei, p. 108; Ching Wu and Chung Ting, pp. 34–36, 39–42; Fairbank, *Trade and Diplomacy*, I, 395.

66.   Ko Yüan-hsü, pp. 84–85.

67.   For Humphrey Marshall, see *NCH* (Apr. 2, 1853), p. 138; (Apr. 9, 1853), p. 142. The other two compradors of the council were Yü Hsia-ch'ing, comprador of the Netherlands Bank, and Chu Pan-san, comprador of Liddell Brothers & Co. Actually, Yü Hsia-ch'ing obtained the greatest number of votes and was elected chairman, but he modestly resigned his chairmanship in favor of Wu Shao-ch'ing. *NCH* (Feb. 16, 1906), p. 346.

68.   At the invitation of K'ang Kuang-jen, brother of K'ang Yu-wei, Cheng Kuan-ying managed the *Tzu-ch'iang pao* (Self-strengthening newspaper) at Shanghai. Cheng Kuan-ying, *Hou-p'ien*, 15: 5–6.

69.   Wang Ching-yü, *Kung-yeh*, II, 970–971.

70.   During K'ang's twenty-day stay at Hong Kong, he lived in the police office for six days and then moved to Ho's home, where he resided for fourteen days (Oct. 6–19). Wang Shu-huai, *Wai-jen yü wu-hsü pien-fa* (The foreigners and the 1898 reform movement; Taipei, 1965), pp. 183–184.

71.   Lo Chia-lun, ed., *Kuo-fu nien-p'u* (Chronological biography of Sun Yat-sen; Taipei, 1958), p. 84. See also Hao Yen-p'ing, "The Abortive Cooperation Between Reformers and Revolutionaries, 1895–1900," *Papers on China* (Harvard University, East Asian Research Center, 1961), 15: 91–114, esp. p. 106.

72.   Cheng Kuan-ying, in his preface to the *Wei-yen*, asserted that the West was superior to China in three key areas—using people's talents to the utmost (*jen chin ch'i ts'ai*), extracting benefit from the soil as much as possible (*ti chin ch'i li*), and expanding the flow of goods (*wu ch'ang ch'i liu*). Cheng Kuan-ying, *Tseng-ting*, 1b. In Sun's petition to Li Hung-chang, he mentioned four categories. The first two were the same as Cheng's, the third was "using every thing to the utmost" (*wu chin ch'i yung*) and the fourth was "expanding the flow of commerce" (*huo ch'ang ch'i liu*). Sun Yat-sen, *Chung-shan ch'üan-shu* (Complete works of Sun Yat-sen; Shanghai, 1927), IV, 1–13. See also Hu Ch'iu-yüan, "Cheng Kuan-ying chi ch'i Sheng-shih wei-yen" (Cheng Kuan-ying and his book *Warnings to a Prosperous Age*), *San-min chu-i pan-yüeh-k'an* (The three people's principles fortnightly), 3: 11 (Chungking, June 1, 1944), available at the Fu Ssu-nien Library, Academia Sinica, Taipei.

73.   Lo Chia-lun, *Ko-ming wen-hsien*, III, 1, 61. For the compradors' connection with Sun's revolutionary movement, see Ch'en Shao-po, pp. 7–8, 23, 30, 32; Lo Chia-lun, ed., *Ko-ming wen hsien* (Documents of revolution; Taipei, 1958–1963), III, 61–79; Feng Tzu-yu, *Ko-ming i-shih* (Reminiscences of the revolution; Chungking and Shanghai, 1939–1947), III, 1–23, 31–122. The first comprador members of the

Hsing-Chung hui included Ho K'uan, Cheng Hsiao-ch'u, Huang Cho-wen, Li Ping-yüan, Liu Hsiang, Lu Ts'an, Wen Fen, Wen Yü-kuei, and Yang Hsin-ju.

74. For Yang Ch'ü-yün, see Feng Tzu-yu, *Hua-ch'iao ko-ming tsu-chih shih-hua* (A history of revolutionary organizations of overseas Chinese; Taipei, 1954), pp. 4–5. For Hsieh Tsan-t'ai, see Frank H. H. King, ed., and Prescott Clarke, *A Research Guide to China-Coast Newspapers, 1822–1911* (Cambridge, Mass., 1965), p. 72.

75. *Tzu-yüeh ts'ung-k'an*, 3: 6.

76. Lo Chia-lun, *Ko-ming wen-hsien*, III, 76.

77. Chu Pao-san, Wang I-t'ing, and Yü Hsia-ch'ing were in charge of finance, communication, and commerce, respectively. *Hua-tzu jih-pao* (Nov. 11, 1911); Huang I-feng, "Chiu Chung-kuo," p. 98.

78. Fang T'eng, "Yu Hsia-ch'ing," p. 47.

79. Li Chung-chüeh, 3: 189–192.

80. Ting Wen-chiang, *Liang Jen-kung nien-p'u ch'ang-pien ch'u kao* (First draft of the chronological biography of Liang Ch'i-ch'ao; Taipei, 1959), I, 314. Wang I-t'ing, Chu Pao-san, and Chu Chih-yao were noted compradors who had been politically active in Shanghai. *Shang-hai yen-chiu hsü-chi*, pp. 155–156.

81. Negishi, *Baiben seido*, pp. 302–303.

82. For a detailed account of the conflict, see *Kuang-tung k'ou chieh ch'ao* (The Kwangtung weapon-impounding crisis), comp. *Hsiang-kang Hua-tzu jih-pao* (Hong Kong, 1924).

83. Fang T'eng, "Yü Hsia-ch'ing," 12.2: 47, 12.3: 62–63. According to Fang T'eng, Yü went to Nan-ch'ang to see Chiang Kai-shek in 1926. Through his arrangement, Chiang would get a loan from the Chekiang financial clique in the amount of sixty million dollars. Chang Yung-ni, who later became vice-minister of finance for the Nationalist government, was then introduced to Chiang by Yü Hsia-ch'ing.

84. See ch. VI.

85. Chang Ts'un-wu, *Kwang-hsü san-shih-i nien Chung-Mei kung-yüeh feng-ch'ao* (The crisis of Sino-American dispute over labor agreement in 1905; Taipei, 1965).

86. See ch. VIII.

87. Lin Ch'ung-yung, *Lin Tse-hsü chuan* (A biography of Lin Tse-hsü; Taipei, 1967), pp. 468–474. Lin maintains that Pao P'eng was definitely a traitor, recommended to Ch'i-shan by George Elliot, but this argument is not entirely convincing.

88. *Ibid.*, p. 483.

89. *IWSM*: TK, 37: 33b; 52: 3b–4; 58: 40b–43. See also Yüan Lang et al., *Nan-hsing chi* (Southern star collection; Hong Kong, 1962), pp. 228–231.

90. *Kuang-tung k'ou chieh ch'ao*.

91. For details, see Hao Yen-p'ing, "Yu shou-chiu tao ko-hsin" (From conservatism to reform); *Ta-lu cha-chih* (Continental magazine), 20.7: 26–27 (April 1960).

92. A sketch of Tong King-sing's life, which originally appeared in the June 1878 issue of *The Far East* (*Yüan-tung yüeh-pao*), is included, in Chinese translation, in Hsü Jun's *Nien-p'u*, pp. 57b–58b. After graduation from the missionary school and before entering the service of the Hong Kong government in 1851, Tong became an assistant at an auctioneer's office in Hong Kong. Giles, p. 715.

93. The foreign connections of Tong King-sing's family were extensive and long-lasting, since for at least three generations the Jardine's comprador position was held by the family of Tong (T'ang). Tong King-sing's son and nephew were selected as students in the educational mission to the United States. The nephew,

T'ang Shao-i, played an important political role in the early Republican period. The son, T'ang Kai-sun (Kwo-on) worked at Kaiping for a number of years after his return from America and subsequently became the first president of the Tsinghua College. Thomas E. LaFargue, *China's First Hundred* (Pullman, Wash., 1942), pp. 19, 99, 117–118.

94. Tong King-sing (Shanghai) to W. Keswick (Hong Kong), Oct. 8, 1868, JMA; Liu Kwang-Ching, "Tong King-sing," p. 165.

95. Cheng Kuan-ying's name was Kuan-ying, his "style" (*hao*), T'ao-chai (Taochai). He was a man of obscure origin, whose birth date is unknown. His writings suggest that he was twenty-six when Dent & Co. went bankrupt, occurred in 1867, according to the *North China Herald*. By the Chinese way of counting age, Cheng was thus born in 1842. At the age of eighty, he was able to write an epitograph for his wife. He died at Macao in 1923 at the age of eighty-one. Cheng Kuan-ying, *Hou-p'ien*, 1: 3b; 8: 42–43; 15: 58; Liu Kwang-Ching, *Steamship Rivalry*, p. 130; *NCH* (Aug. 5, 1867), p. 192; Cheng Kuan-ying, *Tseng-ting* (1965 ed.), p. vi.

96. Hsü Jun, *Nien-p'u*, pp. 2, 8; Cheng Kuang-ying, *Hou-p'ien*, 15: 49b; Nieh Pao-chang, "Ts'ung Mei-shang Ch'i-ch'ang lun-ch'uan kung-ssu ti ch'uang-pan yü fa-chan k'an mai-pan ti tso-yung" (The function of the comprador as viewed from the history of the American firm of Shanghai Steam Navigation Co.), *Li-shih yen-chiu*, 2: 100 (1964).

97. According to the local newspapers (*Hu pao* and *Wan-kuo kung pao*), Cheng Hsiu-shan was a prominent comprador in Shanghai at the time, who invested in the Chinese Glass Works Co., among other modern enterprises. Cheng Kuan-ying, *Hou-p'ien*, 8: 31; Wang Ching-yü, "Fu-ku," p. 66.

98. Cheng Kuan-ying, *Hou-p'ien*, 8: 42.

99. Hsü Jun, *Nien-p'u*, p. 5b.

100. Cheng Kuan-ying, *Hou-p'ien*, 10: 1–1b, 10: 118b.

101. Cheng Kuan-ying, *I-yen*, 1:17, 1: 23b; *Lo-fu ch'ih-ho shan-jen shih-ts'ao* (Poems of Cheng Kuan-ying; Shanghai, 1897), I: 13, 30–31.

102. Young J. Allen (1836–1907), an American missionary, published from 1868 a weekly *Chiao-hui hsin-pao* (Mission news) which was expanded into *Wan-kuo kung-pao* (*The Globe Magazine*). A weekly from 1875 to 1883 and a monthly from 1889 to 1907, it included articles by missionaries such as J. Edkins, William Muirhead, Alexander Williamson, John Fryer, and Timothy Richard. It had wide influence, including influence on the 1898 reform movement, see Wang Shu-huai, pp. 90, 24, 104.

103. Teng Ssu-yü and John K. Fairbank, *China's Response to the West: A Documentary Survey, 1839–1923* (Cambridge, Mass., 1954), p. 113.

104. At Shanghai in the 1870's there were some private classes where English was taught two hours a day. In this manner, an intelligent youth could learn pidgin English in six months. Ko Yüan-hsü, 1: 24. In 1907, some compradors were graduates of government schools. For instance, Yue Ko Ming, comprador to Buheiter & Co. at Shanghai for fifteen years, was "educated at the Tung Wen College." Sung Chung Ying, comprador to Handl & Co. at Tientsin from 1888, "was educated in the Tientsin Torpedo and Naval School." Wright, pp. 562, 752.

105. *NCH* (Sept. 16, 1965), p. 147. According to another version, the Church Missionary Society established the Anglo-Chinese School at Shanghai in 1850. *Shang-hai t'ung-chih kuan*, 1.66 (1933). For the efforts of the London Mission, Shanghai, in educating the Chinese, see *NCH* (Apr. 1, 1880), p. 293.

106. Liu Hsin-sheng, a comprador in Hankow after the late 1870's, learned his English and French from foreign missionaries. Sun Yü-t'ang, *Kung-yeh,* II, 961–963; Wright, p. 723. For Wu T'ing-sheng, see Wright, pp. 543–544, 662.

107. For the Protestant missions in China, especially their educational effort, see Irwin T. Hyatt, Jr., "Protestant Missions in China, 1877–1890: The Institutionalization of Good Works," *Papers on China,* 17: 67–77 (1963), Harvard University, East Asian Research Center.

108. Protestant primary schools gradually grew to secondary level and came to be called "colleges." St. John's College at Shanghai was established in 1878 and was converted to a university in 1907. *Shang-hai hsien hsü chih,* 11: 12. By 1883, it had "six distinct departments": preparatory, college, Anglo-Chinese, medical, science, and theological. *NCH* (Jan. 17, 1883), p. 62.

109. *NCH* (Jan. 17, 1883), p. 63.

110. Yung Wing, p. 50. However, Yung never served as a comprador.

111. Hsü Jun, *Nien-p'u,* p. 16.

112. The initial capital of the *Hui pao* was 20,000 taels, subscribed mostly by the Cantonese at Shanghai. The first newspaper operated by Chinese was the *Chao-wen jih-pao,* established one year earlier (1873) at Hankow. Sun Yü-t'ang, *Kung-yeh,* II, 1003–1004, 1166; Ko Kung-chen, *Chung-kuo pao-hsüeh shih* (History of Chinese journalism; Shanghai, 1927), p. 122; Yao Kung-ho, p. 16; Cheng Kuan-ying, *Hou-p'ien,* 15: 12–13b.

113. Cheng Kuan-ying, *Hou-p'ien,* 15: 14. Cheng gives only Chinese name of the newspaper, and its original English name is unknown.

114. Li Chin-wei, ed., *Hsiang-kang pai-nien shih* (A history of Hong Kong, 1848–1948; Hong Kong, 1949), p. 145.

115. Wright, p. 562.

116. Shen-pao-kuan, comp., *Tsui-chin chih wu-shih-nien: Shen-pao-kuan wu-shih chou-nien chi-nien* (The past fifty years: In commemoration of the Shen-pao's Golden Jubilee, 1872–1922), a special supplement published by the *Shen pao* (Shanghai, 1923), 2: 28. When he was the comprador to the *Shen pao,* Hsi Yü-fu compiled the magisterial *Huang-ch'ao cheng-tien lei-ts'uan* (Political encyclopedia of the Ch'ing), published in 1903 in 500 *chüan.* Hsi's liberal views can be seen from its Preface.

117. Hsü Jun, *Nien-p'u,* p. 31; Yao Kung-ho, p. 16; Sun Yü-t'ang, *Kung-yeh,* II, 1005, 1167.

118. *NCH* (Jan. 10, 1857).

119. For instance, when Ahyute became the comprador to Russell & Co. at Shanghai in 1858, he asked his friend Sunchong "to take half the responsibility and profits," and a written agreement was accordingly made. E. Cunningham (Shanghai) to John M. Forbes (Canton), May 14, 1868, Case 26, RA.

120. Augustine Heard, Jr., "Poisoning," p. 9.

121. *Ibid.,* pp. 9–10.

122. *Ibid.,* p. 10.

123. *Ibid.,* pp. 10–11.

124. *Ibid.,* pp. 11–12.

125. See Cheng's preface to the *Wei-yen* (1893). *I-yen* was revised and reprinted in 1875 and 1881. The 1881 edition is used here.

126. Teng and Fairbank, p. 113.

127. Hsiao San, *Mao Tse-tung t'ung-chih ti ch'ing-shao-nien shih-tai* (The childhood and boyhood of comrade Mao Tse-tung; Peking, 1949), p. 13.

128. In 1898, Cheng published a book of poetry, entitled *Lo-fu ch'ih-ho shan-jen shih-ts'ao* (Poems of Cheng Kuan-ying), which included poems with antiforeign sentiments. In 1905, he published a sequel to the *Wei-yen*, titled *Sheng-shih wei-jen hsü-p'ien*. In 1920, another sequel, *Sheng-shih wei-yen hou-p'ien*, was published. In contrast to the *Wei-yen* and its first sequel, both of which dealt with general reform proposals, the second sequel mainly described the various enterprises in which Cheng had participated. He also collated the T'ang knight-errant stories, which first appeared in 1880 as *Chien-hsia chuan* and were reprinted posthumously in 1937 as *T'ang-jen chien-hsia chuan* (T'ang knight-errant stories; Shanghai, 1937).

129. Cheng Kuan-ying, *I-yen*, 1: 2.

130. Cheng Kuan-ying, *I-yen*, 1: 2, 2: 14b.

131. Cheng Kuan-ying, *Tseng-ting*, 7: 20.

132. Cheng Kuan-ying, *I-yen*, 1: 1, 1: 2b, 1: 10, 1: 17. Cheng deplored the fact, for instance, that the Chinese were seizing on irrelevant articles from the West and rejecting important ones. "As for the 'machinery' which had a vogue in China, besides ships and guns, if they are wasteful items such as watches, music boxes and toys, the Chinese love and buy them; if they are useful things like telegraphs, trains, as well as machines for agriculture, textile and mining, then the Chinese hate and disparage them." *I-yen*, 1: 25b.

133. Among the early reformers who advocated indiscriminate learning from the West was Hung Jen-kan (1822–1864), who in 1859 published his book *Tzu-cheng hsin-p'ien* (A new work for aid in administration). He seems to have evaluated Western clocks and watches as highly as steamships. *NCH* (Aug. 11, 1860), p. 127; Supplements of Aug. 18, 25, 1860.

134. Cheng Kuan-ying, *I-yen*, 1: 38–39; *Hou-p'ien*, *chüan* 1. Two chapters of Cheng's *Wei-yen*, rev. ed., are exclusively devoted to the parliamentary system. See his *Tseng-ting*, 4: 1–6b.

135. Both T'ang Chen's *Wei-yen* (Warnings) and Ch'en Ch'iu's *Tung-yu t'iao-i* (Proposals made during a trip to the east) were published in 1890.

136. Cheng Kuan-ying, *I-yen*, 1: 3b.

137. *Ibid.*, 1: 41, 27–27b; 2:9, 14b. For the Ch'ing-liu Tang, see Hao Yen-p'ing, "A Study of the Ch'ing-liu Tang: The Disinterested Scholar-Official Group,1875–1884," *Papers on China*, 16: 40–65 (1962), Harvard University, East Asian Research Center.

138. Cheng Kuan-ying, *Tseng-ting*, 2: 27b, 2: 37b.

139. Cheng Kuan-ying, *I-yen*, 2: 1b; *Tseng-ting*, 2:20.

140. Cheng Kuan-ying, *I-yen*, 1: 14b; 1: 29b; 2:23–25.

141. Cheng Kuan-ying, *Tseng-ting*, 2: 15–27b.

142. Cheng Kuan-ying, *Hou-p'ien*, 1: 1; 2: 37b; 4: 56b–57; 7: 19; 8: 32, 53.

143. Cheng Kuan-ying, *Tseng-ting*, 2: 18b–19. See also Teng and Fairbank, *Response*, pp. 113–115.

144. In one of Cheng's early works, he declared that the purpose of commerce was to make a profit (*li*), which had been looked down upon by scholar-officials. See his *I-yen*, 1: 11–12.

145. Cheng Kuan-ying, *Tseng-ting*, 4: 15, 42.

146. Chang Ts'un-wu, p. 219.

147. Cheng Kuan-ying, *Hou-p'ien*, 4: 2b.

148. Cheng Kuan-ying, *I-yen*, 1: 10; *Tseng-ting*, 3: 7.

149. Cheng Kuan-ying, *Hou-p'ien*, 1: 60, 2: 63–64b.

150.   *Ibid.*, 1: 31, 2: 63–64b.

IX.   CONCLUSION: SIGNIFICANCE OF THE COMPRADOR AS A MIDDLEMAN BETWEEN EAST AND WEST

1.   In a sense, the Chinese comprador was literally a middleman between East and West, since his activities extended far beyond China and reached other parts of Asia. By the 1870's, the Chinese "John Comprador" was active in Japan, Korea, Cochin China, Bangkok, Rangoon, Penang, Malacca, Singapore, Java, and Manila, and his influence was felt even in India. See Knox, "John Comprador," 57: 427–434 (1878).

2.   See Paul A. Cohen, *China and Christianity: The Missionary Movement and the Growth of Chinese Antiforeignism, 1860–1870* (Cambridge, Mass., 1963).

3.   R. H. Tawney, *Land and Labour in China* (London, 1932), p. 13.

4.   For the role of the dilution of wealth in the downward social mobility in Ming-Ch'ing China, see Ho Ping-ti, *Ladder*, pp. 154–161.

5.   Chang Chung-li, *Income*, p. 197.

6.   M. M. Postan, "Recent Trends in the Accumulation of Capital," *Economic History Review*, 6.1. 2 (October 1935).

7.   A. H. Cole's definition. See *Change and the Entrepreneur*, p. 88.

8.   See Joseph A. Schumpeter, *The Theory of Economic Development* (Cambridge, Mass., 1934) and *Capitalism, Socialism, and Democracy, passim.*

9.   BPP, 1867–1868, LXIX, "Reports on Trade by the Foreign Commissioners at the Ports in China for the Year 1866," p. 111.

10.   F. B. Johnson (Shanghai) to William Keswick (Hong Kong), Aug. 17, 1871, JMA.

11.   Dyce, p. 50. "Noble buildings in Shanghai [have been built]. Few and far between are the mansions now to be found, built in what ancient Canton wits called the 'Compradoric Order.'" *NCH* (Aug. 5, 1867), p. 190.

12.   Hsiao San, p. 13.

13.   For the concept of the "marginal man," see Parsons, II, 1371–1380.

Glossary

Acum, Lin Ch'in 林欽
Ahyue, Lin Hsien-yang 林顯揚, Lin Yao-t'ang 林耀堂
Ahyune. *See* Hsü Jun
Akow, Ch'en Ya-chiu 陳亞九, Ch'en Yü-ch'ih 陳玉池, Chun Yok Chu
Asong, Ch'en Shu-t'ang 陳樹棠
Atai, Ya-ti 亞帝
Ayun. *See* Hsü Jun

ch'a shih 茶師
Chan-yu-chang. *See* Choping
Chang Chao 張照
Chang Chien 張謇
Chang Chih-tung 張之洞
Chang Jen-chün 張人駿
Chang Tzu-piao 張子標, Cheong Chi Pio
Chang Yung-ni 張咏霓
ch'e-p'iao 拆票
Chen-hai 鎮海
Ch'en Chiung-ming 陳炯明
Ch'en Chu-p'ing. *See* Choping
Ch'en Keng-yü 陳賡虞
Ch'en K'o-liang 陳可良
Ch'en Lien-po 陳廉伯
Ch'en San-ku. *See* Samcock
Ch'en Shu-t'ang. *See* Asong
Ch'en Ya-chiu. *See* Akow
Ch'en Yü-ch'ang. *See* Choping

Ch'en Yü-ch'ih. *See* Akow
Ch'en Yü-ts'ang. *See* Choping
Cheng Chi-tung 鄭濟東
Cheng Hsiao-ch'u 鄭曉初
Cheng Hsiu-shan 鄭秀山
Cheng Kuan-ying 鄭官應, 鄭觀應, Cheng T'ao-chai 鄭陶齋, Taochai
Cheng T'ao-chai. *See* Cheng Kuan-ying
Ch'eng Te-ch'üan 程德全
Cheong Chi Pio. *See* Chang Tzu-piao
Chi-i hui 集益會
Ch'i-shan 琦善, Kishen
chia-tsu chu-i 家族主義
Chiang Ch'un 蔣春
Chiao-hui hsin-pao 教會新報
Chiao-she pao 交涉報
chieh-p'an 接盤
Ch'ien-shan-chai 前山寨
Ch'ien Shen An 謙愼安
Ch'ih-chou 池州
Chin-li-yüan. *See* 金利源
Ch'ing-liu tang 清流黨
Ch'ing-shih kao 清史稿
Ch'ing-shih lieh-chuan 清史列傳
Choping, Chan-yue-chang, Ch'en Chu-p'ing 陳竹坪, Ch'en Yü-chang 陳裕昌, Ch'en Yü-ts'ang 陳雨蒼, Chun Yue Chong, Yuechang
Chu Ch'i-ang 朱其昂
Chu Chih-yao 朱志堯

295

Glossary

Chu Lan-fang. *See* Chu Ta-ch'un
Chu Pao-san 朱葆三, Chu P'ei-chen 朱佩珍
Chu P'ei-chen. *See* Chu Pao-san
Chu Sok Pin. *See* Hsü Shu-p'ing
Chu Ta-ch'un 祝大椿, Chu Lan-fang 祝蘭芳
Chu Yu-chee. *See* Hsü Jun
chü-jen 舉人
chuang-p'iao 莊票
chui-p'ei 追賠
Chun Sam Cock. *See* Samcock
Chun Yok Chu. *See* Akow
Chun Yue Chong. *See* Choping
chün-hsien 郡縣
Cohong, Kung-hang 公行

Da Sun, Ta-sheng 大生

feng-chien 封建
Feng Hua-ch'uan 馮華川
Feng Kuei-fen 馮桂芬
fu-ch'iang 富強
fu-pan 副辦

hang. See hong
hao 號
Hao-kuan. *See* Howqua
Heung-shan. *See* Hsiang-shan
Ho Ch'i. *See* Ho Kai
Ho Ch'ien 何乾
Ho Fook. *See* Ho Fu
Ho Fu 何福, Ho Fook
Ho Hsiao-sheng. *See* Ho Tung
Ho Kai, Ho Ch'i 何啓
Ho Kan-t'ang 何甘棠
Ho K'uan 何寬
Ho Lien-yü. *See* Sunchong
ho-mai 和買
Ho Shun-ch'ang. *See* Sunchong
Ho Tung 何東, Sir Robert Ho Tung, Ho Hsiao-sheng 何曉生
hong, hang 行
Hoppo, Hu-pu 戶部
Howqua, Hao-kuan 浩官, Wu Ch'ung-

yüeh 伍崇曜
Hsi Cheng-fu 席正甫
hsi-tsai 細崽
Hsi Yü-fu 席裕福
Hsiang-shan 香山, Heung-shan
Hsieh-ch'ang 燮昌
Hsieh Tsan-t'ai 謝贊泰, Tse Tsan Tai
hsin-fu 心腹
Hsing-Chung hui 興中會
hsing-shang 行商
hsiu-ts'ai 秀才
Hsü Chao-heng. *See* Hsü Yü-t'ing
Hsü Ch'un-jung 許春榮
Hsü Jun 徐潤, Ahyune, Ayun, Chu Yu-chee, Hsü Yü-chih 徐雨之, Yuchee
Hsü Jung-ts'un 徐榮村, Yungkee
Hsü Kuan-ta 徐關大
Hsü Shu-p'ing 徐叔平, Chu Sok Pin
Hsü Wei-nan 徐渭南
Hsü Yü-chih. *See* Hsü Jun
Hsü Yü-t'ing 徐鈺亭, Hsü Chao-heng 徐昭珩
Hsü Yün-hsüan 徐芸軒
Hsüeh Huan 薛煥
Hu Chi-mei 胡寄梅
Hu-chou 湖州
Hu Kuang-yung 胡光墉
Hua chang-fang 華賬房
Hua ching-li 華經理
Hua-hsing. *See* Wah Shing
Hua-i lien-shu 華夷聯屬
Huang Cho-wen 黃焯文
hui-kuan 會館
Hui pao 彙報
Hung-an kung-ssu 鴻安公司
huo ch'ang ch'i liu 貨暢其流

I-shan 奕山
i-wu 夷務

jen chin ch'i ts'ai 人盡其才
Jen-ho 仁和
Jung Hsien-pang 容憲邦
Jung Hsing-ch'iao 容星橋

Glossary

Jung Hung. *See* Yung Wing
Jung Liang 容良
Jung Tzu-ming 容子名
Jung Tz'u-yen 容次嚴

K'ang Kuang-jen 康廣仁
k'ang-pai-tu 糠擺渡
K'ang Yu-wei 康有爲
Kao Ch'ing-t'ang 高慶堂
Kin-lee-yuen, Chin-li-yüan 金利源
Kishen. *See* Ch'i-shan
Kiukee. *See* Koofunsing
Koofunsing, Kiukee, Ku Feng-sheng 顧豐盛, Kukee
Ku Feng-sheng. *See* Koofunsing
kuan-tu shang-pan 官督商辦
Kuang-Chao kung-so 廣肇公所
Kuang-chou fu 廣州府
kung 工
Kung ch'in wang. *See* Prince Kung
Kung-hang. *See* Cohong
Kung-i. *See* Kung-yik
Kung-p'iao chü 公票局
kung-shih 宮市
Kung Shou-t'u 龔壽圖
kung-so 公所
Kung-yik, Kung-i 公益
kuo-chia chu-i 國家主義
Kuo Kan-chang 郭甘章, Quok Ache-ong
Kuo Sung-t'ao 郭嵩燾
Kuo Tsan 郭贊

lao ssu-wu 老司務
Leong A Tien, Liang Tien 梁殿, Liang Ya-tien 梁亞殿
Li Chen-yü 李振玉
li-chiao 禮教
Li Ch'iu-p'ing 李秋坪
Li Hung-chang 李鴻章
Li Ping-yüan 黎炳垣
li-she 理涉
Li Sung-yün 李松云, Soong-yin
Li Wen-yao 李文耀
li-ying she-chi chih-jen 理應涉及之人

Liang-Huai 兩淮
Liang Lun-shu 梁綸樞
Liang Tien. *See* Leong A Tien
Liang Ya-tien. *See* Leong A Tien
Lin Ch'in. *See* Acum
Lin Hsien-yang. *See* Ahyue
Lin Shih-chih 林士志
Lin Yao-t'ang. *See* Ahyue
ling-shih ti 領事的
Liu Hsiang 劉祥
Liu Hsin-sheng 劉歆生
Liu Ming-ch'uan 劉銘傳
Liu Sen-chi. *See* Sunkee
Liu Shao-tsung. *See* Seating
Lo Ch'ang-chao 羅常肇
Lo Ho-p'eng 羅鶴朋
Lo In Tin. *See* Lu Ya-ching
Lo Shou-sung 羅壽嵩
lou-kuei 陋規
lou-shang wei-pi ta-ying 樓上未必答應
Lu Ching. *See* Lu Ya-ching
Lu Ts'an 陸燦
Lu Ya-ching 盧亞景, Lo In Tin, Lu Ching 盧景

mai-pan 買辦; 賣辦
mai-pan chih-jen 買辦之人
ming 名
Mo Shih-yang. *See* See Yong
Mok See Yong. *See* See Yong
Mu Ping-yüan 穆炳元

Nan-hai 南海
nei-hang 內行

One A Cheong, Wen Ya-chang 溫亞章

p'ai-fang 牌坊
pan-fang 辦房
P'an Shih-ch'eng 潘仕成
P'an-yü 番禺
pang mai-pan 幫買辦
pao 保; 包
pao-chung 保中
Pao-hsien chao-shang chü 保險招商局

Glossary

Pao Jen-kuan 鮑人琯

pao-pan 包辦

Pao P'eng 鮑鵬, Pao Ts'ung 鮑聰, Pao Ya-ts'ung 鮑亞聰

Pao Ts'ung. *See* Pao P'eng

Pao Ya-ts'ung. *See* Pao P'eng

p'ao-chieh 跑街

p'ao-lou 跑樓

P'eng Ch'i-chih 彭啓智

P'eng Yü-lin 彭玉麟

ping-chan 兵戰

Ping-pu lang-chung 兵部郎中

Prince Kung, Kung ch'in wang 恭親王

Pu Ting-pang 布定邦

p'u-ai 僕埃

Quok Acheong. *See* Kuo Kan-chang

Samcock, Ch'en San-ku 陳三谷, Chun Sam Cock

Seating, Liu Shao-tsung 劉紹宗

See Yong, Mok See Yong, Mo Shih-yang 莫仕揚, Ya Yang 亞揚

Sha-mien. *See* Shameen

Shameen, Sha-mien 沙面

shang 商

shang-chan 商戰

shang-huo 商夥

shang-tsung 商總

shang-t'uan 商團

Shao Yu-lien 邵友濂

Shen pao 申報

shen-shang 紳商

shen-tung 紳董

Sheng Heng-shan 盛恒山

Sheng Hsüan-huai 盛宣懷

Soong-yin. *See* Li Sung-yün

Ssu-ming kung-so 四明公所

ssu-shih 司事

Sun Chu-t'ang 孫竹堂

Sunchong, Ho Lien-yü 何廉玉, Ho Shun-ch'ang 何順昌

Sung Ts'ai 宋彩

Sung Wei-ch'en 宋煒臣

Sunkee, Liu Sen-chi 劉森記

Ta-Ch'ing hui-tien 大清會典

ta pien-chü 大變局

ta-shang 大商

Ta-sheng. *See* Da Sun

tai-p'ei 代賠

T'ai-chi. *See* Takee

Takee, Taki, T'ai-chi 泰記, Yang Fang 楊坊

Taki. *See* Takee

Tang Kee Shang. *See* Teng Chi-ch'ang

T'ang Chi-ch'ang 唐紀常

T'ang Chieh-ch'en 唐傑臣

T'ang Jung-chün 唐榮俊

T'ang Kai-sun, T'ang Chieh-ch'en 唐介臣, T'ang Kuo-an 唐國安, T'ang Kwo-on

T'ang Kuo-an. *See* T'ang Kai-sun

T'ang Kwo-on. *See* T'ang Kai-sun

T'ang Lung-mao. *See* Tong Loong-maw

T'ang Mao-chih. *See* Tong Mów-chee

T'ang Neng. *See* Tong Loong-maw

T'ang Shao-i 唐紹儀

T'ang T'ing-chih. *See* Tong Mow-chee

T'ang T'ing-shu. *See* Tong King-sing

tao-ch'i 道契

Tao Mai Sen. *See* T'ao Mei-sheng

T'ao Mei-sheng 陶梅生, Tao Mai Sen

Taochai. *See* Cheng Kuan-ying

Te Sheng. *See* Tucksing

Teng Chi-ch'ang 鄧紀常, Tang Kee Shang

Teng Chün-hsiang 鄧君翔

ti chin ch'i li 地盡其利

T'ien-chin tsu-lai-huo kung-ssu 天津自來火公司

t'ien-hsia 天下

Tong King-sing, T'ang Ching-hsing 唐景星, T'ang T'ing-shu 唐廷樞

Tong Loong-maw, T'ang Lung-mao 唐隆茂, T'ang Neng 唐能

Tong Mow-chee, T'ang Mao-chih 唐茂枝, T'ang T'ing-chih 唐廷植

Ts'ai Hsing-nan 蔡星南

Ts'ao Tzu-chün 曹子俊

Tse Tsan Tai. *See* Hsieh Tsan-t'ai

Glossary

Tseng Kuo-fan 曾國藩
tso-ku 坐賈
Tso Tsung-t'ang 左宗棠
tsung-li 總理
tsung mai-pan 總買辦
tsung pan 總辦
Tucksing, Te Sheng 德盛
t'ung-liu 同流
t'ung-shih 通事
T'ung-wen shu-chü 同文書局
Tzu-ch'iang pao 自強報

Wah Shing, Hua-hsing 華興
wai-hang 外行
Wan-kuo kung-pao 萬國公報
Wang Ch'ang-chieh 王昌傑
Wang Huai-shan 王槐山
Wang I-t'ing 王一亭, Wong I. Ding
Wang K'o-ming 王克明
Wang T'ao 王韜
Wang Yüan-tse-t'ang 汪遠澤堂
Wei-hsien 濰縣
Wei Wen-pu 韋文圃
Wei Yü 韋玉
Wen Fen 溫芬
Wen Ya-chang. See One A Cheong
wen-yin 紋銀
Wen Yü-kuei 溫遇貴
Wong I. Ding. See Wang I-t'ing
wu ch'ang ch'i liu 物暢其流
Wu Chien-chang 吳健彰
wu chin ch'i yung 物盡其用
Wu Ch'ung-yüeh. See Howqua
Wu Hsü 吳煦
Wu-i 武夷
Wu Jim Pah. See Wu Mao-ting
Wu Mao-ting 吳懋鼎, Wu Jim Pah
Wu T'ing-sheng 鄔挺生

Wu Yao-t'ing 吳耀庭

ya-hang 牙行
ya-kuei 押櫃
ya-shang 牙商
Ya Ti. See Atai
Ya Yang. See See Yong
Yang Chao-ao 楊兆鋆, Yang Hsin-chih
    楊信之
Yang Ch'ü-yün 楊衢雲
Yang Fang. See Takee
Yang Hsin-chih. See Yang Chao-ao
Yang Hsin-ju 楊心如
Yang Kuei-hsüan 楊桂軒
Yang K'un-shan 楊坤山
Yang Mei-nan 楊梅南
Yang Te 楊德
Yang Tsung-lien 楊宗濂
yang-wu 洋務
Yeh Ch'eng-chung 葉澄衷
Yeh Ming-chai 葉明齋
Yen Lan-ch'ing 嚴蘭卿
Ying-Hua shu-kuan 英華書館
Yowloong, Yu Lung 又隆
Yu Lung. See Yowloong
Yü-hang 渝行
Yü Ho-te. See Yü Hsia-ch'ing
Yü Hsia-ch'ing 虞洽卿, Yü Ho-te 虞和
    德
Yü Shun-en 虞順恩
Yü-yao 餘姚
Yüan-ch'ang 源昌
Yuchee. See Hsü Jun
Yuechang. See Choping
Yüeh-chou 岳州
Yüeh pao 粵報
Yung Wing, Jung Hung 容閎
Yungkee. See Hsü Jung-ts'un

Index

Absorption theory, 107, 108
Acculturation, 9, 219
Achea, 33
Achow, 51, 270n37
Acum (Lin Ch'in), 31, 39, 52; as tea
  merchant, 81, 116, 271n45; and
  upcountry purchase, 83, 252n102; as
  Jardine's excomprador, 87; de-
  falcation of, 95; and Tong King-sing,
  174; business with Jardine's, 252n105
Agency house: main office at Hong
  Kong, 16; decentralization of, 16;
  organization of, 16–17; gigantic, 20,
  21; smaller, 21; expansion of, 68;
  functions as bank, 70; number of,
  101–102. See also Merchants, Western
Agreement between foreign merchant
  and comprador, 161, 162
Agunn, 51
Ahee, 51; as tea purchaser, 81
Ahone: as "big face man," 30, 100; as
  rich silk merchant, 31; and Tong
  King-sing, 86; business with Jardine's,
  250n67; and Russell's, 261n79
Ahyue (Lin Hsien-yang, Lin Yao-t'ang),
  28, 33, 164; his commission, 93; and
  Edward Cunningham, 96
Ahyune. See Hsü Jun
Akit, 51, 53; and exchange business, 74;
  and upcountry purchase, 77; and tea,
  79; squeeze of, 81
Akow (Ch'en Ya-chiu, Ch'en Yü-ch'ih,
  Chun Yok Chu): in Japan, 56; salary
  of, 90; his security chop, 158; agree-
  ment with Augustine Heard & Co., 161
Alcock, Rutherford, 95–96

Aleet, 31, 39; as tea merchant, 116,
  271n45
Allen, Young J., 291n102
Allum, 52
Ambiguity of comprador's status, 95.
  See also Brokers
American merchants and grain tribute
  transportation, 114. See also Augustine
  Heard & Co.; Olyphant & Co.;
  Merchants, Western; Russell & Co.
Aming, 47–48, 51
Amoy, 62
Apunn, 29, 32
Arnold, Julean, 110
Asam, 30, 52
Asia, Chinese compradors in, 44, 55–59
Asia, Southeast: Chinese compradors in,
  119–120; and Cheng Kuan-ying,
  190–191
Asong (Ch'en Shu-t'ang) and China
  Merchants' S. N. Co., 142
Assistant comprador. See Pang mai-pan
Atai (Ya-ti), 40, 76, 272n81
Atchu, 51
Atong, 32, 51
Atow, 52
Augustine Heard & Co.: organization of,
  16; and joint account, 19; diverse
  activities of, 20, 23; number of
  employees, including compradors, 24;
  compradors to, 29–30, 164, 173;
  history of, 30; rivalry with Russell's
  for good compradors, 32; cash account
  with comprador, 41, 71; and Cantonese
  compradors, 51; at Foochow, 51; at
  Canton 51, 71; at Hong Kong, 51, 70;

301

at Shanghai, 51; at Japan, 55, 56, 158; at Saigon, 55; at Korea, 55; plan for house at Yokohama, 60; at Hankow, 70; and upcountry purchase, 77, 78–80, 81; agreement with comprador, 161; purpose of, 247; and steamship business, 272n77

Augustine Heard & Co. Archives, 16

Ayow, 52

Ayun. *See* Hsü Jun

Bank comprador: increasing importance of, 64; salary of, 90; income of, 104; association of, 179. *See also* Banks

Banks: agency houses as, 19; decline of comprador and modern Chinese, 62; compradors' investments in, 133; Tong King-sing tries to set up modern, 273n**91**. *See also* Bank comprador; Banks, foreign; Banks, native

Banks, foreign: development of, in 1860's, 22; as full-fledged institutions, 53; nonexistence before 1846, 70; comprador's income from, 104; comprador's investment in, 133. *See also* Banks

Banks, native: issue of money certificates and credit bills, 25; comprador's connection with, 41–42, 115; orders guaranteed by comprador, 68, 85; insecure at Hankow, 68; and Tong King-sing, 85, 97; role in foreign trade, 115, 271n**41**; and Kiangsu compradors, 176; bankruptcy of, 179. *See also* Banks; Banks, foreign

Bangkok, 55

Banque de l'Indochine, 101

Beale, T. C., 52

Bean products, 114

Bills and drafts handled by compradors, 74

Bohea (Wu-i) and tea, 79

Bourgeoisie, national, capital of, 111, 217

Boxer uprising and comprador's losses, 161

"Boy" (servant): duties of, 66; fear of comprador, 66; Chinese names of, 166

Bridges, H. G.: on Apunn, 32; quoted, 66, 68, 75; at Kiukiang, 75

Britain: minister at Peking, 95; consul at Shanghai, 95; law of, 96; consul of, 98; profit rate in, 109. *See also* Alcock, Rutherford; British merchants; Winchester, Charles A.

British-American Tobacco Co., 62, 183

British merchants. *See* Butterfield & Swire; Dent & Co.; Jardine, Matheson & Co.

Brokers: compradors as, 39, 75; increasing importance of independent, 63; difficulty of distinguishing comprador from, 95; and comprador, 265n**35**. *See also* Middleman

Businessmen, compradors as new type of, 4. *See also* Merchants

Butterfield & Swire, 42; and China Navigation Co., 22–23, 123, 197; rivalry with Russell's, 34–35; loans to its compradors for Yü-hang, 42; and its compradors, 160, 169; and Cheng Kuan-ying, 169. *See also* China Navigation Co.

Canton: as a prefecture, 13; tea of, 18; hong merchants at, 27, 46; rivalry between Russell's vs. Olyphant's at, 33; Western merchants at, 46, 51, 68, 71; and China's foreign trade, 49, 255n**33**; decline of, 49–50; compradors at, 51, 88, 189; Indian silver at, 262n**109**. *See also* Canton Guild; Cantonese

Canton Guild, 84, 188, 189. *See also* Cantonese; Guild

Canton system, 49. *See also* Hong merchants

Cantonese: and compradors, 28, 174; skill as compradors, 49; compradors spread to other treaty ports, 51–52; skill at tea business, 53; challenged by others, 53–54; compradors and coastal trade, 114; rivalry with foreign merchants, 118; as servants at treaty ports, 284n**114**; establish *Hui pao* at Shanghai, 292n**112**. *See also* Canton Guild

Capital: Russell's, supported by Chinese merchants', 27; Heard's scarcity of, 29, 272n**77**. *See also* Comprador capital

Capitalism: Chinese, inhibited by foreign merchants, 99; in treaty ports, 117; compradors and commercial, 148; Lenin on, 269n**2**

Cash account with comprador, 41, 71

Chamber of commerce: British, 61, 178; foreigners', 92, 178; at Shanghai, 92, 189; at Hong Kong, 189; comprador's proposal to establish Chinese, 192; at Canton, 288n**52**; at Hankow, 288n**52**

Index

Chan-yu-chang. *See* Choping

Chang Chao, 98

Chang Chien, 139

Chang Chih-tung: and modern enterprises, 138; asks compradors' help, 191

Chang Tzu-piao, 190

Chartered Bank of India, Australia & China, 173

Ch'e-p'iao. *See* Chop loan

Chefoo: under control of Shanghai, 17; cotton goods imported at, 110; compradors at, 189

Chekiang: compradors from, 28, 53, 54, 112, 113; merchants skilled at silk and banking, 53; compradors challenge Cantonese compradors, 174–175

Ch'en Chiung-ming, 12

Ch'en Chu-p'ing. *See* Choping

Ch'en Keng-yü: as railroad shareholder, 132; as leader of chamber of commerce, 189

Ch'en K'o-liang: investment of, 134; style of life, 181; as social leader, 189

Ch'en Lien-po: as president of Canton Chamber of Commerce, 189; clash with Sun Yat-sen, 194, 195; as traitor, 195, 219

Ch'en Shu-t'ang. *See* Asong

Ch'en Ya-chiu. *See* Akow

Ch'en Yü-ch'ang. *See* Choping

Ch'en Yü-ch'ih. *See* Akow

Ch'en Yü-ts'ang. *See* Choping

Cheng Chi-tung, 196

Cheng Hsiu-shan: investment of, 133, 134; and Cheng Kuan-ying, 197, 291n97

Cheng Kuan-ying (Cheng T'ao-chai, Taochai): and freight business, 34, 42; as comprador, 35, 197, 282n89; investment of, 100, 121, 129, 132, 152; on comprador's income, 104; and social mobility, 105; and Shanghai Cotton Cloth Mill, 129, 145, 147, 148; and railroad, 132, 146; and Kaiping Mines, 144; and Yung Wing, 145; and Sheng Hsüan-huai, 146; and joint-stock system, 147; and *ku-tu shang-pan*, 150, 151; and patriotism, 168, 194; loses money as surety of comprador, 169; and Cantonese compradors, 174; style of life, 181; as gentry member, 184, 287n28, 287n37; as social leader, 186, 190; and Sino-French War, 190; and reform movement, 192, 218; biography of, 196–197, 291n95; and newspaper,

199; writings, 201–202, 293n128; on parliament, 203; on foreign policy, 203–204; on economic reform, 204–205; influences Mao Tse-tung, 222

Cheng T'ao-chai. *See* Cheng Kuan-ying

Cheong Chi Piao. *See* Chang Tzu-piao

Chestnuts, 58

Chiang Ch'un, 97

Chiang Kai-shek, 194

Chief comprador, 83–88

Chin li yüan. *See* Kin-lee-yuen

China Coast Steam Navigation Co., 120, 122; founded by Jardine's, 22; Tong King-sing's shares in, 32; and China Merchants' S. N. Co., 150. *See also* Jardine, Matheson & Co.

China Merchants' Steam Navigation Co.: and Hu Kuang-yung, 4; and Tong King-sing, 4, 122–123, 140–143, 149; and Hsü Jun, 4, 29, 147; its compradors, 5, 42; purchase of Russell's fleet, 99; compradors' investment in, 122–123, 214; investment of, 133; early history of, 138; and Chu Ch'i-ang, 138–139; merchant directors of, 142–143; rivalry with foreign merchants, 150; and Cheng King-ying, 174; studies on, 274n106; R. I. Fearon on, 274n112; and Li Sung-yün, 275n125

China Navigation Co.: founded by Butterfield & Swire, 22–23, 123; and China Merchants' S. N. Co., 150; its compradors, 197. *See also* Butterfield & Swire

Chinese language: foreigners' learning of, 27, 61; and Western merchants' success in China, 32; British consular report on, 61

Chinese manager, comprador as, 63, 68

Ch'ing government: income of, 105; honors compradors, 187; and revolutionary compradors, 193

Chinkiang: controlled by Shanghai, 17; rice business at, 87; Western merchants at, 98, 266n54

Chongfat: business with Russell's, 37; as comprador to Russell's, 52; as broker at Canton, 251n95

Chop loan (ch'e-p'iao), 148, 262n109, 264n16; introduced by compradors, 42, 115; introduction at Shanghai, 85–86; comprador's commission from, 92

Choping (Chan-yue-chang, Ch'en Chu-p'ing, Ch'en Yü-chang, Ch'en

Index

Yü-ts'ang, Chun Yue Chong,
Yuechang), 30, 35; as prominent
merchant, 28, 30, 53, 116, 157; as
Russell's comprador, 28–29, 84;
health of, 34; business with Jardine's,
35; wealth of, 99–100; investment of,
121, 132, 152; and speculation, 150;
and Chekiang compradors, 175; as
gentry member, 186; and the Anglo-
Chinese School, 198
Christianity: and comprador, 183,
197–198, 292n106; gentry's hostility to,
209
Chu Ch'i-ang: and China Merchants'
S. N. Co., 138–139; compared with
Tong King-sing, 143; biography of,
274n107. *See also* China Merchants'
S. N. Co.
Chu Chih-yao: investment of, 135, 136,
152, 214; as comprador, 136; as
independent merchant, 151; as
Catholic, 183
Chu Lan-fang. *See* Chu Ta-ch'un
Chu Pao-san (Chu P'ei-chen): in-
vestment of, 134; as social leader, 189;
honored at Shanghai, 190; and 1911
revolution, 193
Chu P'ei-chen. *See* Chu Pao-san
Chu Sok Pin. *See* Hsü Shu-p'ing
Chu Ta-ch'un (Chu Lan-fang): from
Kiangsu, 54; investment of, 100, 134,
135, 152, 214; and textile mills, 129;
and machine manufacturing, 131;
and modern technology, 146; as
independent merchant, 151; style of
life, 181; as social leader, 189
Chu-u-teng, 51, 59
Chu Yu-chee. *See* Hsü Jun
Chun Yok Chu. *See* Akow
Chun Yue Chong. *See* Choping
Ch'ung-hou, 25
Chungking, 42
Clarke, B. A.: at Hankow, 36, 93; in
Korea, 55, 58
Clerk. *See* Ssu-shih
Cochin China, 55
Coe Lun, 33, 51
Cohong (Kung-hang): and rise of
comprador, 1, 2, 48; abolition of, 1,
65, 178; and Cantonese, 49;
compradors under, 190, 254n16
Cole, William, 17
Colonialism, 5. *See also* Imperialism
Commerce: in late Ch'ing, 2; regional
specialization in, 53, 177; compradors'

role in, 112–120, 211; Cheng Kuan-ying
on, 204–205
Commercial gentry, 218, 222
Commission: Western merchants and,
17–18; comprador's, 90–93;
compradors' total, 102–103
Commission house. *See* Agency house
Complete responsibility (*pao*), 151, 168;
and comprador system, 160; comprador
changes attitude toward, 199–201;
comprador's use of, 220. *See also*
Guarantee
Comprador. See *Mai-pan*
Comprador capital, 112, 217. *See also*
Capital
Comprador-merchant, use of term, 12
Comprador office. See *Pan-fang*
Compradoric architectural style, 220
Comprador's order, 72, 259n30, 259n32
Confucianism: influence on comprador,
182; comprador's indifference to, 189;
Cheng Kuan-ying's criticism of, 205,
206
Consuls, foreign, 98, 111
Contract. See *Pao-pan*
Coolies: under comprador, 47, 65, 166;
and the Hong Kong poisoning case, 172
Copper cash: and comprador, 73, 74;
secured by Tong King-sing, 85,
262n107
Cotton, 2, 110
Cunningham, Edward: and decentraliza-
tion of Russell's, 16; quoted, 20, 21;
as successful managing partner in
China, 26–27; biography of, 28,
249n32; promotion of Shanghai S. N.
Co., 29; tribute rice proposal, 40; on
comprador, 96; and Sunkee's wage,
127; and Russell & Co., 249n32
Currency: transaction of hard, 71;
complexity of, 249n32
Customary fees. See *Lou-kuei*
Customs bank, 116
Customs report, 110, 118

Dallas, Alexander Grant: applies for a
comprador, 30; at Shanghai in 1843,
52; on Takee, 82, 175; and Soochow
system of silk purchase, 82–83
Daly, M. A., 53
Dent & Co.: and Cantonese compradors,
52; activities in Japan, 56; its
compradors, 82, 157, 172; and Yung
Wing, 145; and Cheng Kuan-ying,
197

Index

Deposit. See *Ya-kuei*
Dixwell, G. B., 37
Douglas Lapraik & Co., 85
Duties: at treaty parts, 50; import, 110

E-ho hong. *See* Jardine, Matheson & Co.
East and West: Kipling on, 1, 246n1;
  comprador as middleman between,
  44, 54, 180, 207, 223; and comprador's
  new role, 48; after decline of
  comprador, 63
East India Co., British: end of monopoly,
  46; abolition of, 49
Economic development: business climate
  and, 3; and foreign investment,
  107–108; and foreign trade, 107–108.
  See also Economy, Chinese
Economy, Chinese: and treaty system,
  3; comprador's role in, 5, 210–217;
  booms during World War I, 62;
  inhibited by speculation, 150; and
  foreign economic intrusion, 107–108;
  modern sector of, 210. *See also*
  Economic development
Education: of comprador's children, 8;
  compradors as promoters of, 186; and
  Christian missionaries, 198
Ekee, 31, 39; speculation of, 88; and
  upcountry purchase, 250n66
Emperor Kwang-hsü: and comprador
  Wu Mao-ting, 192; influenced by
  comprador Cheng Kuan-ying, 202
English language: Tong King-sing's
  command of, 84. *See also* Pidgin
  English
Entrepreneurship: lack of, in China, 4;
  definition of, 146–147; and
  Schumpeter's theory, 147; compradors
  and, 215
Exchange business: and Western
  merchants, 19–20; and compradors,
  73
Excompradors: and Jardine's, 31, 37–39,
  87, 102; and Western merchants,
  37–39; market report of, 38
Exports: annual value of, 105; items of,
  116; of tea from Canton, 255n33;
  firms, 257n93
Extraterritoriality: and economic
  development, 3; and Western
  merchants, 98
Ever-Victorious Army: and Takee, 184;
  and compradors, 191

Familism: and comprador system, 25,

54, 172–173; comprador relies on, 171;
  Cheng Kuan-ying's criticism of, 205;
  comprador influenced by, 220
Fearon, R. I.: and comprador, 33; on
  Tong King-sing, 140; on China
  Merchants' S. N. Co., 274n112
Feng Hua-ch'uan, 189
Feng Kuei-fen, 205
Fire Dart, 84, 120
Foochow: tea of, 18, 79, 80; upcountry
  purchase at, 30; compradors at, 30, 52,
  88; opening of, 50, 260n61, 261n78;
  duties collected at, 50; establishment
  of Heard's office at, 51. *See also*
  Upcountry purchase
Forbes, Frank B.: quoted, 21, 28–29, 34;
  cultivation of Chinese merchants, 27;
  and Russell's, 28; on Chinese
  connection and Choping, 28–29; on
  comprador, 34; suspicion of
  Butterfield & Swire, 34; on Tong
  King-sing, 140
Forbes, John M., 33
Forbes, Robert B., 76
Forbes, William, 32
Foreign investments. *See* Investments,
  foreign
Foreign merchants. *See* Merchants,
  foreign
Foreign settlement: at Shanghai and
  Hsü Jun, 100; comprador's home at,
  285n8
Foreign trade. *See* Trade, foreign
France: foreign investment of, 269n7
Freight: brokerage hongs, 42; comprador
  as broker of, 65; commission on, 92
Fryer, John, 197–198
Fu-pan (vice-comprador), 164
Fukien, 176–177
Fung Hien: bankruptcy of, 150; mal-
  practice of, 168, 169

Gay, A. O., 56, 58
Gentry: compradors as members of, 7,
  184–190, 218; income of, 105; hostility
  to Christianity, 209
Gentry-merchant (*shen-shang*), 7
Germany: and comprador, 61, 99;
  foreign investment of, 269n7
Ginseng, 58
Godown-keeper, 47
Gold, 73
Grain tribute, 114
Greaves & Co., 123
Guarantee: as prerequisite for a

Index

comprador, 51, 157–161; advantages to Western merchants, 51; as comprador's function, 63, 66, 68–69; and Tong King-sing, 86. *See also* Complete responsibility

Guild: kinds of, 25; foreign merchants' ignorance of, 25; and comprador, 171, 177–179; foreign merchants' dislike of, 178, 258n129; comprador as leader of, 189. *See also* Canton Guild; Ningpo Guild

Hainan Island, 40, 76
Handl & Co., 101
Hankow: and Shanghai, 17; compradors at, 29, 32, 35, 51, 52, 86, 146, 183, 189, 278n9, 284n116; Heard's at, 32, 37, 51; Russell's at, 32–33; Western merchants' rivalry at, 32–33; Jardine's at, 35, 52; Tong Loong-maw at, 37; Yü-hang at, 42; opening of, 50; financial crisis at, 68–69; upcountry purchase at, 85; Tong King-sing at, 86; Chinese merchants' rivalry with foreign merchants at, 118; Ningpo merchants active at, 175; market report from, 252n98; salt trade at, 270n37; Cantonese at, 284n116
Hankow-Canton Railroad, 146
Heard, Albert F.: in Shanghai in 1861, 16; quoted, 21, 53, 100; on Chinese connections, 29; on comprador, 40, 84; tribute rice proposal, 40; on Choping, 53, 100; at Shanghai, 56; and Heard's business in Japan, 58, 59; on Japan trade, 116
Heard, Augustine, Jr.: writes from Canton, 40; on comprador, 64, 65, 66, 117; and his comprador, 66; on upcountry purchase, 79, 230; on watchmen, 165; and Hong Kong poisoning case, 171
Heard, John: on Chinese connection, 29; on comprador, 37, 42, 93, 155; on tea purchase at Foochow, 79; on squeeze, 93; contrasts Shanghai with Canton business, 167; on Tong Loong-maw, 170–171
Henderson, J., 25
Heung-shan. *See* Hsiang-shan
Hides, 55
Hitch, Frederic D., 27
Ho A-mei, 128, 273n83
Ho Ch'i. *See* Ho Kai
Ho Ch'ien, 55

Ho Fook. *See* Ho Fu
Ho Fu (Ho Fook): investment of, 133; and insurance business, 133; as Jardine's comprador, 173; as social leader, 189; modern ideas of, 276n142
Ho Hsiao-sheng. *See* Ho Tung
Ho Kai (Ho Ch'i), 110
Ho Kan-t'ang: invests in insurance business, 133; as Jardine's comprador, 173
Ho K'uan, 193
Ho Lien-yü *See* Sunchong
Ho-mai (negotiatory purchase), 45
Ho Shun-ch'ang. *See* Sunchong
Ho Tung (Sir Robert Ho Tung, Ho Hsiao-shen): as Jardine's comprador, 31; wealth of, 100; and social mobility, 105; investment of, 113, 133; and insurance business, 133; and his compradorial family, 173; as Cantonese, 177; style of life, 181; Western name, 182; as social leader, 183, 186, 189, 190; honored at Kowloon, 190; and reform movement, 192; peace conference proposal of, 194
Hobson, J. A., 269n2
Hong Kong: Western firms at, 13, 16, 51; compradors at, 45, 51, 71, 88, 173; and war of 1856, 49–50; smuggling at, 50; British Chamber of Commerce at, 61; newspapers at, 61; and opium business, 103; poisoning incident at, 171–172; compradors' association at, 179
Hong Kong poisoning incident: and comprador's duties, 66; and comprador's responsibility, 171–172; and pidgin English, 182; and concepts of responsibility and limited liability, 199–201
Hong merchants: supplanted by comprador, 1; definition of, 2; in late Ch'ing, 2, 3; decline, 4, 48; and Western merchants, 13, 28, 155; and China's maritime trade, 46; compradors under, 46; compradors appointed as, 48. *See also* Canton system; Merchants, Chinese
Hongkong and Shanghai Banking Corp.: Jardine's deposits at, 71; its compradors, 53, 86, 101, 104, 133, 145, 157, 176, 199; its Chinese shareholders, 133; manager of, 169
Hongkong Daily Press, 61
Hongkong Telegraph, 61

Index

Hoo Mei-ping, 114
Hoppo, 13
House comprador, 46–47
Howqua (Wu Ch'ung-yüeh): relations with foreign merchants, 28, 155; and a defaulting comprador, 47; and Russell's, 52, 155
Hsi Cheng-fu: wealth of, 101; as native banker, 115, 157; and Chekiang compradors, 176; his compradorial family, 213
Hsi Yü-fu, 199
Hsiang-shan (Heung-shan), 13, 52, 174
Hsieh Tsan-t'ai (Tse Tsan Tai), 193
Hsing-shang (traveling trader), 7
Hsü Chao-heng. *See* Hsü Yü-t'ing
Hsü Jun (Ahyune, Ayun, Chu Yu-chee, Hsü Yü-chih, Yuchee): and China Merchants' S. N. Co., 4, 123, 142, 147, 149; and Russell's, 29, 142; and Jardine's, 31; as native banker, 42, 115; as Dent's comprador, 52, 56, 69, 84; and Tong King-sing, 84; investment of, 100, 113, 123, 129, 133, 135, 152, 199; style of life, 101, 181; as tea and silk merchant, 116, 271n46; and insurance business, 133, 148; and Kaiping Mines, 144; and joint-stock system, 147; speculation and bankruptcy of, 150; and *kuan-tu shang-pan*, 150, 151; his compradorial family, 161, 172, 213; and Cantonese compradors, 174; as social leader, 178, 186–190 passim; and patriotism, 194; and China's educational mission in U.S., 198; in Shanghai foreign settlement, 286n8
Hsü Jung-ts'un (Yunkee): as Dent's comprador, 52, 172, 197; and traditional beliefs, 182; as social leader, 189
Hsü Shu-p'ing (Chu Sok Pin), 161
Hsü Yü-chih. *See* Hsü Jun
Hsü Yü-t'ing (Hsü Chao-heng): as Dent's comprador, 52, 172; as prominent merchant, 157; and Cantonese compradors, 174; as gentry member, 184; portrayed as a mandarin, 185; as social leader, 188; and war of 1858, 190; and Ever-Victorious Army, 191
Hsüeh Huan, 9
Hu-chow, 53
Hu Kuang-yung: failure to respond to new situation, 4, 139; regarded as comprador, 12; and Ch'ing foreign loans, 105; and China Merchants' S. N. Co., 139; and speculation, 152
Hua chang-fang (Chinese treasurer), 45
Hua-tze jih-pao, 61
Hybrid culture of comprador, 219–221

Imperial Bank of China, 5
Imperialism: and economic development, 3, 99; in China's treaty ports, 3, 212; and compradors, 5, 98, 106–112, 216–217; coming of, 15; inhibits Chinese capitalism, 99; comprador's reaction to, 194; Hobson on, 269n2; Lenin on, 269n2
Imports: decline of, 62; amount of, 103; opium, 103
Income: compradors' total, 99–105; of gentry and Ch'ing government, 105
India, 53
Indo-China S. N. Co., 36
Industrialization: comprador's role in, 5, 211–216; comprador as investor, 120–136; comprador as manager, 136–146; comprador as entrepreneur, 146–153
Industry, Cheng Kuan-ying on, 204
Insurance: and agency house, 19; and Tong King-sing, 85; comprador's income from, 104; comprador's investment in, 133; comprador as pioneer in, 147
Interest, high rate in Shanghai, 120
Interpreter, comprador as, 65, 75. *See also* Linguist
Investments of compradors, 112–136. *See also* Investments, foreign
Investments, foreign: amount of, 105, 108–109; as harmful to underdeveloped countries, 107; profit of, 109; of United Kingdom, 269n7; of France, 269n7; of Germany, 269n7

Japan: Heard's in, 17, 54–55, 56–59, 161; compradors in, 56–59, 101, 119, 161, 177, 256n71; Chinese merchants in, 57; Jardine's in, 57; trade with China, 58; tea business in, 58–59, 248n8; economic development in World War I, 61; compradors' trade with, 116–117; contrasts to China, 152; Cheng Kuan-ying on, 204. *See also* Japanese merchants
Japanese merchants: role in China, 13;

Index

abolition of comprador by, 62; compradors to, 98. *See also* Japan

Jardine, Joseph, 37

Jardine, Matheson & Co. (E-ho hong): organization of, 16; and joint account, 19, 40; diverse operations of, 19, 22–23; founder of China Coast S. N. Co., 22; its compradors, 30–32, 57, 71, 82, 135, 146, 173, 191; effort to improve comprador efficiency, 35–36; and excomprador, 37–39; and Cantonese compradors, 52; in Japan, 57; and upcountry purchase, 81; suit with teamen at Foochow, 95; its insurance companies, 133; and China Merchants' S. N. Co., 140. *See also* China Coast S. N. Co.; Tong King-sing

Jardine, Matheson & Co. Archives, 16

Java, 55

Jenchuan, Korea, 55

Johnson, F.B.: on Russells', 28; and Tong King-sing, 31–32, 84, 85–86, 97, 103; and Choping, 35; and shipping business, 84; on godown man, 101; on opium sale, 103; on costly comprador system, 111; on guarantee of comprador, 159

Joint account: risk-reducing, 19; between compradors and Western merchants, 39-40

Joint-stock company, 109

Jung Hsing-ch'iao, 192, 193

Jung Hung. *See* Yung Wing

Jung Liang, 213

Jung Tzu-ming, 173

Kaiping Mines: and Tong King-sing, 100, 124, 126, 149; compradors' investments in, 124; investment of, 133; as China's first large-scale mining, 214

Kanagawa, 57

K'ang-pai-tu (comprador), 45

Kao Ch'ing-t'ang, 98

Keswick, James J., 36, 93

Keswick, William: on Tucksing, 35; on excomprador, 39; in Japan, 57, 58; on gold purchase, 73; on Tong King-sing as treasurer, 85; and Anglo-Chinese School, 198

Kiangsu compradors, 53, 54, 175–176

Kin-lee-yuen (Chin li yüan): shipping office at, 27; and comprador's investment, 121; site of, 249n38

Kingqua (Liang Lun-shu), 97

Kiukee. *See* Koofunsing

Kiukiang: and Shanghai, 17; tea of, 18; Jardine's compradors at, 36; Heard's compradors at, 48, 51

Knox, Thomas, 55; on comprador, 117, 119

Koofunsing (Kiukee, Ku Feng-sheng): as merchant, 28, 116, 157; as Cantonese comprador, 52; and Japan trade, 116; steamship investment of, 121; reputation of, 250n49

Korea, 55, 58

Ku Feng-sheng. *See* Koofunsing

Kuan-tu shang-pan (official supervision and merchant management): and Kaiping Mines, 144; and compradors, 150; and entrepreneurs, 151–152; Cheng Kuan-ying's criticism of, 205

Kung-hang. See Cohong

Kung-shih (palace purchase), 45

Kuo Kan-chang (Quok Acheong), 121

Kuo Sung-t'ao, 203, 205

Kuo Tsan, 183

Kwangtung compradors, 54. *See also* Canton; Cantonese

Lang, William, 34

Language problem of Western merchants, 25

Law, 96

Lenin, V. I., 269n2

Leong A Tien, 55

Li Chen-yü, 139

Li Ch'iu-p'ing, 183

Li Hung-chang: and Hu Kuang-yung, 4; and China Merchants' S. N. Co., 4, 123, 138; regarded as comprador, 12; and Tong King-sing, 123; and Shanghai Cotton Cloth Mill, 129; compared with compradors, 136; and Kaiping Mines, 143; and North China Imperial Railways, 145; Sun Yat-sen's proposal to, 193; change of attitude toward foreigners, 195–196

Li Sung-yün (Soong-yin), 121, 133, 134, 135, 273n97, 275n125

Li Wen-yao, 128

Liang Lun-shu. *See* Kingqua

Liaison shroff. See *p'ao-lou*

Licensed brokers. See *Ya-hang*

Limited liability: and Chang Chien, 139; learned from Western merchants, 199–201. *See also* Hong Kong poisoning incident

Lin Ch'in. *See* Acum

Index

Lin Hsien-yang. *See* Ahyue
Lin Shih-chih, 274n114
Lin Yao-t'ang. *See* Ahyue
Ling-shih ti (comprador), 45
Linguist: under Cohong system, 46; compared with comprador, 47; new job after Treaty of Nanking, 48; Fukienese as, 177. *See also* Interpreter
Liu Hsiang, 193
Liu Hsin-sheng: wealth of, 101; modern equipment, 146; bankruptcy of, 150; and chamber of commerce, 189; honored at Hankow, 190; missionary education, 198
Liu Kwang-Ching, 251n85, 267n59
Liu Ming-ch'uan, 188
Liu Sen-chi. *See* Sunkee
Liu Shao-tsung. *See* Seating
Lo Ch'ang-chao: as Jardine's comprador, 173; and chamber of commerce, 189
Lo Ho-p'eng, 199
Lo Shou-sung, 133
Loans: comprador and foreign, 104; high interest of, 120
London, 17
Lou-kuei (customary fees), 47
Lu Ya-ching, 195
Luncheong, 100

Macao: compradors at, 46; smuggling at, 50; location of, 174
Machine manufacturing, 131–132
Mai-pan (comprador, purchaser), 1, 44, 45; departure from tradition, 8; as marginal man, 9; limitations of, 10–11, 210–211; decline of, 59–63; abolition of, 62; as salesman, 65; salary of, 89–91, 102; absconding of, 95, 168–169; disputes of, 95–96, 168; number of, in China, 101–102; role in urbanization, 113; Westernization of, 182–184, 199–201; acculturation of, 219, 221; style of life, 220–221; resignations, 268n93, 274n114
Malacca, 55
Malpractice: of Tong King-sing, 95; of comprador checked by foreign merchant, 167–168
Malwa opium: price of, 87; from Shanghai, 118. *See also* Opium; Patna opium
Manager (tsung-li), 45; high official as, 138; gentry-merchant as, 138–139; comprador as, 140–146, 214–215

Mandl & Co., 104
Manfoong Hong, 19
Manila, 55
Manufactured goods, 17
Mao Tse-tung, 222
Marginal man, comprador as, 9
Market: difficulty of estimating, 18; information on, 38, 74; integration of Chinese, 62
Market shroff. See *P'ao-chieh*
Marketeering of Western merchants, 18, 39
Mercantilism, 106
Merchant-partner. See *Shang-huo*
Merchants, Chinese: reluctance to enter new fields, 4; rise of, in Ch'ing, 6–7; compradors and, 6, 7, 94–95; kinds of, 7; difficulty in studying, 13; in Japan, 57; and foreign trade, 62; and foreign merchants, 62, 96; and salt trade, 97; Cheng Kuan-ying on modern role of, 205. *See also* Businessmen; Hong merchants; Merchants, foreign; Merchants, Western
Merchants, foreign: number in China, 101–102; and costly comprador system, 110–112; Russian, 116; rivalry from compradors, 117–120; employment of compradors, 155; and China's modernization, 209–210. *See also* Japanese merchants; Merchants, Chinese; Merchants, Western
Merchants, Western: coming to China, 1; entrepreneurship of, 17; in China, 17–20, 46; diversity of operations, 19; change in business of, 20–23; and comprador, 24–26, 32–36, 39, 40, 62, 64, 208–209; effort to promote Chinese connections, 26–32, 33–36; and Chinese language, 27, 61; rivalry among, 33–36; on Yangtze, 36; and excompradors, 37–39; in Japan, 56; dispute with Chinese merchants, 96; inhibit China's capitalism, 99; expectations of Chinese market, 109; and hong merchants, 155. *See also* Agency house; Merchants, foreign
Middleman: comprador as, 1, 9, 207, 208; and acculturation, 9; between East and West, 44, 54; functions of, 63; and squeeze, 93. *See also* Broker
Ming dynasty, origin of *mai-pan* in, 45
Mining, 124–129
Mitsui Company, 62
Mixed Court, 168, 169

Index

Modernization and entrepreneur, 210
Monetary policy of Chinese officials, 74
Monetary system, Chinese: complexity of, 25; reform of, 62
Moore, T., 74, 96
Morse, H. B., 143
Mu Ping-yüan: and Chekiang compradors, 175; and Opium War, 191; as comprador-traitor, 195

Nagasaki, 56, 57, 117
Nan-hai, 13
Nanking, Treaty of: and comprador, 15, 48, 76; symbolic meaning of, 48, 49
Nanzing, 55; Tong King-sing's investment in, 120; purchased by Tong King-sing, 141
National Bank of China, 133
Nationalism: and comprador, 63; in China and economic imperialism, 106; mercantile, 205
Negotiatory purchase. See *Ho-mai*
Netherlands Bank, 53
New York, 17
Newchwang, 58, 257n80
Newspapers, 198–199
Ningpo, 54, 175. *See also* Chekiang
Ningpo Guild, 189. *See also* Guilds
Norna, 85
North China Herald, 61
North China Imperial Railways, 145
North China Steam Navigation Co., 120, 121

Official supervision and merchant management. See *Kuan-tu shang-pan*
Officials: comprador's report to, 47; dealings with, 75; comprador free from control of, 97; visit compradors, 188
Olyphant & Co.: purchase of tea, 18; and new business trend, 21; rivalry with Russell's for compradors, 33; compradors' investments in, 121
One A Cheong, 55
Opium: and late Ch'ing commerce, 2; Western merchant's sale of, 17, 103, 268n83; as medium of exchange, 19; comprador's market report on, 37, 87, 252n98; comprador's sale of, 81, 92, 103, 170, 190, 268n80, 268n84; and barter trade, 82. *See also* Malwa opium; Patna opium
Opium War, 3, 191, 194
Oriental Bank: compradors' investments in, 133; its compradors, 168, 169, 281n71

Pan-fang (comprador office), 45
P'an Shih-ch'eng, 9
P'an-yü, as compradors' homeland, 13, 46
Pang mai-pan (assistant comprador), 164
Pao. *See* Complete responsibility
Pao-pan (contract), 116
Pao P'eng (Pao Ts'ung, Pao Ya-ts'ung): and Opium War, 190, 288n58; as traitor, 194
Pao Ts'ung. *See* Pao P'eng
Pao Ya-ts'ung. *See* Pao P'eng
P'ao-chieh (market shroff), 164
P'ao-lou (liaison shroff), 164
Patna opium, 87. *See also* Malwa opium; Opium
Patriotism, 11, 194–195
Pawnshop, 100, 112
Peas from Newchwang, 58, 257n80
Peiho, 85
Peking, 101
Penang, 55
P'eng Ch'i-chih: and Shanghai Cotton Cloth Mill, 129, 145; and modern technology, 146
Pepper, 37
Perceval, Alexander, 83
Pidgin English: and Edward Cunningham, 26; and comprador, 155, 180, 277n3; definition, 181–182; as multicultural product, 220; in twentieth century, 286n10; learning of, 291n104. *See also* English language
Politics, 7, 190
Portuguese: "comprador" as a term of, 44, 45; trade in the East, 45
Profit, rate of, 109
Pu Ting-pang, 194
Purchaser. See *Mai-pan*

Quok Acheong. *See* Kuo Kan-chang

Railroad: and compradors, 132, 145; and Kaiping Mines, 144
Rangoon, 55
Real estate: and Hsü Jun, 100; comprador's income from, 104; compradors' investments in, 113
Reform, 192
Regionalism, 25; and comprador system, 54, 173–177; comprador's dependence on, 171; comprador influenced by, 220
Remer, C F., 105, 268n97

Index

Revolution, 192–194. *See also* Sun Yat-sen
Rice, 87
Russell & Co.: organization of, 16;
partners, 17, 26–28; and Shanghai S. N.
Co., 22, 121; effort to woo Chinese
merchants, 26; Kin-lee-yuen of, 27; its
compradors, 27–28, 32, 33, 37, 52, 70,
93, 96, 157, 164, 167; and hong
merchants, 28, 155; rivalry with other
Western merchants, 32–35; business
with excomprador, 37; at Shanghai,
67, 70; at Tientsin, 74; at Foochow,
81, 261n78; and upcountry purchase,
81; fleet bought by China Merchants'
S. N. Co., 99. *See also* Shanghai Steam
Navigation Co.
Russia, 116
Russo-Chinese Bank, 53, 101

Saigon, 55
Salary of comprador, 89–91, 102
Sale of rank and degree, 6
Salesman, comprador as, 65
Salt: and late Ch'ing commerce, 2, 3;
merchants, 2, 4, 97, 246n2; and
comprador, 113–114; Saeki Tomi on,
246; trade at Hankow, 270n37
Sassoon & Co., 69, 119; activities in
Japan, 56; compradors to, 114; and
lawsuit, 169
Satsuma, 19
Schumpeter, Joseph A., 147, 215
Seal: of foreign hong, 95; of comprador,
265n37
Seating (Liu Shao-tsung), 51; salary of,
66, 90, 91; and guarantee
system, 69; as a salt merchant, 114;
investment of, 123; and China
Merchants' S. N. Co., 123, 142
Security chop, 156, 157–159, 169, 170
See Kai, 51
See Yong: and joint account, 40; as
Heard's comprador at Canton, 51;
recommends Tong Loong-maw as
comprador, 77; wealth of, 155
Servant. *See* "Boy"
Shang-huo (merchant-partner), 45
Shanghai: and other treaty ports, 17; as
new commercial center, 21; Municipal
Council, 44; compradors at, 45, 51, 52,
81–84 passim, 88, 92, 173, 179, 193;
rise of, 50; Heard's at, 51; British
Chamber of Commerce at, 61;
Russell's at, 67; sound native bank
system at, 68; and upcountry purchase,

76, 81; Dent's and Jardine's at, 82;
as an entrepot, 83; opium supply at,
87; commission at, 92; taotai, 98, 190;
pawnshop at, 100; contrasts with
Canton, 167; Hsü Jun at, 188;
compradors from, 256n54
Shanghai Cotton Cloth Mill: compradors'
investments in, 129, 214; and Cheng
Kuan-ying, 129, 145, 147; and
insurance, 148. *See also* P'eng Ch'i-chih
Shanghai Steam Navigation Co., 37, 74,
75; established by Russell's, 22; and
Edward Cunningham, 27, 29;
compradors' investments in, 121.
See also Russell & Co.
Shanghai Volunteer Corps, 188, 287n40
Shansi banks, 62
Shen-shang. See Gentry-merchant
Shen pao, 199
Sheng Hsüan-huai: and Cheng Kuan-
ying, 146; and Tong King-sing, 152;
and Hsü Jun, 152
Ship comprador, 44, 46, 47, 253n9
Shipping: and foreign merchants, 19,
22–23, 84; comprador's function in,
74; and Tong King-sing, 84, 85. *See
also* Steamship business
Shroff, 47; in Korea, 55; as money
expert, 73; as clerk, 161, 164; meaning
of, 259n34
Silk: and late Ch'ing commerce, 2; and
Western merchants, 17; Soochow
system of purchase, 53, 82. *See also*
Upcountry purchase
Silver: and exchange business, 73; from
India, 262n109. *See also* Monetary
system
Singapore, 55, 117, 181
Sino-French War, 143, 190
Sino-Japanese War, first: comprador's
income from, 104; and comprador, 191
Sino-Japanese War, second: and decline
of comprador, 62
Smuggling, 50
Social attitude of comprador, 8
Social mobility of comprador, 105, 218
Soochow: compradors from, 54, 175–176.
See also Kiangsu; Soochow system
Soochow system of silk purchase, 53, 82
Sow Moey, 35
Sow-no, 56
Soyseng, 69
Specie, 17
Speculation: of Sunkee, 29; of Ekee, 88;
and comprador, 150

Index

Squeeze: comprador avoids official, 3, 98; by comprador, 61, 93–94, 111; and salt merchants, 97; and complete responsibility, 151
Ssu-shih (clerk), 164
Standard Oil Co., 62
Stationary trader. See *Tso-ku*
Steamship business: and Edward Cunningham, 26–27; compradors' income from, 104; compradors' investments in, 120–124. *See also* Shipping
Succession of comprador, 283n98
Suez Canal, 20
Sugar, 37; of Swatow, 58, 257n80; market report of, 87, 252n98; in coastal trade, 114, 119
Suits: teamen vs. Jardine's, 95; Sunkee vs. Russell's, 96
Sun Chu-t'ang, 274n114
Sun Chung-ying, 101, 181
Sun Yat-sen: and compradors, 193, 219; clash with Ch'en Lien-po, 194, 195
Sunchong, 52
Sung Ts'ai, 103
Sung Wei-ch'en, 135
Sunkee (Liu Sen-chi): as Russell's comprador at Tientsin, 28, 74, 250n50, 277n1; discharged by Russell's, 29, 97, 266n44; speculation of, 29, 97, 150; suit with Russell & Co., 33, 96; wages, 90, 92, 263n5; sale of opium, 103; his hongs at Tientsin, 266n43; his pidgin English, 277n3
Swatow, 58, 99, 257n80
Swire, John Samuel, 123
Sycee, 74; and market custom, 249n32; comprador shroffing, 259n34. *See also* Monetary system

Tael, 62
Taiping uprising: and comprador, 3, 54, 98, 99, 176, 188, 192, 266n50; and Canton, 40, 50; and tea transportation, 81; and grain tribute transportation, 114; and Chu Ch'i-ang, 274n107
Taiwan, 76
Takee (Yang Fang): as Jardine's comprador, 31; as native banker, 42, 115; Soochow system of silk purchase, 53; and upcountry purchase, 82; wealth of, 99; and sale of opium, 103; illustrates social mobility, 105; his pawnshop, 112, 270n25; and Japan trade, 117; speculation of, 150; and

lawsuit, 170; and Cantonese compradors, 175; as social leader, 179, 191; as gentry member, 184; and war of 1858, 190; and Ever-Victorious Army, 191
Tamsui, 76
Tang Kee Shang. *See* Teng Chi-ch'ang
T'ang Chi-ch'ang, 173
T'ang Chieh-ch'en: as Jardine's comprador, 52, 173, 276n140; as railroad manager, 132; and Shanghai-Nanking Railroad, 145
T'ang dynasty and origin of *mai-pan*, 45
T'ang Jung-chün, 191
T'ang Kai-sun (T'ang Kuo-an, T'ang Kwo-on), 291n93
T'ang Kuo-an. *See* T'ang Kai-sun
T'ang Kwo-on. *See* T'ang Kai-sun
T'ang Lung-mao. *See* Tong Loong-maw
T'ang Mao-chih. *See* Tong Mow-chee
T'ang Neng. *See* Tong Loong-maw
T'ang Shao-i, 291n93
T'ang T'ing-chih. *See* Tong Mow-chee
T'ang T'ing-shu. *See* Tong King-sing
Tao-ch'i (title deeds) and guarantee system of comprador, 160
T'ao Mei-sheng, 199
Taochai. *See* Cheng Kuan-ying
Taotai: of Shanghai, 98, 190; comprador as, 184
Taytnabb & Co., 69
Tea: and late Ch'ing commerce, 2; and Western merchants, 17, 79; of Foochow compared with Canton's, 18; market report, 37, 252n98; and comprador, 37, 79, 80, 260n57; and Cantonese, 53; export of, 53, 255n33; at Foochow, 79, 80, 261n78; purchase of, 79; processing of, 80, 248n8; trade in, 118; taster of, 255n47; upcountry purchase of, 260n57. *See also* Upcountry purchase
Teaman: at Foochow, 79; and Heard's, 79; at Shanghai, 81; and Jardine's, 95
Teng Chi-ch'ang (Tang Kee Shang): and Ch'ing foreign loan, 104; and government mills, 146; and chamber of commerce, 189
Teng Chün-hsiang, 101, 266n38
Textile enterprise, 129
Tientsin: and Shanghai, 17; compradors at, 29, 32, 52, 74, 88, 92; Russell's at, 29, 74; Jardine's at, 32, 52; treaties of, 44; comprador's Chinese name at, 45; cotton goods imported at, 110;

Index

customs banks at, 116; Chinese merchants rivalry with foreign merchants at, 118–119
Tiffany, Osmond, Jr., 65
Ting Jih-ch'ang, 9, 273n91
Title deeds. See *Tao-ch'i*
Tobacco, 119
Tong King-sing (T'ang T'ing-shu), 30, 31, 34, 35, 52; and China Merchants' S. N. Co., 4, 122–123, 140–143, 149; and Chinese merchants, 7, 264n31, 265n32; and Jardine's, 31, 40, 252n106; as Jardine's comprador, 39, 83–88, 90, 97, 160, 167, 170, 262n107, 263n117; as native banker, 42, 115; malpractices of, 71, 95, 265n33; and shipping, 85, 94, 120, 121, 140–141, 262n97; and insurance, 85, 133, 148; on squeeze, 94; investments of, 100, 112, 120, 121, 133, 152; and opium sale, 103; illustrates social mobility, 105; and pawnshops, 112, 270n35; and salt, 114, 270n26; and tea, 116; and Kaiping Mines, 124, 143–145, 149; and mining, 127; capability of, 140; death, 144; motivation in developing modern enterprises, 149–150; and *kuan-tu shang-pan*, 150, 151; his English, 155, 265n32; as a comprador surety, 169; his compradorial family, 173, 213; and Cantonese compradors, 174; as social leader, 178, 186, 189; as gentry member, 184; and patriotism, 194; early years of, 196; and *Hui pao*, 199; as entrepreneur, 208; at Chinkiang, 262n97; and modern bank, 273n91; U.S. consul on, 275n135; life of, 290n92; and T'ang Shao-i, 290n93
Tong Loong-maw (T'ang Lung-mao, T'ang Neng): as Heard's comprador, 30, 51, 80, 81, 170, 209; and upcountry purchase, 30, 77–78; business with Heard's, 37; effort to get monopoly license from Taiwan, 76; and tea, 80; as salt merchant, 114; and Russian merchants, 116; and Cantonese compradors, 174; market report of, 251n98
Tong Mow-chee (T'ang Mao-chih, T'ang T'ing-chih), 31, 52; as Jardine's comprador, 32, 170, 173, 283n93; on comprador's income, 90, 264n18; salary as comprador, 90; investments of, 133, 134; death, 173; on his own social activities, 188; as social leader, 189

Trade, 112–114. *See also* Trade, foreign
Trade, foreign: comprador's role in, 3, 114–117; dominated by Cantonese, 49; of tea and silk, 53; with Japan, 58, 257n80; with Korea, 58; and Chinese merchants, 62; with Southeast Asia, 85; amount of, 102–103, 105; and economic development, 107–108, 211; native bank's role in, 115, 271n41; peripheral role of, 210–211
Tradition: comprador's departure from, 8
Traveling trader. See *Hsing-shang*
Treasurer, comprador as, 69; Tong King-sing as, 85
Treaty port mandarin, 9
Treaty ports: Western impact originates at, 1; as new commercial center, 3; and imperialsim, 3, 212; Cantonese compradors at, 51–52; and social mobility, 105; hybrid culture at, 180; as enclaves, 181; modern schools at, 184; peripheral economic role of, 210–211; pecuniary milieu at, 212. *See also* Canton; Foochow; Hankow; Shanghai; Tientsin; Treaty system
Treaty system: and economic development, 3; end of, 44, 63; and imperialism, 107; Cheng Kuan-ying on, 203. *See also* Treaty ports
Tribute rice, 74
Tribute system and China's maritime trade, 45
Ts'ai Hsing-nan, 177
Ts'ao Tzu-chün, 135
Tse Tsan Tai. *See* Hsieh Tsan-t'ai
Tseng Kuo-fan, 136, 198
Tso-ku (stationary trader), 7
Tso Tsung-t'ang, 136; and Hu Kuang-yung, 4; arrests comprador, 98
Tsung-li. See Manager
Tucksing, 35; business with Jardine's, 31, 251n70; sale of opium, 103; letter to William Keswick, 268n82
Tyson, George, 28

Union Steam Navigation Co.: compradors' investments in, 120, 121; compradors to, 273n97
United States: compradors' boycott against, 194; consul at Kanagawa, 256n71; China's educational mission to, 290n93
Upcountry purchase: of tea, 30, 260n57; and joint account, 40; comprador stops handling, 63; comprador's role

in, 65, 75–83, 114, 148; at Hankow, 85; illustrates comprador's integrity, 166; at Shanghai, 260n57. *See also* Foochow

Urbanization: comprador's role in, 113

Vice-comprador. See *Fu-pan*

Walsh, Thomas, 17
Walsh Hall & Co., 56
Wan-hsien, 42
Wang Ch'ang-chieh, 55
Wang Huai-shan: as comprador to Hongkong and Shanghai Banking Corp., 53, 157; introduces "chop loan" system, 86; wealth of, 101; investments of, 113; and Chekiang compradors, 175
Wang I-t'ing (Wong I. Ding): investments of, 134; as painter and Buddhist leader, 182; and 1911 Revolution, 193
Wang K'o-ming, 98
Wang T'ao, 205
Ward, Frederick Townsend, 184, 191
Warden, H. H., 28
Warlords, 194
Wealth, comprador's accumulation of, 89–99
Webb, Edward, 113
Wei-hsien, Shantung, 76
Wei Wen-pu, 134
Wei Yü, 186, 190
Weights and measures, 25
Weller, George F.: on importance of comprador, 24; and upcountry purchase, 77; on Tong Loong-maw, 80
Western merchant. *See* Merchant, Western
Westernization of comprador, 182–184
Whampoa, 46, 47
Whittall, Edward, 57, 74
Whittall, James: on monetary system, 25; inability to cultivate Chinese, 34; on Yakee, 37; on comprador, 83; as Jardine's Head in the East, 85
Willamette, 27
Winchester, Charles A., 95–96
Wong I. Ding. *See* Wang I-t'ing
Wood oil, 87
Woolens, 111
Woosung: opium and silk trade at, 82; A. G. Dallas at, 255n44; comprador at, 268n80; and railroad, 275n134
World War I: accelerates comprador's

decline, 44, 61; and booming of Chinese economy, 62
Wu Chien-chang, 191
Wu Ch'ung-yüeh. *See* Howqua
Wu Hsü, 188, 190, 191
Wu-i. *See* Bohea
Wu Jim Pah. *See* Wu Mao-ting
Wu Mao-ting (Wu Jim Pah): as manager, 132; and Tientsin Gas Co., 133; investments of, 133, 135; and North China Imperial Railways, 145; and government mills, 146; as independent merchant, 151; and 1898 reform movement, 192; as comprador to Hongkong and Shanghai Banking Corp., 276n**146**
Wu Shao-ch'ing: investments of, 133; and insurance, 133; as social leader, 192
Wu T'ing-sheng: style of life, 181; as Christian, 183; as social leader, 189; missionary education, 198
Wu Yao-t'ing, 101
Wun Hing, 35, 36

Y.M.C.A., 183
Ya-hang (licensed brokers), 2
Ya-kuei (deposit), 160
Ya-ti. *See* Atai
Yakee, 31, 52; as Jardine's comprador, 37; and upcountry purchase, 83, 250n**66**; as excomprador, 87; and salt business, 113; and Japan trade, 116
Yang Ch'ü-yün, 193
Yang Fang. *See* Takee
Yang Kuei-hsüan: bankruptcy of, 150; money losses as comprador, 160; guaranteed by Cheng Kuan-ying, 174; absconds, 282n**79**
Yang K'un-shan, 101
Yang Mei-nan: guaranteed by Hsü Jun, 172; comprador history of, 174; and Y.M.C.A., 183; as Christian, 183; and chamber of commerce, 189
Yang Te, 126
Yangtze River: opening of, 17; steamship on, 22, 35; compradors on, 28, 37, 92; and Russell's, 28; and Jardine's, 35; rivalry among Western merchants on, 36; and Heard's, 37; and commission, 92
Yeh Ch'eng-chung: wealth of, 100; investments of, 135; as social leader, 179, 186
Yeh Ming-tsai, 133
Yen Lan-ch'ing, 115

Index

Yokohama: compradors at, 56, 57;
Heard's plan for house at, 60;
comprador trades to, 117
Yokohama Specie Bank: its abolition of
comprador, 62; compradors to, 101,
133; compradors' boycott against, 179
Young, J. R., 98
Yowloong, 31, 52; as Jardine's
comprador, 57, 87; and upcountry
purchase, 250n66
Yü-hang (Szechwan hong), 42
Yü Ho-te. *See* Yü Hsia-ch'ing
Yü Hsia-ch'ing (Yü Ho-te): as bank
comprador, 53; wealth of, 101;
illustrates social mobility, 105; and
shipping, 124; investments of, 124, 152,
214; as independent merchant, 151;
and Chekiang compradors, 175; as
social leader, 179, 188, 189, 190; and
chamber of commerce, 189; Road at
Shanghai, 190; and 1911 revolution,
193, 194; and Chiang Kai-shek, 194,
290n83; and Shanghai Volunteer
Corps, 287n40
Yüeh-chou, Hunan, 76
Yuchee. *See* Hsü Jun
Yuechang. *See* Choping
Yung Wing (Jung Hung), 10; and Cheng
Kuan-ying, 145; and Dent & Co.,
145; and China's educational mission
to U.S., 198; and *Hui pao*, 199
Yungkee. *See* Hsü Jung-ts'un

Zaibatzu, 4

Harvard East Asian Series

1. *China's Early Industrialization: Sheng Hsuan-huai (1844–1916) and Mandarin Enterprise.* By Albert Feuerwerker.
2. *Intellectual Trends in the Ch'ing Period.* By Liang Ch'i-ch'ao. Translated by Immanuel C. Y. Hsü.
3. *Reform in Sung China: Wang An-shih (1021–1086) and His New Policies.* By James T. C. Liu.
4. *Studies on the Population of China, 1368–1953.* By Ping-ti Ho.
5. *China's Entrance into the Family of Nations: The Diplomatic Phase, 1858–1880.* By Immanuel C. Y. Hsü.
6. *The May Fourth Movement: Intellectual Revolution in Modern China.* By Chow Tse-tsung.
7. *Ch'ing Administrative Terms: A Translation of the Terminology of the Six Boards with Explanatory Notes.* Translated and edited by E-tu Zen Sun.
8. *Anglo-American Steamship Rivalry in China, 1862–1874.* By Kwang-Ching Liu.
9. *Local Government in China under the Ch'ing.* By T'ung-tsu Ch'ü.
10. *Communist China, 1955–1959: Policy Documents with Analysis.* With a foreword by Robert R. Bowie and John K. Fairbank. (Prepared at Harvard University under the joint auspices of the Center for International Affairs and the East Asian Research Center.)
11. *China and Christianity: The Missionary Movement and the Growth of Chinese Anti-foreignism, 1860–1870.* By Paul A. Cohen.
12. *China and the Helping Hand, 1937–1945.* By Arthur N. Young.
13. *Research Guide to the May Fourth Movement: Intellectual Revolution in Modern China, 1915–1924.* By Chow Tse-tsung.
14. *The United States and the Far Eastern Crises of 1933–1938: From the Manchurian Incident through the Initial Stage of the Undeclared Sino-Japanese War.* By Dorothy Borg.
15. *China and the West, 1858–1861: The Origins of the Tsungli Yamen.* By Masataka Banno.
16. *In Search of Wealth and Power: Yen Fu and the West.* By Benjamin Schwartz.
17. *The Origins of Entrepreneurship in Meiji Japan.* By Johannes Hirschmeier, S.V.D.
18. *Commissioner Lin and the Opium War.* By Hsin-pao Chang.
19. *Money and Monetary Policy in China, 1845–1895.* By Frank H. H. King.
20. *China's Wartime Finance and Inflation, 1937–1945.* By Arthur N. Young.
21. *Foreign Investment and Economic Development in China, 1840–1937.* By Chi-ming Hou.
22. *After Imperialism: The Search for a New Order in the Far East, 1921–1931.* By Akira Iriye.
23. *Foundations of Constitutional Government in Modern Japan, 1868–1900.* By George Akita.
24. *Political Thought in Early Meiji Japan, 1868–1889.* By Joseph Pittau, S.J.
25. *China's Struggle for Naval Development, 1839–1895.* By John L. Rawlinson.
26. *The Practice of Buddhism in China, 1900–1950.* By Holmes Welch.
27. *Li Ta-chao and the Origins of Chinese Marxism.* By Maurice Meisner.
28. *Pa Chin and His Writings: Chinese Youth Between the Two Revolutions.* By Olga Lang.
29. *Literary Dissent in Communist China.* By Merle Goldman.
30. *Politics in the Tokugawa Bakufu, 1600–1843.* By Conrad Totman.
31. *Hara Kei in the Politics of Compromise, 1905–1915.* By Tetsuo Najita.

32. *The Chinese World Order: Traditional China's Foreign Relations.* Edited by John K. Fairbank.
33. *The Buddhist Revival in China.* By Holmes Welch.
34. *Traditional Medicine in Modern China: Science, Nationalism, and the Tensions of Cultural Change.* By Ralph C. Croizier.
35. *Party Rivalry and Political Change in Taisho Japan.* By Peter Duus.
36. *The Rhetoric of Empire: American China Policy, 1895–1901.* By Marilyn B. Young.
37. *Radical Nationalist in Japan: Kita Ikki, 1883–1937.* By George M. Wilson.
38. *While China Faced West: American Reformers in Nationalist China, 1928–1937.* By James C. Thomson Jr.
39. *The Failure of Freedom: A Portrait of Modern Japanese Intellectuals.* By Tatsuo Arima.
40. *Asian Ideas of East and West: Tagore and His Critics in Japan, China, and India.* By Stephen N. Hay.
41. *Canton under Communism: Programs and Politics in a Provincial Capital, 1949–1968.* By Ezra F. Vogel.
42. *Ting Wen-Chiang: Science and China's New Culture.* By Charlotte Furth.
43. *The Manchurian Frontier in Ch'ing History.* By Robert H. G. Lee.
44. *Motoori Norinaga, 1730–1801.* By Shigeru Matsumoto.
45. *The Comprador in Nineteenth Century China: Bridge between East and West.* By Yen-p'ing Hao.